SOCIAL CHANGE
AND PREJUDICE

SOCIAL CHANGE
AND PREJUDICE

INCLUDING

Dynamics of Prejudice

BRUNO BETTELHEIM

and

MORRIS JANOWITZ

THE FREE PRESS, *New York*

COLLIER-MACMILLAN LIMITED, *London*

Library of Congress Catalog Card Number: 64-11214

Collier-Macmillan Canada, Ltd., Toronto, Ontario

Fourth printing November 1967

PREFACE

Dynamics of Prejudice has been out of print for some time. The decision of a new publisher, The Free Press of Glencoe, to reissue it raised a number of questions in the minds of the authors. The opportunity required rethinking of the original research problem in the light of what had been learned during the last 15 years. We had to assess whether and how well our findings stood up. By restudying our results and comparing them with the pertinent research reports that had appeared since its completion, we were able to identify those that were still relevant and to develop some crucial second thoughts. These questions, and the general problem of how social psychological research related to historical change, tempted us to be more ambitious than would be the case in a new or revised edition.

When the occasion presented itself to prepare a new edition of the *Dynamics of Prejudice*, we considered reworking the original data in the light of new findings, new theories, and recent historical experience so as to present a new report. We rejected this approach because we wanted our readers to have access to the original formulations. Therefore, we decided to reprint the original report together with a separate study evaluating the original effort.

Hence, our purpose in Part One of this volume is to reassess the sociological and psychological findings that we presented in the *Dynamics of Prejudice* (reprinted in Part Two of this volume), in the light of both the social changes and the development in theory that have occurred during the last 15 years. During this time, there has been a deep transformation of attitude patterns toward the Jew and the Negro in the United States. Research evidence accumulated since the close of World War II documents that the level and intensity of ethnic prejudice toward both groups has declined during this period. But while the decline has been marked for both groups, the Negro still remains much more an object of hostility than the Jew. This is not to overlook the short-term countertrends, indicators of latent hostility, or the persistence of the hard-core extremist attitudes.

Such a trend is all the more significant because the period was one in which public attention focused chronically on minority problems with both demands for social change and incidents of tension and violence given wide attention. In short, ethnic prejudice declined at a time when there was great divergence in public opinion on policy questions and when ethnic relations stood in the center of local and national political affairs. It was a period when the issues concerning the elimination of discrimination were transformed once more into a fundamental controversy over the rights and authority of local government as compared with the federal government.

In reassessing our original research efforts, we were guided by the underlying question whether our findings were limited to the particular situation we investigated and to what extent they had broader applicability. During the last 15 years, economic and social conditions in the United States have undergone drastic change. If the propositions which were derived and tested about ethnic prejudice at the end of World War II have no applicability under changed economic, social, and political conditions, then the social scientific analysis of attitudes resolves itself into a sophisticated form of recording contemporary history. Because social science seeks to investigate specific situations for the purpose of producing general knowledge, the reassessment of old data in the light of new circumstances and additional research is a crucial but often neglected procedure.

In *Social Change and Prejudice* we use a number of approaches in assessing the *Dynamics of Prejudice*. Chapter I, "Trends in Prejudice," examines shifts in prejudice toward Negroes and Jews during this period, mainly as revealed by national sample studies. Our purpose is to explore how relevant are some basic economic and sociological variables that were used in the original study in accounting for these trends. In Chapter II, "Consequences of Social Mobility," we further explore the link between social mobility and prejudice. Because the original study set forth an explicit hypothesis about the effect of social mobility on prejudice, a number of parallel studies have been completed during the period by other social scientists. These studies give us more data than is usually available for analyzing the social processes underlying attitude change. We also examine the effects of social mobility on other forms of interpersonal relations because we believe our propositions apply to a broader range of social behavior than ethnic hostility. In Chapter III, "The Psychology of Prejudice," we evaluate developments in psychoanalytic theory as they relate to the analysis of ethnic hostility. Finally, in Chapter IV, "Social and Personal Controls: Theory and Practice," we try once more to link theoretical considerations to issues of policy and social action, as we had done at the end of the original study.

The theory and empirical findings had led us then to make a variety of recommendations for action to deal with prejudice and discrimination. Fifteen years ago was a period in which social scientists emphasized education, mass media, and psychological techniques as the basis for modifying intergroup relations. Our findings, especially those dealing with the role of authority and social control, led us to emphasize legal and administrative leadership. In reassessing the findings of the *Dynamics of Prejudice,* we are concerned with taking another look at the elements involved in planned social change in intergroup relations.

There is still another task to which we must address ourselves: the need for the social scientist to correct subjective distortions. This task has become such a commonplace as to have become a ritual. We are not concerned with arguing the possibility of creating a value-free science nor do we feel the necessity of defending the social sciences from misguided attacks that it is unconcerned with human values. These issues have receded in importance. We find no reason to change the moral and philosophical assumptions on which we launched the original study. We sought to be as objective as possible in the collection and analysis of the data about the factors associated with ethnic prejudice. We were convinced and remain convinced that such an objective study could in the long run contribute to the reduction of intergroup hostility.

We recognized that our biases and our limitations were most likely to emerge not so much in the original conceptualization or actual data collection or even in the initial analysis. We were concerned with inferences and conclusions that we must of necessity draw if our findings were to have relevance for social policy. Therefore, we are concerned not only with the assessment of the scientific aspects of our study but also with a re-evaluation of the distortion that we may have perpetuated as we reasoned out the implications of our objective data.

But this is a task which cannot be left to the authors alone. The republication of the original study in its entirety in this volume is designed to assist this purpose. If we did not do this, we would have to quote extensively from the original study to explain to what we were referring, a tedious task at best, which would have interfered with the readability of both the old and the new. Also, only a reading of the original study will permit assessing on one's own whether our way of looking backward on it is justified.

B. B.
M. J.

University of Chicago
January 1963

CONTENTS

PART TWO: DYNAMICS OF PREJUDICE

PART ONE

SOCIAL CHANGE
AND PREJUDICE

CHAPTER I

TRENDS IN PREJUDICE

Social scientists are hard pressed when they are called upon to describe and analyze, on the basis of their objective research data, how social change fashions and refashions human attitudes. In the past 15 years, the United States has developed further as an advanced industrial society. The trends of advanced industrialization are generally considered to imply social change in the direction of less prejudice because of three sets of variables: higher levels of education, growth of middle-income occupations and professions, and increased urbanization. Even if prejudice was found to have declined during this period, one must raise the question whether the trend was the consequence of these three factors or other ones. For example, it is not easy to separate internal social change from developments in the world arena.

We assumed in our original study that "progress" in industrial development does not automatically carry with it "progress" toward tolerance. We question, therefore, the frame of reference implicit in Samuel Stouffer's comprehensive study of *Communism, Conformity, and Civil Liberties*.[1] He found young age, more education, higher socioeconomic position, and urban residence positively associated with a tolerance of political nonconformity. Thus, he saw contemporary trends in social change as resulting in higher levels of tolerant attitudes. He emphasized that "great social, economic and technological forces are working on the side of exposing ever larger proportions of our population to the idea that 'people are different from me, with different systems of values, and they can be good people.' "[2] Clearly, people's attitudes toward political nonconformity are different from their attitudes toward minority groups. Yet his analysis included both, and he saw these social trends as also weakening ethnic prejudice.

By contrast, we see two aspects of the problem: one of tracing the

---

[1] Samuel A. Stouffer, *Communism, Conformity, and Civil Liberties*, Garden City, N.Y., Doubleday and Co., 1955.
[2] *Ibid.*, p. 220.

consequences of those social trends that work to reduce ethnic hostility, and the other of probing their actual and potential countereffects. Thus, our basic orientation is that in an advanced industrial society where individualistic values predominate, those sociological variables that tend to weaken ethnic hostility have some limits and may even generate countertrends.[3] These same advances in industrialization may also create new societal stresses and personal disruptions. For example, even during a period of high prosperity and relative economic growth, some persons experience downward social mobility—the status of sons becomes lower than their fathers'. And such downward social mobility seems to affect as much as 20 per cent of the male population.[4] Yet downward mobility is but one of the characteristics of an advanced industrialized society which we assume to be a source of ethnic intolerance, as against those sociological trends toward greater tolerance.

DECLINE IN PREJUDICE

THE JEWS. What, then, during these 15 years have been the long-term national shifts in attitude toward Jews and Negroes? Despite the proliferation of national attitude surveys, no comprehensive and systematic body of trend data has been collected over these years. Investigations have been episodic and specialized. With the notable exception of survey findings by the Division of Scientific Research of the American Jewish Committee and the more limited efforts of the National Opinion Research Center, there has been too little emphasis on the repeated use of standardized questions over time to chart contemporary social history.[5] Social scientists engaged in survey research have not assumed the responsibility for writing current social history by means of systematic trend reporting. Nevertheless, there are convincing data to support the proposition that since 1945, for the nation as a whole, there has been

[3] A similar position on "race relations" is argued by Everett C. Hughes and Helen M. Hughes, *Where Peoples Meet*, New York, The Free Press of Glencoe, 1952.

[4] Despite sociological interest in the question of social mobility in the United States, satisfactory data do not exist. The best estimates are derived from a study by the National Opinion Research Center, "Jobs and Occupations: A Popular Evaluation," *Opinion News*, September, 1947; and Richard Centers, "Occupational Mobility of Urban Occupational Strata," *American Sociological Review*, XIII, April, 1948, p. 198.

[5] It must be recognized that standardized questions are only a partial approach to charting trends in ethnic prejudice. The meaning of standardized questions changes and new dimensions of prejudice emerge. On the basis of available evidence from a wide variety of studies, there is no reason to believe that these two limitations contributed in any significant degree to the over-all trend.

a decline in the "average" or over-all level of anti-Jewish and anti-Negro attitudes. But it cannot be asserted there has been a similar marked decline in the percentage of persons with "hard-core" extremist attitudes toward these minorities. The available data from national samples are by far more adequate for charting shifts in the more "normal" levels of mild intolerance toward Jews than for measuring the concentration of intense anti-Semitic attitudes.

While the 15-year period has seen a long-term decline in prejudice toward Jews, much of the change occurred as a sharp shift after World War II, namely, during 1946-1950. Evidence of this shift appears in Table 1(I). It shows responses collected for the Division of Scientific Research of the American Jewish Committee from comparable national samples between 1940 and 1959 to the question: "Have you heard any criticism or talk against the Jews in the last six months?" Although the question has defects as a probe of anti-Semitic attitudes, it is useful because it was repeated in standardized fashion since 1940. Apparently it was designed as a projective question. But even if it reflects an objective shift in public and private discussion about Jews rather than a change in personal feelings of hostility, the two are probably manifestly linked. Despite limitations of the measure, the shift from roughly 50 per cent to 12 per cent "yes" is still very pronounced and striking.

If it is argued that this downward trend is related to basic changes in the social structure of an advanced industrial nation state, it is still necessary to observe and explain the short-term shifts. The body of data underlines that anti-Semitic attitudes have a volatility that is touched off by political and economic events. First, the period of 1940 to 1946 revealed a definite increase in anti-Semitic attitudes that might be ascribed to the tensions of the war and to dislocations after the war. Despite the fact that we were at war with a nation that persecuted Jews, there is reason to believe that anti-Semitic attitudes were strengthened among those elements which believed that the Jews were a major cause of World War II. Second, the most dramatic short-term shift came during the years 1946-1950. The marked decline in "yes" responses during those years cannot be ascribed to changes in technical research methods, although these were at work, since a different field agency collected the data. The same sharp drop around 1950 is also documented by national sample responses to a question designed to measure more extremist attitudes, namely, what groups in this country were considered a "threat to America?" (Table 2(I).) The frequency of the response "yes, the Jews," was 19 per cent in 1945, 18 per cent in 1946, and 5 per cent in 1950. This

Table 1(I)

"Have You Heard Any Criticism or Talk Against the Jews in the Last Six Months?"*

National Samples: 1940-1959†
(Percentage)

	1940	1942	1944	1946	1950	1953	1955	1956	1957	1959
Yes	46	52	60	64	24	20	13	11	16	12
No	52	44	37	34	75	80	87	89	84	88
No opinion	2	4	3	2	1	—	—	—	—	—
Total	100	100	100	100	100	100	100	100	100	100
Number	(3,101)	(2,637)	(2,296)	(1,337)	(1,203)	(1,291)	(1,270)	(1,286)	(1,279)	(1,470)

* Based on samples of total white Christian population plus Negroes. Data supplied by Dr. Marshall Sklare, Division of Scientific Research, American Jewish Committee, New York City.

† Studies for the 1940–1946 period were conducted by Opinion Research Corporation, Princeton, New Jersey; for the 1950–1957 period, by National Opinion Research Center, University of Chicago; the 1959 study was by Gallup Organization, Inc.

short-term shift may well have been influenced by the exposure of Nazi genocide practices. Another possible explanation was the consequences of the "cold war" and the rise of the Soviet Union as an object that

TABLE 2(I)

JEWS AS A "THREAT TO AMERICA"*

National Samples: 1945-1950†

	1945	1946	1950
Yes	19%	18%	5%
Number	(2,500)	(1,300)	(1,250)

* "In your opinion are there any religious, nationality, or racial groups in this country that are a threat to America?"
† 1945 and 1946 data collected by Opinion Research Corporation; 1950 data by National Opinion Research Center.

drained off hostility. On the domestic front, the Jews dropped out of a public prominence associated with World War II. This was also the period of the establishment of Israel, and the image of the fighting Israeli Army may well have weakened anti-Semitic attitudes in the United States. Third, the downward trend continues after 1950, with a short-term rise in 1957, which might be linked to the economic recession.

Long-term data on the decline in prejudice toward Jews are also found in three time samplings of college students by Emory S. Bogardus. Using his social distance scale, he found no difference in attitudes during the 20-year period 1926-1946. But in 1956, he found a decline in feelings of social distance from the Jews, similar to the postwar decline of prejudice shown in the data above.[6]

Data on shifts in the percentage of "hard-core" anti-Semites during this period are not fully adequate. In the *Dynamics of Prejudice*, four attitude patterns were identified for anti-Jewish and anti-Negro attitudes: tolerant, stereotyped, outspoken, and intensely prejudiced.[7] "In-

[6] Emory S. Bogardus, "Racial Distance Changes in the United States During the Past 30 Years," *Sociology and Social Research*, XLIII, November, 1958, pp. 127-34. Similar findings on the relative stability of anti-Semitic attitudes until after World War II are contained in H. H. Remmers and W. F. Wood, "Changes in Attitudes Toward Germans, Japanese, Jews and Negroes," *School and Society*, LXV, June, 1947, pp. 484-87.
[7] See *Dynamics of Prejudice*, New York, Harper and Bros., 1950, pp. 12-14; or pp. 116-118 of this edition.

tensely anti-Semitic" were those persons holding an elaborate range of negative stereotypes and spontaneously recommending strong restrictive action against Jews. As of 1945, the conclusion drawn from 20 national and specialized polls was that not more than 10 per cent of the adult population could be classified as intensely anti-Semitic. More specifically, the well-known *Fortune Survey* of 1946 revealed that 9 per cent of the nation's population had strongly anti-Semitic attitudes. The conclusion was based on the percentage who spontaneously named the Jews either as "a group harmful to the country unless curbed" or who designated Jews as "people trying to get ahead at the expense of people like yourself." (There was no mention of Jews in the questions by the interviewer.)

Unfortunately the type of question used in Table 2(I) has not been used in national polls in recent years. However, in the 1950's the spontaneous remark that Communists are most likely to be Jews became a useful measure of intense anti-Semitism, though with an element of ambiguity. One cannot overlook the fact that among a very small group of sophisticated persons, the high incidence of Jews among the Communist party would be taken for granted as a political and social fact. But this group is probably too small to influence national opinion poll results. Therefore, the general question of which groups are likely to be Communists appears to tap intense prejudice among the population at large. In 1950, a national sample was asked the direct question: "In this country do you think any of the people listed here are more likely to be Communist than others?" Eleven per cent named "the Jews" from the designated list.[8] In 1954, when the question was put in indirect form without specific reference to the Jews, "What kind of people in America are most likely to be Communists?" only 5 per cent of a national cross section said that Jews were most likely to be Communists.[9] But the difference between the two sets of responses could in large measure be attributed to the different form of the question and thus it is impossible to infer any actual decline of extremist anti-Semitic attitudes.

Have there been any significant changes in the stereotypes held about Jews, as well in the level of hostility? Among the original sample, the four most frequent groups of stereotypes were: (a) they are clannish, they help one another; (b) they have the money; (c) they control every-

---

[8] Data collected by National Opinion Research Center, from a sample of 1,250 white Christians.

[9] Data collected by American Institute of Public Opinion and National Opinion Research Center from a sample of 4,933 persons.

thing, they are trying to get power; and (d) they use underhanded business methods.[10] More contemporary patterns of stereotypes were revealed in the 1957 and 1959 national surveys by those who volunteered what criticism they had heard of the Jews within the last six months. The striking change was that the "clannish" stereotype had become very infrequent, while the other three stereotypes persisted with the same order of frequency. A comparison of stereotypes among Princeton undergraduates of 1932 and 1949 reveals that there was a "fading of highly negative group stereotypes."[11]

Additional evidence of changing stereotypes comes from direct questions in the 1957 and 1959 national samplings. No pronounced shifts were expected in a two-year period, yet these data show that stereotypes fluctuate. Direct questions probed the stereotypes that Jews spoil neighborhoods and that Jewish businessmen are so shrewd and "tricky" that other people do not have a fair chance in competition. (Table 3(I).) In 1959, there was much more belief that Jewish businessmen are shrewd and "tricky" than that Jews spoil neighborhoods (30 per cent agreed strongly about business, in contrast to only 11 per cent about neighborhoods). But while both stereotypes weakened to a statistically significant degree in the short two-year period, the pattern of change differed. In the case of Jews spoiling neighborhoods, the shift was in the more tolerant direction among all attitude groups. There was an increase among those who disagreed with the stereotype and a decrease among those who agreed with it. In the case of the stereotypes about Jewish businessmen, there was a drop in the percentage of those who agreed, but no corresponding rise among those who disagreed. The shift away from acceptance of the stereotype merely produced more uncertain responses. In other words, the decline in the stereotype about neighborhoods was more pronounced than the one about Jewish businessmen.

Stereotypes about the behavior of the Jews—namely, in spoiling neighborhoods—seem much more likely to weaken under the impact of direct contact than do those involving group characteristics that are illusive and hard to disprove—namely, that Jewish businessmen are shrewd and "tricky." Another plausible explanation of these shifts (if in fact the shifts are significant) is that Jews have become more integrated into residential communities and voluntary associations. And during the same period, the Negro was becoming more of a "threat" to many prejudiced

---

[10] See *Dynamics of Prejudice, op. cit.*, pp. 32-47; or pp. 136-151 of this edition.

[11] G. M. Gilbert, "Stereotype Persistence and Change Among College Students," *Journal of Abnormal and Social Psychology*, XLVI, April, 1951, pp. 245-54.

persons by pressing for residential movement into white areas. This pressure may well have been felt as more of a threat, so that resentment toward Jews moving into non-Jewish neighborhoods weakened. Jewish neighbors, previously shunned, may now appear as relatively acceptable as compared with Negro neighbors. Since stereotypes are to some degree based on social reality, there has also been a parallel corroding of the stereotyped symbol of the "clannish Jews" living in a private world of high social solidarity—enforced though it may be by the non-Jewish world. Such an explanation flows from the assumption that those stereotypes which are easiest to check against direct experience are also most likely to change as the intensity of prejudice declines. Conversely, the

TABLE 3(I)

STEREOTYPES ABOUT JEWS: HOUSING AND BUSINESS

National Samples: 1957-1959 (Percentage)*

	Nation	
	1957	1959
Jews Spoil Neighborhoods†		
Strongly agree	7	2
Agree	12	9
Uncertain	25	26
Disagree	44	46
Strongly disagree	12	17
Total	100	100
Number	(1,058)	(1,294)
Jewish Businessmen Are Shrewd and Tricky††		
Strongly agree	12	6
Agree	25	24
Uncertain	15	22
Disagree	38	38
Strongly disagree	10	10
Total	100	100
Number	(1,058)	(1,294)

* Sample of Christian white persons. Data collected by Gallup Organization, Inc.
† "The trouble with letting Jews into a nice neighborhood is that sooner or later they spoil it for other people."
†† "The trouble with Jewish businessmen is that they are so shrewd and tricky that other people do no have a fair chance in competition."

more remote stereotypes, such as "they control everything" and "they are trying to get power," would be expected to, and in fact do, persist most strongly.

THE NEGROES. The pattern of change in "typical" attitudes toward the American Negro can be inferred from data collected by the National Opinion Research Center of the University of Chicago in its periodic national samplings since 1942. At four intervals, comparable national samples, excluding Negroes, were asked, "In general, do you think Negroes are as intelligent as white people—that is, can they learn things just as well if they are given the same education and training?" The results summarize a basic transformation in attitudes toward the Negro.[12] (Table 4 (I).) For the total white population in the United States, attitudes have risen from 41 per cent who answered "yes" in 1942 to 76 per cent in 1956. A change of attitude among Southern whites on this question is equally marked during the same period, shifting from 21 per cent to 59 per cent answering "yes."

TABLE 4(I)

CHANGING ATTITUDES TOWARD NEGROES
National Samples: 1942-1956 (Percentage)

	Northern White Population	Southern White Population	Total U.S. White Population
*"Yes, Negroes Are as Intelligent as Whites"**			
1942	48	20	42
1944	47	28	44
1946	60	33	53
1956	82	59	77

* "In general, do you think Negroes are as intelligent as white people—that is, can they learn things just as well if they are given the same education and training?" Data collected by the National Opinion Research Cener.

Residential and school integration became focal points for measuring changing attitudes about discrimination. In 1942, two-thirds of the population, as measured by national sampling, objected to the idea of living in the same block with a Negro; but by 1956, a majority declared that

[12] Herbert Hyman and Paul B. Sheatsley, "Attitudes Toward Desegregation," *Scientific American*, December, 1956, pp. 35-39.

they would not object.[13] In 1942, fewer than one-third of the respondents in the nation favored school integration; by 1956 almost half endorsed the idea. This shift took place in both the North and the South. In the North, support for school integration had risen among white people from 41 per cent in 1942 to 61 per cent in 1956. In the South in 1942, only 2 per cent of the white people favored school integration; by 1956, the figure had increased to 14 per cent.

Even after 1956, as "massive" resistance to school integration temporarily developed, the national trend toward tolerant responses on this item continued, though perhaps at a slower pace. By 1959 the over-all national level expressing support for integration stood at 56 per cent as compared with just under half in 1956.[14] This slight upward trend was at work in both the North and the South. But what changes took place in the South were in the "Border States" as compared with the "Deep South." Breakdowns within the South reveal 4 per cent of the Deep South approving school integration and 23 per cent in the Border South.

Although adequate data are lacking, it is necessary to raise the question whether attitude change concerning school integration is connected with the growth of suburban, private, and parochial schools. With the growth of these school systems it may well be that more white parents are willing to express approval of integrated schools because there is little or no likelihood that their children would attend such schools.

Trends in response to "social distance" questions from national samples highlight the intensity and persistence of prejudice toward the Negro even during this period of social change. From 1948 to 1958, whatever the changes that took place in attitudes toward racial intermarriage, they hardly produced extensive tolerance. In answer to the blunt question, "Do you approve or disapprove of marriage between white and colored people," 4 per cent approved as of 1958 and most of the approval was among college graduates. By contrast, there was the marked decline in prejudice against Negroes as neighbors as measured by attitudes expressed in surveys. In 1942, two-thirds of the population objected to the idea of living in the same block with a Negro. But by 1956 a majority did not object, and in 1958, 56 per cent answered "no" to the question, "If colored people came to live next door would you move?"[15] In his

---

[13] *Ibid.*, p. 38.

[14] American Jewish Committee Research Report, *The Nationwide Poll of 1959*, p. 5. Data collected by Gallup Organization, Inc., from 1,297 white Christians.

[15] Data collected by American Institute of Public Opinion, from 1,650 whites.

study of college students, Bogardus found that between 1946 and 1956 "social distance" between these students and Negroes declined somewhat, as measured by his questionnaire tests.[16]

What, then, has changed and what remains stable in American attitudes toward the Negro during the last 15 years? Gunnar Myrdal coined the phrase the "American Dilemma" to emphasize the white man's involvement in race relations. In his comprehensive study of the position of the Negro in the United States before World War II, Myrdal stated that the majority's sense of conscience—its commitment to the creed of equality and dignity—created a powerful dilemma that was a constant source of pressure for social change. He believed that the "American Dilemma" operates with greater force among community and political leaders, but exists also as a moral norm for society at large. The greater the sense of a "dilemma," the more likely the person seems to be saying that the Negro is being treated unfairly.

How strong is this awareness of an "American Dilemma"? What changes have reshaped these attitudes since World War II? The question, "Do you think most Negroes in the United States are being treated fairly or unfairly?" supplies a crude but revealing index. (Table 5(I).)

TABLE 5(I)

CHANGING ATTITUDES TOWARD NEGROES
National Samples: 1944-1956 (Percentage)*

	Northern White Population	Southern White Population	Total U.S. White Population
"Yes, most U.S. Negroes are treated fairly"†			
1944	62	77	66
1946	63	76	66
1956	63	79	69

* Data collected by National Opinion Research Corporation.
† "Do you think most Negroes in the United States are being treated fairly or unfairly?"

It is crude because it mobilizes defensive sentiments; it is revealing because on this score, United States attitudes have changed little over the years. As of 1944, 66 per cent of a national sample thought that the Negro was being treated fairly (or the "American Dilemma" was being

[16] Emory S. Bogardus, *op. cit.*, p. 131.

felt by much less than a majority.)[17] And as expected, the percentage answering "fairly" was greater in the South than in the North (77 per cent in the South, 62 per cent in the North).

Moreover, neither the great transformation in attitudes toward Negroes nor the actual change in practices of the last 15 years has brought any measurable changes in this response pattern. In 1946, the national percentage remained at 66; by 1956, it had risen only to 69. The greater tendency of Southerners to say "fairly" persisted. In short, there was no increase of popular sensitivity to the "American Dilemma" even during this period of greater agitation for equality within the United States, and of a greater salience of race in international affairs. One plausible explanation is that the social, economic, and political progress of the Negro during this period has served to prevent any increase in a sense of moral dilemma.

Attitude patterns toward the United States Supreme Court decision that "racial segregation in the public schools is illegal" also indicate the extent to which there has been a resistance to attitude change, particularly in the South, in the face of legal and administrative changes. In 1954, 24 per cent of the Southern population approved of the decision, and by 1961, the percentage remained at the same level. The highest it had reached was 27 per cent in 1957. During the same period for the nation as a whole, the per cent rise was from 54 per cent in 1954 to 62 per cent in 1961.

AGE, EDUCATION, AND SOCIOECONOMIC STATUS

To what extent are these recent trends in prejudice, as revealed in national opinion surveys, related to basic changes in the social structure during the last 15 years? To explore this question, the social changes produced by advanced industrialism can be crudely highlighted by the key variables of age, education, and socioeconomic status. If the data were adequate, we could assess how important these variables, singly and in combination, may have been in accounting for the trend toward less prejudice. Unfortunately, the available data are hardly adequate for this purpose, but they do offer some revealing findings.

In the original study we assumed—and the data supported the conclusion—that particular sociological variables such as age, education and socioeconomic status *per se* would not be very powerful in accounting

---

[17] Hyman and Sheatsley, *op. cit.*, p. 39.

for patterns of ethnic hostility; a more dynamic and interactive analysis would. Fifteen years later Melvin Tumin, in his review study of empirical work on American anti-Semitism, comes to the same conclusion.[18] "We are led first to the realization that no single sociological characteristic will suffice to give adequate understanding or prediction of where we will encounter the greatest amount and intensity of anti-Semitism. Not age, nor income, nor education, nor region, nor any other (sociological factor) by itself, is adequate. Nor can valid statements be made about the impact of various combinations of these characteristics, unless we specify the situational context."

Nevertheless, while the impact of the variables is likely to be complex and interactive, each of the key variables permits a general trend hypothesis about its effect on prejudice. First, younger persons are likely to be less prejudiced than older persons; second, better educated persons are likely to be less prejudiced than less well-educated persons; and third, higher socioeconomic status is likely to be associated with less prejudice than is lower status.[19] To what extent does new research evidence support or throw doubt on these general hypotheses? Moreover, to what extent have changes in the age, education, and socioeconomic structure of American society contributed to shifts in prejudice patterns during the last 15 years? We have already seen that an important amount of the shift in attitude toward Jews took place in a short time span after the close of the war, and must therefore be linked to specific events—both domestic and international. On the other hand, the struggle for desegregation in the South after 1956 seems to have slowed but not stopped the trend toward greater tolerance toward Negroes. Despite these short-term shifts, we still need to explore the underlying shifts in social structure that might account for the longer-term trends.

AGE. A fundamental rationale for the hypothesis that younger persons are less prejudiced than older persons lies in the conflict between the generations.[20] The older generation is the carrier of basic values and norms in society, while the younger generation is being socialized into

---

[18] Melvin Tumin, *Inventory and Appraisal of Research on American Anti-Semitism*, New York, Freedom Books, 1961, p. 28.

[19] Of course, in empirical studies of prejudice, more educated persons or those of high status may be more skillful in obscuring their prejudices.

[20] The sample used in the *Dynamics of Prejudice* was not meant to be representative but rather to concentrate on the young age group. Nevertheless, it was possible to divide the sample into younger and older veterans; the general hypothesis held that the young were more tolerant.

accepting these values. Invariably there is tension and struggle between the generations and this is greater in an advanced industrialized society as the standards of the older generation are more quickly made obsolete by the tempo of social change. Attitudes toward minority groups become one aspect of this tension, just as do styles of clothing and standards of morality. In the search for identity, the younger age groups tend to assert their independence from the older groups, and greater tolerance toward ethnic groups is a frequent expression of this assertion. Thus, where the general trend in society is toward tolerance, the younger age groups are apt to be even more tolerant. In this sense, age is an index to the broader processes of social change. That is, the hypothesis that younger persons are less prejudiced than older persons is more than just a symptom of the conflict of generations. All of the changes of a more advanced industrialized society, such as in the United States, that might result in a decline in prejudice are likely to affect younger persons most. Numerous studies of specialized samples have found this relation between age and attitudes toward minority groups. There are historical and political conditions that have produced a reversal of this trend, however, as for example, in Germany where younger age groups were more Nazi than older groups.

This pattern of tolerance is also at work for political attitudes as well. Thus, Samuel Stouffer in his extensive national sample study of tolerance for political nonconformity found that young people were clearly more tolerant than older people. The concentration of "more tolerant" responses in the age group twenty-one to twenty-nine was 47 per cent, and it dropped systematically with age. Those persons sixty years and over revealed only 18 per cent in the tolerant category.[21]

In contrast to the findings on age grading, there is no adequate body of empirical data dealing with the life cycle of the individual and his attitudes toward minority groups. Is there any basis for speculating that as a person grows older his attitudes toward minority groups become less tolerant? It seems very plausible that they do. Impressionistic accounts of the political behavior of older people emphasize a rigidity of outlook and more extremistic demands. However, older people tend to focus on concrete economic issues and to show less concern with minority groups and the social order in general.

Given a link between age grading and prejudice, the basic question

[21] Samuel A. Stouffer, *op. cit.*, p. 92.

remains: To what extent can the decline in ethnic hostility during the last 15 years be explained by shifts in age composition among the population at large? Examination of the changes in gross age composition during this period, marked though they were compared with other periods in history, shows them to be unimportant factors in the trends in prejudice. The age structure is still relatively stable, decade by decade, and those changes that have occurred were in the age groupings under seventeen and over sixty-five. Neither one would explain the trend toward greater tolerance.[22]

The analysis of age structure and prejudice requires a more refined approach involving cohort analysis. Are the new cohorts of young people entering the adult population reducing the over-all level of prejudice because they are replacing the old cohorts above sixty years of age, who are dying off and who are more prejudiced than the middle and younger cohorts? We have no adequate cohort data but we presume that they are. Although such a cohort analysis would be important, it would not explain the process of attitude change. In particular, it remains to be shown whether growing older tends to produce a rigidity of attitudes toward minority groups, even during a period of greater tolerance.

The relationship between age and tolerance is complicated by the results of education. Young persons are more likely to be better educated and to have an education compatible with ethnic tolerance. In fact, one could argue that the general hypothesis of younger persons being more tolerant rests to some degree on the fact that the younger are better educated. That makes education the second basic variable in assessing trends toward greater tolerance.

EDUCATION.   Education correlates with a wide variety of social behavior, from consumer behavior to political attitudes. But in analyzing the consequences of education and an ever rising level of attainment, we must distinguish between education in its "intellectual" and moral value con-

[22] During the 1950-1960 decade, the median age of the population declined for the first time since 1900; it dropped from 30.2 years in 1950 to 29.3 years in 1959. But the median is a poor measure of the changes in age composition. The important changes that have occurred are those in the age groupings under seventeen years and those over sixty-five years. While the total increase in population during the decade was 17.2 per cent, those under seventeen years and over sixty-five years grew at a much faster rate (fourteen to seventeen years, 30.7 per cent; sixty-five years and over, 26.1 per cent). Middle-age cohorts remained relatively stable or grew at a rate lower than the national rate.

tent, and education as a precondition for occupational mobility. How-ever, the rationale for the hypothesis that better educated persons are likely to be less prejudiced does not rest solely on the argument that education is an index to socioeconomic position. Education should be positively correlated with tolerance both because of what is socially ex-perienced during the educational process and because of the selective processes that determine who will receive advanced schooling. It can be assumed that the effects of education will be different for different social groups. For example, the higher the socioeconomic position a person starts from, the less effect education will have on intolerant atti-tudes, because for such persons family and social background have already operated to influence the extent of their tolerant attitudes. But education in a political democracy is designed *per se to* strengthen one's personal controls and to broaden one's understanding of social reality (in Karl Mannheim's term "substantive rationality"). And both of these social processes are assumed to weaken ethnic prejudice.

The very fact that a significant portion of college graduates still hold stereotypes and support discrimination reflects the limits of the educa-tional system in modifying attitudes. Yet on the basis of some 25 national sample surveys since 1945, the positive effect seems to be real, not spuri-ous. The lower levels of prejudice among the better educated seem to involve the social experience of education specifically and not merely the sociological origins of the educated. Throughout most of the United States outside of the South, the content of education involves some in-doctrination in a tolerant outlook toward minorities. Thus, to speak of the impact of education involves more than the effort to increase intel-lectual skills and aptitudes; it involves also exposure to a specific liberal content. In parts of the South where the education system does not con-tain such a content, the effects of education would be different.

However, the impact of education is not a simple process. The avail-able data underscore areas in which education operates to reduce prej-udice. But the same body of data highlight the persistence of prejudice among the educated, as well as some instability of attitudes. These data are relevant in accounting for the persistence of a "hard core" of very prejudiced persons.

In his careful review of the effects of schooling on prejudice, Charles H. Stember concludes that the better educated are: (a) less likely to hold traditional stereotypes about Jews and Negroes, (b) less likely to favor discriminatory policies, and (c) less apt to reject casual contacts with minority group members.[23] Education seems to reduce a provincial outlook and to weaken primitive misconceptions. On the other hand, the more educated, according to Stember, are also: (a) more likely to hold highly charged and derogatory stereotypes, (b) more likely to favor informal discrimination in some areas of behavior, and (c) more apt to reject intimate contacts with minority groups.

Thus, for example, the better educated are more prone to accept the stereotypes that Jews (a) are loud, arrogant and have bad manners, (b) are shady and unscrupulous, and (c) have too much business power. Moreover, the question administered in 1952: "In this country do you think any of the people listed here are more likely to be Communists than others?" revealed that a higher concentration among the college graduates than among those with only grammar school education answered "Jews" (17 per cent for college education; 10 per cent for grammar school). Evidence that this is not merely a politically sophisticated response comes from the findings that the better educated are also more likely to perceive Jews as a "threat to the country" and as unwilling to serve in the armed forces.

The limits of social acceptance often are sharply drawn by better educated people. Covert discrimination continues to be acceptable and the desire to keep minorities at some social distance remains. These findings need to be interpreted in the light of available data which reveal that college-educated persons (and thus persons of higher socioeconomic status) have more actual contact with Jews than do less educated persons. Moreover, the better educated show no greater concern with the problem of discrimination than others, on the basis of national sample studies. In particular, better educated persons show marked concern about sending their children to school with Negroes, presumably because the educational standards are assumed to be lower in such schools. There is an important regional difference in this finding. In the South, Melvin Tumin found that among his sample in Guilford County, North Carolina, the best educated were the most prone to accept integration in the public schools.[24]

The data on education and stereotypes confirm the theory and find-

[23] Charles H. Stember, *Education and Attitude Change: The Effects of Schooling on Prejudice Against Minority Groups*, New York, Institute of Human Relations Press, 1961, pp. 168 ff.
[24] Melvin Tumin, *Desegregation: Resistance and Readiness*, Princeton, N.J., Princeton University Press, 1958, p. 193.

ings of the *Dynamics of Prejudice*. Since stereotypes are rooted in social and psychological needs, schooling alone does not consistently bring a rejection of stereotypes. The better educated are more likely to reject certain kinds of stereotypes, but new ones emerge and old images persist. Apparently, the attitudes of the educated are more liable to change under the impact of particular events. The less educated seem more stable in their attitudes. Clearly, these data indicate the persistence of prejudice despite the rising United States level of education.

In recent years, there has been, of course, swift progress in raising the educational level of the United States. During the period 1940–1957, the proportion of the population classified as functional illiterates (less than five years of elementary school) decreased by one-third. Shortly before 1940, the average citizen was a graduate of elementary school. By about 1965, the average citizen will be a high school graduate. These dramatic changes are important ingredients in the over-all decline in prejudice, although the pattern of decline is different toward Jews than toward Negroes. Each increase in education seems to be linked to less prejudice; but in the case of anti-Negro attitudes there seems to be a threshold: College-level education is necessary before attitudes toward Negroes change significantly.

Findings on education must also be assessed in the light of a crucial observation based on repeated surveys: Education as a separate factor has less consequences at the upper social levels. Within the upper socio-economic groups, educational differences make less of a difference in prejudice (toward both Negroes and Jews) than at the lower levels. Again education seems to have built-in limitations as an agent of social change for reducing prejudice; those who get the most education have been and are the least likely to be influenced by it *per se*. If the trend toward a "middle class" society continues, it may well be that the future effects of expanding education will not be as powerful as in the recent past. Or, to put it differently, the specific content of education and its personal impact as opposed to amount of it will grow in importance.

We have spoken here of the consequences of education. However, both access to education and the effects of education depend on a person's socioeconomic status.

SOCIOECONOMIC STATUS. A number of sociological arguments would lead one to anticipate that persons of middle and upper socioeconomic status would be less prejudiced than those of lower status. It can be argued that higher social position may make for greater personal security and therefore the person may feel less threatened by out-groups. Higher social position, like education, also serves to broaden personal perspectives and in turn to reduce prejudice. In the same vein, upper status groups have a greater stake in the existing social arrangements and are therefore less likely to hold extremist attitudes, including those toward minority groups. The same reasoning can be extended to portions of the middle class, especially those in the new bureaucratic occupations. But it can be argued that there are other portions of the middle class vulnerable to economic competition and social change and therefore likely to be more exposed to factors increasing ethnic intolerance.

As a result, it is not possible to postulate simple and direct relations between social class and prejudice. Likewise, to explain the trends of the last 15 years, these differences make it necessary to reject a simple economic conflict model of prejudice, although economic pressures are clearly important. Specific ethnic and religious differences within the middle class, as well as within the lower class, strongly modify the class patterns of ethnic intolerance. Finally, it was originally assumed in the *Dynamics of Prejudice* that to locate a person in the over-all stratification system—as measured by his income or occupation—was only a first step.[25] We then had to investigate the dynamics of mobility by which a person reached his socioeconomic position.

National surveys reveal that for the population as a whole and for very broad socioeconomic groupings a limited association with very general forms of ethnic prejudice does emerge. The upper social groups are at least more inhibited in their expression of ethnic intolerance. But much more relevant is what can be learned by selecting a particular metropolitan community instead of a national sample. Within the metropolitan community the interplay of social stratification and ethnic prejudice can be seen more precisely. Important regional differences are ruled out—the South versus the other regions of the country. The differences between urban and rural areas are also controlled, for there is a gradual decrease in the level of ethnic intolerance as one goes from rural areas and small towns to cities under a million to cities over a million. The use of metropolitan community samples focuses more sharply on the realities of social stratification in what we now call the mass society.

Thus, it appears that within the metropolitan community, when occupation is the measure of socioeconomic status, the difference in levels of prejudice within the middle and working classes emerge. Data col-

[25] See *Dynamics of Prejudice, op. cit.*, pp. 57-61; or pp. 161-165 of this edition.

lected by the Detroit Area Study in 1957, for a representative sample
of the adult population, allow for a breakdown of anti-Negro attitudes
by heads of households. (Table 6(I).) In these data, the concentration

TABLE 6(I)

SOCIOECONOMIC STATUS AND NEGRO PREJUDICE

Detroit Metropolitan Area Sample: 1957
(Percentage)

	Tolerant	Mildly Intolerant	Strongly Intolerant	Total Percentage	No.
Professional, managerial, and proprietors	32.6	53.3	14.1	100	(92)
Clerical, sales, and kindred	28.9	44.6	26.5	100	(83)
Craftsmen and foremen	31.7	50.0	18.3	100	(82)
Operatives, service, etc.	30.0	33.8	36.2	100	(80)
Number	(104)	(154)	(79)		(337)

of persons in the tolerant category remains relatively stable, and the
shifts by socioeconomic status are in the strongly intolerant category.
The top of the social structure—the professional and managerial group—
displayed the lowest amount of strong intolerance, while the very bottom
—the operatives and service, etc.—had the highest amount. There was,
however, no straight line progression in the intolerant category as one
moved down the hierarchy. While the professional and managerial category roughly represented the upper-middle stratum with less prejudice,
the lower-middle stratum (clerical, sales, and kindred workers) revealed
a markedly higher level. Crossing the white collar-blue collar line, the
upper working class stratum (craftsmen and foremen) was more tolerant
than the lower-middle class stratum and much like the top professional
and managerial group. The lower working class group, the most intolerant, was more prejudiced than even the lower-middle class, which is
often described impressionistically as being especially prone to extremist
attitudes.[26] This pattern of ethnic prejudice in which the upper strata

[26] Stratification in the metropolitan community involves not only the occupational
category but also differential risks of unemployment. The incidence of unemployment
falls heaviest on the lower socioeconomic strata. The Detroit Metropolitan area
during the 1950's was representative of the urban center where unemployment has
persisted. The higher level of ethnic hostility expected among the unemployed, as
compared with the employed labor force, was found present.

of both the middle and working classes are less prejudiced than the lower strata of the same classes runs parallel to the distribution of the authoritarian syndrome in representative national samples.[27]

In the metropolitan community, personal contacts between majority groups and minority groups are stratified. These contacts influence stereotypes and ethnic hostility. The Jewish minority is essentially a middle and upper class group, although a Jewish "proletariat" exists in the largest metropolitan centers. By contrast, Negroes in the urban centers are predominantly a lower and lower-middle class group. These patterns of contact help explain the higher incidence of certain stereotypes about the Jews among the better educated and upper socioeconomic status groups. Earlier, we pointed out an over-all decline in frequency of the stereotype that the Jews are "clannish" and stick together. This decline may well be linked to the greater social integration of the Jews into the metropolitan community, mainly through residence and membership in voluntary associations. Nevertheless, the "clannish" Jew is one of those select stereotypes more likely to be mentioned by upper status persons as compared with working class persons.[28] Middle class persons have most contact with Jews, and this is a case where contact does not necessarily result in weakening a stereotype. It is plausible that they are more observant of the ambiguities that result from the interplay of Jewish demands for social equality and the practice of social withdrawal into Jewish communal life. Therefore, while this stereotype decreases in the over-all measures, it reveals a greater incidence as one moves up the social structure.

A very similar reaction was found in the case of the "inferior intelligence" of Negroes. This again is one of the select stereotypes about Negroes that increases with higher socioeconomic status. Presumably, middle class persons have more chance to observe and judge the consequences of the Negro's lack of cultural preparation for higher education. For defensive reasons, middle class persons are then more prone than lower class persons to label the Negroes as inferior in intelligence.

To summarize, since World War II there has been a downward trend in the United States in prejudiced attitudes toward minority groups, as measured by attitudes toward Negroes and Jews. This trend can be

---

[27] Morris Janowitz and Dwaine Marvick, "Authoritarianism and Political Behavior," *Public Opinion Quarterly,* XVII, September, 1953, pp. 185-201.

[28] Based on data collected from 3,000 Christians by Ben Gaffin, *Catholic Digest Religious Study,* 1952.

linked to changes in the social structure of an advanced industrial society; namely, changes in the age structure, higher levels of education,
and a broadening of the middle strata. While the consequences of
changes in the age structure are equivocal, the higher levels of education and the broadening of the middle strata have operated to weaken
ethnic prejudice. But these variables, singly or in combination, cannot
account for the modification of patterns of prejudice over the last 15
years. Changes in the structure of social controls, such as the law, political organization, and the mass media, must be brought into the analysis.
More important for our analysis at this point is the conclusion that
these basic sociological variables as they change under advanced industrialism do not automatically result in "progress," if by progress we
mean the further reduction of ethnic prejudice. The consequences of
these variables are complex, and we have observed limits on their impact,
particularly in the case of education. Changes in the stratification system under advanced industrialism also reveal similar limitations, and
even indicate countertrends when we examine—as we do in the next
chapter—the consequences of social mobility.

CHAPTER II

CONSEQUENCES OF SOCIAL MOBILITY

How valid are our hypotheses linking selected aspects of social mobility to ethnic intolerance in the light of the new research reports that have appeared in the last 15 years? As implied in our original analysis, might these hypotheses apply to a broader range of social behavior than ethnic hostility?

In studying the effects of social mobility, we called our approach that of personal and social control, because we were interested in how inner and interpersonal processes interact with patterns of social control. Our underlying assumption was that the effects of social mobility on beliefs and attitudes, including prejudice, derive not only from differing group norms but also from how the person responds to group norms. We were interested not only in explaining how group norms evolve, but in understanding the range of attitudes held by persons within a relatively homogeneous group as well.

By personal controls, we mean the internalized patterns that regulate and influence human predispositions and emotions and thereby condition overt behavior. By social control, we mean the institutionalized patterns regulating and influencing groups as they pursue social values and social goals. The approach of personal and social control was used to compare and contrast the correlates of prejudice against Jews and Negroes.[1] We hardly sought to contribute to a unified theory of behavior that would be applicable to prejudice. But neither did we give priority to either social or psychological variables. Our frame of reference was interdisciplinary and our objectives were limited. We believed that the concept of control—personal and social—supplied a useful coordinating device. By using a sociological approach to prejudice and its correlates, we felt that psychological mechanisms could be studied as medi-

---

[1] See *Dynamics of Prejudice*, New York, Harper and Bros., 1950: Chapter VII, *Tolerance: A Function of Control*, and Chapter VIII, *Condoning Intolerance: Anti-Negro Attitudes*, pp. 94-161; or pp. 198-265 of this edition.

ating variables. For example, one of our central hypotheses was that downward social mobility would increase ethnic intolerance. Downward social mobility is seen as a sociological process which has effects on psychological processes connected with personal control. We are aware, of course, that psychological processes contribute to mobility, particularly to mobility different from dominant societal trends. But the underlying rationale was that downward mobility as a social process would increase feelings of subjective deprivation and insecurity, which in turn would contribute to hostility and prejudice. Likewise, from a psychological orientation, the sociological variables would lend understanding of the context. We believe the same approach would be relevant for a range of social behavior broader than ethnic intolerance.

This approach of personal and social control stems from the work of Émile Durkheim, who focused attention on the disruptive consequences of social mobility in his classic study of suicide.[2] Durkheim sought to explain in social terms what was looked on as a psychological act. For him, the higher incidence of certain types of suicide indicated a weakening of the social bond or of "collective representations." He recognized that a special type of suicide could also be linked to overintegration and overrigidity of social norms.

Durkheim saw a weakening of social bonds as a result of the growth of the industrial division of labor, which alters the basic institutions of society. For him, social mobility was a specially important manifestation of the industrial division of labor. He felt it would weaken the collective representations on which social stability rests. Therefore, he expected—and found—higher rates of suicide among groups with greater social mobility.

In retrospect, we would note three limitations of Durkheim's analysis. First, he overlooked the positive contribution that social mobility with its widening horizons can make to personal well-being and social stability. This takes the forms of releasing personal and group creativity, a process that we still understand only dimly. Second, he underestimated the potential of social institutions and of new social inventions to contain, and even overcome, the disruptive effects of social mobility. Third, he did not concern himself with the interpersonal mechanisms by which a person may give up old values and incorporate new ones. He overlooked the variation in the capacity of human beings with similar social back-

---

[2] Émile Durkheim, *Le Suicide: étude de sociologie*, Paris, F. Alcan, 1897. (In English: *Suicide: A Study in Sociology*, New York, The Free Press of Glencoe, 1951.)

grounds to develop requisite new personal controls and incorporate new norms.

In our analysis, a person with stronger personal controls—as opposed to rigid inner controls—would be a person who was able to adjust to varying conditions connected with social mobility; that is, he would have a stronger ego and more effective psychological resources for coping with the personal consequences of social change. He would be able to withstand the pressure and disruption of social mobility more than would a person with weaker personal controls. Moreover, since Durkheim's time, the "world view" toward mobility has changed. Social mobility has emerged as a desirable social goal in the United States, an end to be sought after by "good" people. Thus, in our efforts to study the consequences of social mobility on ethnic prejudice, we sought to go beyond the frame of reference supplied by Durkheim; we sought to incorporate—directly or indirectly—a person's reactions to mobility, that is, his definition of the situation.

Our hypotheses about social mobility and ethnic prejudice were limited by the following considerations. First, we were concerned with the effects of personal mobility; that is, the movement of persons and families from one social stratum to another. Social shifts in the position of a whole group, as they affect prejudice, provide a closely related but distinct issue, although we did not focus on this problem in *Dynamics of Prejudice*. In the writings of Robert E. Park,[3] one finds a discussion of prejudice and group mobility. For him, prejudice was a social response—a resistant response—to change in the social order. When Negroes as a group moved up the social scale, there would necessarily be an increase in social competition and therefore in social prejudice, as a defensive reaction for maintaining the older social order. But our materials on social change and prejudice, over the last 20 years, do not support the view that a rise in social position for the Negro directly increases prejudice. The process seems to be more complex, more varied, and more interactive. Higher social position, including social benefits won by direct action, as by the "sit-ins," also brings greater respect for the particular minority group. Thus, group mobility is an important influence on ethnic prejudice. Nevertheless, our empirical data dealt with a narrower problem: namely, that as a society moves into advanced industrialism, personal mobility is fundamental to the process of social change. In investigating trends that might slow or even operate against

[3] Robert E. Park, *Race and Culture*, New York, The Free Press of Glencoe, 1950.

the growth of tolerance, personal mobility is of special importance.

Second, in the original study and in evaluating the various new studies, we speak of a particular time and place. Our focus was on the United States as an advanced industrial society. We were concerned with social mobility in the metropolitan community, where the bulk of the American population resides. The changes that take place in urbanization, in moving from the agricultural sector to the urban sector, are not directly covered by our hypotheses. We do not believe our hypotheses are directly applicable to rural areas. They might not apply directly to the South with its special historical traditions.

Third, the period during which we were studying social mobility was one of economic expansion and without prolonged economic depression. On historical and theoretical grounds, we rejected the assumption that the effects of upward and downward mobility would be the same. There was every reason to believe that downward mobility would be the more disruptive. It not only would weaken social bonds, but would forcibly confront the person with the fact that his social experience was at variance with the cultural ideal and with major societal trends. Both pressures would weaken or strain his personal control and increase his feelings of deprivation and insecurity. These psychological mechanisms would increase his level of prejudice, even above what existed in the group he was entering.

Upward social mobility during this recent period would not have had the same effect. A moderate amount of upward mobility is widespread and in a sense typical or "normal." With this pattern so widespread, there was no reason to suppose that moderate upward mobility would create high levels of social and personal disruption. Only among persons who had experienced extreme upward mobility could we expect to find the consequences described by Durkheim. What is required is a measure of normal or "expected" upward mobility so that mobility beyond that is extreme or "abnormal."

We were, of course, fully aware that certain social institutions, such as voluntary associations and religious groups, operate to contain the disruptive consequences of social mobility. Yet, on balance we expected both downward mobility and extreme upward mobility to have the over-all effect of increasing the incidence of high ethnic hostility. We rejected, as not being overriding, the reverse proposition that ethnic prejudice would influence these patterns of mobility because there was no theoretical rationale to support it; neither did it seem plausible. This might operate for some cases but not as a systematic factor, especially not for extreme upward mobility.

Fourth, social mobility variables cannot explain the historical genesis of ethnic prejudice in any particular social group. They are relevant only in explaining the mobile person's deviation from or conformity to group norms.[4] In the original study and in all of the subsequent studies, the research approach was to focus on the correlates of high versus low ethnic prejudice. This was done by cross-sectional analysis at a particular time period. It meant that the norms of ethnic prejudice had to be identified for each group—that is, the group's central tendency and its range from high to low. Thus, the more we know about the "norms" of intolerance in a particular group, the more precisely can we identify the effects of mobility. To study these effects in national samples is highly complex, because the norms of the many social groupings become much harder to identify. That is why relatively homogeneous samples were necessary to test our hypotheses.

In summary, no simple assumption can be made about the effects of mobility on prejudice, or for that matter on other types of social behavior. In the search for generalizations, we must keep in mind the direction and extent of movement, the norms of the groups to and from which the person is moving, and the economic context of the mobility process.

DOWNWARD SOCIAL MOBILITY

Efforts to study the hypothesis that downward social mobility increases ethnic hostility have been rewarding. They also demonstrate that sociological investigations can be cumulative. The seven relevant efforts to restudy the problem have produced evidence to support the hypothesis, at least for the period of the last 15 years of economic expansion. (See Table 1(II).) At the same time they help to reformulate the original proposition by more clearly identifying which social groups are most vulnerable to the disruptive effects of mobility.

It was assumed in the *Dynamics of Prejudice* that a single variable can explain only limited aspects of ethnic prejudice. This makes a multivariate analysis appropriate. Since the original study was completed,

---

[4] We focused on social mobility because we were concerned with social change and not because we considered it to be the "key" sociological variable in understanding prejudice.

TABLE 1(II)

REPLICATION STUDIES

PROPOSITION: DOWNWARD SOCIAL MOBILITY INCREASES ETHNIC PREJUDICE

Investigator	Sample	Instrument	Target Group	Prejudice Measure	Type of Mobility	Comparison Group	Replication
Bettelheim and Janowitz[1]	150 World War II veterans of Chicago, under 35 years, interviewed 1945	Intensive structured interviews	Jews; Negroes	Typology based on 12 response categories	Intra-generation	a. No mobility b. Upward mobility	a. Confirmed b. Confirmed
Curtis[2]	Probability sample of Detroit Area Study, interviewed 1954	Standard survey research interview	Negroes	Coding of spontaneous references	Inter-generation	a. No mobility b. Upward mobility	a. Confirmed b. Confirmed
Greenblum and Pearlin[3]	Representative sample of 664 adults from Elmira, N.Y., interviewed 1948	Standard survey research interview	Jews; Negroes	Responses to individual questions	Inter-generation	a. No mobility b. Upward mobility	a. Confirmed on 6 items; tied on 1 item b. Not confirmed
Silberstein and Seeman[4]	Sample of 665 persons of Morgantown, West Virginia, published 1960	Standard survey research interview	Jews; Negroes	Anti-Semitic and anti-Negro scale of authoritarian personality	Inter-generation	a. No mobility b. Upward mobility	a. Partially confirmed b. Confirmed
Lenski[5]	Probability sample of 640 adults, interviewed 1959 in Detroit Area	Standard survey research interview	Negroes	Responses to individual questions	Inter-generation	a. No mobility b. Upward mobility	a. Confirmed b. Confirmed

Pettigrew[5]	180 New England adults and 186 Southern adults from Carolina and Georgia, interviewed 1955	Standard survey research interview	Jews; Negroes	8-item scale of anti-Semitic; 12-item measure of anti-Negro	Inter-generation	a. No mobility	a. Confirmed for Northern sample; reversal for Southern sample
Tumin[7]	Sample of 287, Guilford County, North Carolina, published 1958	Standard survey research interview	Negroes	6 Gutman type scales	Inter-generation	a. No mobility b. Upward mobility	a. Partially confirmed b. Confirmed
Leggett[8]	375 blue collar male heads of households in Detroit, interviewed 1960	Intensive structured interview	Negroes	Coding of spontaneous references	Intra-generation	a. No mobility	a. Confirmed

[1] Bruno Bettelheim and Morris Janowitz, *Dynamics of Prejudice*, New York, Harper and Bros., 1950, pp. 59, 150.
[2] Richard F. Curtis, *Consequences of Occupational Mobility in a Metropolitan Community*, Unpublished Ph.D. dissertation, University of Michigan, 1958, p. 196.
[3] Joseph Greenblum, and Leonard I. Pearlin, "Vertical Mobility and Prejudice: A Socio-Psychological Analysis," in Reinhard Bendix and S. M. Lipset (eds.), *Class, Status and Power*, New York, The Free Press of Glencoe, 1953, pp. 480-91.
[4] Fred B. Silberstein and Melvin Seeman, "Social Mobility and Prejudice," *American Journal of Sociology*, LX, November, 1959, pp. 258-64.

[5] Gerhard E. Lenski, Special tabulations prepared on data presented in *The Religious Factor: A Sociological Study of Religious Impact on Politics, Economics and Family Life*, Garden City, N.Y., Doubleday and Co., 1961.
[6] Thomas F. Pettigrew, "Regional Differences in Anti-Negro Prejudice," *Journal of Abnormal and Social Psychology*, LIX, July, 1959, p. 33.
[7] Melvin M. Tumin, *Desegregation: Resistance and Readiness*, Princeton, N.J., Princeton University Press, 1958, p. 130.
[8] John Carl Leggett, *Working Class Consciousness in an Industrial Community*, Unpublished Ph.D. thesis, University of Michigan, 1962.

however, such techniques have been greatly improved. We sought a partial solution by using a relatively homogeneous sample. Our sampling procedures de-emphasize the difference in levels of prejudice at the extremes of the social structure. We sought to reduce or eliminate the special problems of studying prejudice at the very top of the social structure. And by excluding Negroes, we reduced representation from the very bottom. Nevertheless, it needs to be emphasized that to the extent that prejudice varies between social status groups, we sought to correct these differences in testing our mobility hypotheses.

The first test of our downward mobility hypothesis was to compare levels of prejudice between those who were stationary in the middle classes, and those who were downwardly mobile from the middle class. But, the downward mobility hypothesis could be put to a more severe test. We could examine whether persons who move downward are not only more prejudiced than the group they left but also more prejudiced than the lower status group they enter. It is a more severe test because prejudice in the stationary, lower status groups is usually greater than in the middle status groups. The downwardly mobile were also compared with those moving upward.

Using the more stringent test, these seven studies produced a general pattern of confirmation (Table 1(II)). Four studies produced clear-cut confirmation; two yielded partial confirmation. Uniform measures of statistical significance were not possible because of how the data were collected and published; however, two samples were significant at the .01 level or better. (Partial confirmation implies either that results were in the predicted direction but did not achieve statistical significance, or that the relationship could be observed for the more limited test of the middle class stables versus the downwardly mobiles.) The seventh study confirmed the proposition at the statistical level for its Northern sample, while the finding was reversed for its Southern sample. Of the six Northern samples, there was not a single reversal, only one partial confirmation, and all the remaining were confirmed. When comparing the downwardly mobile with the upwardly mobile as another test of the proposition, roughly similar results were obtained.

The samples covered a variety of populations and methodologies. Three samples represent the Northern urban metropolis; two of them were drawn from the Detroit Area Study by the Department of Sociology of the University of Michigan, which used probability sampling and standardized interview procedures (Richard F. Curtis and Gerhard

Lenski). A third made use of an urban working class population (John Leggett). Another sample studied by similar research procedures was the one used by Joseph Greenblum and Leonard I. Pearlin in their reanalysis of the Elmira voting study data. The special relevance of this latter study is that it reflects attitudes among the minority of the population who live in small industrial communities. Silberstein and Seeman interviewed a group of residents of Morgantown, West Virginia, for the specific purpose of probing the relationship between social mobility and prejudice. Two studies involved Southern samples: one included a North-South comparison, undertaken by Thomas F. Pettigrew; the other, by Melvin M. Tumin, made possible a very careful study of attitudes toward desegregation in North Carolina.[5]

Both John Leggett and Richard Curtis used spontaneous expressions of hostility as their operational measures of ethnic prejudice. Leggett's work in particular is an interesting example of the field approach required for studying ethnic and moral values, especially among working class persons. His study was designed to probe class consciousness—not in a rigid Marxian sense, but in the concrete realities: style of life, job opportunities, and political power in the daily life of a worker in a metropolitan community. His particular insight was that class consciousness in the working class—the person's awareness of the class-based limitations on his style of life (or of limitations imposed by the social order)—depends on the ethnic factor. He found, holding income and skill constant, that Poles were more class conscious than Germans, and Negroes more class conscious than Poles. In general terms, the lower the ethnic status the higher was the level of class consciousness. The order was Negroes, Poles, Germans.

While probing social class consciousness, Leggett had an ideal opportunity to elicit expressions of anti-Negro hostility among white members of his working-class sample. Because his sample was sociologically homogeneous, and because the interview probed effectively for levels of hostility, the results were noteworthy in that the downwardly mobile work-

---

[5] While these studies used a variety of operational measures of prejudice, all the findings point in the same direction. However, the findings were most revealing and most significant when relatively homogeneous samples were used, and when the measure of prejudice was not a response pattern to a standardized direct probe, but spontaneous expressions of ethnic hostility on neutral or indirect questions designed to elicit expressions of hostility. This device isolated the very intolerant on a more meaningful basis than by arbitrary statistical measures of limited and highly structured responses. Both devices were used in the *Dynamics of Prejudice*.

ers were most prejudiced. Among the workers with stable mobility backgrounds, 26.9 per cent gave spontaneous responses that were anti-Negro as against 43.3 per cent among the downwardly mobile.

Curtis' findings had further relevance. He was able to measure the extent of downward mobility—moderate, high, and extreme—on the basis of a more refined occupational stratification code than was used in most of the other studies (but similar to that employed in *Dynamics of Prejudice*). This enabled him to confirm the proposition that more extensive downward social mobility was linked to higher levels of ethnic intolerance. His findings indicate that the downward mobility proposition operates both within and between the white collar and blue collar stratification system.

Greenblum and Pearlin's re-examination of the downward mobility hypothesis took the supplementary step of studying subgroups. The proposition was validated for the entire sample: men and women, for the subsample of the gainfully employed; for males only; and for gainfully employed males under thirty-five. They also broke down their data by social class of origin into manual stationary, downwardly mobile, and nonmanual stationary. Again the findings were that the downwardly mobile are more prejudiced than the stationary, manual or nonmanual.

Silberstein and Seeman introduce a related distinction between two different outlooks on status—those stressing mobility and those stressing achievement. They report that the distinction "lies in the fact that the latter tend to give status and prestige a lower value—i.e., they choose to emphasize the relative importance of, for example, friendship, political freedom, community life, or intrinsic interest in the job as compared with the value of social rank."[6] For our purpose, this distinction is relevant for locating those persons most vulnerable to the disruptive effects of downward mobility. They offer the hypothesis that among the downwardly mobile, those persons who stress mobility would be more prejudiced than those stressing achievement. Empirical results support this proposition when objective measures of mobility are used.[7]

---

[6] Fred B. Silberstein and Melvin Seeman, "Social Mobility and Prejudice," *American Journal of Sociology*, LX, November, 1959, p. 259.

[7] The authors' attempts to show that mobility orientations are more important than actual mobility patterns are subject to two reservations. The data on ethnic intolerance collected by the scales of *The Authoritarian Personality* do not permit the analysis of variance as performed. More fundamentally, the issue is a theoretical one. The authors seek to develop a theory of prejudice based on status striving. We feel that such a concept is relevant, but it is much too narrow a theoretical base for explaining ethnic hostility and prejudice.

UPWARD SOCIAL MOBILITY

By contrast to the extensive restudy of the downward mobility hypothesis, new data on upward social mobility are limited and incomplete. In retrospect, we attribute this in part to our not being more explicit about the link between rational inner controls and the effects of upward mobility. Added to this, full replication requires both direction and extent of mobility, and only one of the seven studies examined both.

Our central hypothesis did not state that upward social mobility would increase prejudice. Upward social mobility is widespread in the United States, and there is no reason to expect a moderate amount to be particularly stressful or disruptive. The linkage of upward mobility and ethnic intolerance was based on extent of mobility; i.e., if a person had experienced extreme (not just moderate) upward mobility, one would expect higher levels of prejudice on the basis of an approach seeking to link personal and social controls to levels of prejudice.

What prediction could be made about moderate or average upward mobility? In the original research, it was found that for our sample of young veterans, the total group of upwardly mobile persons (characterized mainly by moderate upward mobility) were more tolerant than those who had experienced no change in social position. Among the rapidly upward subgroup, a higher level of ethnic intolerance was found. We have no theoretical grounds for stating, as a general proposition, that moderate upward mobility would reduce prejudice for the period studied. We can merely suggest that moderate upward mobility would be associated with levels of tolerance equal to *or* higher than those of the nonmobile group. The approach of personal and social control implies that moderate upward mobility would not create inner pressures that would show up in greater prejudice; either no change would take place or else prejudice would decrease. One can argue that, given American values which legitimate gradual social mobility, both economic and status, the moderately upwardly mobile person is likely to have relatively effective personal controls. Likewise, the process of moderate social mobility is likely to strengthen the personal controls under which the individual functions.

Of the seven studies, one did not investigate upward mobility (Leggett). Of the remaining six, five included Northern samples. In three of these five cases, results demonstrated that the upwardly mobile group as a whole was more tolerant than the nonmobile. (For both the Curtis and Lenski samples, the findings are clear-cut; the Silberstein and Seeman study is a partial confirmation in that some subsamples were equal to that of the nonmobile group, but there were no significant reversals.) Only one Northern sample presents a clear-cut case in which the upward mobility group is more intolerant than the stable group (Greenblum and Pearlin). This alternative pattern appears partially due to the reported structure of prejudice in Elmira. There, in contrast to general expectation, a very low level of ethnic intolerance was found in the lower class, particularly as to residential location of Negroes.

Of the two Southern samples, the larger and more comprehensive study by Tumin indicates that upward mobility was linked to lower levels of prejudice than in the stable lower class groups. The Pettigrew sample, which is more limited in scope, did not confirm the hypothesis.

Thus, the evidence gathered from these new studies goes a long way to support the minimum observation that moderate upward mobility does not increase ethnic prejudice and often brings some decline in hostility.

For the more important theoretical proposition that rapid and extreme upward mobility would increase prejudice, only the study by Curtis can be cited. In his Detroit sample, he found that persons who had experienced extreme upward mobility had markedly higher levels of ethnic hostility. Since it was the only study to collect comparable findings, no case can be built to confirm this hypothesis. But the lack of adequate data does not cancel its relevance.

In summary, our investigation of sociological variables was designed to determine which trends in an advanced industrialized society operate for and against greater ethnic tolerance. New studies strongly support the view that under advanced industrialism downward personal mobility operates against the general social trend toward ethnic tolerance. Estimates of the impact of automation on the occupational structure indicate new sources of downward social mobility for displaced workers, along with higher levels of skill being required of other population segments. We cannot estimate the magnitude of these trends from available data. But one can speculate that their effects on attitudes toward ethnic minorities are likely to be felt, despite the generally higher levels of education in the society.

MOBILITY AND SOCIAL CONTROL

Findings on the relation between mobility and prejudice also integrate with new research on social stratification. There is no reason to believe that the effects of mobility on ethnic intolerance differ widely from its effects on mental health, family relations, and even political behavior. It was never our assumption that prejudice could be understood as a distinct phenomenon apart from other types of social and psychological behavior. On the contrary, our concern with personal and social controls represents our conviction that to study prejudice is simply one approach to an understanding of human behavior and of conformity or deviance in modern society.

Ours was not an approach which sought to study mass psychopathology or mass behavior in a global fashion, whereby one problem area could be substituted for another. We did not assume that the variables helping us to understand prejudice could apply directly in explaining mental health, family disorganization, or political extremism. Each of these problem areas has its own generic factors. But by using the framework of personal and social controls, we believed that some of the key variables relevant for understanding prejudice would also illuminate other problem areas and would be useful for other investigations. Social mobility is just such a variable, having wider relevance than prejudice and therefore of significance for understanding social structure and personality patterns.

In the past, research on social structure in the United States has concentrated mainly on describing social stratification patterns and on isolating the positive and negative factors that affect social mobility. Only a handful of past empirical works have focused rigorously on tracing out the consequences of American mobility. Since publication of *Dynamics of Prejudice,* there has been a quickening of interest in the dynamics of social stratification. Therefore, it is now possible to place the original and subsequent study of prejudice in the context of a broader understanding of social stratification in the United States.

The popular image of the impact of upward mobility in the United States has been a positive one. Social mobility is a mechanism through which a person pursues his self-interest and at the same time helps improve society while it maintains its fundamental equalitarian values. By contrast, academic sociologists have often stressed its negative aspects.[8] But to focus attention on the disruptive aspects of social mobility is equally one-sided. If mobility produces inconsistencies and strains in social behavior and tradition, there is reason to believe that a person or a social group which remains immobile is not spared its own forms of social pain and discomfort. More important, although we are interested in the disruptive consequences of mobility, we must not overlook its positive consequences. What we also need to explain is why social mobility has not produced even higher levels of social disorganization and prejudice. If mobility is mainly disruptive in its impact, then the present rates of personal and social disorganization should be even higher.

Under which circumstances does social mobility add to disorganization and under which circumstances does it strengthen consensus? Stratification is present in all societies.[9] Changes in technology, in production and consumption, in the educational system, and in political decision-making influence stratification and social mobility. Moreover, there are pervasive social and psychological factors that select certain persons for mobility—up or down. There is also reason to believe that constitutional factors—levels of energy and vitality—may be involved. In turn, the effects of mobility, from the point of view of personal and social controls, are manifested through and modified by the basic group structures of an industrialized society. At a minimum, the primary group as well as community structures and bureaucratic organizations act to control and to modify those effects.

For an understanding of contemporary social change, the simple classical distinction between primary and secondary group structures will suffice for integrating empirical data on the effects of social mobility in the United States.[10] The consequences of mobility on primary group structures (for example, family, work groups, friendship cliques) can

[8] Melvin Tumin, "Some Unapplauded Consequences of Social Mobility in a Mass Society," *Social Forces*, XXXVI, 1957, pp. 32-37.

[9] Pitirim Sorokin, *Social Mobility*, New York, Harper and Bros., 1927; Talcott Parsons, "A Revised Analytical Approach to the Theory of Social Stratification," in *Class, Status and Power*, edited by Reinhard Bendix and Seymour M. Lipset, New York, The Free Press of Glencoe, 1953. For a review of the empirical literature, see Reinhard Bendix and Seymour M. Lipset, *Social Mobility in Industrial Society*, Berkeley, University of California Press, 1959.

[10] Charles Horton Cooley focused attention on the sociological significance of the primary group. Out of his work and the efforts of others such as Elton Mayo and Edward A. Shils, the distinction between primary and secondary group structure has emerged. Charles Horton Cooley, *Social Organization*, New York, Scribner's, 1927.

be very different from its effects on secondary group structures (community organization, religious association, or political parties). On the basis of this distinction, available findings of empirical research, which seem highly diffuse and even contradictory, assume convergence in two important ways. Two propositions may help in summarizing the present state of research on the consequences of social mobility, recognizing that selective factors such as motivation and intelligence may predispose persons toward mobility.

One: Social mobility has often been found to have disruptive implications for the structure of primary group relations and related interpersonal processes, and thus to carry socially disruptive and maladjustive consequences. The findings that support this conclusion do not offer precise data about differential rates of mobility. Nevertheless, it has been documented that both upward and downward mobility have socially disruptive consequences for primary group structures. The social and psychological processes at work are the same as those that link ethnic hostility to social mobility. On *a priori* grounds, as in the case of ethnic prejudice, one expects greater disruption to flow from downward mobility than from upward mobility, and the empirical findings give support to this conclusion.

Two: For the consequences of social mobility on the nature and extent of participation in secondary group structures, a markedly different order of inferences can be made. Here, social mobility does not necessarily have negative effects on participation in secondary group structures. In fact, upward social mobility, especially within the middle class, tends to orient and incorporate mobile groups into many types of secondary group structures and thus enhances the pursuit of self-interests. By contrast, downward mobility does not seem to produce effective involvement in secondary group structures. It should be kept in mind that these consequences for secondary group structures refer mainly to research findings accumulated during the post-World War II period of relative economic security and expansion, and could be different during periods of mass economic depression. The underlying assumption is that the involvement in secondary group structures is an essential device of social control, which contains or counteracts the disruptive consequences of mobility on the primary and interpersonal processes.[11]

[11] A similar formulation is presented by Eugene Litwak, "Occupational Mobility and Family Cohesion," *American Sociological Review*, XXV, February, 1960, pp. 9-21.

In other words, from the point of view of a theory of personal and social control, the effects of social mobility are influenced by the interplay of primary and secondary group structures.[12]

One interesting and comprehensive effort to investigate the effects of mobility on participation in primary and secondary group structures is that of Richard Curtis in his study *Consequences of Occupational Mobility in a Metropolitan Community*.[13] Curtis undertook an extensive secondary analysis of a number of the annual surveys of the Detroit Area Study. Despite the fact that the data were limited for his purposes, his findings supply suggestive confirmation of the differential effects of mobility.[14] Among mobile persons he found a lower rate of social participation in primary groups, such as contacts with extended family, relatives and friends, and higher amounts of family disruption. Downward social mobility and extreme upward mobility, as anticipated, were the most likely to produce the "Durkheim" effect of weakened social bonds. However, Curtis concluded that the extent of these relationships was often small and at times without statistical significance. Aside from the

[12] Empirical research on social stratification in the United States makes possible the following observations about the social context within which the consequences of social mobility on primary and secondary group structures operate: (a) The United States has been characterized by a high rate of social mobility, and there is no basis for concluding that these rates are declining. (b) The high rates of upward social mobility have been simultaneously accompanied by lower but significant rates of downward social mobility. (c) The avenues of social mobility change, and higher education seems of increasing importance as a precondition for social mobility. (d) For research purposes, it is convenient to describe the occupational or prestige characteristics of individuals, although such an approach does not present a comprehensive base for analyzing patterns of mobility. Even before the development of contemporary field methodology, Joseph Schumpeter, in his brilliant essay on "Social Classes in an Ethnically Homogeneous Enrivonment," focused attention on the family as a basic unit for describing the processes of social mobility. Social mobility involving all members of a family shifting from one stratum to another is likely to have different consequences from social mobility involving one member of a family. We have one form of social mobility when the son whose father is a skilled worker and whose mother is a housewife enters the engineering or accounting profession, and another form of mobility if the son's father was a skilled worker and his mother a public school teacher. In an industrialized society, it is useful to describe mobility by investigating the occupational background of both the man's mother and wife. Unfortunately, the research studies that trace out the consequences of social mobility on primary and secondary structure have usually described social mobility in terms of the individual, not the family.

[13] Unpublished Ph.D. dissertation, University of Michigan, 1958.

[14] Curtis' data were limited for two reasons: Strict probability sampling produced a heterogeneous sample which obscured the effects of social mobility; the number of cases available were limited because questions were seldom repeated from one year to the next, and because respondents with rural backgrounds had to be eliminated. Curtis himself emphasizes the difficulty of getting adequate measures of primary group participation by the standard survey method as compared with patterns of participation in secondary associations.

special character of the sample, which obscured the effects of mobility, Curtis was anticipating a greater disruptive effect than would be warranted by the approach of personal and social controls. Moreover, he was studying the effects of mobility between the generations which were expected to be less disruptive than mobility within a generation.

The Curtis study is of particular interest because his findings confirm that social mobility, particularly upward, does not produce markedly lower rates of participation in secondary group structures.[15] In some selected areas, the mobile persons were more involved, for example, in sports clubs; and church attendance was higher among those persons with church affiliations.

Paralleling Curtis' work are a series of more delimited studies that tend to give additional support to the differential effects of mobility.

PRIMARY GROUP RELATIONS

The work of Julius Roth and Robert F. Peck confirms the above findings on the disruptive effects of mobility on primary group relations by focusing on family instability. The downwardly mobile spouses produced the most unstable marriages. Interestingly enough, if both spouses were upwardly mobile, there was no negative effect. indicating a limiting condition to the disruptive implications of mobility on family relations.[16]

Evelyn Ellis found a sample of mobile career women to have markedly more disruptive interpersonal and primary group relations as compared with a comparable sample of nonmobile career women; mobile career women had fewer attachments to their parents, reported fewer intimate friends, drank more often, had more psychosomatic illness, and more conflicts with parents over religion, politics, careers, and personal conduct.[17] Since intensive case studies can often illuminate these processes, Bossard and Sanger traced out in detail the effects of social mobility on children due to marked and sudden upward changes in social position. They report development not only of feelings of insecurity and isola-

[15] Richard F. Curtis, "Occupational Mobility and Membership in Formal Voluntary Associations: A Note on Research," *American Sociological Review,* XXIV, December, 1959, pp. 846-48; and "Occupational Mobility and Church Participation," *Social Forces,* XXXVIII, May, 1960, pp. 316-19.

[16] Julius Roth and Robert F. Peck, "Social Class and Social Mobility Factors Related to Marital Adjustment," *American Sociological Review,* XVI, August, 1951, pp. 478-91.

[17] Evelyn Ellis, "Social Psychological Correlates of Upward Social Mobility Among Unmarried Career Women," *American Sociological Review,* XVII, 1952, pp. 558-63.

tion, but also compensatory mechanisms such as increased verbalization.[18]

Family contacts and friendship patterns are another relevant dimension of primary group processes disrupted by social mobility. Both Curtis and Litwak report that upwardly mobile persons have somewhat lower rates of extended family contacts including visiting patterns. The phrase "somewhat lower" needs to be emphasized, for the mobility processes hardly denude the family of such primary contacts but weaken and attenuate them. These effects were greater in the blue collar group, which relies more heavily on family contacts, than in the middle class. In some of this research, there is an effort to control for geographical mobility. It is mainly among younger middle class families that upward mobility is likely to lessen primary contacts with neighbors, friends, and work associates. However, it is precisely for this group that such contacts are an important source of integration with the large community and they seem most vulnerable to these effects of upward mobility.

Following the specific direction of Durkheim's research, suicide, and likewise mental illness, and psychopathology can be taken as indicators of primary group processes that have been affected by social mobility. Although it is generally accepted that mobility increases mental strain and mental disease, empirical validation is far from impressive. Extensive statistical analysis of suicide and homicide by Henry and Short confirms the extreme disruptive consequences of social mobility, although their measures were indirect since they were based mainly on fluctuations in the business cycle.[19] Porterfield and Gibbs found that in New Zealand the mobility patterns of persons who committed suicide were predominantly downward, but some conformed to the upward mobility pattern as well, confirming the original formulation of Durkheim.[20] "Summary of Studies on the Incidence of Mental Disorders," by Rose and Stub reviews 65 studies, none of which used mobility as the basis for delimiting incidence groups.[21] Much of the work on ecological distribution of mental illness by Faris and Dunham relates indirectly to

[18] James H. S. Bossard and Winogene Pratt Sanger, "Social Mobility and the Child: A Case Study," *Journal of Abnormal and Social Psychology*, VL, 1949, pp. 266-71.

[19] Andrew Henry and James Short, *Suicide and Homicide*, New York, The Free Press of Glencoe, 1954.

[20] Austin L. Porterfield and Jack P. Gibbs, "Occupational Prestige and Social Mobility of Suicides in New Zealand," *American Journal of Sociology*, LXVI, No. 2, September, 1960, pp. 147-52.

[21] Arnold Rose, ed., *Mental Health and Mental Disorders*, New York, W. W. Norton, 1955, pp. 87-116.

the consequences of mobility.[22] Hollingshead and Redlich sought to describe the class stratification of schizophrenia, and their findings confirm those of Faris and Dunham; namely, that schizophrenic patients are concentrated in the lowest social strata, but they found no relationship between social mobility and schizophrenia.[23] Finally, Ruesch has presented an ingenious analysis pointing to the conclusion that the disruptive effects of upward mobility on psychosomatic illness differs from the effects of downward mobility.[24] Upward mobility, he reasons, predisposes psychosomatic illness while downward mobility predisposes alcoholism. Thus, in partial summary, data are available to indicate the disruptive consequences of social mobility on a variety of social behaviors linked to primary group relations.

SECONDARY GROUP RELATIONS

In modern industrial society, a person's social participation in secondary groups is linked to activities at his place of residence and his place of work. The common problems of earning a living or rearing a child and of consumer consumption orient in varying degrees one family to other families and to those organizations and institutions that are ecologically based in the residential community. The requirements of family life create common tasks for parents and establish even in the most industrialized centers intimate and relatively stable social relations which have some limiting effect on the disruptive impact of mobility. New patterns of etiquette have to be learned, participation in voluntary associations come to supplement family and kinship relations. Lloyd Warner has focused attention on the role of friendship cliques in this process of adult socialization. Social scientists have not overlooked the role of the church, community agencies, and units of the government that come into existence in support of the family.

A great deal of research on assimilation of immigrant groups in the

[22] R. E. Faris and H. W. Dunham, *Mental Disorders in Urban Areas*, Chicago, University of Chicago Press, 1939.

[23] August B. Hollingshead and Frederick Redlich, "Social Stratification and Schizophrenia," *American Sociological Review*, LIX, June, 1954, pp. 302-306. Their results are difficult to evaluate since 92 per cent of the patients were in the non-mobility category, a percentage at variance with all other studies and in no way to be accounted for by their careful sampling procedures.

[24] Jurgen Ruesch, "Social Technique, Social Status and Social Change in Illness," in *Personality in Nature, Society and Culture*, edited by Clyde Kluckhohn and Henry A. Murray with the collaboration of David M. Schneider, New York, Alfred A. Knopf, 1953, pp. 123-36.

United States is relevant for tracing out how these secondary group structures assist family organization. The process of assimilation among immigrant groups generally involves social ascent. It is difficult to separate changes in social behavior and social values that result from assimilation into a new society, from those changes that derive from upward mobility. Initially, some of these immigrant groups are subject to considerable personal and social disorganization.

Case studies of the assimilation of ethnic groups, since Thomas and Znaniecki's classic study of *The Polish Peasant in Europe and America,* trace out the mechanisms by which, over the short run, ecological segregation of these groups is an integrative factor during the process of assimilation and upward social mobility.[25] With physical separation from the "cultural ghetto," especially by the sons and daughters of immigrants, family units become especially exposed to the disruptive consequences of mobility as adjustment to new norms and modes of behavior is required. But movement from one residential neighborhood and community to another is not merely a process of social strain and heightened instability. There are special mechanisms within the residential community that act as counterweights. Thomas and Znaniecki anticipated later research by analyzing community structures, large-scale organizations (the church and the benevolent fraternal organizations in their particular case), as well as the mass media as social structures for containing and limiting the disruptive effects of mobility.

Of the various organizations operating in the United States residential communities—old, transitional, and new—organized religion is the most persistent element of social cohesion. Thus, instead of assimilation (aside from the Negro minority), the restructuring of United States society has resulted not in an ethnic melting pot society, but in a triple-religious melting pot. Within the same religion, various ethnic groups intermarry. Regardless of the theological content of religion in the United States today, from the point of view of social mobility, religious life is both community based and highly organized along bureaucratic lines. The many-sided institutions of organized religion have supplied standards of behavior and institutional support for the mobile sons and daughters of lower class immigrant groups as they entered into the lower-middle class. Today, religious organizations play the same role in middle class suburbs.

---

[25] William I. Thomas and Florian Znaniecki, *The Polish Peasant in Europe and America,* Chicago, University of Chicago Press, 1918, 4 vols.

As mentioned above, Curtis found that among white Protestant men who were church members, the mobile persons were more likely to be frequent attenders than nonmobile men. This finding was independent of age or present social status. Lenski's study of religious behavior confirmed the finding both for mobile middle and working class men.[26]

It is interesting that the relationship did not appear for Protestant women; it could be argued that the interpersonal problems of mobility are less severe for them. Likewise, the consequences of social mobility on church attendance were not present for Catholics, perhaps because of the more generalized structure of the Catholic church. Curtis also found that the average level of formal voluntary association membership of most mobile persons is not unusually low. The same finding was confirmed in an earlier study by Sykes.[27] In other words, persons can substitute social participation in secondary groups more easily and more rapidly than in their primary relations. While Sykes did not find that upwardly mobile families were more active in PTAs, Curtis found that upwardly mobile men participated more actively in sports teams and hobby clubs—institutional arrangements which serve as a basis of communications among men of widely varying status. However, one can speculate that participation in voluntary associations, and especially the pursuit of leadership position in them, for some persons is only a continuation of mobility aspiration rather than a device for social integration.

Studies of the effect of mobility on social participation in secondary groups linked to the work place are limited to trade union participation.[28] Upward mobility tended to decrease trade union participation. But more important, downward mobility generally did not increase it, and therefore did not imply the development of greater working class cohesion.[29]

[26] Gerhard Lenski, *The Religious Factor: A Sociological Study of Religious Impact on Politics, Economics and Family Life*, Garden City, N.Y., Doubleday and Co., 1961.

[27] Curtis, *op. cit.*; Gresham Sykes, *Social Mobility and Social Participation*, unpublished Ph.D. dissertation, Department of Sociology, Northwestern University, 1954.

[28] Seymour M. Lipset and Joan Gordon, "Mobility and Trade Union Membership," in *Class, Status and Power, op. cit.*, pp. 491-500; Richard F. Curtis, "Note on Occupational Mobility and Union Membership in Detroit: A Replication," *Social Forces*, XXXVIII, October, 1959, pp. 60-71.

[29] Political behavior is a form of secondary group activity related to the process of social mobility. Since publication of the *Dynamics of Prejudice*, four studies of national elections produced the same results: Persons who have experienced downward mobility as between the generations are more likely to support Republican candidates than nonmobile people. The differences are not great for national samples but are clear-cut in more delimited samples. A. Kornhauser, H. L. Shepard, and A. J. Mayer, *When Labor Votes*, New York, University Books, 1956, p. 43; 1952 and

Geographical mobility, in an advanced industrial society, is generated by the same underlying processes of social change that produce social mobility. Geographical mobility is also linked to the family cycle and to changing needs and aspirations for housing. Like social mobility, it has both positive and negative consequences on primary group attachments and participation in secondary groups.

Despite the extensive popular discussion of suburbanization, as a dramatic form of geographical mobility, there is hardly an adequate body of literature for our purposes.[30] On *a priori* grounds, the same orientation we employed for analyzing the consequences of social mobility should apply to geographical mobility. We believed that geographical mobility would disrupt certain types of primary group attachments; and that disruption would be most relevant for personal and social controls among families who move frequently in comparison with those who make few, or a "normal" amount of moves.

The available research literature tends to confirm such thinking. For example, Peter Rossi concluded his study of *Why Families Move* by observing that in areas of high family mobility "the opportunities for friendship and association on an informal level seem slight in a situation

1956 Survey Research Center, University of Michigan, data reported by S. M. Lipset and H. L. Zetterberg; International Sociological Association, *Transactions of the Third World Congress of Sociology*, III, London, 1956, p. 174; Eleanor Maccoby, "Growth and Political Change," *Public Opinion Quarterly*, XVIII, Spring, 1954, pp. 23-39. Downward mobility also produces a more conservative ideology among workers: R. Centers, *The Psychology of Social Classes*, Princeton, N.J., Princeton University Press, 1949, p. 180; Harold L. Wilensky and Hugh Edwards, "The Skidder: Ideological Adjustment of Downward Mobile Workers," *American Sociological Review*, XXIV, April, 1959, pp. 216-31. Two election studies and one study of political opinion report that upwardly mobile persons also produce a drift toward the Republican presidential candidate and toward conservative ideology during this period: Bernard R. Berelson, Paul F. Lazarsfeld, and William N. McPhee, *Voting*, Chicago, University of Chicago Press, 1954, pp. 90-91; Eleanor Maccoby, *loc. cit.*; Patricia S. West, "Social Mobility Among College Graduates," *Class, Status and Power, op. cit.*, p. 478. None of these studies distinguish between conservative and radical right ideology, for it may be the case that extreme mobility contributes to extreme political behavior.

These studies cannot be considered as a comprehensive basis of linking social mobility to political behavior. Yet it does appear that during a period of full employment and the re-emergence of conservative political action, upward social mobility, or at least moderate upward mobility, adds to the growth of conservative values. Apparently downward mobility did not produce during the same period such intense interpersonal pressures as to generate the need for developing radical political behavior—either of the left or of the right. In other terms, the political system worked adequately enough to contain the pressures of downward mobility.

[30] Peter H. Rossi, *Why Families Move: A Study in the Social Psychology of Urban Residential Mobility*, New York, The Free Press of Glencoe, 1955—an empirical study containing a summary of the literature available at the time of publication.

of diverse population types and impermanency."[31] These observations are important because they indicate that the consequences of geographical mobility depend not only on the experiences of the particular family but also on the over-all extent of mobility in the community the family enters.

Rossi's study of the consequences of geographical mobility is particularly relevant because it deals with participation in community affairs and voluntary associations. His data, based on community leaders, indicate that extensive mobility presents a problem to voluntary associations, but that they are often able to adjust their activities to the needs of their more mobile clients. Likewise, the consequences of geographical mobility on participation in local community affairs may be less marked in middle class than in working class communities. In middle class communities, new families get "involved" by cultivating personal friends, and by associations linked to relatives and occupational ties. Herbert Gans presents a similar picture of the middle class suburb, where voluntary associations, especially those associated with religious institutions, help to integrate the newcomer. In this process the specialized mass media, the community press—both urban and suburban—support the voluntary associations as devices of social control.[32] Thus, on the basis of the very limited available data, the effects of geographical mobility lend themselves to the same type of analysis as those of social mobility.

In the analysis of mobility and social behavior, a final limiting observation is necessary. One can speculate that there are conditions under which the disruptive consequences of social mobility make selected persons accessible to social change in the direction of tolerance. This can occur when the disruption of primary group relations exposes persons to mass media influence or legal and governmental norms that emphasize tolerance and equality. Thus, tradition-bound Southerners seem less accessible to national norms than those who have experienced forms of mobility that have removed them from conventional primary group pressures.

In over-all summary, there is a convergence between the consequences of social mobility in general and the effects of mobility on ethnic intoler-

---

[31] Peter H. Rossi, op. cit., p. 181.
[32] Morris Janowitz, The Community Press in an Urban Setting, New York, The Free Press of Glencoe, 1952, passim.

ance. For our purposes, the theory of personal and social controls is a reasonable basis for analysis. Social mobility, especially downward mobility, is a form of social change that operates against the social trend toward tolerance. Downward social mobility produces disruption of primary group relations and increases tension and anxiety. But these consequences, in turn, may vary with the ability of secondary group structures to contain their disruptive character. In this sense, the effects of social mobility on ethnic prejudice are not fundamentally different from those in other areas of social behavior.

It is true that we are interested not only in ethnic attitudes—implicit and explicit—but also in actual patterns of discrimination. In this respect, the institutional structures of an industrial society, such as voluntary associations, churches, and political parties, as well as the mass media, are crucial not only indirectly, as they condition ethnic attitudes, but also directly, as they can develop new norms of behavior for their members.

CHAPTER III

THE PSYCHOLOGY OF PREJUDICE

When 15 years ago we undertook to study the dynamics of prejudice, our intention went beyond an exploration of a most troublesome social problem. The investigation of this significant social issue was also an effort in the integration of dynamic psychology based on psychoanalytic theory, and existing sociological research. Following Harold D. Lasswell and other pioneers in the application of psychoanalysis to social problems, it was felt that an understanding of social phenomena would be enhanced if psychoanalytic findings could be applied to the study of social processes. That is why we—a psychoanalyst interested in social problems and a sociologist aware of psychoanalysis—joined forces in a common undertaking.

At the time of this investigation, psychoanalytic theory was developed mainly as a therapy and as a closed theoretical system for explaining personal development with little regard to social influences. Its main emphasis was still on the effects of early childhood experiences on later life; that is, on personal development and neurosis but not on the elucidation of social problems. In 1950 we said, "In choosing psychoanalytic theory, it was recognized that the application of the theory beyond the individual, and particularly to the larger organization of society, was relatively undeveloped." As of now no fundamental change regarding such application has occurred. But one aspect of psychoanalytic theory, ego psychology, has experienced an important development during these intervening years. Hardly existing in the 1940's, it seems to have become the center of psychoanalytic theory in the 1960's. Earlier psychoanalytic theory shied away from viewing man in the context of his society, concerned itself mainly with the "inner" man, and disregarded man "in society." These earlier formulations, to quote Rapaport, "may at times have given the impression that the organism is totally autonomous from its environment."[1] Concentration on the unconscious led, comparatively

---

[1] David Rapaport, "The Structure of Psychoanalytic Theory," *Psychological Issues*, II, New York, International Universities Press, 1960, pp. 58ff.

speaking, to a far-reaching lack of interest in the influence of the social environment on the individual.

This emphasis on the inner world of man still continues, so much so that as recently as 1962 a prominent theoretician of psychoanalysis, on surveying the psychoanalytic scene remarked: "the habitual reference to man's environment as an 'outer world' attests, more than any other single term, to the fact that the world of action is still foreign territory to our [i.e., psychoanalytic] theory. This term, more than any other, represents the Cartesian straitjacket which we have imposed on our model of man, who in some of our writings seems to be most himself when reflecting horizontally—like a supine baby or a reclining patient; or like Descartes, taking to his bed to cogitate on the extensive world."[2]

THE PSYCHOANALYSIS OF PREJUDICE

When we were planning the *Dynamics of Prejudice*, our design was to remove psychoanalysis from its social isolation, to apply it to the field of social analysis, and to show that it has application to the field of social action. Unfortunately, the state of psychoanalytic theory at that time made this a difficult task and, despite progress in theory, continues to do so. Since the middle of the 1950's, the notion of the relative autonomy of the ego from its environment has been questioned by a few but prominent psychoanalysts. But unfortunately, to regard the ego as devoid of energy and initiative, and to view its function as reconciling the demands of the id, the superego, and reality, remained and remains the dominant view. But very slowly, beginning with Hartmann's paper of 1950[3] and his addition of 1952,[4] a change in the conceptual orientation to the ego began to take place. Up to then, following Freud, the main emphasis was on the ego's defensive functions in its fight against reality, superego, and id. Since then, theory has been slowly changing to allow the possibility, or even likelihood, that reality shapes not only the ego but even the underlying drives. Thus, the drives which previously were conceived of as unchanging are now subject to the impact

[2] Erik H. Erikson, "Reality and Actuality," *Journal of the American Psychoanalytic Association*, X, July, 1962, p. 453.

[3] Heinz Hartmann, "Comments on the Psychoanalytic Theory of the Ego," in *The Psychoanalytic Study of the Child*, New York, International Universities Press, 1950, Vol. V, pp. 74-96.

[4] Heinz Hartmann, "The Mutual Influences in the Development of the Ego and Id," in *The Psychoanalytic Study of the Child*, New York, International Universities Press, 1952, Vol. VII, pp. 9-30.

of the environment. While these changes are highly theoretical, they actually have far-reaching consequences. They will eventually bring sociological and psychoanalytic theory much closer together and may even contribute to their integration.

The implications of these developments in psychoanalytic thinking have not yet been applied to social problems. Hence, as will be discussed below, ethnic prejudice is still viewed by psychoanalysts as mainly the consequence of defensive efforts of the ego or superego. Contrary to such older formulations, the newer theory postulates that what happens in society can and does influence both the drives (in this case hostility) and the manner in which the ego deals with them. According to the older theory, society and social organization could at best inhibit hostility, redirect it, or lead to the exchange of one defensive mechanism (for example, in the case of prejudice, that of projection) for another. The new theoretical position assumes that society and social organization may reduce hostility and make the use of projection unnecessary or unacceptable; or conversely, social events may increase hostility. But these are as yet only our general inferences of what these new psychoanalytic formulations may imply for the study of prejudice. They remain to be spelled out in greater detail for this and other social issues.

In a recent treatise devoted mainly to a discussion of prejudice, a prominent psychoanalyst made the following statement: "Every war is a dramatization of man's inner war, the externalization of his inner conflicts. Man feels temporarily relieved of tensions when there is outside trouble in the world. He can postpone finding a solution to his own conflicts as long as the outside world offers a more stirring emotional drama in which he can play a role."[5]

Thus, the typical psychoanalytic study of war and peace continues to disregard social, political, historical, and economic factors. War is simply the externalization of inner conflicts. Such reductionism of social events into inner psychological ones will do as little for our understanding of war, or prejudice, as the opposite reductionism of ascribing all psychological phenomena to the impact of societal forces.

Psychoanalytic explanations of prejudice and scapegoating that disregard social forces result in equally simple conclusions: "Scapegoatism is a universal defense against inner weakness; it is universal because

[5] Joost A. M. Meerloo, *That Difficult Peace*, Great Neck, N.Y., Channel Press, 1961, p. 16.

once we all were babies and weak and dominated by others,"[6] and hence "we may say it [i.e., prejudice] is nearly man's second nature."[7] These are reductions *ad absurdum*. Certainly men are born helpless infants. But the student of society is interested in what happened since our emergence from childhood. Such a traditional view leads of necessity to the view—and it is probably unfortunately true—that prejudice is part of our nature, but this formulation is no great help to those interested in social reform, to those who wish to understand what nurtures prejudice, and how it could be changed. Adults who engage in scapegoating or hold prejudiced views do so not because they had been weak as babies, as had been all those others who as adults are free from prejudices, but because of what happened to them in their social interactions as they grew up and became adults. Despite Freud's observation on the strains that civilization imposes on the individual, and the discontent that is created, his views on the interrelation between the individual and his society did not lead to parallel psychoanalytic studies of specific social phenomena, such as prejudice. The traditional psychoanalytic outlook remains one of seeking causes inside the individual only, with little respect to his social situation and the stresses within his society.

Such a solipsistic view when applied to prejudice makes for a one-sided analysis and precludes any social action. The consequences may be seen in the following quotation. Bird, investigating the etiology of prejudice, says: "The venting of hostility against one group or individual is created as a defense against envy and hostility felt toward another individual or group. In terms of the oedipal situation, which all [i.e., psychoanalytic] authors agree is at the root of the disorder, prejudice represents an attack upon a less desired parent or younger sibling, occurring in place of an attack upon the desired parent. . . . The cause in any case of prejudice should be looked for not only in the relationship between the subject and the object of prejudice, but mainly the cause should be looked for in an unsuspected rivalrous relationship to a third party—a more fortunate or desired third party."[8]

Although this statement deals with the inner cause of prejudice in the individual, it fails to explain why certain groups and not others are selected as the object of prejudice. Moreover, short of prolonged

---

[6] *Ibid.*, p. 63.

[7] *Ibid.*, p. 92.

[8] B. Bird, "A Consideration of the Etiology of Prejudice," *Journal of the American Psychoanalytic Association*, V, 1957, pp. 493 ff.

psychoanalysis, it is difficult to see how one could look for and find this desired third party. The few who have been analyzed but nevertheless remain prejudiced (and there are quite a few of those) as well as the large number of prejudiced people who have not been analyzed, can hardly derive any benefit from such type of understanding of unconscious causes.

PREJUDICE AND EGO PSYCHOLOGY

By contrast, the contribution of psychoanalysis to understanding prejudice becomes more relevant with the shift from the psychology of the unconscious to the emerging contributions of ego psychology. Unfortunately, efforts to apply ego psychology are still mixed with the older views and lead to strangely contradictory evaluations of prejudice. As mentioned above, Meerloo generally views prejudice as a reflection of the inherent weakness of the ego, as a defensive mechanism (projection) that further weakens the person in his tasks of meeting reality on a rational basis. But on the rare occasions when he applies ego psychology, he also recognizes the ego-strengthening propensities of prejudice and points out, for example, how prejudice "represents the deep fear of being a lonely individual,"[9] and how escaping such loneliness through prejudice can be an ego-strengthening experience: "Several egoless patients of mine became (in their own estimation) new personalities when the Nazis, who occupied their homeland, gave them the opportunity to feel real hatred. The reality hatred cured them of their obsessive defenses against their inner hostility."[10] This confirms observations by Ackerman and Jahoda, who observed that "it is conceivable that the successful adaptation to reality in the work sphere is related to the outwardly directed orientation of aggression."[11] Thus, prejudice permits the prejudiced person to function better in society than he might without being prejudiced. This is possible if society accepts or condones such prejudices; otherwise to be prejudiced would lead to further aggravation of difficulties. Thus, prejudice strengthens or weakens a person within himself, depending on the prevailing social norm toward his particular prejudice. Though this is an obvious conclusion, it is absent in these discussions because they are directed

---

[9] J. A. M. Meerloo, op. cit., p. 92.
[10] Ibid., p. 69.
[11] Nathan Ackerman and Marie Jahoda, "The Dynamic Basis of Anti-Semitic Attitudes," Psychoanalytic Quarterly, XVII, 1948, pp. 240ff.

solely to the individual, as if he were living only in a solipsistic world
not part of the larger society.

Finally, of particular importance for understanding the ego-strengthening implications of prejudice was Hartmann's and Kris' introduction
in 1952 of the concept "regression in the service of the ego." When
we apply this concept to the study of prejudice, it seems that in certain
critical phases of the inner life of the individual, projection (or simple
discharge of tension through ethnic hostility) is such regression in the
service of the ego, permitting a re-establishment of the threatened ego
control over the rest of the instinctual forces, as exemplified by Meerloo's
patients.

Because our study was undertaken during the aftermath of World
War II and the mass persecutions of Hitler, it was difficult to view
prejudice as anything but a destructive or disintegrating phenomenon.
We also found it difficult to view prejudice as an integrating psychological force, though we were not unaware of this possibility. In holding such views, we may have been influenced by our values rather
than holding sufficiently to a detached point of view. Today, we are
even more bent on leaving an old world of particularism. Ethnic hostility and prejudice are part of a particularistic way of life which
protects the continued existence of social units by binding them even
more closely together, and by inuring them against universalistic tendencies. The dangers of particularism, at a time when economic, technological, and social developments make increased universalism an
essential aspect of solution of the pressing problems, led us to deplore
ethnic hostility. Because of our concern with social reform, we might
not have been equally sensitive to how great are the desires of many
to hold on to the comforts particularistic group life can offer, and how
prejudice seems to offer them protection against losing their feeling of
selfhood.

In any case, because of the new psychoanalytic conceptual system,
we now better understand the conditions under which ethnic hostility
can prove ego strengthening. We were not unaware of this issue in
the original study, as our discussion of the relationship between anxiety
and intolerance suggests. We stressed that the greater the underlying
anxiety of a person, the more prejudiced he is, because the pressure of
his anxiety weakens his personal controls. Thus weakened, he seeks
relief through prejudice, which serves to reduce anxiety because prejudice facilitates the discharge of hostility, and if hostility is discharged
anxiety is reduced. Prejudice reduces anxiety because it suggests to

the person that he is better than others, hence does not need to feel so anxious. We also analyzed the psychological value of prejudice to the person if he can project on others unacceptable tendencies within himself. But we did not adequately recognize the ego-strengthening consequences these responses may have for the person. To see this process clearly seems so much easier now than 15 years earlier, partly because of the change in the social scene, the increased distance from Hitler's persecutions, the progress made in combating discrimination, and because of the advances in ego psychology.

Even if the concept of regression in the service of the ego had been available when we conducted our study, it is doubtful whether our findings would have been any different. We discussed how medieval man's greatest fear appears to have been the fall from grace, and hence the threat of such danger to the person was dealt with through religious prejudice and persecution. We analyzed how in modern times the psychological threat of social and economic deprivation reinforced prejudice against minorities. We spoke implicitly of how prejudice serves as a regressive response to combat feelings threatening integration and emotional well-being. To go into any greater detail about inner dynamic processes such as, for example, specific infantile experiences that may predispose one person to take recourse to prejudice to master anxiety, while another infantile experience may preclude such recourse for another person, seemed then outside our research interests and does so now. It was a deliberate choice to select a methodology that avoided investigation of inner processes and interpretations which did not also have social implications. As a result, our focus was on ego control and on social control, rather than on ego strength or regression. The interviewers questioned the subjects about their social experiences (in the army) and expectations (economic conditions, jobs) rather than about their inner emotional experiences. They asked the veterans how their parents brought them up, rather than their feelings about their parents.

If we were to repeat our study today, or to conduct a similar one, we might take advantage of these new concepts of ego psychology. For example, it would be important to probe how the subjects feel when they compare themselves to members of the minority groups we investigated. Such questions would further our understanding of the ego-bolstering effects of ego regression represented by prejudice. But despite such enlargement of the investigation, we still would not have a sufficiently improved psychoanalytic conceptual structure for our purposes, because, as Rapaport says in his survey of psychoanalytic ego psychology,[12] so far no "systematic study of ego psychology, containing a precise definition of the ego and a full listing of ego functions . . . has been published." Without a more precise redefinition of the ego and an analysis of all of its functions, sociological findings in regard to prejudice cannot yet be put into an appropriate framework of ego psychology.

The state of theory is quite different in regard to another development of psychoanalysis which very definitely sees human development not only under the frame of reference of the development of biological drives and inner psychological institutions of the mind, but views it also under the frame of reference of the individual's social development. In the same year in which *Dynamics of Prejudice* appeared, with its effort to bring psychoanalysis to bear on social reality, Erikson published a book in which he elaborated his theory of the role of social reality in personality formation and made it a core element of his psycho-social theory of development. The new trend is epitomized by the title of the book, *Childhood and Society*.[13] As Erikson's thinking developed, the problem of identity came to occupy him ever more strongly, as the title of his later monograph indicates, "Identity and the Life Cycle."[14] His concept of mutuality as applied to psychoanalytic theory specifies as crucial the coordination between the individual's stage of psycho-biological development and the impact of his social environment on him. In a parallel vein, we stressed the interrelation that exists between the incidence of prejudice in individuals and the societal orientation toward prejudice.

PREJUDICE AND THE SEARCH FOR IDENTITY

In the original study, we said that "ethnic hostility is a symptom of the individual's effort to maintain balance in his psychic economy."[15] Thus we were aware that the expression of prejudice can help a person to protect his individuality. But seen under the frame of reference of present-day ego psychology, we did not stress sufficiently that as a person develops his need for securing his identity, this need may feed

[12] David Rapaport, "A Historical Survey of Psychoanalytic Ego Psychology," in Erik H. Erikson, "Identity and the Life Cycle," *Psychological Issues*, I, New York, International Universities Press, 1959, pp. 5-17.
[13] Erik H. Erikson, *Childhood and Society*, New York, W. W. Norton, 1950.
[14] Erik H. Erikson, "Identity and the Life Cycle," *op. cit.*
[15] See *Dynamics of Prejudice*, New York, Harper and Bros., 1950, p. 95; or p. 199 of this edition.

ethnic hostility and prejudice. The search for identity, and with it the search for ego strength and personal control, might very well involve as a detour the desire to find one's identity, or to strengthen it, through prejudice. And those who fail to achieve an effective personal identity might temporarily or permanently come to use this devious method to establish some kind of identity. Prejudice then might be likened to the tumultuous solutions triggered by the adolescent's search for a personal identity, a search that often continues after the age of adolescence. As many persons seem to get stuck permanently in adolescence because they fail to establish their identity, so many get stuck in prejudice in our society where, for many persons and for particular social groups, finding one's identity is very difficult. The traditional approaches to finding one's identity, for example, through clear location within a hierarchical structure or through one's occupation or religion have become less readily available. Thus, in modern society, reasons persist which tempt a person to seek to secure this identity (or in its absence, at least a feeling of identity) in various ways, including the devious ways of prejudice.

Despite our increased understanding that an important psychological root of prejudice is in the struggle for identity, were we to repeat our study today we could not do an effective analysis of prejudice in terms of ego psychology, because even in this regard the conceptual tools are not yet adequate. To quote Rapaport, "Erikson's theory (like much of Freud's) ranges over phenomenological, specifically clinical psychoanalytic and general psychoanalytic-psychological propositions, without systematically differentiating among them. Correspondingly, the conceptual status of this theory's terms is so far unclear. To systematize this theory and to clarify the conceptual status of its terms is a task for ego psychology in the future."[16]

Nevertheless, Erikson paid special attention to the problem of identity formation and to the danger to the personality of identity diffusion. He pointed out the contribution intolerance makes as a defense against identity diffusion. Speaking of adolescence, he says: "The danger of this stage is identity diffusion; as Biff puts it in Arthur Miller's *Death of a Salesman*, 'I just can't take hold, Mom, I can't take hold of some kind of a life.' "[17] Such inability to "take hold" is not restricted to adolescence; on the contrary, it is to be found in various segments of society.

[16] David Rapaport, "A Historical Survey," *op. cit.*, p. 16.
[17] Erik H. Erikson, "Identity and the Life Cycle," *op. cit.*, p. 91.

Where it coincides with strong doubt about one's ethnic, social, personal, or sexual identity, prejudice is one readily available psychological outcome. This reaction is involved in the prejudice the beat holds against the squares, the Jew against the gentiles, or the boy against the girls. Therefore, no social psychological study of ethnic hostility and of prejudice can afford to overlook the contribution that fear of identity diffusion makes to intolerance. "In general," Erikson holds, "it is primarily the inability to settle on an occupational identity which disturbs young people. To keep themselves together they temporarily overidentify, to the point of apparent complete loss of identity, with the heroes of cliques and crowds. On the other hand, they become remarkably clannish, intolerant, and cruel in their exclusion of others who are 'different,' in skin color or cultural background, in tastes and gifts, and often in entirely petty aspects of dress and gesture arbitrarily selected as *the* signs of an in-grouper or out-grouper. It is important to understand (which does not mean condone or participate in) such intolerance as the necessary *defense against a sense of* identity diffusion."[18] Erikson has spelled this defense out for the adolescent age group, but it is not restricted to this group. Whoever has not yet reached a secure personal identity of his own is threatened by feelings of self-doubt, by confusion about who he is, a nagging anxiety that he may be a "nobody." This fear he tries to silence by telling himself, "At least I am not a Negro, or a Jew; and this makes me at least something more than a nobody."

Below we shall discuss *West Side Story* in terms of what it reveals about prevailing popular attitudes about ethnic hostility. Here we note that the play also expresses in popular terms the need for group belonging by the person who feels deficient in personal identity. It suggests how such a person tries to overcome his feelings of isolation and lack of competence by belonging to a group which, through its prejudice of out-groups, achieves a precarious sense of identity. In the lyrics the boys sing that when you are a Jet you have a brother around and that you are a family man and you are never alone. They go on to say that as a Jet a little boy is a man and a little man is a king. Such a sense of identity is precarious because, as the song suggests, the reason for joining the group is the feeling that, by oneself, one is really only a little boy, but through identification with the group one

[18] *Ibid.*, p. 92.

becomes a man, a king. Thus, this song correctly expresses both the feeling of insignificance (little boy) which leads to joining a prejudiced group, and how this feeling of isolation, of lacking identity and of personal incompetence, is overcome through identification with the group.[19]

Prejudice as a projection has been widely studied.[20] Prejudice as a means to buttress a weak sense of identity has found less attention in psychoanalytic studies, while prejudice as a defense against identity diffusion or total loss of identity has hardly been studied. We believe that to understand prejudice as a psychological phenomenon and to combat it successfully both through psychological and social means, more attention must be paid to its ego-supporting propensities and to the protection it offers the individual against identity diffusion or total loss of identity. Unless other means of ego support are found for the person seeking identity and fearing its loss, prejudice can be expected to continue to exist in one form or another.[21]

If prejudice can bolster a weak sense of identity, the loss of this psychological supportive mechanism may threaten a weak identity. Efforts at racial integration threaten not only the social status and economic security of a prejudiced group but actually the inner sense of identity of its members. Steps toward integration mean criticism of their prejudices—a criticism that increases certain guilt feelings they may be unable to admit even to themselves. As a result they may feel psychologically trapped, because now both criticism and guilt threaten their sense of identity. At a loss in seeking to protect their identity,

---

[19] As *West Side Story* seems to express present-day feeling about the nature of ethnic prejudice, so did a book (and movie) represent German feelings of incompetence and personal isolation in the pre-Hitler years. Hans Fallada's book *Little Man, What Now?* (New York, Simon & Schuster, 1933) describes the "little man" with his feelings of incompetence, his lack of personal identity, and how he becomes the easy victim of Nazi ideology because of his need to find identity at all costs, even at the cost of becoming a Nazi.

[20] For prejudice as a protection against intrapsychic dangers, see for example, *Dynamics of Prejudice, op. cit.*, pp. 42ff; or pp. 146ff of this edition.

[21] An illustration from recent history may suggest how political events can be misunderstood so long as the tremendous value to the individual of bolstering his lacking sense of identity through prejudice and hostility to an ethnic out-group is disregarded. Many Americans found it difficult to understand that Castro could count on the loyalty of segments of the Cuban people despite the hardships his regime imposed on them. What was overlooked was the degree to which economic and political deprivation can be compensated—at least temporarily—by psychological satisfactions. The deprivation the regime imposed was in part compensated by the enhanced feeling of competence derived from identification with Cuban nationalism, from engaging in a common prejudice against Americans, and from the feeling that the Cuban nation had achieved world political significance.

such prejudiced persons may try to further buttress it by maintaining their prejudice.

The fighting liberal and the deeply prejudiced person are therefore, psychologically speaking, at cross purposes. To seek his own identity, the fighting liberal battles for social justice, and against prejudice. Through this fight he actually enhances his feeling of identity, so he cannot comprehend the resistance of the deeply prejudiced person even though the latter is actually seeking to achieve exactly the same psychological end as the fighting liberal. As long as two such groups encounter each other in their fight for and against integration they cannot possibly understand each other, though they both, in opposing each other, try to gain the same psychological advantage for themselves: a heightened feeling of identity. The fighting liberal through his endeavors increases his feelings of well-being, since he engages in actions designed to make ever more secure his identity as a protagonist of good causes. The identity of the deeply prejudiced person, which rests in large part on his feeling superior to the group he discriminates against, is severely threatened by the actions of his opponent. While for the former, what is at stake is an increased sense of identity, the latter has to fear that he may lose the very basis on which this feeling of identity rested. Thus, the fighting liberal has much to gain—namely, securing his identity by fighting against prejudice—but the prejudiced person fears he may lose even more—namely, one of the bases on which his sense of identity rested. If he should give up his prejudice this would require him to create for himself an extremely new and different identity, a tremendous task at the least.

Psychologically speaking, the fighting liberal tells the prejudiced person: relinquish that which gives you a feeling of identity, so that by your doing so I can combat the threat of identity diffusion which I feel in me and thus make my own identity secure. However just such a request may be on a moral plane, to the prejudiced person it seems extremely unfair on the psychological one. Fighting against prejudice as a means to buttress one's own threatened identity is an ineffective way to eliminate it in others, because those who are prejudiced feel the self-seeking nature of this pressure. The enlightened attitude of the educated or socially secure person who joins with the fighting liberal out of his sense of justice does not help matters much, because he is already envied for his greater sense of identity.

The prejudiced person does not remain unaware of the underlying motives of his opponent. To the extent that he feels he is attacked because of the benefit the attacker derives from it, he will feel entitled to derive parallel benefits from maintaining his prejudices. Thus, for example, the Negroes' own fight against discrimination produces more dramatic and lasting results than, for example, the exuberant endeavors of some white college students who want to gain psychological advantages for themselves; namely, feeling superior to narrow-minded and prejudiced people. Some students are attracted to the fight against discrimination, since to fight against discrimination is also part of an adolescent revolt against their parents. The prejudiced person recognizes that this is as much a self-seeking effort as it is a fight for social justice. To tell others how immature they are is unlikely to help them reach maturity. But this is what very often happens in the discussions between the fighting liberal and the prejudiced person.[22]

In our study we dealt with these problems by means of concepts which may have been too broad: security and ego strength on the one side, and feelings of deprivation and a sense of incompetence on the other. No doubt an adequate sense of identity is part of integration, and fear of deprivation, part of anxiety about identity diffusion. Thus, while our conclusions are compatible with the advances in ego psychology, these reformulations—most of all Erikson's study of the problem of identity—would have led us to collect data on and paid greater attention to issues of personal and social identity.

THE STRUGGLE FOR TERRITORY

In view of the great attention which the problem of segregation in housing has received, it seems strange that no scientific investigation

[22] In practice, motives and results are often mixed. Some persons engage in the fight against prejudice for unselfish motives. Their sense of identity is sufficiently secure so that they do not need to secure it through such endeavor. Others desire to fight discrimination because of their need to buttress a weak sense of identity. But by engaging in this fight they gain inner security, which then permits them to be much more open-minded about the social issues at stake.

By and large there is an easy gauge to separate the self-seeking fighters against discrimination from those others who engage in this battle out of a sense of justice, and not mainly to support their weak egos. The first are deeply prejudiced, despite their open battle against it. They are prejudiced in their inability to understand and make reasonable allowances for the historical and social causes of prejudice, and they are so hostile against the prejudiced person that they are ready to ride roughshod over him because of his prejudice.

The person who does not need to buttress a weak ego will act quite differently. He will be able to maintain at all times a much more balanced judgment, despite his fight against discrimination. He will understand the needs of the prejudiced person and will try to help him meet his needs, as he is also trying to help the person discriminated against.

of this issue has been related to Erikson's insights on the fear of identity diffusion. Nor has the fight for turf been understood as the human counterpart of the animal "instinct" for territory.[23] The combination of these two ideas, germinal for our understanding of ethnic relations, has found telling expression in a recent musical play.

We cannot look to popular art or the personal insights of the authors of plays to elucidate complex social phenomena. But they become important when millions respond to them with the immediate feeling that they express well what the audience feels on this issue. Therefore, when a musical dealing with complex psychological and social problems in general, and with ethnic hostility in particular, has world-wide and lasting success, we are told much about prevalent popular attitudes. The musical to which we are referring is *West Side Story*. The way it was unquestionably accepted by such a large audience suggests that they intimately felt that here was a dramatic statement of the problem of an ethnic conflict, exploding in gang war, which was in line with their own feelings of what it is all about. The success of the story is its statement that there is much more to ethnic prejudice than juvenile delinquency, than one group feeling superior to the other, than slum conditions and poverty. It not only shows two ethnic groups fighting each other for the same territory, but more importantly—that both the fight for territory or "turf" and ethnic hostility are, on a deeper level, the consequences of a fight for self-realization, for personal identity; and that once these are gained ethnic hostility evaporates all by itself and defense of territory seems no longer important.

Insecurity behind ethnic hostility is thus both social and emotional. If one is insecure, one can find identity through adherence to a group that finds its justification only through fighting another group. Neither

---

[23] By contrast, recent psychological and ecological studies of the protoculture of animals have investigated the role that the fight for, and defense of, territory plays in animal life. The more we learn about it, the more striking become the parallels between animals' fight for territory and the degree to which recent ethnic issues have become centered on segregation versus integration of living areas. Even the problem of school integration in the Northern cities is largely an issue of territory. Local segregation continues to a considerable degree because of separate living areas. To our knowledge, so far the findings of animal ecology have only incidentally and inferentially been applied to the study of human behavior in general, and not at all in any systematic way to patterns of ethnic hostility. The fight for territory is only an aspect of insecurity and of lack of identity, but it seems so prevalent among animals, and particularly primates, and it played such a tremendous role in the formation of political units such as states, that we cannot simply relegate the so-called instinct of defense of territory to the animal world only. Had these studies been available then as they are now, they undoubtedly would have altered our plan of investigation.

the police officer and the candy-store owner, nor the judge and social worker, understand this. Therefore, the boys make fun of them. These boys are fighting for their self-respect and to make certain that they are not "nobodies." Thus the fight of the American Jets against the Puerto Rican Sharks under the railroad tracks serves to secure their personal identity as worthwhile human beings, much as fighting in the Spanish Civil War did for the American volunteer of the International Brigade and much as fighting poverty and disease does now for the volunteer of the Peace Corps in the tropics of Africa. The end result will obviously be different for the prejudiced gang boys of the Jets and the Sharks, when compared with a member of the Peace Corps. But in each case, initial conception of the meaning of personal identity was radically different.

If prejudice serves to test one's identity against the "nonself," frequently such a test of becoming a "somebody" at first involves fighting *against* something. Such fight can result in becoming a "somebody" only if in the end the fight is *for* something of social value. As long as it remains a battle against being a "nobody," it matters little whether the prejudice is directed against another minority group, or the capitalists, or the communists, or any other out-group. Only after he has been able to secure his identity does a person become able to use Erikson's terminology, to "share being oneself with another self." Thus, a person formerly beset by ethnic prejudice may move to maturity and identity as the two protagonists of the *West Side Story* do in the end. Because each has become certain of his personal identity, they both can transcend ethnic hostility.

It is worthwhile to compare *West Side Story* with another musical, *South Pacific*, which related to the period when we studied the *Dynamics of Prejudice*. Perhaps one should not overinterpret the differences between these two expressions of popular art. Still, it is important to note that *West Side Story* takes prejudice far more seriously and recognizes that if we want to reduce it we have to dig at roots that go very deep indeed. An obvious and crucial difference is that *South Pacific* dealt with interethnic relations not by presenting opposing groups *and* a pair of lovers, but on a personal basis alone, the love of two people. In fact, ethnic prejudice is always a group phenomenon. But in *South Pacific*, the ethnic conflict separating the protagonists has to do only in the most incidental way with the social conditions that shape their lives. More important, no deeper psychological or social cause is given for prejudice. It serves no inner needs, and hence hangs in mid-air socially and psychologically. Prejudice is viewed as merely the result of a conditioning process. But nowhere is any reason offered why anybody should be conditioned in this fashion; it just happens. According to *South Pacific*, ethnic tensions occur when an inherently innocent man is perverted by somebody without rhyme or reason.

In comparing these two plays, one might say that the public temper of 1950 was one of naive ignorance about the real causes of ethnic hostility, whereas *West Side Story* by comparison reveals an impressive degree of sophistication. In *South Pacific*, ethnic hostility is not related to the search for identity, the need to find security in the in-group, the fear of the stranger, or the defense of territory. On the contrary, according to one of *South Pacific's* most famous songs, which represents the view of one of the most enlightened characters (and obviously the authors), it requires special and deliberate efforts on the part of evil adults to condition man to engage in ethnic hostility. According to *South Pacific*, hate and fear of those whose eyes are differently shaped, or whose skin color is not your own, have to be carefully nurtured, "drummed" into you "before you are six or seven or eight." But there is no reason why anybody should want to teach prejudice.

In *South Pacific*, the hero was never prejudiced in the first place, and as soon as his prejudiced girl finds out that he is a war hero, her prejudice disappears and ethnic hostility no longer poses any problems. Since prejudice is viewed as improper conditioning without any basis in the individual's psychology or his social conditions, all that is necessary is to find out that one person of the group against which you held prejudices is a fine person.

This is quite different from *West Side Story* in which the love of two people for each other makes a personal difference only for them. It fails to solve any of the problems created by prejudice as a social condition. In *West Side Story*, ethnic hostility is viewed not as arbitrary conditioning but as the "natural" consequence of individual background, social conditions, psychological pressure, and fight for "turf." Though the two lovers who belong to inimical groups can and do overcome these divisive forces, though they find themselves as individuals with individual identities, they are destroyed in the end.

The viewers of *South Pacific* were left with the feeling that ethnic prejudice is really no problem at all; after having seen *West Side Story*, nobody could dismiss its message so easily. Appropriately, the scene has shifted from a faraway island to a neighborhood in a big city. Thus, we have become much more aware of the seriousness of the problem and of how close it hits home. The change in social conditions, the influence of social research into prejudice, as well as the difficulty of reducing discrimination by social action, all make it possible for a popular musical to present a much more complex and realistic image of the problems posed by ethnic hostility.

NEW RESEARCH FINDINGS

New research on the psychology of prejudice related to the *Dynamics of Prejudice* covers a variety of themes. One of our important psychosocial findings; namely, the correlation between rapid social mobility and emotional disturbance—and with it, prejudice—was unexpectedly corroborated by some recently published psychiatric studies. As part of the impact of the newly developed ego psychology discussed above, psychoanalysis has begun to free itself from its origin in the study of pathology, and to concern itself as well with the mentally healthy personality. This is significant for the study of prejudice because of the widespread tendency to view prejudice as a sign of mental disturbance; our findings indicated that it seems "normal" for the average man to follow the prejudice of his group.

The psychiatric studies of normal individuals have not dealt explicitly with prejudice. But they corroborate our findings that both those who are markedly upward mobile, and those who move downward on the socioeconomic scale, tend to be more emotionally disturbed; while those who are only moderately upward mobile are the most emotionally stable group. We approached this problem by means of our scales measuring adequacy of controls, feelings of deprivation, and degree of tolerance. These are obviously quite inadequate scales for measuring mental health in a psychiatric sense. Therefore, it is striking that our findings about the emotional stability of the only moderately upward mobile group has been fully corroborated by elaborate studies, using the most up-to-date techniques of dynamic psychiatry. A recent study by Grinker contains a description both of the social stability of these mentally healthy young men and of the psychiatrists' startled reactions to them.[24] The author remarks:

I often described my subject population to various social and professional groups characterized by driving social upward mobile or prestige seeking

---

[24] R. Grinker, Sr., with the collaboration of R. Grinker, Jr., and John Timberlake, "Mentally Healthy Young Males," *Archives of General Psychiatry*, Vol. VI, 1962, pp. 405-53.

people, who, although outwardly serene, were consumed with never satisfied ambitions. The invariable comment was, those boys are sick, they have no ambition. [He continues], Intense commitment to change in itself may be one of the elements in neurosis building. Change is accelerating at a rapid pace, as the students of the modern American family have so well documented. The "healthy" population demonstrates little participation in this rapid pace, nor have their parents: they move ahead slowly at a pace which does not overly strain them.

The cultural and family background of our subjects was conducive to growth and change without difficulties that precipitate crises or overt conflict. . . . Biological and psychological growth or maturation is not naturally associated with crises. Rather it is the rapid shifts within environments or sudden movements of the individual among two or more external social and culturally dissimilar environments that precipitate crises. Whatever changes took place in the worlds of our subjects were gradual and could be absorbed without too much strain. . . . They are goal directed and earnestly strive toward achievement of success and avoidance of failure. Upward mobility is obvious in that they are in college as contrasted with their poorly educated parents, yet their image of future social and economic position and kind of life remains fixed to the level which they experienced at home in childhood.[25]

Thus, it seems that our findings about the emotional stability of the stable and moderately upward mobile group among the veterans based on the analysis of interviews and a simple measure of social mobility is borne out by a most careful psychiatric study of individuals.

In terms of more specific psychological investigations of prejudice, there seems no question that the *Studies in Prejudice* series of which *Dynamics of Prejudice* was one volume was instrumental in encouraging or at least in influencing a large number of empirical research reports. These efforts have produced a considerable body of data substantiating the relevance of specific psychological mechanisms in accounting for differences within and between groups in their levels of ethnic intolerance. However, these studies do not seem to deeply extend our understanding of the psychological basis of prejudice, and their contribution to explaining the trends in prejudice during the last decade and a half are limited.[26]

---

[25] *Ibid.*, pp. 446-49.

[26] Much of the response to the *Studies in Prejudice* has been relatively unconcerned with the social context in which attitudes are mobilized and expressed. In fact, influenced by formal psychological theory, there has been a trend to disregard social context when studying the psychology of ethnic attitudes. Thus, for example, Milton Rokeach in his volume *The Open and Closed Mind* (New York, Basic Books, 1960) concludes that attitude structures are either open or closed (prejudiced or unprejudiced. Although such dichotomies make for clear and distinct categories, they fail to do justice to the wide variations, depending upon the subject on which

Considerable research in the psychology of prejudice during the last decade has been devoted to examining and often to refuting the conclusions of *The Authoritarian Personality* study written by Theodore Adorno, *et al.*[27] Both *The Authoritarian Personality* and subsequent research bear on the psychological aspects of the *Dynamics of Prejudice.* In particular, *The Authoritarian Personality* seeks to link prejudice and political ideology by means of personality variables. In response, Edward A. Shils has pointed to the limitations of its theoretical framework. which describes political issues in a simple continuum from liberal to conservative.[28] His criticisms from the point of view of political philosophy point out how such a simple continuum has the consequences of obscuring the ideological components of both the radical right and the radical left. Despite the increase in empirical studies of political attitudes since the publication of *The Authoritarian Personality,* we still did not have adequate studies which distinguish between the radical right and conservative ideology and between liberal and radical left ideology. As a result, we are not adequately able to relate political ideology to ethnic intolerance. Such studies of political ideology remain indispensable if we are to have a firmer grasp of the structure of modern ideological trends. But it must be recognized that the authors of *The Authoritarian Personality* were aware of authoritarianism of the left even though they focused on authoritarianism of the right.[29]

Much of the research in response to *The Authoritarian Personality* has been methodological, and this literature has been evaluated by Herbert H. Hyman and Paul B. Sheatsley, and Richard Christie.[30] These authors raise fundamental methodological issues, particularly the observation that the findings are most applicable to specific segments within the white middle class. The findings have been criticized on the basis that high

---

a mind is open or closed. Hence, such an approach throws little light on the changes in ethnic intolerance which have taken place in the United States, or for relating specific attitude changes to social practice.

[27] T. W. Adorno, Else Frenkel-Brunswik, Daniel J. Levinson, and R. N. Sanford, *The Authoritarian Personality,* New York, Harper and Bros., 1950.

[28] Edward A. Shils, "Authoritarianism: 'Right' and 'Left,'" in *Studies in the Scope and Method of "The Authoritarian Personality,"* edited by R. Christie and M. Jahoda, New York, The Free Press of Glencoe, 1954, pp. 24-49.

[29] An effort to distinguish operationally between conservatives and extreme conservatives is contained in H. McClosky, "Conservatism and Personality," *The American Political Science Review,* LII, March, 1958, pp. 27-45.

[30] Herbert H. Hyman and Paul B. Sheatsley, "'The Authoritarian Personality'— A Methodological Critique," and R. Christie, "Authoritarianism Re-examined," in R. Christie and M. Jahoda, *op. cit.,* pp. 50-122, 123-96.

scores on the basic authoritarian scale are related to low education. Now, the available data give no basis for believing that the essential components of the authoritarian personality syndrome—as measured by its subscales—can be accounted for by education. In fact, there is reason to believe that among very selected samples of highly educated persons, the authoritarian personality may be positively associated with a particular form of exaggerated pro-tolerant outlook. In addition, it is doubtful whether all the psychological component elements investigated by the Berkeley group add up to an authoritarian personality. Nevertheless, one essential finding of *The Authoritarian Personality* has been adequately documented in extensive replication studies, leaving little doubt that "authoritarian submission" is mildly related to strong prejudice.

From the point of view of our theoretical concerns with personal and social controls, the controversies generated by *The Authoritarian Personality* are not directly relevant or productive. We do not believe that there is such an entity as the prejudiced, or authoritarian, personality. We even doubt the value of these concepts as ideal types. We did not try to establish the upward (or downward) mobile person as an entity. Instead, we sought to relate degrees of social movement to degrees of prejudice. Likewise, the *Dynamics of Prejudice* was concerned with investigating a series of specific personality mechanisms rather than a personality type that might be linked to ethnic prejudice.

First, we did not believe that the significance of these mechanisms could be understood without reference to the context of the social structure and social values of the groups in which the veterans were members. These psychological mechanisms would not "explain" prejudice. At best, they would help us understand why persons had levels of ethnic prejudice markedly higher or markedly lower than the norms of their social group. Second, we did not investigate personality structure as did the Berkeley group. Conceptualization of personality structure for social psychological research is far from adequate. There are no adequate techniques for the collection of data on personality structure that can readily be applied to large groups, or at least those groups large enough to study social behavior patterns such as prejudice. More fundamentally, we did not believe that we could postulate a personality structure which would be directly related to higher or lower levels of prejudice. To the contrary, we anticipated that a number of different personality structures could be linked to patterns of prejudice. The most that could be postulated was that persons with stronger personal controls would be less likely to blame others irrationally for their own difficulties and with that would be less hostile toward minority groups. Personal controls were defined in terms of ego psychology but always with regard to the social context. The structure of personal controls is conditioned largely by childhood experiences and those later educational and social experiences which modify them. And a wide variety of child-hood—and later—experiences, social, economic, political, educational, and personal, can make for achievement of inner controls. Obviously, the processes of socialization continue beyond childhood, that is, when the personality is not extremely rigid or otherwise pathologic. In any case, a variety of constellations of psychological mechanisms, not a single personality structure, would be involved both in strong personal controls and the opposite tendency to hold strongly prejudiced opinions.

Thus, two steps are involved in assessing the recent literature on psychological mechanisms associated with prejudice. First, it is necessary to review the research that bears on the specific psychological mechanisms investigated in *Dynamics of Prejudice*. These were personal insecurity, subjective feelings of deprivation, anxiety, and hostility. Second, it is necessary to examine those researches which bear on the concepts of ego strength and personal controls, or which can be translated into this frame of reference.

In the original study, personal insecurity, subjective feelings of deprivation, anxiety, and hostility were found to be positively and meaningfully linked to prejudice. We employed these concepts, fully aware that the state of psychological theory did not permit logically exclusive operational definitions in all cases. By means of intensive interviews, however, significant indicators of these psychological reactions could be encountered. Unfortunately, most of the parallel work—and we include not only those designed specifically to test our hypothesis but also those which independently focused on similar psychological concepts—was generally performed by means of less intensive interviewing techniques and by a major reliance on questionnaire responses. Nevertheless, a limited body of data emerges from these researches into the psychological bases of prejudice, which corroborates the relevance of personal insecurity, subjective deprivation, anxiety, and hostility. As correlates of higher levels of ethnic prejudice, while these findings are generally statistically significant and theoretically relevant, they seldom are very noteworthy in their magnitude.[31]

---

[31] Although more than 300 studies on the psychological bases of prejudice have been done since *Dynamics of Prejudice*, the bulk is so limited in theoretical scope

Careful research, confirming the association of prejudice with personal insecurity, is presented, for example, by Nancy Morse and Floyd H. Allport, and in the work of Harrison G. Gough.[32] An alternative approach is to experimentally induce frustration and to observe the consequences on levels of intolerance. If one makes the assumption that persons suffering the highest levels of personal insecurity are most likely to respond more strongly to frustration, then the research work by Miller and Bugelski, and by Gardner Lindzey is relevant.[33] Persons most likely to express experimentally induced frustration demonstrated increased prejudice. The same results were encountered by Cowen, Landes, and Schaet.[34] Fishbach and Singer tried to refine this experimental approach by making a distinction between a personal threat and a shared threat. It is interesting that their experimental evidence producing a personal rather than a shared threat showed greater increase in social prejudice.[35]

On the basis of data collected by intensive interviews, at least two studies replicate and amplify the relationship between ethnic prejudice and subjective deprivation. Using materials gathered from patients undergoing psychotherapy, Haimowitz found that hostility was linked to feelings of deprivation in the past.[36] In a British working class sample, Robb found that prejudice was associated with subjective feelings of deprivation. More directly replicating the formulation of *Dynamics*

---

that we do not feel much would be gained by discussing them in any detail, though a few of them focus on important issues.

[32] Nancy Morse and Floyd H. Allport, "The Causation of Anti-Semitism: An Investigation of Seven Hypotheses," *Journal of Psychology*, XXXIV, October, 1952, pp. 197-233. Harrison G. Gough, "Studies of Social Intolerance; I. Some Psychological and Sociological Correlates of Anti-Semitism," *Journal of Social Psychology*, XXXIII, May, 1951, pp. 237-44; "II. A Personality Scale for Anti-Semitism," *Ibid.*, pp. 247-55; "III. Relationship of the Pr Scale to Other Variables," *Ibid.*, pp. 257-62; "IV. Related Social Attitudes," *Ibid.*, pp. 263-69.

[33] N. Miller and R. Bugelski, "Minor Studies of Aggression: II, The Influence of Frustrations Imposed by the In-Group on Attitudes Exposed Toward Out-Groups," *Journal of Psychology*, XXV, 1948, pp. 437-42. Gardner Lindzey, "An Experimental Examination of the Scapegoat Theory of Prejudice," *Journal of Abnormal and Social Psychology*, XLV, April, 1950, pp. 296-309; and "Differences Between the High and Low in Prejudice and Their Implications for a Theory of Prejudice," *Journal of Personality*, XIX, September, 1950, pp. 16-40.

[34] Emory Cowen, J. Landes, and D. Schaet, "The Effects of Mild Frustration on the Expression of Prejudiced Attitudes," *Journal of Abnormal and Social Psychology*, LVIII, January, 1959, pp. 33-38.

[35] S. Fishbach and R. Singer, "The Effects of Personal and Shared Threats Upon Social Prejudice," *Journal of Abnormal and Social Psychology*, LIV, 1957, pp. 411-16.

[36] M. Haimowitz, "The Development and Change of Ethnic Hostility," unpublished Ph.D. thesis, University of Chicago, 1951.

of Prejudice, he reported that subjective feelings of deprivation were more indicative of intense levels of prejudice than the actual experience of objective deprivation.[37]

We postulated that the relation between anxiety and prejudice depends on the individual's pattern of personal controls in that, all other things being equal, stronger personal controls would produce less intolerance.[38] However, much of the research concerning generalized anxiety seeks to describe this psychological dimension without relation to ego functions. Nevertheless, one can identify in the literature those research reports which reveal that in limited psychological test situations, persons with higher levels of ethnic intolerance display higher levels of anxiety. Altus and Tefejian include obsessive-compulsive traits, paranoid tendencies, and antisocial tendencies among groups scoring high in ethnic prejudice.[39] Likewise, the data collected by Milton Rokeach indicate anxiety manifestations among his more close-minded or prejudiced subjects.[40]

INTIMATE CONTACT AND PREJUDICE

As far as hostility is concerned, the most relevant investigations of psychological hostility in ethnic intolerance relate to those studies which seek to change prejudiced attitudes by some form of psychotherapy or group work. Since the publication of *Dynamics of Prejudice,* some large-scale social experiments have been undertaken designed to influence directly the interpersonal and psychological processes underlying ethnic orientations.

Since we found that intimate contact with members of the minority group does not seem to disintegrate prejudices held in regard to this group, studies attempting to improve relations among groups through intimate contact and equal status should provide corroboration or refutation of our thesis. Observations at an interracial boys' camp where Negro and white children lived, ate, and played together are reported by Paul H. Mussen.[41] Intimate contact was assured because there were

---

[37] J. H. Robb, *Working-Class Anti-Semite,* London, Tavistock, 1954.
[38] See *Dynamics of Prejudice, op. cit.,* pp. 94-95; or pp. 198-199 in this edition.
[39] W. D. Altus and T. T. Tefejian, "MMPI Correlates of the California E-F Scale," *Journal of Social Psychology,* XXXVIII, August, 1953, pp. 145-49.
[40] M. Rokeach, *op. cit.,* pp. 347-65.
[41] Paul H. Mussen, "Some Personality and Social Factors Related to Changes in Children's Attitudes Toward Negroes," *Journal of Abnormal and Social Psychology,* XLV, July, 1950, pp. 423-41.

about as many Negro as white campers and there was no racial segregation in any of the activities or in the cabins. The results conform to our findings. Getting to know members of the discriminated group is not likely to change attitudes, since the white group as a whole did not change its attitude toward Negroes after having been in intimate contact with them for four weeks. Like the veterans we studied, the boys who were highly prejudiced before intimate contact with Negroes had more aggressive and dominance needs, were more hostile, and had more resentment against their environment than boys who were low in prejudice.

So far as social controls are concerned, it is interesting that boys who increased in prejudice after intimate contact with Negroes were those who revealed great needs to defy authority. They also felt that they themselves were the victims of aggression and had a generally unfavorable view of society in general; they were boys who were more dissatisfied with the camp situation itself and with their fellow campers. Those who decreased in prejudice had relatively few aggressive needs and their attitudes toward their parents and others in the environment were generally favorable. They tended to be generally satisfied with the camp and their fellow campers and were, in turn, well accepted by others.

The author concludes that his findings make it clear that intimate contact with Negroes *per se* does not insure a decrease in prejudice. Whether a child increases or decreases in prejudice following such an experience seems to be related to his personality structure and whether or not the camp situation is felt to be a rewarding one.

If deliberate efforts of "therapeutic" group work—that is, efforts at changing patterns of hostility and at increasing personal controls—are added to merely getting acquainted and living together, then the results are different. For example, Marian Radke Yarrow has reported on the experimental efforts to operate a summer camp for two weeks on a desegregated basis designed to reduce interethnic hostility.[42] The camp which served children of relatively similar backgrounds afforded a carefully controlled experiment in attitude change, since it was possible to organize one group of cabins on a desegregated basis and another on a segregated basis.

The objective of the administrative leaders was to observe the consequences on personal controls when the camp was run on the basis

<hr/>

[42] Marian Radke Yarrow, "Interpersonal Dynamics in a Desegregation Process," Special Issue, *Journal of Social Issues,* XIV, No. 1, 1958.

of an equalitarian environment within the experimental cabins. First the desegregated cabins did produce a significant reduction in prejudice as measured by early and late sociometric interviews. Second, the desegregated cabins had a more positive tone as measured by expressed desires of the children to expand their stay.

While there are additional studies indicating the positive consequences of effective "group work," this particular study is relevant for the general hypothesis concerning prejudice and hostility because the authors recorded the emotional tension which emerged during the process of group work and which required an interpersonal solution.[43] Among the desegregated cabins, where attitude change took place, there was low social cohesion as reported by the counselors. These cabins had more group explosions and more individual expression of hostility. Desegregation brought to the surface underlying anxieties and hostilities that had to be dealt with in order to create the conditions for changing attitudes. The variable accounting for such change seems to have been the counselors' ability to establish rapport with the children and to deal with their problems of expressing hostility and strengthening their personal controls. Similar observations can be found in the play therapy studies with children by Axline and by Mussen.[44] Haimowitz found related reduction of personal hostility as an essential prerequisite for changing attitudes toward minority groups in individual psychotherapy.[45]

The interrelated syndrome of personal insecurity, subjective deprivation, and varying manifestations of anxiety and hostility bespeak an absence of adequate controls. One would also infer that such persons had low self-respect and a weak or poorly integrated sense of self-identity. Thus, it is interesting to note that Himelhoch found that generalized ethnic prejudice varies directly with self-rejection.[46]

PREJUDICE AND SOCIAL AUTHORITY

While the above-mentioned studies confirm the original specific findings of *Dynamics of Prejudice,* they supply only indirect measures of

[43] For a summary of these researches, see George E. Simpson and J. Milton Yinger, *Racial and Cultural Minorities,* New York, Harper and Bros., 1958.
[44] Virginia M. Axline, "Play Therapy and Race Conflict in Young Children," *Journal of Abnormal and Social Psychology,* XLIII, July, 1948, pp. 300-10; P. Mussen, *op. cit.*
[45] M. Haimowitz, *op. cit.*
[46] Jerome Himelhoch, "Tolerance and Personality Needs: A Study of the Liberalization of Ethnic Attitudes Among Minority Group College Students," *American Sociological Review,* XV, February, 1950, pp. 79-88.

the underlying question of relations to authority and the acceptance or rejection of authority in psychological terms. In our thinking, these psychological dimensions are central issues in personal control and ego function. In this regard, it becomes necessary to discriminate at the personal level between controls based upon external controls, superego controls, and ego controls over hostile tendencies.

In the original study we said that "the source of the individual's control lies in the impact which societal authority makes on his developing personality." Thus, it becomes necessary to study the individual's relationship to authority if we are to probe in a meaningful way the interrelationships between personal controls and ethnic prejudice. In terms of modern ego psychology, relation to authority is in essence one of the central aspects for understanding personality processes.

It is at this point that our fundamental differences with the theoretical perspective of *The Authoritarian Personality* emerge. The empirical findings of *The Authoritarian Personality* and the *Dynamics of Prejudice* are antithetical. Perhaps it would be more correct to state that there appears to be a contradiction in the results. According to *The Authoritarian Personality*, those persons are prejudiced who accept society as it is, who approve of its values, and who conform and are conventional; we found, however, that those are prejudiced who resist society, who reject its fundamental values, and who have no feelings of consensus with social institutions.

One possible resolution of this contradiction is suggested by Nathan Glazer in his brilliant review article on the series *Studies in Prejudice*.[47] There he points out that *The Authoritarian Personality* deals mainly with specialized groups within the middle class; namely, the better educated. By contrast, our sample was a lower and lower-middle class one. Glazer feels that this might be a basis for the apparent contradiction. We agree with his inference that "for example, nonconformity in the middle class might be considered the expression of a rational outlook towards the world that sees through conventional values as inconsistent, harmful, and irrelevant; this would be the outlook of the unprejudiced person. In the less favored lower classes, nonconformity might be the sign of a resentful personality, rather than an enlightened one, and the resentment here would tend to well up and spill over on institutional authorities and all other conspicuous targets."[48] There is some empirical

[47] Nathan Glazer, "The Authoritarian Personality in Profile: Report on a Major Study of Race Hatred," *Commentary*, IV, June, 1950, pp. 573-83.
[48] Nathan Glazer, *op. cit.*, p. 581.

evidence to support this finding, particularly the work of Earl Zack, which carefully compares the significance of the authoritarian syndrome in the middle class and in the lower class and finds, while there is a positive association between authoritarianism and prejudice in the middle class, it is absent in the lower class.[49] His study is of particular relevance because he used a sample in which the age factor is held constant.

Glazer speculated that both sides might reject this resolution of the differences. We certainly do not reject it, though we believe it does not completely account for the different findings. We certainly feel that to some extent the social class basis of the samples in *The Authoritarian Personality* helps explain the authors' findings on the crucial issue of relations to authority.

The difficulty is the theoretical formulation of *The Authoritarian Personality*, which rests on the assumption that tolerance is only or mainly an expression of nonconformity. Our broader formulation seeks to develop an interplay between social class and type of personal control. In the lower social strata it could be that submission to external authority and superego control are the central psychological mechanisms. On the middle social stratum, with a higher level of education, superego and rational ego controls are more likely to operate. Tolerance based on rational ego controls would involve a rejection of overconformity. But basically in both social strata, we are dealing with effective personal controls. If some nonconformists display a high level of tolerance, it may well be the result of a reaction formation or displacement of hostility generated by unsatisfactory relations with authority. It is not farfetched to call these persons false tolerants, for while they may be tolerant of minorities, they often are intolerant of accepted ways of social life.

Thus, the issue runs deeper as Nathan Glazer so correctly points out. Our feeling is that the efforts in *The Authoritarian Personality* to describe the structure of personality lead away from the underlying dynamics involved in ethnic tolerance. Our methodology, both for measuring ethnic attitudes and describing attitudes toward authority, indicate that we were tapping, as Glazer points out, deeper levels of personality. We concur with *The Authoritarian Personality* group in the emphasis on the importance of initial frustration in childhood socialization as leading to strong aggressions, personal hostility, and the failure

---

[49] Earl Zack, "'Class Differences in Prejudice," abstract of Ph.D. thesis, New York University, 1953.

of "internalization." But we add the process of adult socialization as well. Likewise, it is not enough to describe manifest orientation toward authority. Instead, it is necessary to analyze the interplay between the levels of personal hostility and effects of the controlling institutions. It may well be that for some individuals weak levels of social control are adequate to control low levels of personal hostility. But for the population at large, the strength of the controlling institutions must be powerful enough to counterbalance the levels of personal hostility.

In terms of ego psychology, it is possible to speak of ego strength as representing the outcome between the adequacy of the individual's controls and the social pressure on his controls. Thus we hypothesized that ego strength should in general be positively associated with ethnic tolerance. While it is clear that ego strength has to be studied in the context of the social environment, the proposition is a general one. We felt and we found that in more cases than not, ego strength is directly associated with tolerance.

Thus it becomes important to examine the research efforts which seek to continue and amplify the investigation of the relationship between personality dimensions and ethnic intolerance in terms of ego psychology. It is unfortunate that during the last decade, as mentioned at the beginning of this chapter, most of the psychological literature stimulated by contemporary ego psychology has been highly speculative and hence unrelated to our central proposition; namely, of a direct relationship between ego strength and low intolerance, for any given social subgroup.

Some tentative inferences can be drawn from sociological studies. While there are important deviations and exceptions, the weight of evidence rests on the side that acceptance of authority of the controlling institutions go hand in hand with the inhibition of expression of extremist attitudes and a predisposition to accept social change toward more tolerant practices. This emerges in the studies of attitude variables related to acceptance of desegregation in the South, both in the work of Melvin Tumin and equally in the case of the research by Killian and Haer.[50] There is also evidence that when one probes into the influence of religious institutions, for example, especially at the lower educational levels, that more active church involvement is positively linked to higher levels of tolerance. This would not include involvement in some minor fundamentalist religions. This does not mean that at some higher

---

[50] Melvin Tumin, *op. cit.*; Lewis M. Killian and John L. Haer, "Variables Related to Attitudes Regarding School Desegregation Among White Southerns," *Sociometry,* XXI, June, 1958, pp. 159-64.

social levels tolerance is linked necessarily to the rejection of religious authority. To the contrary, the data from religious institutions fit the general pattern that at the lower levels of the social structure we are dealing with submission to external control and superego control, while at the higher level the incidence of superego control or more rational ego control is likely to be the basis for tolerance.

Thus, the research literature that has appeared since the publication of the *Dynamics of Prejudice* extends our knowledge of the psychological dimensions of prejudice. The psychological variables involved are not always as precise and well-defined as seem required, and in some cases they may explain only a limited amount of the phenomenon. Furthermore, they generally become much more meaningful and significant when viewed in their interaction with social reality and sociological variables. But, for theoretical and particularly for social action purposes, their utility remains crucial.

CHAPTER IV

SOCIAL AND PERSONAL CONTROLS: THEORY AND PRACTICE

The *Dynamics of Prejudice* was an early interdisciplinary study combining variables from dynamic psychology and from sociological theory dealing with some aspects of group life in a modern, industrialized society.[1] Our theoretical framework focused on the interaction of personal and social controls as these controls influence the genesis and expression of ethnic prejudice.

Implicitly, our frame of reference rejected a general theory of human behavior for explaining prejudice. Some such theories are general in the sense that they seek to fuse together psychological and sociological variables into one conceptual framework, or at least they seek to translate sociological and psychological variables into one common unified language. We rejected such efforts not as a long-term goal, although even as a long-term goal they seem more utopian than realistic. Our indifference to a general theory of human behavior was based upon both scientific and policy reasons. First, general theory in the social sciences is deficient because it is unable to guide empirical research with sufficient precision. Such theories are rubrics for observing reality rather than hypothetical statements about sources of personal and social change that can be tested and verified. They generally leave open or avoid the crucial questions of presumed causality. Second, general theories seem to us too remote from social reality to incorporate our value preferences and the social goals we seek to strengthen by the use of scientific knowledge. Social reality must be analyzed in categories that relate to policy issues and social goals.

We realize that our scientific aspirations in the *Dynamics of Prejudice*

[1] The distinctive contribution of sociological and psychological analysis to the understanding of anti-Semitism was set forth in an early article by Morris Ginsberg, "Anti-Semitism," *Sociological Review*, XXXV, Nos. 1–2, January-April, 1943, pp. 1-11. He did not concern himself, however, with the potentialities and limitations of interdisciplinary research.

were modest and limited as compared with the enthusiastic claims set forth by the "behavioral sciences" in the period immediately after 1945. Today, however, social science goals are viewed differently. Unified and general theories combining sociological and psychological concepts have not achieved general scientific acceptance. In fact, at the intellectual level a reaction is leading toward an excessive concern with disciplinary purity.

In particular, we were concerned with improving our ability to assess the outcome of alternative policies for reducing prejudice. In the period immediately after World War II, psychologists increased their efforts in the study of social issues. The initial outpouring of "policy-oriented" literature emphasized attitude and communication variables as the basis of public policy designed to modify prejudice and discriminatory practices. The *Dynamics of Prejudice* was one of the few studies of that period to conclude that certain social structural changes, such as changes in the legal system and new administrative practices, were crucial. During the last 15 years, this point of view has gained acceptance until it is now fashionable even for psychologists to claim that they are not primarily interested in attitudes.[2] Instead, they claim they are interested in overt behavior, and their recommendations emphasize almost exclusively legal sanctions and administrative changes.

We reject such an orientation as being incompatible with the values of a free society. In a free society, attitudes and sentiments are important and they must inherently support the demands of human dignity. As a basis for social policy, we shall argue that in the next decade the variables dealing with attitudes and personality will grow in importance, although we shall continue, as we did in the *Dynamics of Prejudice*, our emphasis on legal and social change.

On a theoretical level we reject the view that changes in social practice must invariably precede attitude or personality changes. We shall argue that important progress has been made and needs to be made in reducing prejudice.[3] It is a serious oversimplification to assume that changes in

[2] See for example, Kenneth B. Clark, "Desegregation: An Appraisal of the Evidence," *Journal of Social Issues*, IX, No. 4, 1953, passim; Stuart W. Cook, "Desegregation: A Psychological Analysis," *American Psychologist*, XII, January, 1957, pp. 1-13. For a similar point of view of a sociologist, see Arnold M. Rose, "Intergroup Relations vs. Prejudice: Pertinent Theory for the Study of Social Change," *Social Problems*, IV, No. 2, 1956.

[3] See William C. Bradbury, "Evaluation of Research in Race Relations," *Inventory: Research in Racial-Cultural Relations*, V, Nos. 2-3, 1953, pp. 99-133, for an interpretation of the relationship between research and policy which avoids reductionism, either sociological or psychological.

overt behavior necessarily bring about desired changes toward increased tolerance. Such a view rests on data collected from laboratory experiments. In the real world of social and political movements, attitude patterns can become not only rigid but explosive and destructive under the pressure of social change. There are many areas of society in which broad sectors of the population change their overt behavior before their attitudes, but where the strategy of change involves mobilizing leaders, interpersonal influences, and attitude changes often anticipate overt political and social behavior. Thus, it becomes necessary to assess the policy implications of our research on both the levels of social and personal controls. The issues of social action can be stated in other terms. If we consider our goal to be desegregation, the elimination of barriers, we are concerned mainly with social controls and institutional arrangements. If we are to have integration as our goal, then the effectiveness of personal controls and the content of attitudes become more important.

SOCIAL CONTROLS

Changes in attitudes toward Negroes and Jews during the last 15 years can be called dramatic, even though the results fall far short of democratic ideals. In evaluating the frame of reference of personal and social controls, it is necessary to ask how adequate this frame of reference has been in accounting for these changes in attitudes toward ethnic minorities. It is abundantly clear that the structure of personal controls and changes in these personal controls alone do not adequately explain the changes of the last 10-15 years. In short, changes in underlying psychological mechanisms do not account for the decline in hostile attitudes toward Jews and Negroes, although such changes were operative. During this period, changes in social controls were crucial in producing attitude changes.

The limitations of personal controls and underlying psychological mechanisms in explaining changes in mass attitudes has been long emphasized by psychoanalytic writers. In answer to the question whether psychoanalysis could account for the development of anti-Semitism in Germany, Otto Fenichel replied with a question: "Is the instinctual structure of the average man in Germany different in 1935 from what it was in 1925? Surely not. The psychological mass basis for anti-Semitism, whatever that may be, existed in 1925 too, but anti-Semitism was not a political force then. If one wishes to understand its rise during these ten years in Germany, one must ask what happened there during these ten years, not about the comparatively unaltered unconscious."[4]

Fenichel singled out the growth of political propaganda to explain the rise of anti-Semitism in Germany. Undoubtedly, political propaganda was an important instrument but, in retrospect, it was the articulation of political propaganda with overt coercion that was crucial. Moreover, in retrospect, it is necessary to analyze the underlying changes in the social and political organization of Germany, which, first, produced the unprecedented flow of political propaganda, and, second, induced the population to accept these appeals. The spread and acceptance of political anti-Semitism in Germany involved a change in the outlook of various elite groups whose approval or at least whose acquiescence was a precondition for the changes in attitudes that took place.

To explain the changes in prejudice in the United States, some sociological students of race relations have made use of the "mass society" concept. These writers make the assumption that social trends in modern society bring about depersonalization and destruction of intimate primary group relations, which has the consequence of increasing prejudice. For them it is the social institutions and broader political processes that produce changes in race relations and prejudice. Arnold Rose, in an article entitled "Intergroup Anxieties in a Mass Society," analyzes these processes and the consequent frustration from economic and political insecurity.[5] His analysis does not explain the decline in prejudice that has occurred, and to the contrary, by implication he anticipates a growth in prejudice. Dietrich Reitzes, in a similar type of mass society theory, characterizes attitudes as relatively unimportant and argues that the pressures of modern society produce self-contradictory behavior, especially in race relations.[6]

To account for the decline in prejudice in the United States, sociological theories of mass society are obviously inadequate. First, there is a growing body of data which indicates that depersonalization *per se* is not the invariant outcome of industrialization. Primary groups are

---

[4] Otto Fenichel, "Psychoanalysis of Anti-Semitism," *American Imago*, I, No. 2, 1940, p. 25.

[5] Arnold M. Rose, "Intergroup Anxieties in a Mass Society," *Phylon*, XII, No. 4, 1951, pp. 305-18.

[6] Dietrich C. Reitzes, "Institutional Structure and Race Relations," *Phylon*, XX, No. 1, 1959, pp. 48-66. See also Joseph D. Lohman and Dietrich C. Reitzes, "Notes on Race Relations in Mass Society," *American Journal of Sociology*, LVIII, 1952, pp. 240-46.

attenuated and restructured but not destroyed by modern industrial society. Second, and more closely related, these mass society theorists cannot account for the decline in prejudice attitudes over the recent years.

In terms of social control a more adequate analysis is presented by J. Milton Yinger and George E. Simpson in their functional analysis of the pressures for desegregation.[7] They see the secular trends pressing toward increased desegregation. They conclude, "Although it will not disappear quietly or immediately, segregation is crumbling," because of urbanization, industrialization, and large-scale migration, as well as political realignments and new international relations.

Similarly, our point of view is that industrialism and urbanism and the attendant processes of social change are preconditions for the decline of segregation and the modification of prejudiced attitudes. But, as we sought to demonstrate in Chapters I and II, advanced industrialism also produces social change, which can contribute to prejudice and ethnic hostility. Moreover, in addition to the underlying social trends of industrialization and urbanization, we find it necessary to add the processes of decision-making and action by organizations operating in an advanced industrial society. These organizations and their leaders are able to speed the processes of change or mobilize the attitudinal resistances and residues to maintain existing practices. These decision-making processes are perhaps secondary variables in accounting for long-term trends but their impact is significant, especially in the immediate period under consideration.

Of course, organizational sources of change do not remain constant. In the 1930's, organizations seeking to modify intergroup relations—both practices and attitudes—were the trade unions, federal government agencies, and to a lesser extent, voluntary associations. The sociological history of the New Deal period is yet to be written. Such an analysis would trace out the role of the trade unions, which with governmental assistance unionized unorganized workers and thereby changed the social and economic status of the Negro. The welfare programs of the New Deal were designed to meet specific economic needs, but they also had the effect of raising the social status of the Negro and other minority groups. During this period, the political parties in the North operated informally to repress extreme intergroup tensions, and raised the self-

---

[7] J. Milton Yinger and George E. Simpson, "Can Segregation Survive in an Industrial Society?" *Antioch Review*, XVIII, No. 1, 1958, pp. 15-24.

esteem of minority group members by giving them opportunities to participate in politics. At the same time, voluntary associations concerned with intergroup relations were developing. But essentially, it was both the trade unions and government economic and welfare agencies that were the main organizational sources of change.

World War II brought an increase in the tempo of managed social change because of more extensive intervention by the federal government. Economic mobilization broadened the opportunities for employment under wartime conditions.[8] Governmental activity also had consequences in wide areas of social relations because of the stronger national commitment to equal treatment for most minorities during a crisis period. The first steps in eliminating segregation in the armed forces were taken, but these efforts were halting and did not mature until the Korean conflict. During World War II, semiofficial organizations, particularly Mayor's Commissions, developed to handle wartime-generated tensions. The expansion of governmental and semigovernmental activities marked the beginning of a transition from "removing barriers" toward an orientation of positive intervention.

After World War II, planned social change in intergroup relations shifted toward governmental legal action and a wider range of activities by voluntary associations, particularly by local community organizations. Social change was facilitated by full employment, which brought about a further weakening of discrimination against Negroes in a variety of occupations as well as the removal of barriers against Jews in selected occupational and professional groups. The trade union movement became less an agent of change in the occupational area; instead, state fair employment activities and administrative action by the federal government in connection with government contract work became more significant.

The most dramatic legal step was taken in 1954, when the Supreme Court called for the elimination of discrimination in the school system. Voluntary associations also spread the base of their demands. They developed new tactics as for example the dramatic Montgomery bus boycott and the spread of sit-ins among Southern Negro college students.[9]

[8] Everett C. Hughes, "Queries Concerning Industry and Society Growing Out of Study of Ethnic Relations in Industry," *American Sociological Review*, XIV, April, 1949, pp. 211-20.

[9] The tempo of these social changes conforms to the "natural history" of a revolutionary movement. At first, demands are limited; only with success do they become more militant. In the 1930's, progress was limited and demands for change were persistent; in retrospect they seem limited. Only after the important progress made

In the last 15 years two additional elements of social control have
been important as organizational devices to modify race relations and
attitudes: the national political parties and the mass media. First, both
of the major political parties have had candidates committed at the
national level to democratic goals and objectives. Campaign rhetoric
is important in setting the moral tone of political life. Both political
parties have been pledged to continuous social change toward the
elimination of discrimination and prejudice, although there may be
important differences as to tactics and desired rate of change. This issue
has been eliminated from the national political arena. Instead, there
has been a constant flow of statements by political leaders about the
goals of human rights. Of course, the cold war has accelerated this political development because of the need to present the United States
as a nation moving toward equality in the treatment of minority groups.

Second, the mass media, by making use of official and unofficial
statements on race relations and by linking racial equality to religious
tolerance, have created a new "definition of the situation" for its mass
audience. Most sociological and psychological studies of the mass media
deal with short-term effects and do not encompass the long-term consequences of these fundamental changes in the presentation of minority
groups in the mass media over the last 15 years.[10] While we recognize
the inherent limitations in the mass media for direct and immediate
modification of attitudes, this revolution in content has had at least a
powerful negative effect of repressing extreme prejudice and creating
the conditions under which governmental agencies and voluntary
associations can operate to bring about social change.

Despite these stronger and more effective social controls, the efforts

---

in the 1940's did the demands for social change and social equality develop. Mili-
tancy among Negroes began increasing sharply after 1954, when the Supreme Court
decision was passed, and reached a high point in 1958 and thereafter.

This observation is also documented in a study by Robert Lee Eichhorn entitled
"Patterns of Segregation, Discrimination, Interracial Conflict: Analysis of a Nationwide Survey of Intergroup Practices," *Dissertation Abstract*, XV, 1955, pp. 163-64.
On the basis of questionnaires with race relations officials in 248 cities, he pointed
out that Negroes react most militantly to segregation and discrimination in cities
where some gains have been made.

[10] For a study of these specific experimental and survey type studies of the impact
of the mass media, see Joseph T. Klapper, *The Effects of Mass Communication*,
New York, The Free Press of Glencoe, 1960. See also Edward A. Suchman, John P.
Dean, and Robin M. Williams, Jr., *Desegregation: Some Propositions and Research
Suggestions*, New York, Anti-Defamation League, 1958, Chapter 3, which contains
an analysis of the mass media in broad sociological terms. Melvin M. Tumin,
"Exposure to Mass Media and Readiness for Desegregation," *Public Opinion Quarterly*, XXI, Summer, 1957, pp. 237-51, points out that involvements in the mass
media predispose persons in the South toward a willingness to accept desegregation.

of the last 15 years have not been uniformly successful and without setbacks. In the decade ahead, issues in the educational system and in housing patterns will be paramount. In order for laws and regulations to become fully effective, new forms of social controls at the community level will be required. The areas of resistance to change indicate the need for greater personal controls, if new forms of social control are to be successful and rapid.

Desegregation of the school system is taken to be essential if the Negro is to enter fully the mainstream of American life. In the South, resistance to desegregation has been massive in the sense that the progress so far made has had to confront the most deep-seated personal attitudes. Violence has occurred because strong enough social controls were not mobilized to overcome both spontaneous and organized resistance. In the North, because of residential segregation, school segregation continues to be part of the practices of social control. Therefore, the school is seen by some public leaders as a device for weakening and overcoming segregation rooted in residential patterns. In the school setting, the importance of personal control is highlighted. If the white middle classes continue to send their children to private and parochial schools and to move to suburban school districts which, because of housing conditions, are generally all white, desegregation of the schools as enforced by law or administrative practice will do little to overcome segregation in residential patterns. Only when societally enforced regulations become—through such influences as the mass media—an inner moral stance (i.e., also part of personal control) can societal control fully achieve its goals.

At the same time, the school will be a crucial institution for change in race relations in the decade ahead because of the emerging patterns of occupational stratification. The school becomes the central vehicle for social mobility as well as for enhancing the self respect of deprived minorities. Education *per se*, however, is not a cure-all. Because of occupational discrimination, Negroes in the North with comparable education still earn significantly less than whites, and this holds true for young and recently educated Negroes.[11] Moreover, a high school education is not sufficient to insure access to changing job opportunities; some college is essential for many of the new occupational categories. The university-educated Negro is also a positive symbol to both the white and the Negro communities. He reflects the fact that Negroes

[11] Basil G. Zimmer, "The Adjustment of Negroes in a Northern Industrial Community," *Social Problems*, Spring, 1962, pp. 378-86.

can achieve superior status. But all efforts at educational integration will remain sterile unless Negroes take successful advantage of them.

At a point, the goal of desegregation of education blends into the broader problem of the cultural values of the lower class, especially the lower-lower class. The American school system, despite a decade of social criticism, still operates on the assumption that social mobility and entrance into the middle class is the central cultural value. Without denying the desirability and actuality of an expanding "middle majority," a segment of the population must be prepared to lead dignified lives as wage earners. The cultural and humanistic education of this group, which is composed mainly of minority groups, is a topic with which professional educators have not concerned themselves sufficiently: partly because to do so is incompatible with the value of social mobility, and partly because it would require far-reaching changes in underlying philosophy and curriculum content. Where there have been experimental efforts to enhance the education of the so-called "culturally deprived," the results indicate that they have much greater capacities for cultural growth and development than most educators have assumed.

In the decade ahead, a key social policy question will be the extent to which the school system can be used as an instrument of social control to bring about desegregation of residential communities and still remain a relatively autonomous sector of a free society. Our knowledge of the school system, which would be appropriate for understanding its potentialities to change patterns of community segregation, is most inadequate. In fact, research on the school as a social system has so far only partly met our needs. Such research is essential in order to broaden our understanding of the educational system as a device of social control.

There are some findings available on the specific effects of interracial housing. These studies invariably show that the experiences of living in interracial housing can be conducive to reducing hostile attitudes.[12] But these studies deal with limited and specific housing projects where the pattern of social control is such that outside community pressures could be eliminated. Because of shortages of housing or because of

[12] See, for example, Morton Deutsch and M. Evans Collins, *Interracial Housing: A Psychological Evaluation of a Social Experiment*, Minneapolis, University of Minnesota Press, 1951; Daniel M. Wilner, Rosabelle P. Walkley, and Stuart W. Cook, "Residential Proximity and Intergroup Relations in Public Housing Projects," *Journal of Social Issues*, VIII, No. 1, 1952, pp. 45-69; Daniel M. Wilner, Rosabelle P. Walkley, and Stuart W. Cook, *Human Relations in Interracial Housing*, Minneapolis, University of Minnesota Press, 1955, pp. 167 ff.

existing administrative authority, managers of such housing projects could enforce some system of quotas and thereby prevent mixed housing units from becoming all Negro. These results must be matched with the day-to-day experiences when whole neighborhoods undergo changes in ethnic or racial composition.[13] In reality, the general pattern at the neighborhood level is that of increasing hostility, because the residents believe that the trend of "invasion" is irreversible, uncontrollable, and certain to lead to a predominantly Negro residential area.

Ethnic hostility in housing is influenced by minority group demands. In the area of residential preference, the demands of minority groups are subtle and ambiguous. In order to estimate Negro preferences as residential segregation weakens, the experiences of Jewish preferences and practices seem relevant. The Jews, who suffer fewer restrictions, have a pattern of demands and preferences that seems to be outright contradictory. They wish to reside in unsegregated communities, yet they prefer to have close association with other Jews, which they often feel requires a majority of Jews in their community. In essence, they fundamentally wish to have gentiles as neighbors but in the minority, and only a small fraction are prepared to live in overwhelmingly non-Jewish areas.

Likewise, it seems that only a minority of Negroes are prepared to live in overwhelmingly white communities. The idea that a quota system should be used to limit Negroes to 10 per cent in a white community is unacceptable to Negro leaders and rejected by the bulk of the middle-class Negroes who have thought about the issue. Moreover, a rigid and formal quota system is indefensible on moral grounds, since it would subject the Negro to a permanent minority group status in his residential community. However, it is possible to speak of the patterns of desegregation which would give expression to current housing preferences of Negroes if barriers were in effect removed. One possible pattern is that a small percentage would move into overwhelmingly white communities, a larger proportion would live in communities where Negroes constitute a sizable segment of the residents, and the bulk would live in communities where Negroes were at least the majority group. If such a pattern of housing were realized, it would in turn generate new preferences and demands. Again, as in the case of the desegregation of schools, we are dealing with an interaction of race and class factors. In a society where social class is highly stratified, social

[13] Alvin E. Winder, "White Attitudes Toward Negro-White Interaction in an Area of Changing Composition," *Journal of Social Psychology*, XLI, 1955, pp. 85-102.

discrimination may well be more easily reduced and eliminated. However, in the United States, the goals are both those of an open class system and the elimination of race discrimination and segregation.

Social experimentation to modify the self-perpetuating cycle of community invasion and succession can take various directions. The desegregation of the school system can be used to bring about new patterns of community relations. One approach is to abandon the community-based school and permit parents to transport their children (or require the school authorities to transport children who wish such transportation) so that segregated schools based on community residence are reduced or eliminated. Such a strategy is being attempted by some educational authorities. While it seems to be a device for reducing overcrowded schools, it is cumbersome to administer, and it seems to touch only a limited portion of the school population. No scientific data are available to evaluate the social and personal consequences of this approach; some speculations are presented below in the section on personal controls.

Another potentially comprehensive approach to developing interracial communities is to make use of urban renewal. This is clearly an official objective of urban renewal and urban planners who sought to identify the potentials and barriers involved in the use of various forms of urban renewal as a technique of social change.[14] As of 1962, this goal of urban renewal had been achieved only in token areas, that is, in individual housing projects. One of the only major exceptions in the United States where urban renewal has been integrated into comprehensive interracial community planning has been the University of Chicago sponsored Hyde Park-Kenwood renewal project. This effort has succeeded in developing a stable interracial community which involves not only housing and educational institutions but religious and social facilities and other amenities of urban life. Although the politics of this urban renewal program have been studied, there are no available systematic trend data on the changes in attitude structures during the period of redevelopment.[15] There is every reason to believe that this project has succeeded mainly on the basis of self-selection of people, and to a lesser extent on the modification of attitudes.

[14] For an interesting analysis of the problematic issues, see Mel J. Ravitz, "Effects of Urban Renewal on Community Racial Patterns," *Journal of Social Issues*, XIII, No. 4, 1957, pp. 38-49.

[15] Peter H. Rossi and Robert A. Dentler, *The Politics of Urban Renewal*, New York, The Free Press of Glencoe, 1961.

However, a number of conclusions emerge from this experiment as to the social controls that are essential for an urban interracial community. First, the financial resources and leadership of an institution such as a university or a major hospital which has close ties in the local community through its staff and clients are essential preconditions. Neither industrial, commercial, nor banking and business enterprises, although they are essential for the success of such ventures, have succeeded in supplying the required leadership. Second, even if physical standards are achieved through reconstruction or enforcement of housing regulations, there is no guarantee that the automatic working of the economic marketplace for housing will produce or maintain an interracial community. Elaborate community organizations are required to achieve some form of managed integration. These include private consortiums for buying and selling real estate, area-wide associations of business and real estate interests, as well as community and block organizations of residents. These block organizations serve as a device for developing new norms and for persuading white residents not to leave the area. The argument can be made that an interracial community is a form of political bargaining unit and there is danger if one major, unified organization seeks to manage the differing interests. Bargaining seems best achieved if the major economic interests are organized apart from the residents and tenants in the area and if an informal set of rules for resolving disputes is developed. All of these organizations must interact with and modify the community power structure and the local political system.

During the last five years considerable research has been undertaken by sociologists and political scientists on community decision-making and community power structures. Although much of this literature has focused on the physical reconstruction of the metropolitan community, this research points to a more realistic understanding of political factors in changing ethnic and race relations. Community decision-making is an expression of community power structure, which can best be described as a pluralistic structure because of the variety of interests it must serve. But more important, it is pluralistic because it represents a balance between two types of leaders: the economic dominants and what has come to be called the "public leaders."[16] The economic dominants are the owners and top managers of the major industrial, banking and

---

[16] Robert O. Schulze, "The Bifurcation of Power in a Satellite City," in *Community Political Systems*, edited by Morris Janowitz, New York, The Free Press of Glencoe, 1961, pp. 19-80.

commercial firms, both local and absentee. The public leaders are the spokesmen of the racial, ethnic, and religious groups, as well as of the professional, social welfare, and civic associations. These public leaders include many businessmen, but they tend to be the owners not of the largest economic units but rather of middle-sized enterprises. In addition, public leaders comprise lawyers, professionals, and political leaders who come to act as community "brokers."

The view that community power is tightly dominated by a small group of top business leaders has been found to be oversimplified. The pressures of corporation life limit business leaders in the amount of time and energy they have available for participation in community affairs. Within the largest business enterprises there are conflicts of interest, which contribute to the pluralism of community affairs. When the economic dominants enter community life, they represent a particular economic, social, or religious outlook rather than a unified business point of view.

Depending on the issues at stake, different sets of community leaders come to the fore, but there is enough overlap so as to speak of a leadership "cadre." At the center of the community leadership cadre are the professional politicians, who formally and informally must seek to develop consensus on community decisions. From the point of view of an effective democratic procedure, the problem of community decision-making centers not on the concentration of political power. To the contrary, most observers emphasize that pluralism has tended to proceed to the point where it produces deep fractionalization of community interests. The political task is to create conditions in which effective decisions required for social change can be made and to mobilize community support on behalf of these decisions.

This is particularly the case in ethnic and race relations. Economic dominants have in the past either resisted or more likely displayed a lack of concern in the elimination of prejudice and discrimination. Progress has been made mainly by public leaders and political leaders. However, there are signs of a broader perspective on the part of selected industrial companies, public utilities, merchandising and commercial groups.

But at the level of community organization it is clear that the existing local legislative bodies are not viable enough to supply a forum for all community interests. The American political system sets limits on legislative action and legislative effectiveness. Already the demands for social progress have led Negro groups to such direct actions as sit-ins and the less dramatic but highly effective economic boycotts. Such pressures can be expected to continue and even to intensify as metropolitan communities grope toward new forms of social control.

The term *community development* need no longer be limited to village work in new nations; it applies directly to race and minority relations in the largest metropolitan centers of the United States. It involves the development of new leadership skills and new devices for coordinating the unrelated activities of private agencies and for bridging public and private agencies. Social control in a democratic society at the community level does not require the development of one roof organization with the danger of remoteness from the public and arbitrary concentration of power. But it does require more explicit forms of community management than currently found in the United States. Undoubtedly, the existing official coordinating bodies, especially the Mayor's committees on race and human relations, supply a useful focal point, but only if their tasks are very broadly defined and only if there is national support for their work. The analogy with economic affairs and with labor-management relations is striking. What seems required is a President's conference on community race relations for evolving policy and knowledge to guide community development. In thinking about new forms of social control to achieve change, we must also include in our goals the development of more effective personal controls.

PERSONAL CONTROLS

Efforts to modify ethnic prejudice by direct intervention into personal controls or psychological mechanisms—both emotional and cognitive—have been extensive during the last 15 years. First, there has been a continuous effort to investigate attitude change by means of laboratory experimental and quasi-experimental studies.[17] Second, there have been field experiments and systematic observation of natural settings; for our purposes they seem to be of greater importance. George Simpson and J. Milton Yinger, in their compendium on race relations, *Racial and Cultural Minorities: An Analysis of Prejudice and Discrimination,* and Gerhart Saenger in his volume *The Social Psychology of Prejudice,* present significant evaluations of portions of this literature.[18]

[17] For a theoretical overview of this literature, see Daniel Katz, ed., "Attitude Change," *Public Opinion Quarterly,* XXIV, Summer, 1960, pp. 163-65.
[18] See especially Chapter 22, "The Reduction of Prejudice and Discrimination: Changing the Prejudiced Person," in George Simpson and J. Milton Yinger, *Racial*

Third, there has been a growth of widespread action programs both with and without follow-up research evaluation. The growth of an intercultural education curriculum in the school system represents a mass social psychological experiment. Recreational, social welfare, and community programs with interracial objectives have grown in scope and complexity to the point where we can speak of mass "treatment" programs. Voluntary organizations—religious, social welfare, and recreational—consciously seek to handle interracial relations with a concern for the personal controls of the individuals involved. A propositional analysis of some type of "action" experiences are presented by John P. Dean and Alex Rosen in *A Manual of Intergroup Relations*.[19]

Because of the previously discussed emphasis on sociological reductionism there is a strong tendency by research scholars and professional personnel to view such large-scale efforts of attitude change to be of secondary consequence. As a result, there has been little effort to develop a body of theory about attitude and psychological change that would assist the practice-oriented professionals, such as the educator, social worker, and the like, in handling interracial tension at the interpersonal level.

From our point of view, it is essential to develop such "doctrine" if a democratic society is to mobilize its full resources for social change. Programs of social change designed to speed desegregation require concern with psychological mechanisms and attitude formation in order to reduce extreme tension and violence. For example, Arnold Rose, in an analysis addressed to psychiatrists, offered the realistic expectation that some degree of violence is to be expected in the American scene during desegregation unless explicit attention is paid to the emotional predisposition of the persons involved.[20]

Furthermore, concern with the dimensions of personal control arises from the fact that in many areas desegregation is no longer a goal. The objective of a free society is to achieve some form of managed integration, and integration does not come about automatically. Effective integration would fail if it had to rely exclusively on administrative decree. It necessarily involves the attitudes and sentiments of those involved.

---

and Cultural Minorities: An Analysis of Prejudice and Discrimination, New York, Harper and Bros., 1958, pp. 647-95; Gerhart Saenger, *The Social Psychology of Prejudice: Achieving Intercultural Understanding and Cooperation in a Democracy*, New York, Harper and Bros., 1953, pp. 304 ff.

[19] John P. Dean and Alex Rosen, *A Manual of Intergroup Relations*, Chicago, University of Chicago Press, 1955.

[20] See Arnold Rose, "Desegregation: Its Implications for Ortho-Psychiatry," *American Journal of Orthopsychiatry*, XXVI, July, 1956, pp. 445-49.

Already in particular areas of employment, especially where fair employment legislation has been rigorously enforced for a number of years, Negroes have been hired in such numbers that the prospects of creating Negro employment ghettos are real. Thus, in the employment area as in housing, if the self-defeating cycle of invasion and succession perpetuating segregation is to be broken, attitude change is required.

In the public school system, a major effort is being made to modify ethnic group attitudes by means of direct interpersonal intervention. Much of the effort to modify these attitudes is grounded in a concern with cognitive processes of learning. But the climate of the classroom, the attitude of the teacher, and the whole structure of the educational system supply the context in which attitude formation takes place.

Students of social change are likely to underestimate the extent to which the school system in its organized curriculum has become involved in modifying intergroup attitudes. Since 1945, there has been a widespread effort to introduce into the public school system special instructional material designed to deal with Negroes and minority groups in a democratic context. These efforts have had some success. One large-scale evaluation study by Robert Floyd Corder,[21] based on a sample of approximately 3,000 high schools, of which some had intergroup programs and others did not, revealed by means of a before-and-after study that for even a one-year period these intergroup curriculum programs had definite and significant effects on attitudes.

During the first years of college, the impact of the formal curriculum has particular effect on intergroup attitudes. It is then that young people leave home and begin to explore their own attitudes and orientations. The content of undergraduate social science courses—sociology, anthropology, and psychology—all have significant effect in fashioning attitudes. As Professor Paul F. Lazarsfeld has shown in his study of *The Academic Mind*, the teachers of these subjects are strongly liberal in their orientation.[22] Although they consider themselves to be scientists, they believe that intergroup attitudes is an area in which the results of social science make it possible for them to develop democratic values. These social science courses are now a central part of undergraduate education, and their impact on ethnic attitudes is particularly strong among those middle class students who have previously had little direct

[21] Robert Floyd Corder, "A Factoral Approach to Anti-Democratic Attitudes," *Purdue University Studies in Higher Education*, No. 82, 1954.

[22] Paul F. Lazarsfeld and Wagner Thielens, Jr., *The Academic Mind: Social Scientists in a Time of Crisis*, New York, The Free Press of Glencoe, 1958.

contact with minority groups, especially with Negroes. Teachers in the big-city colleges and universities report that students recruited from the lower-middle and working classes, and who have had extensive contact with minority groups, are uninterested in this phase of social science and are less likely to modify their attitudes.

In assessing the impact of the school system, particularly the primary and secondary levels, on ethnic attitudes, a number of factors outside of the curriculum seem to be important. One factor is the type and effectiveness of the school curriculum and a second is the authority relations between teachers and students and between teachers and the supervisory level. A third factor is the relative proportion of minority group members in a school and the type of contact between majority and minority group members.

On a common-sense basis, effective and meaningful desegregated schools should produce the least hostile students. But there are limits to what the school system can accomplish. Thus, one study points out that in a school with 10 to 15 per cent Negro children, there was still evidence of self-rejection by the Negro children, partly attributed to the fact that the children were still a minority under these circumstances.[23] In fact, it can be argued that the impact of preschool family experience is overriding as compared with that of the social composition of the classroom. Self-rejection by children is often based on their views of their own families as inferior. Thus, as long as Negro children view themselves as coming from undesirable families when compared to the whites, self-rejection may be increased rather than decreased by such measures to manipulate the racial composition of a classroom by transfers from one school to another. If they are considered to be transfer students (unwelcome; a group for which special arrangements have to be made) the result may well tend to increase self-hatred and feelings of inferiority.

Clearly, learning tolerance is not the result simply of having some minority group members in the same school. Our common-sense observations seem to emphasize the need of avoiding wherever possible gross underrepresentation or overrepresentation of the minority. But within these limits, clearly the quality of contacts and not the relative concentration of number is of primary importance. The quality of contacts depends on a wide variety of factors, ranging from economic standards of living and the physical well-being of the students to the

[23] Marion Radke, Jean Sutherland, and Pearl Rosenberg, "Racial Attitudes of Children," *Sociometry*, XIII, May, 1950, pp. 154-71.

professional skill of the teachers in creating an appropriate classroom climate.

But in order to develop personal controls appropriate for a democratic society, we must consider the changing goals of the school system in the United States. The present dilemma of the American school system rests in the difficulties inherent in maintaining a balance in its goals of intellectual attainment and the socialization of the next generation. Along with its vocational and academic programs, the school system has traditionally been involved in molding the personal controls and attitudes of its pupils. In the past, however, the task of socialization was very closely articulated with that of intellectual development. This was the case for a wide variety of reasons, the most important of which was that the kind of socialization required by the social order could be accomplished as a by-product of a simplified and common education system. The long-term trend has been toward a shift in the social structure that requires a more differentiated educational system, and new and higher levels of personal control.

To achieve those personal controls required to contain and repress ethnic hostility, the school system must assume greater institutional responsibility than it did in the past. In our frame of reference, a democratic society now requires a much higher level of internalized personal control. It is not enough to rely on submission to external authority, a simpler task which the older school system sought to and could achieve. Given the complexity of modern society and given our emphasis on individualism, it becomes necessary to develop an orientation toward minority group members that is more and more based in internal controls. Nevertheless, constitutional factors, childhood experiences, and the cultural attitudes—particularly in the lower income groups—mean that submission to external authority will remain for some time an essential element of personal control for ethnic tolerance. To expect and strive for a system based entirely on internalized personal control seems not only possible but also likely to result in disruption of orderly and effective social change.

Along with the mass school system, mass "socialization," or "treatment" programs of social work, group work, and community organization have emerged. It is difficult even to estimate the number of professional social workers involved and the large numbers of voluntary workers who are mobilized. The special target of these activities are, of course, young people. If one includes Boy Scouts, Girl Scouts, the YMCAs, settlement houses, church-affiliated groups, and the extensive arrangements of summer camps, it can be estimated that, directly or indirectly, over half of the youth of this country have had some exposure to these group activities. In general these program are committed, except in the deep South, if not to the practices, at least to the goal of interracial equality. Available research evidence indicates that some of these programs, especially those camp programs in which children are removed from their natural home environment, do reduce ethnic hostility if they are based upon desegregated practices and if they are managed by professionals.[24]

Group therapy programs, even if they are brief, also have been shown to reduce intergroup hostility.[25] But these efforts can encompass only very minute audiences. More important are community-based programs, both public and private, which extend welfare and recreation services to a variety of clients and which have consequences for ethnic hostility to the extent that they are concerned with interpersonal process. John P. Dean and Alex Rosen, in their book *A Manual of Intergroup Relations,* highlight the importance of these agencies for intergroup relations.[26] As part of their research effort they collected data on the attitudes of officials in more than 200 organizations throughout the United States, attitudes that could be rated in terms of effectiveness. One of their crucial findings is that the more professionalized the officials in these organizations were, the more effective they were in their day-to-day activities.

Along with the increased involvement of the teaching and welfare professions in race relations and minority group problems, there has been a somewhat similar development in police work. Many large-city police departments have special details for human relations problems and conduct in-service training programs. The changes in police work represent the pattern in which a variety of professions, for example, the clergy, industrial relations, personnel specialists, and nursing, begin to see active intervention on the race relations front as one of their professional responsibilities. These developments involve recognition of the existing practices of the profession either in recruitment of new personnel or in the treatment of clients and programs of planned changes. On the other side of professional development, a group of specialists

[24] Marian Radke Yarrow, ed., "Interpersonal Dynamics on Desegregation Process," *Journal of Social Issues,* XIV, No. 1, 1958.
[25] David Pearl, "Psychotherapy and Ethnocentrism," *Journal of Abnormal and Social Psychology,* L, March, 1955, pp. 119-227.
[26] John P. Dean and Alex Rosen, *op. cit.*

in intergroup relations have emerged and formed the National Association of Interracial Relations Officials. After a gradual development, the organization has emerged with considerable vitality, and its members are heavily involved in governmental agencies and programs designed not only to enforce new practices but to develop new norms appropriate for the elimination of segregation and discrimination as well.

But there are limits in a democratic society to the role and potentials of professionals in intergroup and racial relations. The supply of professional agents is limited and often these professionals tend to adopt a technical outlook. The standards they must set are high and, as a result, limit services.

In the years ahead, the task of professionals in intergroup relations is to mobilize citizen leadership and citizen participation in order to strengthen both appropriate social and personal controls. In theoretical terms: if stable integration is to be achieved, more than desegregation is required. Social controls must operate to strengthen personal controls to produce attitudes and sentiments of mutual self-respect. In practical terms, we are emerging from a period of token demonstration and from a period in which legal and administrative decrees were the prime instruments of change. We are entering a period of organizational effort and community involvement which will penetrate the entire fabric of our urban society. The theory and practice of social and personal controls does not require "mass" involvement, for the term "mass" is vague or undefinable. It does require a much wider involvement and sharing of responsibility for positive social change than has been the case to date.

PART TWO

DYNAMICS OF PREJUDICE

A PSYCHOLOGICAL AND SOCIOLOGICAL
STUDY OF VETERANS

PREFACE

ALTHOUGH the plan of this study reflects the period in which it was conceived and executed, the problems of intolerance and ethnic prejudice are, unfortunately, not bound to any year, or world political constellation. A study of war veterans, their anxieties about adjustment in a postwar world, and how they related to intolerance, showed that in the end these anxieties have much deeper roots than the fear of immediate tasks. It also showed that intolerance is as likely to be present in times of war as of peace, of full employment as of depression, since it fulfills important functions in maintaining the integration of the intolerant person.

In 1944, Max Horkheimer, then Director of the Department of Scientific Research of the American Jewish Committee, developed plans for a comprehensive study of the problem of anti-Semitism. He hoped that such an investigation would add not only to our understanding of this particular and important problem of human relations, but would also permit greater insight into intolerance, "fascist" agitation, and, last but not least, into the structure of a society which permits so asocial a phenomenon as ethnic intolerance to persist. The task at hand seemed too extensive for any one group of researchers, and it was decided to set up a series of projects, each of which would select a specific area for independent investigation.

At Mr. Horkheimer's invitation Bruno Bettelheim undertook to serve as director for one of these research projects. Various plans were investigated at first before a final decision was reached. For example, the possibility was initially explored of comparing the ethnic attitudes of psychotic individuals with those of a normal group of people of comparable intelligence, education, family background, etc. The purpose would have been to learn whether a disintegrated person would prove free of ethnic intolerance, or whether, in his case, intolerance would take different forms from those observed among normal persons.

Interesting as this and several other alternative projects seemed, they were discarded as a basis for this research—particularly after the surrender of Germany and the prospect of peace. With the end of the war in view, and in terms of the then prevalent assumption that readjustment to a peacetime economy would be difficult, it was felt that recently discharged veterans might become a group of much social import. It was therefore decided to single them out for careful study as to the origin, nature, and external forms of their ethnic intolerance. Once the study was under way, it became clear that a cross section of such veterans would be tantamount to a cross section of the younger age groups of our male urban population.

Edward A. Shils joined the project as codirector shortly after its inception. Full credit is due to him for an equal share with the director of the project in the construction of the original hypotheses, the selection of the variables and indices to be studied, the construction of the interview schedule, and the execution of the study. Unfortunately other duties took him to London after the data had been collected and after the main decisions regarding their coding and tabulation, in which he assumed a major responsibility, had been completed. He cannot be blamed for the shortcomings of this report, since he could not participate in the evaluation of the findings, as they are contained in this book.

Morris Janowitz, who joined the study in its early stages, assumed major responsibility for the actual collection of the data and their analysis.

Ruth Shils assisted in the construction of the interview schedule and in the training and supervision of the interviewers. Sebastian de Grazia directed the interviewers for a short period of time during the pilot phase of the project. Lucia Ackron, Susan Caudill, Ruth Chapin, Jane Luebbing, Meryl Rogers, and Betty Jane Tullis interviewed the men. Natalie Rogoff participated in the coding and analysis of the interview records and in the construction of the main indices.

The study itself was sponsored by the Social Science Research Committee of the University of Chicago and the authors wish to express their gratitude to Ralph W. Tyler, chairman of the Committee, for his valuable suggestions and active support of the project.

The American Jewish Committee financed the study by a grant from its Department of Scientific Research. We are greatly indebted to Mr. Horkheimer, who first as director and later as chief scientific consultant of the Department, but much more so as a friend, helped in developing the plan for the research, and made invaluable suggestions during its execution. The cooperation of Theodore W. Adorno in shaping the plan of the study is also deeply appreciated. After Samuel H. Flowerman joined the Department of Scientific Research of the American Jewish

Committee, of which he later became director, his patient understanding and helpfulness gave us support in presenting in this book a large segment of the material accumulated. We are especially obliged to Ruth Soffer for her endless battle for clarity of style which she waged so kindly.

THE LIMITATION OF AGGRESSION IS THE FIRST
AND PERHAPS THE HARDEST SACRIFICE WHICH
SOCIETY DEMANDS FROM EACH INDIVIDUAL.

Sigmund Freud

CHAPTER I

DYNAMIC APPROACH TO INTOLERANCE

An attempt has been made in this study to present an objective analysis and a systematic interpretation of the particular type of group hostility known as ethnic intolerance. Although this analysis is primarily an effort to contribute to a scientific theory of human behavior—its social basis and psychological motivation—we hope that the diagnosis so arrived at will prove useful in planning a cure for one of the major disorders in contemporary American society: ethnic discrimination and aggression. The authors believe that "pure" science, without the practical applications implied in its findings, is a sterile abstraction. True, the development of social science depends upon objective study unbiased by any wish for immediate practical applications. But research into the significant problems confronting society today must, necessarily, arrive at findings which have important implications for social planning and action.

Hostilities among groups—nations, classes, ethnic groups, or families—are alike in being directed by members of one group against those of another group in the name of certain collective symbols of identification. Such group hostility can thrive very well alongside of friendly, even intimate, relations between individuals of the two hostile groups, the accepted individual being considered an exception to his group. It is true that in many important respects the kinds of hostility among social groups differ widely. The particular goals that groups strive for, the particular social contexts in which they interact, all affect the forms of hostility. But if human behavior is to be understood and explained, the principles of group hostility in general must be determined. In other words, it is necessary to formulate and establish propositions which will cover the whole range of intergroup hostility and which will have a generalized explanatory value, even though they may not explain particular variations. They may even be derived from the intensive study of only one or a few types of group hostility.

The plan for any type of research must assume a theoretical framework, a body of hypotheses with central bearing on the phenomena under investigation. If the research produces significant results, these validate, to some degree, the hypotheses which were initially assumed; if the research does not produce such results either the hypotheses or the research procedures are proved inadequate or invalid. For the research reported and discussed in these pages, particular hypotheses were selected which seemed likely to help in answering the central question: *What are the factors essentially associated with anti-Semitism and are these factors also associated with anti-Negro attitudes?* Obviously, the hypotheses had to be part of a central theory of human behavior and social organization, since the purpose of the study was to clarify their interconnection with anti-Semitic and anti-Negro attitudes. Since no such theory has as yet found general acceptance, a tentative choice was made. The body of theories chosen to analyze human motivation was that of the dynamic theory of personality. In choosing psychoanalytic theory, it was recognized that the application of the theory beyond the individual, and particularly to the larger organization of society, was still relatively undeveloped. Yet it was our conviction—and especially so after having finished the study—that this theory seemed an exceedingly fruitful one in accounting for certain aspects of human behavior in society. This does not mean that, in basing our investigation on the psychoanalytic theory, the theory was regarded as a closed and finished system of propositions. On the contrary, it was assumed that a vast labor of reformulation and systematic testing remained to be done; indeed this study represents, among others, an effort to test the validity of dynamic theories of human behavior as they apply to phenomena of group interaction.

Compared with the relatively comprehensive formulation of psychoanalytic theory as applied to the individual and his motivation, no single view of the modern social organism within which the individual functions seemed equally adequate to cover the problems under investigation. Hence it was necessary to utilize various theoretical formulations on the organization of group life in a modern, industrialized society.

On the basis of these considerations, the following major hypotheses were evolved, which were then to be tested in an intensive study of a relatively small, but homogeneous, group.

First, hostility toward outgroups is a function of the hostile individual's feeling that he has suffered deprivations in the past.

Second, hostility toward outgroups is a function of the hostile individual's anxiety in anticipation of future tasks, as inferred from his expectations of deprivation.

From the first and second hypotheses followed certain sub-hypotheses: (1) Past or anticipated deprivation leads to intolerance only if the individual has initially felt an obligation to succeed in mastering the task at hand. (2) Self-respect and self-love prevent an individual, so situated, from accepting failure as his own and he therefore ascribes it to aggressive and/or amoral behavior by an outgroup. (3) Once the individual has blamed a particular outgroup for his own failure to gain self-respect, those characteristics within the individual which are unacceptable to himself are fought by externalizing them and projecting them onto members of an outgroup.

The *third* hypothesis was that when the individual blames the outgroup for his failure at mastery of past and future experiences, and projects undesirable characteristics denied in himself onto members of the outgroup, such behavior is the consequence of a lack of ego strength and of inadequate controls which favor irrational discharge and evasion rather than rational action.

Related to this hypothesis was the sub-hypothesis that the individual blames his own inadequate integration on existing authorities. He feels that they do not provide the strong support he needs to be able to ignore or to deny his own ego weakness and often they are attacked with a simultaneous demand for stronger authorities.

Ethnic intolerance can be viewed in terms of the individual's position within the social structure either statically or dynamically. Therefore, as a *fourth* major hypothesis, it was assumed that ethnic intolerance was related more to the individual's dynamic movement within the structure of society than to his societal position at a particular moment. It was assumed that ethnic intolerance was more related to the individual's mobility within the social structure than to his economic situation, or his political or religious attitudes at any one time. As a sub-hypothesis it was assumed that intolerance would be more related to downward social mobility, while it was assumed that upward social mobility would be associated with ethnic tolerance.

At this point, it should be emphasized that these hypotheses were to be tested in a community where at least two important ethnic minorities were present, and that there are other communities where only one important minority is involved. It was expected that all phenomena connected with ethnic intolerance which seem to be concentrated on a single minority, where only one is present, would be separated among the various minorities, where more than one is present. Such findings, though testable only in part, would tend to confirm the underlying assumption of the hypothesis that intolerance is a function of the structure and needs of society and not a function of the presence or absence of a particular ethnic minority.

It may be added that no claim is made that these hypotheses are universally applicable. They seemed useful in understanding hostility within modern industrialized communities which are characterized by a complex division of labor. Group hostilities take on different aspects in primitive cultures, in predominantly agricultural societies, and in cultural areas which are in a period of particular transition. Under those conditions other hypotheses might be required for understanding the particular forms in which group hostility may operate. In particular, the whole complex of special factors and conditions of the South, with its particular historical traditions and its transitional economy, were ruled out. However, it may well be that the question of ethnic hostility and of its political consequences, particularly in their relation to fascism, will in the main be decided in the big cities. Urban population is most subject to the instabilities of industrialism and urban areas contain the bulk of the population.

Despite the foregoing, it was felt that theoretical considerations of economic, social, and psychological hypotheses alone were not a sufficient basis for planning procedures in social research. They had to be supplemented by a backward look at the context in which similar phenomena have been appearing in the past, in order to correctly assess the more or less relevant contexts for the study at hand.

In recent times, the outstanding instance of ethnic intolerance, anti-Semitism, had its roots in Germany after the first World War. The chief promoters and followers of the anti-Semitic movement were former soldiers, unable to reintegrate themselves successfully into society. If ethnic intolerance should approach critical limits in the near future, and in this country, the reasons may well be similar to those which accounted for its development in Germany. Thus, theoretical as well as practical considerations suggested demobilized soldiers as the particular group of individuals to be studied.

Since a basic hypothesis was that persons who believe they have experienced deprivations are more disposed to ethnic intolerance, and since it was plausible that ex-soldiers who had undergone major deprivations in varying degrees might be specially responsive to intolerant agitation, it seemed fitting to study ex-soldiers, rather than other groups. In this context, it should be realized that the army experience was not only one of deprivation but also one of security in the case of basic necessities and, for much of the time, orderliness of living.

The followers of Hitler had a strong desire to see violent change in the structure of a society which they felt had let them down, and they wished also to regain those advantages which the army had offered: the opportunity for hostile discharge against an enemy; a regulation of their lives which made it unnecessary to assume responsibility or make choices; security as regards food, shelter, clothing, and spending-money; and a relief from responsibility for their families.

Precisely because veterans have experienced all these things and also because of the prestige they once enjoyed, they may become a pivotal group in shaping postwar policy if and when the social and economic situation should lead to dissatisfaction and a desire for change. For the same reason, veterans as a group may become pawns in the formation of pressure groups.

It was not intended, of course, to compare soldiers with civilians and thus to arrive at specific differences in their attitudes. It was felt that it would be sufficient to study the veterans who then formed the most active part of the male population. Moreover, the problem of matching veterans with civilians of the same age, experience, personality characteristics, etc., had become nearly insoluble with the almost universal conscription of young men in the United States. The selection of veterans as the sample to be studied had several other advantages. It made it possible to hold certain variables relatively constant such as those of recent experiences, age, and, most important of all, the need to remake one's place after having been away in the army. Nor did military service interfere in the determination of factors underlying ethnic intolerance.

Therefore, the group selected for intensive study was a random sample of 150 male veterans of World War II who were residents of Chicago. Because of the added complexity of studying both urban and rural veterans, the sample was limited to an urban area. Therefore the conclusions on intolerance in this study do not necessarily apply to rural populations.

Veterans who had been officers were excluded from the study since their war experiences were sharply at variance with those of enlisted men. Most of the former came from social and economic backgrounds which differed markedly from those of enlisted men. Because of this restriction, the sample tended to represent the economic lower and lower middle classes more adequately. This was not unrealistic, for recent German history has shown that it was from these classes that the most ardent and energetic supporters of anti-Semitic parties were recruited. The men who tended to become officers were also more likely to possess some leadership qualities and overt intolerance among such individuals, if it developed, would be likely to take another pattern. However the facilities of the study were not large enough to sample adequately both officers and enlisted men and the former were excluded.

Other limitations, as to age, length of service, and the like were included in order to enhance the homogeneity of the sample. (Full details of the sampling procedure are described in the Appendix.) Members of those ethnic groups toward which hostility is most frequently directed were not included, i.e., Negroes, Jews, Chinese, Japanese, and Mexicans.

PATTERNS OF ETHNIC INTOLERANCE

THE PLAN OF THE RESEARCH

In recent years, a number of attempts have been made to estimate the extent of anti-Semitic attitudes in the United States. Since underlying hostility may reveal itself verbally, the responses collected in nationwide public opinion polls have been used repeatedly as an indirect measure of anti-Semitic hostility. Because of technical limitations, these efforts to measure anti-Semitism have failed to produce exact answers. At best they tell us how many persons verbalize negative reactions to Jews on a general, abstract level. But in a problem area such as that of intolerance, numbers are often less important than intensity of feeling or the importance of anti-Semitism in the emotional economy of the anti-Semite. Moreover, from a practical point of view, intensity of feeling is less relevant than readiness to action. Polls reveal little about the intensity of anti-Semitism, or about readiness to act, since the verbal statements they gather, most of them superficial in nature, are unreliable measures of an actual desire to take action against a minority.

Despite these limitations, national polls offer clues to the over-all incidence of anti-Semitism in the United States. The conclusions drawn from about twenty or thirty of them[1] indicate that not more than 10 per cent of those sampled spontaneously made anti-Semitic statements. One of the polls most frequently quoted bears out this observation. The *Fortune* Survey of February, 1946, revealed that 8.8 per cent of the nation's population was strongly anti-Semitic. This conclusion was based on the percentage who spontaneously named the Jews either as "a group harmful to the country unless curbed" or who spontaneously designated the Jews as "people trying to get ahead at the expense of people like yourself."

In addition to this "core" of almost 10 per cent, nationwide poll data have indicated that from 30 to 60 per cent offered various anti-Semitic responses when questioned directly about the Jews. Their anti-Semitic

[1] Flowerman, Samuel, and Jahoda, Marie: "Polls on Anti-Semitism," *Commentary*, April, 1946, pp. 82-86.

remarks were not made spontaneously and were, generally speaking, less drastic in their criticism of Jews.

Gordon Allport, in 1944, found a similar distribution of anti-Semitic attitudes. He estimated that of our national population, "5 to 10 per cent are violently anti-Semitic, while perhaps 45 per cent are mildly bigoted in the same direction."[2]

The patterns of ethnic intolerance are, however, vastly more complex than one might expect if one were to accept the limited responses to public opinion polls at their face value. Equally, the reasons for intolerance are much more subtle than the simple rationalizations produced in response to poll questions, or in an effort to justify personal intolerance. Obviously it is not enough to merely discriminate between those who spontaneously make anti-Semitic remarks, those who make them only in response to a specific stimulus such as the naming of Jews, and those who make no anti-Semitic statements even when their attention is directed toward the problem.

A distinction must first be recognized between those persons who merely hold negative stereotyped value judgments about the Jews to be true, and those who openly express a desire to have Jews restricted, either politically, economically, or socially. But even there our study shows that an important differentiation can and must be made if one wishes to assess anti-Semitic attitudes correctly. There is a great difference between the man who says spontaneously that the Jews should be curbed (and insists that laws be passed or unlawful pressure exercised to that end), and another who may say the same thing at first but may realize, on further reflection, that such actions would be contrary to our basic liberties and form of government. The first may well be considered more of a danger to the well-being of the community than the second, unless the total situation should change so radically that the latter is no longer interested in safeguarding our basic institutions.

Some people make strongly anti-Semitic statements, only to change their opinions on further reflection. There are others who are prevented by their reflections from revealing their underlying attitudes in this matter to others—or even to themselves. In the latter case underlying attitudes remain repressed, unconscious at the moment, but may reveal themselves dangerously as soon as the repression ceases to be effective. Although there are wide circles of our society for whom ethnic intolerance is a part of the mores, written into the law, enforced by the main institutions of

[2] Allport, Gordon: "The Bigot in Our Midst," *Commonweal*, October 6, 1944, p. 583.

social control and supported by the channels of mass communication, the same mores caution that intolerance is better left unmentioned. Moreover, if intolerance is institutionalized or generally accepted much of the motive for discussing it disappears. The situation becomes quite different if Jews compete on the job or live next door.

Whether the average individual is ready to express his hostility toward minorities to a stranger will depend on many factors. One of them is the degree to which such discussion is an approved custom within his own circle. It must be realized that in many respects the public opinion poller is a stranger to his randomly selected subjects, many of whom do not feel close enough to him to discuss what they consider personal matters. It is another thing to express prejudice to closer associates, to those in whom one has confidence.

DESIGN OF THE INTERVIEW

The interests of the social researcher in studies such as this are not limited to statements made for public record. At least as important are the subject's full range, intensity, and shading of attitudes and the motivations which account for his public behavior. Although the subject may try to conceal some of them from all-too-public inspection, it is possible to understand them through an interview if the interviewer has first succeeded in gaining the confidence of his subject by establishing what is technically known as positive rapport. Only then can he gather information which may lead to an adequate understanding of the attitudes under investigation.

Interviewing people in connection with anti-Semitic attitudes is complicated by the fact that many people hold at least two different sets of attitudes on the question, one for general consumption, and another for private expression. Moreover, as with many other problems in which the individual's emotions are strongly involved, the reaction depends more or less on the context in which the problem appears. One man's outlook may be so constituted that the word-stimulus "Jew" evokes no strong reaction in connection with intellectual matters, while the same word-stimulus may arouse strong emotions in the context of economic practices. For another person, the reverse may be true. As a matter of fact, the study seemed to reveal that the intensity of anti-Semitism could not be adequately gauged on the basis of the veteran's reaction to the word-stimulus "Jew" in a single and particular context even if this simple reaction was of great violence. Rather, intense anti-Semitism could be determined only when the negative reaction to the word-stimulus was persistent in the different contexts in which the Jew was presented throughout the interview.

For reasons discussed in the preceding chapter, this study of ethnic intolerance in general, and of anti-Semitism in particular, was based on the reactions of a group of 150 veterans of enlisted rank from the city of Chicago. In view of the character of the group, it seemed plausible that good rapport could be established by offering the veteran an opportunity, in the course of a pleasant though intensive interview, to express his personal views on the problem of adjustment to civilian life and a chance to recount his wartime experiences. It was expected that an informal talk with a woman interviewer about the current difficulties of adjustment and the hardships experienced in the war would aid rapport by permitting the veteran to express some of the tension which may have accumulated in him during his years of service.

In most cases, the understanding attitude of the interviewer and her interest in the interviewee's fate and difficulties produced two results: first, it lowered the individual's defenses, since this seemed a "safe" situation, in which one might speak freely; second, it relieved the feeling of discomfort at least about the present situation. Many statements by veterans indicated that they were open with interviewers on matters which had been preying on their minds for a long time, and about which they had had little opportunity to express themselves. Such statements seem to corroborate that the interview achieved its purpose in this regard. For example, one veteran declared:

"It was swell I think. You get a chance to say things that you don't get a chance to say except to friends."

In a number of cases, veterans revealed details of their wartime sex experiences which, they were quick to add, they did not wish made known, especially to their girl friends or wives. Thus it seems that the study succeeded in putting the subject at ease and in lowering the individual's constraint with regard to the admission of attitudes he thought should not be communicated.

This mode of approaching the veteran had two effects: By setting the individual at ease, he was enabled to express his hostile feelings more freely. On the other hand, the same ease did away with some of his superficial frustration and hostility and therefore decreased the need for discharge of hostility, whether through anti-Semitic remarks, or otherwise. This was in keeping with the purpose of the study which was less interested in fleeting expressions of anti-Semitism due to chance annoyance than in underlying anti-Semitism, which would be present even if the immediate setting were not frustrating.

While the discharge of tension by way of anti-Semitic remarks was thus less necessary or attractive, it should not be overlooked that many of those interviewed may have been searching for common ground on which to meet the interviewer. There was just a chance that this factor may have been conducive to anti-Semitic remarks, but careful study of the records reveals that such was rarely the case. Moreover, a subject who felt that anti-Semitism was an easy and convenient meeting ground for forming personal relationships thereby revealed his conscious or unconscious conviction of the widespread character and general acceptance of anti-Semitic attitudes.

It was not the object of this research to study the individual's *readiness* to discharge tension in a hostile manner against any stimulus which was presented, but to study, instead, the individual's *habit* of discharging hostility chiefly by means of ethnic intolerance. If the first object had been chosen for study, it might have proved best to remind the individual, before long, of the unpleasantness of his past war and present adjustment experiences and, at the height of his annoyance over them, to introduce the word-stimulus "Jew." Since it was the second problem which was selected, the interview situation was handled quite differently.

Steps were taken to insure that superficial hostility, which might be discharged at random against any casual stimulus, would not be discharged in an anti-Semitic manner simply because the subject's attention had been directed toward the Jews. This was particularly important when interviewing a group of men who during the recent past had undergone the frustrations of military service and were currently undergoing the frustrating experience of adjustment to civilian life. Therefore, the stimulus "Jew" was presented only after many other topics had been introduced, such as politics, employment, marriage, and the army. These topics offered sufficient outlets for random discharge of hostility. If, during these portions of the interview, hostility was spontaneously discharged by means of anti-Semitic remarks, one could be more certain that an individual would reveal anti-Semitic hostility in many other contexts. It was felt that if the bulk of the interview avoided ethnic topics, it would then be possible—after rapport had been established and maintained—to include indirect and finally direct questions on ethnic attitudes. The stimulus "Jew," could then be introduced without having to fear that reactions would be due to the presentation of the stimulus rather than to underlying permanent attitudes.

Such a procedure required that the interviews be extremely long and detailed and be administered by highly trained and skilled interviewers, well able to establish and maintain rapport. In view of the particular group studied, a small number of women were employed who were psychiatrically trained social workers with experience in public opinion surveying. Their skill in interviewing, combined with their ability to establish rapport, made the interview an interesting experience for most of the veterans.

The long interview took from four to seven hours and in several cases was administered in two sessions.[3]

In order to obtain data which would allow for comparative analysis, the interviews were carried out in as standardized a fashion as was compatible with maintaining rapport and insuring spontaneous reactions.[4] The interviewer approached the veteran either by telephone, or, on the occasion of a home visit, by asking him whether he would be willing to be interviewed for a public opinion survey of veterans. She explained that this survey was being conducted by the University of Chicago in order to learn about veterans' opinions. Anonymity was assured and the veteran was told that the survey was not seeking the views of the individual veteran. The survey, he was told, was interested in finding out as a whole the opinions of the veterans living in the metropolitan area of Chicago. No promise was given that the men's answers would lead to a remedy of their complaints, but they were informed that all findings would be published and the veterans' feelings thus conveyed to the community at large.

DEGREES OF INTOLERANCE

On the basis of exploratory interviews with a small group of veterans who were not included in the final sample, it was found that for purposes

---

[3] A copy of the interview is to be found in the Appendix on pages 213-218. There were more than 160 predetermined questions, excluding the neutral probes which were introduced to encourage the veteran to continue or to elaborate his statements.

[4] Details on the procedures are found in the Appendix on pages 189, 190. As noted there, the following elements of the interview were standardized: (1) the person of the interviewer, (2) the method of approaching the subject, (3) the place of the interview, (4) the method of asking the predetermined questions and of probing for associative material, (5) the technique for recording the entire interview, and (6) the time period in which the interview took place.

of the study it would be necessary to distinguish four types of veterans on the basis of their attitudes toward Jews. These four types were designated as *intensely anti-Semitic, outspokenly anti-Semitic, stereotyped anti-Semitic,* and *tolerant* toward Jews.

Briefly, the four types may be defined as follows:

1. The *intensely anti-Semitic* veteran was spontaneously outspoken in expressing a preference for restrictive action against the Jews even before the subject was raised. For example, he might have advocated Hitler's solution to the Jewish problem here in America, when asked whether there were any groups of people trying to get ahead at his expense. When questioned directly about the Jews, he maintained his outspoken preference for restrictive action. For example, he might have objected to having Jews as next-door neighbors, to working on the same job with them, or he might have advocated prevention of intermarriage with Jews. Finally, he also displayed a wide range of unfavorable stereotyped opinions about the Jews.

2. The *outspokenly anti-Semitic* veteran revealed no spontaneous preference for restrictive action against the Jews. Instead, outspoken hostility toward the Jews emerged only toward the end of the interview when he was questioned directly. As in the case of the intensely anti-Semitic veteran, his thinking contained a wide range of unfavorable stereotypes.

3. The *stereotyped anti-Semitic* veteran expressed no preference for hostile or restrictive action against the Jews, either spontaneously or when questioned directly. Instead, he merely expressed a variety of stereotyped notions about the Jews, including some which were not necessarily unfavorable from his point of view. For example, he might have thought Jews clannish, or that they are people who engage in shrewd business methods. But he felt, for any number of reasons, that these characteristics did not justify aggressive action against the Jews, by the government or by society at large.

4. The *tolerant* veteran revealed no elaborate stereotyped beliefs about the Jews although even the most tolerant veterans expressed isolated stereotypes from time to time. Moreover, neither spontaneously nor when questioned directly, did he advocate restrictive action against the Jews. In fact, on policy questions, the tolerant person either denied any just grounds for differentiating between Jews and non-Jews, or affirmed his lack of concern about such differences.

On the basis of the experience gained in the exploratory study, the

interview situation was so constructed that the responses to questions
would permit a clear delineation of these four types.[5]

CONTENT OF INTERVIEW

A description of the interview in broad outline may indicate how such
delimitation was achieved. The first portion of the interview was designed to offer the veteran an opportunity for the spontaneous expression
of hostility against the Jews without leading the veteran's attention to the
subject.

After some casual initial talk intended to create a pleasant, conversational atmosphere, the recorded portion of the interview opened with
very general questioning as to how the veteran thought that "things were
going to turn out now that the war is over," and what and who "would
interfere with the veteran's having a decent life." His answers were followed by detailed probing and produced a first chance for verbal discharge of tension or hostility.

The interview then turned from the problem of a decent life for all to
problems more particular to the veteran's readjustment to civilian life.
In this connection and in order to bring to light hostility directed against
persons and groups, the veteran was asked whether he thought there were
any groups of people who might be harmful unless curbed, and what
groups, if any, were trying to get ahead at the expense of people like
himself. A specific chance was offered for expressions of hostility by asking whether some people or groups got "all the breaks," whether de-
servedly so, and who they might be.

Next, the veteran was questioned on his attitudes toward political parties, employment, economic security, and the last depression. Some of
these questions supplied further indirect opportunity for the spontaneous
expression of hostility toward the Jews and other minorities. The discussion of economic security led easily to the problem of seniority on the
job. In this context, ethnic stimuli were introduced for the first time in
the interview, by querying whether veterans, white people, native-born
Americans, or Gentiles should receive employment preferences when
jobs were scarce.[6]

These questions concluded the first portion of the interview, which was
designed to permit discrimination between spontaneous and nonsponta-

[5] The full methodological and statistical details of this procedure may be found in
the Appendix on pages 195-208.
[6] More than forty questions not mentioning minority groups had been asked
previously.

neous readiness to discharge tension by means of ethnic intolerance. This first section of the interview was designed to throw light on the subject's generalized attitudes, his generalized dissatisfaction, fears, and apprehensions of a less personal nature. Its purpose was also to assess the veteran's feeling either of competency or of being overpowered by the political or economic system; it also permitted evaluation of his feelings of deprivation and of his attitudes toward symbols of authority.

Questions on occupational and financial aspirations for the future led up to the second part of the interview which was more personal in character. Questions on marital status and expectations, and on plans for child rearing, were followed by a detailed inquiry into the man's army experience. In this second portion of the interview, and especially in connection with army experiences, there were extended opportunities to display stereotyped thinking and thereby contribute to the differentiation of the various types of anti-Semites. This was particularly true of such questions as who the veterans thought were the "troublemakers" and "goldbrickers" in the army.

The third and last portion of the interview contained the direct questions on Jews and Negroes. It was designed to determine which men consistently displayed tolerant attitudes. This section began with a series of questions on international topics and foreign countries, which were related to the previous discussion about army life. At this point, the stimuli "Negro" and "Jew" were introduced directly; first in connection with what kinds of soldiers they made, and then in regard to the subject's preference or nonpreference for social and economic association with them, as well as his views on the modification of current interethnic patterns.[7]

Charting the subject's attitudes as to the proper limits of his social contacts with Jews and Negroes—that is, technically speaking, his social distance from them—supplied an indirect measure of his disposition towards discrimination of members of these groups. One method of studying social distance is to probe for the limits of social contact common and relevant to the everyday living of the individuals involved. In this sample it would have been pointless to ask whether Jews should be excluded from membership in "social register" clubs, since almost none of the veterans themselves would have been eligible. Instead, social distance was measured in terms of approval or disapproval of common employment, neighborhood residence, and intermarriage.

[7] This final series of direct ethnic questions came after more than 80 per cent of the attitude portion of the interview had been completed.

At this point, the part of the interview intended to evoke associational answers ended. Further questions were asked requiring direct and factual answers about age, length of domicile, family extraction and composition, income, education, reading and listening habits, and so on.

TABLE 1(II)

DISTRIBUTION OF ANTI-SEMITISM

	Number	Percentage
Tolerant	61	41
Stereotyped	42	28
Outspoken	41	27
Intense	6	4
Total	150	100

In order to adequately characterize the anti-Semitic and anti-Negro attitudes as they were gathered from each individual, and before the individual cases are compressed into over-all statistical conclusions for each of the four categories on the tolerance-intolerance continuum, excerpts from one characteristic case in each category will be presented.

The number of men who fell into each of the four categories can be seen from table 1(II).

From this table it is evident that less than half of the subjects were tolerant, while slightly more than a fourth were stereotyped and another fourth outspokenly anti-Semitic. Only a very small fraction were intensely anti-Semitic. In this sample of veterans, the approximately 60 per cent who displayed some measure of intolerance toward Jews was roughly the same percentage found in national opinion polls. The number falling within the intensely anti-Semitic category was quite small, and they are therefore analyzed together with the outspokenly anti-Semitic veterans throughout this study. However, since they are potential activists whose political role might be significant, should their dissatisfaction increase and be channelized into organized anti-Semitic agitation, it is important to examine one of their number along with the other more frequent types.

TYPICAL EXAMPLES

CASE ONE: AN INTENSELY ANTI-SEMITIC VETERAN. As defined above, the *intensely intolerant* veteran spontaneously declared a preference for restrictive action against Jews, and, in addition, expressed a range of unfavorable stereotypes about them.

Mike, a thirty-two year old switchman, was born in Chicago, of Irish Catholic parentage, as one of six children. His father was a conductor on the elevated lines. After four years of high school, Mike became a beverage salesman. He married shortly after he went into the army, where he served as an airplane mechanic. Thereafter he was separated from his wife for most of the four and one-half years of his army life.

On his current job he earned approximately $55.00 per week. The *Chicago Tribune* was his regular newspaper and he was a member of the Veterans of Foreign Wars and of the Switchmen of North America.

Attitudes toward Jews. As was typical for the few intense anti-Semites, Mike's hostility toward minorities emerged spontaneously and explosively in the initial portions of the interview.

His remarks were pessimistic from the outset, and he took frequent opportunity to denounce politicians and big business for the difficulties in which Chicago, the United States, and the world found themselves. After an outburst in which he characterized the capitalists as the people who really run the government and who got the United States into war, the question was put to him: "As things stand, would you say that some people get all the breaks and others get none?" His answer was:

"Yeah, the Hebes. (And without probe or other encouragement, he elaborated:) I think Hitler did a good thing. They're born that way, they can make a dollar where a white person starves. Where they come in, the niggers follow and knock the property down. They're awfully clannish for another thing. Take the Irish, they don't trust each other. The Jews patronize each other."

Thereafter, and throughout the interview, he described the Jews in outbursts of negative character and urged that repressive measures be used against them. When, in a probe following the above response, he was asked whether he felt that the Jews deserved the breaks they got, he declared:

"No, I think they should put them all in Africa. Yeah, I certainly would. (Pause.) Conscientious objectors is another thing. They should take their citizenship and deport them. If this country isn't good enough for them to fight for, it isn't good enough to live in. They had a lot of jobs in the army where they didn't have to carry a rifle."

His views on the role of the Jew in the army were dominated by the fact that his outfit had had a Jewish chaplain.

"We had a Jewish rabbi for group chaplain, and we had a Catholic priest come around three times a week. . . . I don't see why they gave us that Jewish chaplain. There were only about ten Jews in our outfit of 2,500 men. They'd never make good regular army soldiers. They're below the average. They just aren't cut out for military life. (In the army) I've only seen about four Jews that I know of. One of them was kill crazy. . . ."

At the end of the interview, when questioned directly about the Jews, Mike reiterated his demand that Jews be deported, and gave as his reason:

"They're too clannish, they don't mix. All your big industries are controlled by them. Your movies are all controlled."

He favored the prevention of intermarriage: "You get half-castes." He objected to living next door to Jews. He was opposed to working on the same job with a Jew:

"If I could get away from it I would. They kill a job. They overproduce. A Negro will never try to get ahead of a white man where a Jew would."

Finally, as a solution to the problems of interethnic relations, he advocated:

"Get a Hitler over here, he'd take care of them. (Laughs.) They should curb them somehow, they should not let any more in. No matter what country they get into, they get into money."

Among other opinions frequently held to be true by extreme anti-Semites, Mike suspected that President Roosevelt was of Jewish ancestry:

"Sometimes I think Roosevelt was part Jewish—he sure took care of them Hebes. We cheered over in England when he died. They're piggish. They demand the best, but then when they get the bill they kick."

Attitudes toward Negroes. Negroes too, were spontaneously used as objects for discharge of intense, verbal hostility, and restrictive measures were advocated. First spontaneous mention of Negroes occurred early when he recalled his army experiences in England. The lack of a clear color line there was a source of annoyance:

"I could talk all night about England. Being in England is like living on Maxwell Street.[8] In the small towns they have no plumbing, a toilet outside and several families use it. . . . It's a backward country. . . . Another thing was the color line. There wasn't any. It was common to see a Negro with a white girl."

The Negro as a symbol of sexual rivalry recurred spontaneously in the

[8] A slum thoroughfare in Chicago crowded with shops and stalls which are chiefly Jewish-owned.

interview even after the discussion of interethnic relations was guided into other areas. When, in the portion of the interview dealing with economic expectations, he was asked about equal employment treatment for Negroes, he replied:

"That's a delicate question. I hate them myself. They should put them in one section of the city and keep them in there. They're giving them too much independence. (In which way?) It was disgusting over in England. You could walk down the street and see a beautiful English girl go down the street with a nigger and wheeling a colored baby. They'd write home to get underwear to give these girls. It was disgusting. (Pause.) I talked to a corporal in the infantry that saw them in combat and said they weren't up to par in fighting either."

On the direct questions designed to probe the limits of his social distance from Negroes, he scored the highest possible intolerance score. He objected to intermarriage: "It would do away with the white race entirely. You won't have a white race left." He objected to Negroes moving in next door to him. "It ruins a neighborhood, lowers it." He objected to working on the same job with a Negro. "That's the reason I left the post office. That place was lousy with them, about eight to one." In fact, he said, he would only eat with Negroes if he had to.

Finally, he viewed the solution of Negro-white relations in terms of strict segregation.

"The only trouble with colored people is the way they increase. They don't care how they live. And you know yourself you see them in department stores where you didn't a few years ago. . . . As long as they're all over the country now, put them in one section and don't let them out."

CASE TWO: AN OUTSPOKENLY ANTI-SEMITIC VETERAN. As defined above the *outspokenly anti-Semitic* veteran responded to direct questions by declaring a preference for restrictive action against Jews, and, in addition, expressed a range of unfavorable stereotypes about the Jews.

Peter, a thirty-five year old semiskilled worker in a machine shop, was born in Chicago of Italian-Catholic parentage, as one of three children. His father was a laborer. After four years of high school, Peter went to work in a machine shop with no special technical training. He had never married; while in the army for three and one-half years, he served as a military policeman in the European theater.

On his current job Peter earned $35.00 per week. The *Chicago Tribune* and *Herald American* were his favorite newspapers; he was not a member of any organization.

Attitudes toward Jews. Although Peter's stereotyped characterizations of the Jews emerged only after he was questioned directly, his stereotyped attitudes led him to advocate a variety of restrictions. His first mention of Jews was in the middle portion of the interview dealing with economic expectations and the question of employment preference for Gentiles during periods of depression. (This may be contrasted with Mike's interview, in which Jews were mentioned spontaneously in the initial portion of the interview.) Peter was convinced of the inevitability of another depresson in about seven years. "The unemployment will be bad enough so that we'll have to have war with Russia to bring us out of it." He saw himself unequipped to deal with the effect of a depression except by going on relief. When asked whether Gentiles should be given first chance if there were not enough jobs to go around he laughed nervously and said:

"They (the Jews) usually go into business for themselves. They have money and stick together. I've only known two that ever worked in a factory. The Gentiles will stick to a job while if a Jew gets $500 he'll quit and open a store."

He felt that:

"The Jews in the army did right well for themselves. They were treated all right. Our first sergeant was Jewish. He didn't qualify for it, he got it through drag."

As a solution to the Jewish problem, he suggested deportation:

"Personally I would send them all back to Jerusalem. They're not a creative race, they're always counting their money. It was the Germans, Irish, and the Italians and the Russians that built up this country. These races aren't too proud to work. The Jews control the money and stick together."

When, toward the end of the interview, Peter was questioned directly on his attitudes toward Jews in different social situations, he was predominantly, if not completely, hostile. He objected to intermarriage, not on racial grounds but "because of religious difficulties" and was opposed to working with Jews. "They're not experienced and wouldn't be dependable on a job. It requires skill that they don't have because they don't work on jobs." On the other hand, he was tolerant of the prospect of Jews living next door to him. "He could have his business, and I could have mine. We could keep to ourselves."

Attitudes toward Negroes. Peter made no spontaneous mention of Negroes. When the subject was introduced by the interviewer, he revealed a thoroughly stereotyped attitude and made repeated demands for restrictive action against them.

Discussion of employment rights of Negroes produced the following outburst:

"Well, Mussolini said that if white people didn't watch out, the colored people would rule the world. I'm not prejudiced though. I think the Negroes should have their place. I don't know, the Negroes today, the majority of them are lazy and they don't seem to be able to get away from their ancestry, although we try to educate them. They have their peculiar ways and carry on just like wild men. You should see them in their own neighborhood. White people should get preference. The Negroes are expanding, they have no birth control, and if we aren't careful they'll take over in about a hundred years."

In describing the Negro in the army, he said:

"The Negroes were treated very well. Most of them had physical handicaps and got good jobs. They were put into the Quartermaster Corps. They abused their jobs. They were the ones that sold our supplies and cheated. . . . They didn't do any fighting. We got along with them as long as they stayed in their place. We didn't associate with each other. They kept on the other side of the line. . . ."

The full meaning of Peter's attitudes emerged as he commented on the question of social distance:

"They're like their ancestors. They're lazy and of different color and from a different climate. They'll never acclimate to this climate or to the ways of the white man. They're slow in education. Their ancestors were cannibals and wild, and they haven't gotten over that."

He was emphatic in urging prevention of intermarriage.

"That wouldn't help to keep the ideals of America up. It would change the whole evolution of this country. When you speak of an American, you speak of a white person. Overseas the Negroes called themselves 'American Indians.'"

When asked about having Negroes as next-door neighbors, he said:

"We have them in my own neighborhood, and I know from personal observation that their habits are very bad, they're dirty, loud, and filthy. . . . (As fellow workers.) They're careless and lazy. I would have no confidence in them. They're wild and they're not clean. Their body has aroma of a bad smell. A white person might be more untidy than a Negro, but I could tolerate that. I have observed them personally, and I don't think they'll ever work into the ways of the white man and this is because of their ancestors. They (the Negroes) should be isolated in different states and put them there to stay and let them have the same privileges as the whites in those states. (Pause.) I guess that wouldn't be very democratic. They might want to live in states that weren't set aside for them. They should be allowed to live in any state that they wanted to. Maybe it would be better to isolate them in different sections of the different states."

Case Three: A Stereotyped Anti-Semitic Veteran. The *stereotyped anti-Semite* has been defined as an individual who expressed a range of unfavorable stereotypes about the Jews, but who rejected the notion of any restrictive action against the Jews.[9]

George, a twenty-eight year old bank clerk, was born in Chicago of German-Lutheran parentage, as one of two brothers. After four years of high school and one term in a banking school, he went to work as a bank clerk. His four years of army service were mostly spent in combat in the Far East. He returned home to be married, and took up a bank clerk's job which was currently paying $43.00 per week. His wife was also employed.

The *Daily News* and the *Tribune* were his regular newspapers. George was a member of the American Legion.

Attitudes toward Jews. George made no spontaneous mention of the Jews in response to any of the indirect questions designed to elicit ethnic hostility. His mild stereotypes about the Jews first emerged when, toward the end of the interview, he was asked for his opinions about their behavior in the army. He replied:

"We didn't see many of them in the front lines. Those that were there had all the privileges anyone else did. I don't believe they were mistreated. Most of them were in the Medical Corps and base sections."

"Yes, they did (make good soldiers). . . . In some cases they were as good as the next man. A few were killed in the front lines. It is true that a Jew tries to use his brain to get him out of things and is sly. It usually worked, too."

He also held stereotyped opinions of the Jew in business and finance:

"They got hold of all the financial ends in this country. I don't dislike them, but I don't like them because a Jew has no scruples when he's out to get ahead. It's at his best friend's expense that he'll get ahead. I don't care to deal with Jews, but nowadays you can't help it because they're in every business field."

Despite these stereotypes, he showed little aggressiveness on the question of what should be done about the Jews:

"There's nothing much you can do about it. They have as much right to live here as anybody else. . . . You can't force anybody to leave the country, but I don't believe we should take any more in."

[9] The absence of demands for restrictive action was easily established by questions as to whether such action should be taken. However, subjects who stated that no restrictive action should be taken because there was no way to assure their success, were subsumed in the category of the outspoken anti-Semites.

This last opinion was in line with his more general views on immigration. He was opposed to any further entries into the United States and felt that the European refugee problem should be handled by the shipment abroad of American Red Cross supplies.

The range of social distance questions completed a picture of passive acceptance, toward the Jews. He was opposed to the prevention of intermarriage. "No, you can't stop that. It's up to the individual. He makes his nest and he's got to lie in it. There are plenty of white men marrying Jewish women nowadays." He had no objection to having Jews move next door to him. "No, it all depends upon what type he is. I have a friend who is a Jew—one of the finest types of persons I know. I don't know why he shouldn't move in next door to me." Finally he expressed no objections to working with a Jew.

Attitudes toward Negroes. George's attitudes toward Negroes contained a mixture of individual stereotypes, a mild personal tolerance toward them, and a belief that the conditions of Negro life ought to be bettered. At the same time, he insisted that segregation was more and more required if only because of the attitudes of other whites.

When the Negro was mentioned, he declared:

"I don't believe in difference between race. No matter what color a person is, providing he's a good citizen, he should have an equal chance at the job. I don't believe in inequality there. It's true some things will have to be done about the colored people because the problem is becoming acute. Pretty soon they'll have to segregate them because there are people who can't stand them to live next to them. But there are a lot of colored people who're cleaner and neater than white people."

As a solution to Negro-white relations, he stated: "I believe that a Negro sooner or later will have to live in certain parts of the city. I could get along with them, but the average white man can't. He's here, he's human, he must have a place to live and work. He should be taught to live clean. That might help."

His personal tolerance of the Negro extended to numerous areas of personal contact. He opposed prevention of intermarriage.

"It's up to the individual. If a white person likes a Negro and wants to marry, why shouldn't he? That's his problem. But I don't believe a white man would care to do a thing like that: I wouldn't. Not that I have any feelings against them."

He would accept Negroes as neighbors.

"If he's a good neighbor, a good clean man, does things to keep up his property—better than a dirty, white man." (As fellow workers:) "I've worked with them already. Good workers and they've got to earn a living just like any-body else. After all, our natives are colored, and we worked with them. They were our best friends over there."

George's stereotypes about the Negro included the oft-encountered ones of the inability of Negroes to be combat soldiers, and of general laziness:

"From the reports I've heard they didn't stand up under combat. . . . I think they got the makings of smart people if they get rid of their lazy streak, get their homes and persons cleaned up."

CASE FOUR: A VETERAN TOLERANT TOWARD THE JEWS. The *tolerant veteran* was defined as an individual who held no stereotypes or only an occasional isolated stereotype about Jews and who denied the desirability of restrictive action against them.

John, a twenty-six year old mechanic, was born in Chicago of Austrian-Evangelical parentage, as one of eight children. His father was an orna-mental ironworker. After four years of high school, John went to work as an apprentice in an ironworks factory. He was single; while in the army for three years he served as a light ordnance maintenance mechanic. On his current job, as a mechanic in a crane factory, he earned $65.00 per week. He was a regular reader of the *Chicago Tribune*, a member of the American Federation of Labor, and of the social club of his church.

Attitudes toward Jews. John made no spontaneous mention of ethnic minorities during the initial portion of the interview, or in response to any of the indirect questions. When, toward the end of the interview, the subject was raised directly, he displayed a pattern of tolerance toward the Jews despite one isolated stereotype. On the other hand he employed a wide range of stereotypes about Negroes, and although he declared himself for equal treatment of Negroes, he insisted on segregation.

John's isolated stereotype about Jews emerged in connection with army life: "They were treated all right as far as I know. They all seemed to get pretty good jobs—either clerks or in the medics—postal clerks, company clerks and things like that." Nevertheless, when asked "How did the fellows in your outfit get along with Jews," he responded, "The ones in our outfit mixed right in. There was no ill feelings. Everybody got along."

In the various questions concerning interethnic relations, John dis-played consistent and tolerant attitudes toward the Jews. He had no objection to intermarriage, in fact, he favored it as a policy to improve interethnic relations. "Don't think any harm can come to the Gentiles marrying the Jews. It may cause better relations between the two if more were to marry."

With regard to employment preference, he would favor:

"The person that can do the job and has been there the longest. As far as any race, color, or creed—that shouldn't interfere in any way."

He summarized his attitude toward the Jews associatively as follows:

"I don't think there's any reason for ill feeling between the Jews and the Gentiles. That's caused a lot of trouble as in Germany, and I think we should overcome it. They say Jews have all the money—well, some of them do, but there are many who don't. It's just one of those things that grew. And here it shouldn't make any difference what the race, color, or creed of a man is."

Attitudes toward Negroes. John's opinions on the position of the Negro in the army showed a strange mixture of stereotypes combined with a limited amount of personal observation.

"It's true that they were kept apart. They had the same rights as the whites, I think, even though they were segregated."

To the question of whether Negroes made good soldiers, he replied:

"They made good combat soldiers if they were mixed in with the whites. There at the last they were mixed in, given infantry training, and ten or twelve put in with a white company. Then they were good; but when they were a whole division by themselves, they weren't. (In what way?) Don't know why. It seemed like they needed the leadership or the courage of the whites."

It is interesting to note the line which separated demands for tolerance toward the Negro from those for anti-Negro segregation and restrictions. John objected to intermarriage:

"Well, that's something I don't approve of. (Pause.) But it's entirely up to the individual. As far as the government interfering—it shouldn't. Every man should have the right to his own opinion."

He objected to Negroes moving in next door to his house:

"Yes, I would. I'll tell you, it's just the idea that as soon as one moved in all the rest would soon follow suit and then you'd be the only white left. There is that and the fact that property evaluation would go down. They just don't take care of their homes the way a white man does. It just seems Negro nature, the greatest percentage of them. He just doesn't have the initiative that the white man does to keep up his house. All his money goes into clothes, drinks, or something like that. That is, not all of them. There are some different, but that's the greatest per cent."

But on employment preferences, he expressed opposition to restrictions:

"I think they should be given the same advantages as the whites to make a living. You do find some very brilliant Negroes, and I don't think they should be hindered just because they're colored."

His response to the question of what should be done about the Negro in this country revealed his more general underlying attitude.

"They should be given freedom of speech and of the press. They should have all those rights. I think they should stay in their own restricted areas for the simple reason that as soon as they get in a neighborhood, the property evaluation goes down. The whites move out. If they could just move anywhere, they would soon ruin the city. But outside of that they should have all the rights."

John's general level of tolerance may be inferred from his answer to the question, "In your experience in the army, what kind of fellows were the biggest 'goldbrickers'?"

"Well, they were just individuals. All kinds. Some from the South and others from the North. Don't think you could say that one was more toward 'gold-bricking' than the other."

COMPARISON OF ANTI-SEMITIC AND ANTI-NEGRO ATTITUDES

From these case studies it appears that attitudes of tolerance or intolerance are generalized to some degree, since almost all those who were intolerant of Jews were also intolerant of Negroes, but the intensity of intolerance varied. Although anti-Negro attitudes are separately discussed in Chapter VIII, an analysis of the interrelation of these two expressions of ethnic hostility seems fitting at this point. The same method used in analyzing the nature and degree of intolerance toward Jews was used with some slight modifications in the analysis of anti-Negro attitudes. (See Appendix.)

Table 2(II) shows that one-sixth of the veterans had attitudes which

TABLE 2(II)

DISTRIBUTION OF ANTI-NEGRO ATTITUDES

	Number	Percentage
Tolerant	12	8
Stereotyped	40	27
Outspoken	74	49
Intense	24	16
Total	150	100

were intensely anti-Negro, while half of them were outspokenly so. One-fourth held unfavorable stereotypes about Negroes to be true; at the same time nearly all of them called for equality of rights and opportunity but under conditions of segregation. Less than a tenth of the veterans could be classified as tolerant toward Negroes.

Merely to note that the incidence of intolerance is higher for the Negro, as these data indicate, does not fully reveal the association which exists between intolerance toward the Negro and intolerance toward the Jew. In the majority of cases, for example, tolerance toward Jews was coexistent with stereotyped and even more marked intolerance of the Negro. (See Chart A.) As the degree of intolerance toward the Jew increased, it was generally accompanied by an even greater degree of intolerance toward the Negro. The reversed pattern—that is, tolerance toward the Negro accompanied by outspoken anti-Semitism—occurred in only *one* case. This case may be explained by the fact that this man's hostility toward the Jews was limited to a special subclass of Jews—namely, alien Jews.

Other interesting differences in intolerance can best be seen by a comparative examination of how the Jew and the Negro fared with respect to demands for restrictive action generally, and also in specific areas of interethnic relations.

For obvious reasons, the questions designed to reveal intolerance toward the Jews were not equally likely to reveal anti-Negro feeling. For example, on general questioning as to the solution of the Jewish problem, outspoken and intense anti-Semites often recommended specific and detailed restrictions such as the curbing of immigration or even deportation, especially to Palestine. For the Negro, expressions of restrictive desires were vague and undifferentiated. Instead of concrete demands of a repressive nature, such statements were made as: Negroes should be kept in their place; they have too much liberty. Or: Since sending them back is impossible, they should be kept at a distance.

It required more specific questions to determine a subject's concrete attitudes in this respect. Therefore, a series of four questions was asked dealing with situations likely to occur in the everyday life of the veteran. (See Table 3(II).) The tabulation shows that the character of expressed hostility depended on the area of interaction. There was only one question which evoked the same degree of intolerance for Jews and Negroes, namely, whether they should be forced to leave the country. Obviously, none but the most intolerant persons would welcome such extreme action. While the outspoken anti-Semite could rationalize his discriminatory

CHART A

INTERRELATION BETWEEN ANTI-SEMITIC ATTITUDES
AND ANTI-NEGRO ATTITUDES

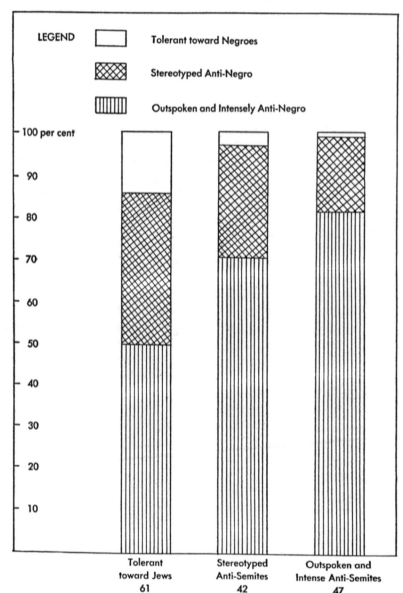

LEGEND — Tolerant toward Negroes

Stereotyped Anti-Negro

Outspoken and Intensely Anti-Negro

Tolerant toward Jews	Stereotyped Anti-Semites	Outspoken and Intense Anti-Semites
61	42	47

demands by claiming that the Jews themselves want to leave the country, no such claims could be—or in fact were—made in the case of the Negroes.

With respect to common employment with Negroes or Jews, greater prejudice was shown toward the Negro. Ten per cent said they would be

TABLE 3(II)

ATTITUDES TOWARD MINORITIES
(on Selected Questions)

	Attitude toward Jews		Attitude toward Negroes	
	No.	Percentage	No.	Percentage
Should Jews (Negroes) Be Forced to Leave the Country?				
Yes	16	11	25	17
Yes—particular class[a]	14	9	2	1
No	114	76	115	77
Don't know and Other[b]	6	4	8	5
Would You Be Willing to Have A Jew (A Negro) Work in the Same Job That You Are Doing?				
Yes	120	80	71	47
No	16	11	75	50
Don't know and Other[b]	14	9	4	3
Would You Object to A Jew (A Negro) Moving in Next Door to Your House?				
Yes	25	17	123	82
No	116	77	17	11
Other[b]	9	6	10	7
Should Jews (Negroes) Be Prevented from Intermarriage?				
Yes	10	7	114	76
No	130	87	32	21
Don't know and Other[b]	10	6	4	3

[a] Includes alien Jews, recent Jewish refugees, etc.
[b] Includes only responses which could not reliably be classified as "yes" or "no."

unwilling to have a Jew work on the job with them, but more than half were unwilling to work with Negroes under any circumstances, or only if Negroes were in inferior positions. In other words, 40 per cent more of the veterans were hostile toward the Negroes than toward the Jews in this regard.

The greatest difference between attitudes toward Jews and Negroes was found to exist on the question of intermarriage. It was to be expected that the feeling against intermarriage between Jews and non-Jews as against intermarriage between Negroes and whites would differ considerably in degree. Three-fourths of the veterans were opposed to intermarriage between Negroes and whites, a figure which was almost 70 per cent higher than those who rejected intermarriage between gentiles and Jews.

Contrary to popularly held notions, the level of hostility toward intermarriage was most similar to that displayed against close residence with Negroes. Over 80 per cent of the sample objected to having Negroes as next-door neighbors; a figure which is 65 per cent higher than the number who objected to having Jews move in as next-door neighbors.[10]

Thus, we see that attitude patterns toward Jews and Negroes with regard to intermarriage and mixed housing present a similar level of hostility for each minority and may indicate a common underlying sentiment. It seems difficult to maintain the usually proffered explanation that segregation in housing is carried out mainly for economic reasons, while marriage restrictions are supposed to result from sex attitudes. Two such different explanations will not suffice to explain the similarity of attitude toward these seemingly different aspects of living together.[11]

It has been recognized that sexual rivalry and fear, as well as suppressed desires, are often projected onto members of an outgroup. However, it is striking to note the degree to which this type of hostile projection is concentrated on the Negro group and is *not* directed toward the Jew.[12] In the main, responses on intermarriage with Jews were conspicuously free of sexually oriented symbols from which one could have inferred projection of repressed sexual desires. Neither in response to the question of intermarriage, nor in any other part of the interview were the Jews characterized as persons who engaged in sexually immoral or deviant behavior. This stands in sharp contrast to an important element of European anti-Semitism and anti-Semitic agitation which stressed the Jew's supposed sexual immorality.

The fact that the interviews were conducted by women interviewers

[10] The difference between the number of those who objected to Negroes moving in next door and of those who thought intermarriage with Negroes should be prevented is below statistical significance.

[11] Currently, it is a focal point of democratic policy to eliminate segregation in housing. It is felt that changes in interethnic patterns are possible in this area, even while underlying prejudice about sexual and marital relations remains unchanged. This position seems difficult to maintain in view of the interrelatedness of these attitudes as indicated by the similarly high level of hostility.

[12] For a fuller discussion of this observation see Chapter VIII.

cannot explain the absence of this characterization. A number of those interviewed discussed illicit sex relations on the part of soldiers. (These remarks were not simply bravado, since the topic was usually discussed with reluctance and expressions of guilt.) Moreover, sexual allusions to the Negro were not infrequent. In characterizing the Negro as a soldier, he was repeatedly described in terms of his sexual behavior while serving overseas.

The overall pattern of hostility toward the Negro and the Jew suggests that when each minority is presented in different contexts and in different interethnic situations, different amounts of hostility are mobilized. In terms of these differential quantities, the Negro received *proportionately* more hostility than the Jew as the sphere of interethnic relations became more private, more intimate, less secular and less commercial. The measures of restrictive demands indicate that Negroes as compared to Jews fared least poorly in employment and worst in housing.

STEREOTYPING THE MINORITY

A discussion of patterns of intolerance cannot disregard the reasons which the individual himself brings forward to justify his animosity. Among social scientists there is now general agreement that verbal expressions of hostility need not directly reveal their real causes. But many efforts to combat intolerance have been blind to this fact and have concentrated on disseminating correct information and on disproving the accusations of the intolerant. One of the basic hypotheses of this study is that intolerance is a function of deprivation and anxiety, while the intolerant person's accusations are ways to justify his aggressions. Nevertheless, a dynamic interpretation of the processes at work in the biased person should not lead one to neglect those reasons by which he justifies his aggressive tendencies.

Nor will it do to dismiss the intolerant person's stereotyped opinions in an off-hand fashion with such statements as: If there were no Jews they would persecute all those who have red hair. Such an approach overlooks the fact that even some psychotic persons can still exercise a modicum of reality testing. In order to justify his persecution of the red heads, the biased person must avail himself of rationalizations quite different from those employed to rationalize anti-Semitism; and they must be of such a nature as to permit a minimum of reality testing. These rationalizations, moreover, will condition the ways in which hostile feelings against the particular minority can be discharged. Similarly, the accusations which the intolerant person directs against Jews or Negroes must contain traces of testable observations; and these, too, will affect the manner and conditions under which hostility manifests itself.[1]

[1] German history provides a tragic example. Jewish extermination was decided upon at a relatively late moment in the annals of National Socialism, as documented by the proceedings of the Nuremberg trials. So long as the accusation that Jews possessed wealth and power could be justified by a minimum of fact (i.e., as long as some relatively wealthy and influential Jews remained within Germany), discrimination by expropriation and defamatory laws satisfied most anti-Semites in their need for the discharge of hostile feelings. When such accusations could not longer be backed up even by shreds of evidence, the accusations became more and more extravagant. While propaganda had previously emphasized the Jewish control of business and finance within Germany, the emphasis then shifted to the thesis of a secret world conspiracy, an accusation no longer testable by the average German.

Freud has convincingly demonstrated that any delusional belief must rest upon some psychological reality (and it may be added here that this reality may be objectively insignificant when compared with the delusional bias). Some very hostile persons need intolerance as outlets for hostility which, if not somehow discharged, would destroy the integration of their personalities. If they are approached with requests to submit these beliefs to reality testing, their dim feeling that such testing would deprive them of much needed outlets for hostility will lead them to greater anxiety and thus more intense hostility.

Moreover, the prejudiced person senses that the reasons by which he justifies his prejudices are not the source of his actions. Therefore, all attacks on his reasoning seem only to demonstrate a lack of appreciation and understanding of his real motives. This convinces him that those who question his prejudices do not really understand him at all and he does not feel compelled to accept their arguments.

All intolerant veterans in the sample avoided reality testing to some degree. They seemed not quite able to see Jews and Negroes as individuals in their own rights, and as unique persons. Each of them made some statements about minorities which showed that they ignored the individual's uniquely personal characteristics; in short, they used stereotypes. As was to be expected, those who were only moderately biased, i.e., men who applied stereotyped thinking to ethnic minorities without being outspoken in their demands for restrictions, retained more ability to test reality. They were able to evaluate correctly those individuals whom they met, but clung to stereotyped thinking about the rest of the discriminated group. One veteran, for example, who was asked about "goldbricking" in the army, said that Jews were the greatest "goldbrickers," but elaborated that there were "some fine Jewish boys" in his outfit, for whom this was by no means true. Another man said:

"If there was a Jewish officer in the outfit he'd have a Jewish fellow with him; if there was any easy work to be done, he'd get a Jewish fellow to do it. I don't know what there is in it, but they always think they're superior. There was one Jewish fellow in our outfit whom I liked especially. He wasn't like the ordinary run of Jews, that's why I remember him."

Thus attitudes were frequently found to indicate that while uncritically accepted and repeated opinions (nearly always unfavorable in character) were considered the rule, the individual's contrary experience was viewed as the exception. In this way it remained possible to retain the stereotyped attitudes which permitted discharge of hostility despite contrary actual experience.

Such limited amount of reality testing, however, did not seem to be available to strongly biased individuals. Their intolerance signified a much stronger underlying need for hostile discharge which had to be totally protected against possible disintegration through real experiences. In these cases the stereotype became their defense, and since the pretension of reality testing had to be maintained, the Jew was no longer tested against reality. On the contrary, instead of testing whether a Jew, or the majority of Jews, conformed to the stereotyped picture of the Jew which was used to justify anti-Semitism, the reverse procedure took place. Whoever fitted the stereotyped picture of the Jew was accepted as such and used to support the validity of the stereotype. On the other hand, whoever eluded the pattern was either not recognized as a Jew, or declared a rare exception. The classical expression of this attitude was voiced by the man who led the first modern party based almost exclusively on political anti-Semitism, the late nineteenth century Viennese lord mayor, Lueger. When questioned about his private and professional associations with individual Jews he declared: "I decide who is a Jew and who is not."

But even for the individual who must avoid any extent of reality testing, it is incompatible with his self-esteem to realize that he is waging a war of persecution against a comparatively helpless minority. Therefore, in order to fight it with justification and without damage to his self-esteem, he sometimes invents the existence of a powerful and threatening conspiracy aimed at his own well-being. This rationalization, in the case of anti-Semitism, takes the form of accusations, which in their mildest expression involve a widespread belief in Jewish "clannishness." This belief found its most exaggerated form in the Nazi's conviction that there existed an international conspiracy of Jewish plutocracy which was waging war against Germany.

However, the intolerant person cannot rely upon any obvious signs for demonstrating the existence of this powerful organization, since neither the Jews nor the Negroes have, for instance, any army to speak of—nor are they in positions of power among the great nations. Therefore, the existence of a secret organization has to be postulated, and this is exactly what many extremely intolerant persons do.[2]

[2] Here again the delusional mechanisms determining ethnic intolerance become obvious. In his claim that there exists a secret conspiracy, the thinking of the intolerant person may be compared with the rationalizations of the paranoid patient who uses the fact that nobody else recognizes the existence of his enemies to reinforce his belief in their cunning.

The more violent the aggressions of the intolerant person are, the more he must justify them with a stereotyped belief in the danger of the minority's power. The greater he believes this power to be, the greater his anxiety becomes, which then spurs him to even more violent action. Thus he is caught in the vicious circle of his delusional system, which may be one of the reasons why, once interethnic aggression becomes rampant, it proceeds with self-perpetuating vigor. The violence of the persecution demands new and stronger justification. It also creates guilt feelings, which add to the anxiety already created by the stereotyped belief in the power of the outgroup.

The testimony of two men may exemplify the differences in degrees of reality testing which were found among them. One biased man who retained his ability to test reality to some degree said about the Jews in the army:

"They shirk their duty, they're not combat men. Some will fight, I'll give them that credit, but most of them are out for themselves. If he has a chance to save himself, he'll save himself. A Jew will never give you nothing for nothing either. (But) I've found a couple of good Jews, like in any nationality, but only a few."

On the other hand, confronted with the fact that in his own experience Jews behaved like other soldiers—namely that some tried to avoid the danger of combat, while others were courageous, another strongly biased man was still able to protect his stereotype from being dented. The average Jewish soldier, he implied, was incompetent, and the others, bloodthirsty. Thus he was able to negate the courageous Jew's behavior by means of another unfavorable stereotype.

Because the intolerant person's rationalizations are closely, though not obviously, connected with the reasons for his intolerance, he must find means to protect them. On the other hand, they also reveal the nature of his underlying anxieties. According to Freud, "The delusion is found like a patch on that spot where originally there was a tear in the relation between the ego and its outer reality."[3] A study of stereotyped opinions about ethnic minorities may be likened to a removal of this "patch" in order to find the "tear."

Among the veterans studied, as everywhere, stereotypes and stereo-

[3] Quoted from Simmel, E.: "Anti-Semitism and Mass Psychopathology" *Anti-Semitism*, E. Simmel, ed., New York, 1946, p. 53. Besides the papers in this book, another psychoanalytically oriented discussion of anti-Semitism may be found in Fenichel, O.: "Psychoanalysis of Anti-Semitism," *Am. Imago*, 1: 2, March, 1940.

typed thinking revealed the individual's view of minority groups and
indicated the blocks to the individual's ability to test reality. No statistically significant relationship emerged between the pattern of particular
stereotypes which the individual held to be true of a minority group, and
the degree of his hostility against that minority, as indicated by his demands for restrictions. But it was found that the more outspoken and
intense the individual was in his feelings against Jews (or Negroes) the
larger was the total number of stereotypes he employed (see Table 1
(III) below).[4]

TABLE 1(III)

DISTRIBUTION OF STEREOTYPES

Number of Stereotypes Used	Anti-Semites Classified as "Stereotyped"		Outspoken and Intense Anti-Semites	
	No.	Percentage	No.	Percentage
0–3	14	33	11	23
4–6	18	43	11	23
7–9	9	22	18	39
10 or more	1	2	7	15
Total	42		47	

A comparison of the patterns of stereotypes used to characterize the
Negro and the Jew revealed several important differences in the structure
of group hostilities. The various stereotypes employed by the sample to
characterize ethnic minorities are summarized in Tables 2(III) and
3(III) below.

An examination of the five most frequent Negro and five most frequent
Jewish stereotypes reveals strikingly different results, with each set presenting a more or less integrated pattern. For the *Jew*, the five most
frequent stereotypes were:

THEY ARE CLANNISH; THEY HELP ONE ANOTHER

"The Jewish are cliquish. I heard that they have a lodge that will appropriate
money for one of its members to start a business and then he repays it. If we're

[4] The analysis of stereotypes was based on a content analysis which combed the
entire interview record for the presence of stereotyped assertions. Several questions,
including some dealing with army life, were designed to reveal stereotyped thinking.

TABLE 2(III)

STEREOTYPES CHARACTERIZING JEWS

	No. of Veterans Mentioning Stereotypes
General	
They have the money	26
They control everything, (or have an urge to control everything); they are running the country	24
The Jew in business and industry	
They use underhanded or sharp business methods	24
They control most business	18
They are mostly in business for themselves	15
They monopolize industry; own most of the factories	13
They have the best jobs; they always get to the top	11
They control particular businesses	9
The personal characteristics of the Jew	
They are clannish; they help one another	37
They don't work; they don't do manual labor	19
They are overbearing; they are forward	17
They are dirty, sloppy, filthy	17
They are interested only in money	11
They are smart, especially in business	9
They are energetic	8
They are loud, noisy, and cause commotions	7

all created equal, it looks like the Jewish are in the driver's seat. . . ." (Veteran twenty-seven years old; one year high school.)

THEY HAVE THE MONEY

"They're pretty shrewd operators, I guess. Maybe I'm prejudiced against them. The one that screwed me up was a guy from California who said he had more reason than anybody to go back because he had a business to take care of. No family or anything else. He was a smart fellow, had a college education. He had a lot of money and would loan it to the guys and charge them interest. Any other guy would just hand it out and if he forgot to pay it back, O.K., you never asked him for it. Money is their God. This one got more passes than anyone else. Of course he was in the orderly room so he just wrote one for himself whenever he wanted one. He had a brand new Buick up at camp and drove it all around. He managed to get out before it was over. He went to the hospital every day; said it was his nerves. Probably was worrying about his business." (Veteran thirty-two years old; four years high school.)

They Control Everything

"Everybody blames the Jews. In a way that's right because they have everything. They control everything. They're in all the right places—in the offices, in politics. They're the ones running things. They always manage to get in at the top of everything. Like the Jews in the army. There were just three Jewish boys in our company, anyway. Then at the point of embarkation, just when we were ready to pull out, what did they do but yank them two off the ship. So those two Jews got left behind—no reasons given, they weren't sick or anything. That's the way it is with them all the time.

Table 3 (III)

Stereotypes Characterizing Negroes

	No. of Veterans Mentioning Stereotypes
General	
They are taking over; they are forcing out the whites	25
They have low standards; they are a lower class	18
The personal characteristics of the Negro	
They are sloppy, dirty, filthy	53
They depreciate property	33
They are lazy; they are slackers in work	22
They have low character; they are immoral and dishonest	18
They are ignorant; have low intelligence	18
They are troublesome; the cause of disturbances	14
They smell bad; they have a body odor	11
They carry diseases	10
They spend their money on a good front; they don't save	8

"They control all the liquor—that's one I know about. Just take a look around at the liquor stores, see one on this corner run by a Dago and he ain't got nothing, neither has the Irish or whatever else he may be—but look at the one that's got plenty and you'll see it's a Jewish place. They control it all. If your name is Goldberg, you get all you want—otherwise you don't get nothing. . . . 95 per cent of the liquor companies they still keep the same names, but the Jews got them now. It's the same in all business; but the liquor business is the one I know about." (Veteran thirty-three years old; less than eight years of school.)

"It seems like Jews are in back of every big outfit." (Veteran thirty-eight years old; four years high school.)

"They have power all over the world—in all the industries. Everything is Jewish. Marshall Field and all the big stores in Chicago are Jewish." (Veteran twenty-seven years old; two years high school.)

They Use Underhanded Business Methods

"I have a lot of trouble with the Jews, too. They're hard to deal with. They're too tight. Every time you go up to deliver something to them you have to have a fight with them first before you can collect your money." (Veteran thirty years old; two years high school.)

They Don't Work; They Don't Do Manual Labor

"Well, most of the Jewish people have all the factories so the white people are working for them. You don't see Jews working." (Veteran twenty-six years old; two years high school.)

For the *Negro*, the five most frequent stereotypes were:

They Are Sloppy, Dirty, Filthy

"He's lazy and he smells. Don't do any good for him to take a bath, he's born with it. . . . I just couldn't stand being near a nigger and I don't see how anybody could. They're colored, we're white. We just shouldn't marry them, we have no business doing it. They have a country, let them go back to Africa." (Veteran twenty-six years old; two years high school.)

"They should be taught where their place is, taught to be clean. Then you could stomach them more easily." (Veteran twenty-two years old; four years high school.)

They Depreciate Property

"Why is it when a bunch of niggers moves into a building, it gets all broken down so fast? I just got no use for them. You can always tell one by his smell." (Veteran twenty-nine years old; two years high school.)

They Are Taking Over; They Are Forcing Out the Whites

"I just don't like niggers, they're getting too big, will be wanting to take over. All these groups getting them to think they're so big—pretty soon, if they don't watch out, there's going to be a race riot. Why they push you off the street, now. Everywhere you go there's a bunch of niggers. You go downtown to a big department store and they're all over. Of course they got to buy things too, but it's sure getting bad. All these politicians are trying to get the nigger vote by putting them in white neighborhoods. Let them live together . . . they say. But there'll be a race riot if they keep up that stuff. Guess that's about all there is to do—get a riot going, start killing them—that's all. Then when 400 or 500 of them get killed, they'll find out that they got to stay in their place." (Veteran thirty-three years old; less than eight years education.)

They Are Lazy; They Are Slackers in Work

"There are Negroes working for my company but you always have to keep chasing them to keep them working." (Veteran twenty-five years old; four years high school.)

THEY ARE IMMORAL

"Well Negroes are an awful dirty class of people. There's more trouble with Negroes than with anyone else. They're always getting in hold-ups." (Veteran twenty-six years old; three years high school.)

"The trouble with them is they have no morals. If they're with whites, we can't trust the morals of the whites either, and we don't want a generation of mulattoes." (Veteran twenty-seven years old; two years high school.)

The composite pattern of stereotypes for the Jew did not stress personally "obnoxious" characteristics. Jews were not predominantly characterized as forward, pushy and overbearing, or loud and noisy by the members of this predominantly lower and lower middle class sample. In the main they were represented in terms of a powerful, well-organized group which by inference, threatened the subject. The most frequently mentioned stereotype was that Jews were clannish, and that they helped one another. In itself such a stereotype might be colorless, or it might indicate an underlying positive emotion. Contextual material almost invariably indicated that what the veteran was actually revealing was his social and personal isolation; he was decrying what he considered to be the unfair advantage in business and politics which accrued to the Jew who enjoyed greater social solidarity than himself. The following statement represents this attitude in its extreme form:

"Well it may not sound good, but I think Hitler had the right idea. Kill them all off. They make life miserable for everybody else. All they do is to look out for themselves." (Veteran twenty-two years old; one year college.)

The power of the Jews, it was felt, lay not in their strength; for that matter, neither physical nor intellectual ability was stressed. The Jews' power to control was felt to lie in their cooperation with one another (their clannishness) and in their possession of money. The wide range of stereotyping which surrounded the power and wealth of the Jew highlighted his ability to amass and keep wealth, largely through underhanded business methods and general cunning. Complementary to this was the observation of the stereotyped and aggressive veteran that Jews do not work, since they do not do manual labor.

On the other hand, the stereotypes of the Negro in this sample stressed the individual, personally "offensive" characteristics of the Negro. Just as the stereotypes of the group characteristics of the Jews implied a threat to the values and well-being of the intolerant white, so the stereotypes about the Negro were used to describe a conception of the Negro as a threat to the white man's economic and social status, particularly because the Negro was "forcing out the whites"—for example:

"I say that the white race should get the jobs because I believe that they live at a higher standard than the colored and it would give the white race a more superior feeling over the colored than we've had in the last few years. I believe that the colored race is growing too strong. During the war they were kept in their place. Now they're learning white ways and stepping out of place. This was very evident in the service." (Veteran twenty-three years old; four years high school.)

While both stereotyped and outspoken anti-Semites used by and large the same kinds of stereotypes, there was, nevertheless, some marked difference in the frequency with which members of these two groups mentioned particular stereotypes. The greatest difference in the use of stereotyped thinking (between stereotyped anti-Semites and outspoken anti-Semites), occurred in connection with the charge that Jews exercise control. Twice as many outspoken anti-Semites made this statement as did stereotyped anti-Semites. Another stereotype made much more frequently by outspoken anti-Semites was that Jews are clannish and help one another. Stereotypes about Jews having all the money, using underhanded business methods and not doing manual labor were as frequently used by stereotyped anti-Semites as by outspoken ones. Thus stereotypes which may be related to superego tendencies were used twice as frequently by outspoken anti-Semites, while stereotypes related to id tendencies (shirking of hard labor, cheating, and hoarding money) were equally frequent among both groups.

These data may be compared with the frequency distribution of stereotypes applied to Negroes. The greatest difference in the use of stereotypes between stereotyped anti-Negro and outspokenly and intensely anti-Negro veterans was found as regarded the accusation that Negroes were sloppy, dirty and filthy. (Twenty-three per cent of the stereotyped anti-Negro men made such statements, while twice as many of the outspoken and twice as many of the intense anti-Negro men made such assertions.) Thus in the case of the Negro, stereotypes related to id tendencies were used much more frequently by men whose anti-Negro bias was more intense.

A comparison of the distribution of stereotypes applied to Jews and Negroes, as indicated by this enumeration, with those used by the National Socialists in Germany permits certain observations. In Germany the whole list of stereotypes were applied to the Jews, which in the United States were divided between Jews and Negroes. In German anti-

Semitic propaganda, Jewish dirtiness and lack of morality were greatly emphasized. Thus there is additional evidence that within Western European-American culture the selection and use of stereotypes seems to depend on the needs of the person applying them, although the patterns revealed by the veterans permitted some significant qualification.

In the United States, where two or more ethnic minorities are available, a tendency has emerged to separate the stereotypes into two sets and to assign each of them to one minority group. One of these two sets indicates feelings of anxiety over the first minority's power of control (Jews exercising control, having power). The other set of stereotypes indicates anxieties aroused by the second minority's assumed ability to permit itself the enjoyment of primitive, socially unacceptable forms of indulgence or gratification (the Negroes'—and one might add the Mexicans'—dirtiness and immorality). Moreover, it would seem that when the two minority groups differ in physical characteristics, such as skin color, the minority showing greater physical difference is used for projecting anxieties associated with dirt and sex desires.[5] The minority whose physical characteristics are more similar to those of the majority becomes a symbol for anxieties concerning overpowering control.

According to psychoanalytical interpretation, ethnic hostility is a projection of unacceptable inner strivings onto a minority group. Projection is a mechanism by means of which one tries to solve a conflict within oneself by ascribing to another person emotions, motives, and behavior which actually belong to oneself. For instance, if we hate another person without justification, that creates a conflict within us if our conscience does not approve of the emotion of hatred. Instead of solving this conflict by overcoming our hatred, we may try to get rid of it through projection. We project our hatred into the other person so that it appears to us not as if we hate him, but that he hates us. Thus in a devious way we not only try to get rid of an emotion which is not acceptable to our conscience (superego), we are also now justified in hating the other person if we so desire, because we think he is hating us.

Any survey of those characteristics to which the members of the ingroup object in members of the outgroups is frequently a list of all those characteristics which they fear in themselves.[6] The outgroup provides

[5] It may be mentioned that stereotypes frequently used by the veterans in speaking about Mexicans followed closely the pattern of Negro stereotypes.

[6] "For example, in the German concentration camp situation, both Jewish prisoners and Gestapo guards acted as if psychological mechanisms comparable to paranoid delusions were at work in them. Both believed that the members of the other group were sadistic, dirty, unintelligent, of an inferior race, and that they indulged in sexual perversions. Both groups accused each other of being interested only in material goods

subjects onto which they can project the rejected part of those tendencies which created an inner conflict. Thus they try to free themselves of the conflict and to reestablish their personality integration which has been endangered by demands of which their superego, for example, did not approve. That this is so can be seen from the fact that the outgroup is always accused of satisfying needs which are common to all men. No child wants to be and remain clean; everybody would like to live at a leisurely pace, to have money, and to enjoy sexual gratification. But often our conscience does not permit us to give in to these instinctual demands and fights against them.

Personal integration can be threatened by two opposing psychological entities: superego and id. Superego, by definition, controls human behavior in line with social standards. The economic system, particularly the necessity to work, and to work hard, seem suitable to represent superego demands, many of which the individual feels unable to meet. The indulgence in primitive desires represents id gratifications, the desire for which is felt by many individuals as a threat to their integration.

In the metropolitan area studied, there seemed to be a tendency, among the intolerant, to select the Jew for projecting onto him those tendencies rejected by the superego (for instance, the individual's desire to take advantage of others), while id desires were projected onto the Negro, whose supposed greater irrationality seemed to make him a suitable representative of the pressures originating in the irrational id. However, a projection may easily show features of both opposing forces since in all conflicts they are intertwined. Still, in each case one of the two opposing tendencies will dominate.

It frequently happens that the impact of the environment on the individual may force him to change the objects onto whom he projects unapproved inner tendencies. Thus the question arose of the possible effects of army experiences with Jews and Negroes upon patterns of projection, as revealed in stereotyped thinking. In the absence of prewar interviews, only limited inferences could be drawn.

Men brought into the army the forms of stereotyped thinking which they made use of in civilian life. In the army, enough of the practices and forms of civilian life were continued to permit ready application of

and of having no respect for ideals, or for moral and intellectual values. In the case of each group there may have been individual justification for some of these beliefs. Nevertheless this strange similarity indicates that the two groups were availing themselves of analogous mechanisms of defense." Bettelheim, B.: "Dynamism of Anti-Semitism in Gentile and Jew," *Journal of Abnormal and Social Psychology*, 42: 2, April 1947.

existing stereotypes. Moreover, at the time of the interview the men were back in civilian life, trying to regain their places. This would have tended to revive attitudes previously formed in civilian life. In addition, the pressure of army life was likely to increase many individuals' need for protecting their personal integration by the use of defensive mechanisms, including projections.

Nevertheless, the army experience threw many men into new and varied contacts with Jews and, to a lesser extent, with Negroes. Such experiences could have been viewed as new opportunities to realistically test their conceptions of minority groups. In particular, the fact that men were asked to join with these minorities in a common task might have led them to re-examine their attitudes. Thus whether associations with Jews in the army influenced the patterns of projection is an important issue for the understanding of intolerance.

TABLE 4(III)

CHARACTERIZATION OF SOLDIERS

	Jews		Negroes	
	No.	Percentage	No.	Percentage
They were not used in combat (had rear-echelon jobs)	30	20	19	13
They were poor combat soldiers	25	17	65	43
They fought like others	87	58	39	26
Don't know and other	8	5	27	18
Total	150		150	

Analysis showed that the stereotyping of Jews in the army was in good measure an extension of the conceptions of civilian life onto army experiences. Table 4(III) above presents the veterans' responses to the question: "Did the Jews make good soldiers?" From this table it can be seen that the number of veterans who were free of negative stereotypes in their characterization of Jews as soldiers equaled the number of men tolerant toward the Jew as measured by the overall index of intolerance (approximately 60 per cent in both cases).[7]

Closer examination of the interview records of intolerant men reveals

---

[7] Since this question was included in the construction of the overall index of anti-Semitic attitudes, some association was to be expected. However, the percentage was almost the same for this question as for the overall index, composed of eleven groups of questions, each consisting of several items.

how civilian patterns of stereotypes were uncritically applied to the army setting and that the experience of living together did not markedly influence these patterns.

The civilian characterization of the Jew as a powerful figure, with business ability and cunning, was merely enlarged to signify a series of traits which enabled the Jew to succeed regardless of the context in which he found himself. To intolerant men, being a Jew meant possessing this basic ability. This emerged clearly in many of the statements about the Jew in the army. For example:

"There were only a few Jews in our outfit. One of them was a master sergeant. They did get up faster in rank and promotion, but we couldn't do anything about that. They would do favors for the officers and get promoted." (Veteran twenty-two years old; two years high school.)

Even if personal attachment and respect bound a man to a particular Jew, the stereotype of his greater ability "to get things" remained.

"Oh, there was one Jew, Lt. ———— . . . almost forgot about him. He lived right over here a few blocks, too. He took pictures of me and a buddy of mine the day before he was killed. He knew somebody on the *Sun* and was always sending in pictures of the guys. He was really white. At first I didn't like him and he knew it and picked on me at first too. But then I changed my mind. He took care of his platoon all right. To show you how much they liked him, they all got together at Christmas time and bought him one of those fancy lined sleeping bags—which is something, cause otherwise none of the G.I.'s did nothing like that for the officers. He took good care of his men. He saw to it that they had things they needed. They had cigarettes all the time when there weren't many around. *That's the Jew in him—he was good at getting things like that.* He'd do anything for his men and they'd do anything for him." (Veteran thirty-three years old; less than eight years of education.)

Again, in the army as in civilian life, the Jew's power position was ascribed to his special characteristics—in particular, money and education.

The equation of the Jew as civilian to the Jew as soldier was summarized by one thirty year old corporal: "The Jews don't work or fight."

In the case of the veterans' views of the Negro soldier, the stereotypes seemed also to follow the previously mentioned pattern of stressing the Negroes' personally obnoxious traits. The fact that Negroes were in fact used chiefly as rear-echelon and service troops, tended to reenforce the existing stereotypes about the Negro's being lazy and inefficient.

"I have yet to see a good Negro soldier. Well, for instance, when we were aboard ship we had three white companies and one Negro company; and every time we had a drill, it would take three minutes for the white companies to be at their stations, and fifteen minutes later the Negro company was not at their stations."

The actual position of the Negro in the army appears to account in part for the 13 per cent of the sample who responded that the Negroes were not used in combat (Table 4(III)). More important was the fact that the characterization of the Negro in the army was colored by the sexual mores which developed between white women and the Negro troops in the European theater of operations. To complete the foregoing analysis of attitudes Table 5(III) summarizes the men's responses to the question, "How did the fellows in your outfit get along with the Jews (with the Negroes)?"

TABLE 5(III)

"HOW DID THE FELLOWS IN YOUR OUTFIT GET ALONG WITH THE JEWS (WITH THE NEGROES)?"

	Jews		Negroes	
	No.	Percentage	No.	Percentage
Had little contact	6	4	59	39
Did not get along	26	18	45	30[a]
Got along all right	96	64	35	23
Got along very well	11	7	3	2
No answer	11	7	8	6
Total	150		150	

[a] Includes responses: "Got along as long as they stayed in their place."

For negative answers, the reason most often volunteered in the case of the Jews was their clannishness. For Negroes, however, allegations of friction hinged around the topic of Negro-white sexual relations. Those who expressed attitudes on this subject were uniform in their condemnation, not of the white women, but of the Negro soldiers.

"There was lots of trouble, lots of fighting and shooting. The main trouble was about girls—they was taking out the white girls all the time, in Italy and in France. They told the white girls they were American Indians. They don't know any better. The girls thought they were pretty good, I guess, because the niggers would buy them a lot of things. They were so anxious to get girls that they would spend a lot on them. And they were there close to all the supplies so that they would steal stuff to the girls. . . .

"Sometimes, maybe one company would come into a small town where a big colored unit had been stationed for a long time, and we'd just stay to ourselves and not go into the town at all. It would just start a lot of children. Like one time a guy was talking to a girl and a colored soldier came walking down the street, she said so long to the white guy, I have a date with him, and went walking off with the nigger. But what could you do about it? So we just stayed away from them. Course there were plenty of fights, a hell of a lot of shooting." (Veteran thirty-three years old; less than eight years of education.)

"Negroes were scared of their own shadow in combat. The Negroes went out with white girls in England; in fact you'd see 'em kissing white girls. Boy, those fool girls thought they were American Indians, but as soon as more white troops landed we took care of that. I remember one incident. A white guy was dancing with an English girl and a Negro came in and the girl left the white guy for the Negro. They'd do it over there. Well, the white guy got mad and came up asking what the big idea was, that that man was a Negro. The Negro was mad too, and told him that when he got home, he'd be going out with the guy's own sister. . . ." (Veteran twenty-five years old; two years high school.)

These data and many similar statements support the hypothesis that the individual's stereotypes are not only vitally needed defense mechanisms, but are persistent, even under the impact of such immediate and realistic experiences as service with Jews and Negroes under conditions of war. But were there more basic life experiences which forced the individual toward a new and different integration of hostile and anxious impulses? This raised the question of which types of life experiences are likely to modify an individual's intolerance? If we were to find significant differences between the life experiences of tolerant and intolerant men, we might assume that some of these experiences favored ethnic tolerance. The task of the investigator thus became one of isolating those life experiences which were associated with intolerance.

CHAPTER IV

SOCIAL STATUS

In view of the widespread notion that intolerance can be explained by social and economic factors, a first task was to determine whether the men's social and economic history could account, either in whole or in part, for their ethnic intolerance. The most basic analysis of social factors concerned itself with whether or not significant differences in intolerance could be associated with different social and economic attributes. Those characteristics singled out for preliminary study were: age, education, religion, political affiliation, income, and social status.

The data as set forth below suggest that—subject to certain limitations —these factors cannot of themselves account for differences in the degree or nature of intolerance. With some few exceptions, other studies offer little assistance on this point. One of them, a carefully controlled survey poll on anti-Semitism which was conducted by Angus Campbell on a nationwide sample of 316 cases, tended toward the same conclusion.[1] It was found, for example, that when attitudes toward Jews were classified according to the various social and economic characteristics of those interviewed (age, sex, religion, education, and income), the relationships were for the most part slight, and in some cases negligible. While that study was based on a cross section of the nation's population, the present investigation had selected a relatively homogeneous group of veterans. This made possible a sharper testing of the findings mentioned above because it permitted certain important factors to be considered constant for the group.

AGE.   To investigate a possible correlation between the subject's age and the degree of his anti-Semitism seemed pertinent, since ethnic intolerance is apparently absent in early childhood. Moreover, although elderly people are often intolerant, they rarely join violent mobs, perhaps because they are less volatile, or just less physically fit.

Recent German history has shown that the age groups between 16

[1] Newcomb, T., and Hartley, E.: *Readings in Social Psychology.* New York, Henry Holt and Company, Inc., 1947, pp. 518-27.

and 40 were those most ready to take part in violent anti-Semitic action. The *Fortune* opinion poll (February, 1946) indicated that both men and women in the age group of 35 to 49 tend to be slightly more anti-Semitic than those between 21 and 34. However, the Campbell study referred to above concluded that there was no consistent relationship between anti-Semitism and age.

Although the basis for selection in our sample limited the age-range it was still possible to divide the veterans into groups of younger and older men, and also into groups of three-year age intervals. When comparing the degree of anti-Semitic attitudes in the various age groups, no statistically significant difference appeared, although the older veterans tended to be slightly more anti-Semitic[2] (see Table 1(IV) below).

This table permits another observation: From the sample it appears that those born between 1910 and 1926 showed no significant difference with regard to anti-Semitism. Men born after 1918 went through their formative adolescent years in the 1930's when National Socialism and its program of anti-Semitic persecutions were widely discussed. Nevertheless, their attitudes toward the Jewish problem did not differ significantly from those of veterans who were born before 1920 and had therefore reached maturity before Hitler and his anti-Semitic policies made headlines. The implication seems to be that world events which have no direct impact on the individual do not significantly influence the development of his anti-Semitic attitudes.

EDUCATIONAL LEVEL. Whether a higher degree of general knowledge is positively correlated with tolerance is a question of great import. If it were so, then an educational program, such as the dissemination of correct information, would seem an adequate means of promoting tolerance. To date, opinion polls have not settled this problem, although it was found that for the nation as a whole, anti-Semitism seemed to be slightly related to educational level; those most educated were least anti-Semitic. A good case could be made for denying the existence of such a difference beyond mere verbalization, since those with more education may be expected to qualify their statements more carefully, while their underlying attitudes and behavior may be the same as that of persons who express themselves more bluntly and thus appear less tolerant. This may explain why veterans with at least some college education appeared slightly more tolerant, but not markedly or significantly so on the continuum (see Table 1(IV)).

[2] The Chi-square test was employed to determine the significance of various attributes. Throughout the text, where a *significant* difference is reported it is at least at the .01 confidence limit unless otherwise specifically mentioned.

TABLE 1(IV)

SOCIAL CORRELATES OF ANTI-SEMITISM

Age	Under 28 Years	29–36 Years	
	Percentage	Percentage	No.
Tolerant	44	34	61
Stereotyped	27	30	42
Outspoken & Intense	29	36	47
Number	94	56	150

Education	Did Not Complete High School	Completed High School	Some College or More	
	Percentage	Percentage	Percentage	No.
Tolerant	35	39	51	61
Stereotyped	31	28	23	42
Outspoken & Intense	34	33	26	47
Number	65	46	39	150

Religion[a]	Catholic	Protestant	No Present Religious Denomination	
	Percentage	Percentage	Percentage	No.
Tolerant	40	48	33	61
Stereotyped	28	25	33	41
Outspoken & Intense	32	27	33	46
Number	103	33	12	148

[a] Two cases of Greek Orthodox not included.

RELIGION. Religious denomination showed no significant relation to degree of anti-Semitism (Table 1(IV)). Nor did any significant association between religious extraction—if this term may be used—and degree of anti-Semitism emerge when the religious denomination of the veterans' parents were also examined (see Appendix, Table 4(A)). Finally, it was noted that veterans in whose homes two religious denominations contended for dominance showed no higher degree of anti-Semitism.

The relatively high percentage of Catholics among the group studied was a function of the sampling procedure which emphasized lower income groups. In the city studied, these groups are predominantly Catholics. (Negroes were not interviewed, and thus could not increase the percentage of Protestants in the sample, although they are overwhelmingly a Protestant group in Chicago.)

Since professed religious denomination is probably not a valid basis for analyzing the association of religious conviction with interethnic attitudes, a number of projective questions were employed, most of which dealt with soldiers' religious behavior in the army.

Among other questions dealing with army experiences, the men were asked: "How did the fellows feel about religion?" This opened a discussion of religion during which additional questions probed religious practices, such as church attendance in the army and in civilian life.

TABLE 2(IV)

"How Did the Fellows Feel About Religion?"

	Tolerant		Stereotyped		Outspoken and Intense		Total	
	No.	Percentage	No.	Percentage	No.	Percentage	No.	Percentage
Religion was important in army	26	43	15	36	11	23	52	35
Most soldiers followed their own habits	22	36	19	45	28	60	69	46
Most soldiers didn't go to church	7	11	5	12	7	15	19	13
Don't know and Other	6	10	3	7	1	2	10	6
Total	61		42		47		150	

Veterans who answered the central question by stressing the acceptance and importance of religion in the army were *significantly* more tolerant than the rest of the sample (see Table 2(IV) above). It was assumed that the subjects were obviously projecting their own feelings about the importance of religion in the army and not basing their answers on carefully observed behavior in others. Those who replied that "no one in the army was really religious" were equally distributed as to anti-Semitism. Intolerance, however, was concentrated in the group whose answers indicated their indifference to religion by statements to the effect that "most soldiers followed their own habits" or "everybody has his own opinions."

Thus it appears that men whose religious attitudes were characterized by vague and ambiguous statements about nonspecific "little differences" and "everybody having his own opinions" were those who were most intolerant.

That this correlation between stable religious beliefs, either positive or negative, and tolerance was of long standing appears to be a plausible hypothesis. Responses to the question, "Do you think your attitude toward religion was changed in any way by army life," appear to support this contention (see Appendix, Table 5(A). Intolerant veterans claimed to have been strengthened in their religious conviction by the army experience *significantly* more often than the tolerant men.

The conclusion seems to be that while permanent religious attitudes correlated positively with tolerance, vascillation on this score was accompanied by a higher degree of anti-Semitism.

POLITICAL AFFILIATION.   Just as religion (or religious conviction) in itself bore no relation to tolerance, but only the stability of such convictions, so political affiliation in itself seemed without bearing on the question. The lack of differences between the party affiliations of tolerant veterans and outspokenly anti-Semitic veterans confirms the often reported observation that political affiliation for the rank and file, in the United States, does not depend on party program. Only 50 per cent of the men had clear enough political convictions to call themselves either Democrats or Republicans. Of the tolerant veterans roughly 30 per cent were Republicans, while the percentage of outspoken anti-Semites among the Republicans was almost the same (26 per cent). Comparable percentages of tolerant veterans (69 per cent) and intolerant veterans (74 per cent) claimed to be Democrats.

FAMILY COMPOSITION.   In addition to religious and political attitudes those of intolerance are also moulded under family influence. Therefore, an effort was made to determine whether family composition (as distinguished from family attitudes) was associated with intolerance. Gross comparisons of family composition failed to produce any correlates with anti-Semitism. The percentage of divorce among the men's families (about 10 per cent) indicated that the group as a whole was one in which family disorganization was not high. There were too few cases of divorce among the veterans themselves to determine whether this factor exercised any influence on tolerance.

Intolerant men were just as likely to be single as married. The size of the veteran's own family, as well as that of his parents, was unrelated to anti-Semitism. Moreover, the fact that he came from a large family, with three or more children, exercised no influence on his degree of intolerance toward the Jew; neither did it make any difference whether he was the only child or had one sibling.

As another index of family integration, the relative permanence of residence was considered since frequent moving interferes with the stability of interpersonal relationships. However, when the length of family residence in the current dwelling unit was related to the degree of intolerance, no significant difference was noted. The spread among the sample in this respect ranged from 43 per cent, who had been dwelling in their homes for less than one year, to 32 per cent, who had lived in theirs for longer than ten years.

The question of family disruption was also studied as a possible factor in the development of intolerance. Nor did the absence of any relationship between gross indices of family organization and anti-Semitism settle the issue. It merely meant that the answer was not to be found in the formal state of the family, and that further investigation of the impact of the family on the individual was indicated (see Chapter VII).

NATIVITY OF PARENTS. In past years, it has been a popular belief that anti-Semitism, as well as many other interethnic hostilities, found its roots in the struggles of European life, and that it was transplanted to the United States by relatively uneducated immigrants. This was one of the many ways in which man safeguarded his own self esteem by blaming undesirable attitudes on an outgroup. If this assumption had been true, the "Americanization" of immigrant groups would have been the most effective method for improving interethnic relations.

Since it is true that anti-Semitism took a much more violent form in some European countries than it ever did in the United States, it seemed relevant to learn how the sons of native-born parents differed in questions of tolerance from the sons of foreign-born parents. It was found that the degree of ethnic intolerance proved unrelated to the nativity of the veterans' parents; in the metropolis studied, the sons of immigrants were no more intolerant than those of native-born parents (see Appendix Table 6(A)).

However, it was observed that whereas it made little difference whether both parents were foreign- or native-born, an increase in the degree of anti-Semitism was observed in cases where only one parent was foreign-born, although the difference was not great enough to be statistically significant. Only a tentative explanation of this phenomenon may be suggested, namely that a union of native-born and foreign-born parents may have made for less family cohesion, which may in turn have increased the son's insecurity and led him to seek aggressive outlets for his frustrations and/or to adopt more outspoken attitudes.

Similarly, those subjects who had one native- and one foreign-born parent tended to be somewhat more intolerant toward the Negroes. Thus the tendency toward greater intolerance among children with one foreign-born parent could not be ascribed to patterns formed in Europe (where anti-Semitism was rampant), since these parents came from Central and Eastern Europe, where discrimination against Negroes was virtually unknown. (See Appendix Table 13(A).)

READING AND LISTENING HABITS. Attitudes expressing themselves in social interaction are no longer shaped by the family and the church alone. While the family still moulds the basic personality, and while, consciously or unconsciously, most fundamental values are derived from the religious and moral teachings of childhood, how the personality expresses itself in action and how moral convictions are implemented in everyday living is now strongly influenced by propaganda. Although the bulk of empirical observations and the limited number of controlled experiments on this subject indicate that mass communications tend to be less important than basic personality and environmental factors in modifying attitudes, the German example certainly demonstrated that once slumbering hostility is aroused by environmental factors it can easily be directed against a specific goal. Though mass communication does not as yet seem to influence basic attitudes such as aggression, isolation, and feelings of competence or incompetence, it certainly influences the manner in which they are expressed, and channelizes their expression.

Undoubtedly, mass communications perform a significant role of buttressing and providing elaboration for existing attitudes. The impact of these defense processes is difficult to assess, but the individual's selectivity reveals itself in the way he chooses, from the variety of available communications, those whose symbols are most readily incorporated into his existing frame of reference. In this sense, therefore, the reading and listening habits of the individual are significant social characteristics which help to maintain his current beliefs, and limit all attempts at modification which are contrary to their tendencies. In an analysis of intolerance, these social characteristics have special significance. First, various sources of mass communications present different amounts of material designed to maintain existing prejudices.[3] Secondly, various media of mass communication give different "news slants" to the general social and political process. Therefore the veteran's reading and listening habits were investigated rather to determine how his selectivity reflected on his tolerance than to find whether ethnic attitudes reflect the impact of chosen types of communication.

Specifically, the men were asked which newspapers they read regularly, and which were their favorite radio programs and magazines. Statistically, the findings were negative. No significant relations between intolerance and the favoring of one newspaper, type of magazine, or radio program could be established. The replies indicated that almost as many men declared their favorite newspaper to be one of the two New Deal papers in town, the *Chicago Sun* and the *Chicago Times,* as preferred the opposing *Chicago Tribune* or the local Hearst paper. The rest, a small minority, preferred the middle-of-the-road *Daily News.* It may be added that the Hearst paper and the *Daily News* were the only papers preferred more by outspoken and intense anti-Semites than by tolerant men, while for both the *Chicago Tribune* and the New Deal papers the reverse was true. The numbers in each case were too small to permit conclusions, particularly since the difference was not statistically significant.

SOCIOECONOMIC STATUS. To determine the relationship between the varying degrees of anti-Semitism and socioeconomic status, four different status criteria were employed: (1) amount of *income* of the subject at the time of the interview; (2) type of *job* held by the veteran, ranked according to the Alba Edwards socioeconomic classification;[4] (3) type of *job* held by the subject's *father*; and (4) the indirect measure of the veteran's *rank* at the time of his *discharge* from the army. Anticipating the discussion of these criteria it may be said here that none of these factors seemed associated with intolerance among the members of the sample since none

[3] Berelson, Bernard, and Salter, Patricia: "Majority and Minority Americans: An Analysis of Magazine Fiction," *Public Opinion Quarterly,* Summer, 1946, present a statistical analysis of the frequency with which ethnic stereotypes are contained in magazine fiction.

[4] Edwards, Alba: *A Social-Economic Grouping of Gainful Workers of the United States,* Washington, Government Printing Office, 1938, p. 2.

of them were significantly different for the tolerant, the stereotyped, or
the outspoken anti-Semite. (Table 3(IV).)

TABLE 3(IV)

SOCIOECONOMIC CORRELATES OF ANTI-SEMITISM

Current Salary	Up to $2,500	$2,500 to $3,000	$3,000 and Over	Not Applicable	
	Percentage	Percentage	Percentage	Percentage	No.
Tolerant	39	39	43	45	61
Stereotyped	33	24	18	35	42
Outspoken and Intense	28	37	39	20	47
Number	59	43	28	20	150

Socioeconomic Status	Unskilled and Semi-skilled	Top Four Groups[a]	
	Percentage	Percentage	No.
Tolerant	38	42	61
Stereotyped	33	24	42
Outspoken and Intense	29	34	47
Number	80	70	150

Rank in Army	Privates and Corporals	Sergeants	
	Percentage	Percentage	No.
Tolerant	38	42	61
Stereotyped	26	31	42
Outspoken and Intense	36	27	47
Number	80	70	150

[a] Includes students on G. I. Bill of Rights and veterans engaged in on-the-job training.

Salary distribution among the veterans was skewed by the underrepresentation of high incomes which was due, of course, to age differen-
tials and the absence of former officer personnel. For the same reason,

as far as type of job held was concerned, the professional and managerial groups were not proportionally represented. Nevertheless, a detailed breakdown by degree of anti-Semitism, amount of salary earned, and type of job held failed to reveal any group in which outspoken anti-Semitism was significantly concentrated. The lack of a relation between type of job held by the veteran and anti-Semitism was particularly noteworthy in the case of clerks and kindred worker categories where it was presumed that anti-Semitism might be concentrated. Some studies have stressed that anti-Semitism is prevalent among the lower middle classes, or the upper classes, while workers are supposedly less contaminated. This study seems to indicate that for this sample socioeconomic status as such is not correlated with intolerance. (See Appendix Tables No. 7(A) and 8(A) for more detailed breakdown of income, socioeconomic status, and intolerance.)

Because status causation of anti-Semitism has been so frequently accepted, and because the veterans' status in civilian life was still so new, another gauge of status was also investigated, namely, rank at discharge. In this case too, there was no difference to be found between the degree of intolerance among privates, and the lower versus the higher ranks of noncommissioned officers.

The conclusion as to socioeconomic status and its relation to anti-Semitism bears comparison with the situation in pre-Hitler Germany. Contrary to widely held notions, anti-Semitism there was by no means restricted to the petty bourgeoisie, but was widespread among sectors of all classes, including the working class.[5]

SOCIAL MOBILITY. The picture so far presented begins to change when the static concept of status is replaced by the dynamic concept of social mobility. Social scientists define social mobility as upward or downward change in the social position of an individual over a period of time, or as compared with the position of his family. If the effect of social mobility on anti-Semitism is studied, rapid change in status becomes more significant. Slow changes need not lead to aggressive behavior nor will a change of society as a whole produce such feelings. If societal change embraces all members of society, appropriate societal cushioning will usually protect the individual. In the case of individual changes in status, a slow

---

[5] It should be pointed out again that this sample permits no generalizations about the top social strata. The *Fortune* survey of February, 1946, it is true, indicates increased anti-Semitism on the upper income level, but there are no statistical studies to support the point. However, some impressionistic observations support this contention, although anti-Semitism in the "upper classes" may be somewhat different in causation and content.

rate of change will allow him time for adjustment and also permit him to
direct slowly accumulating frustrations into socially acceptable channels.
Sudden frustrations promote the tendency to react to deterioration of
status through discharge in hostility. This was exemplified in the rapid
succession of inflation and deflation in pre-Hitler Germany and the
attendant increase in anti-Semitism. Therefore, a study of the consequences of relatively sudden status change seemed indicated.

Social mobility was viewed as a shift in the veteran's socioeconomic or
occupational position from that of his immediate prewar position to that
of his position at the time of the interview.[6] Most men felt they were
entitled to return to a position which was better than, or at least equal
to, the one they had left on enlistment. They felt that their service to the
country, the hardships they had experienced, and especially the loss of
opportunity for regular advancement more than justified such expectations. Therefore, a current status lower than the one enjoyed before enlistment was not only an injury to their self-esteem, as loss in status always
is, but was also viewed as an unjustified mistreatment by society, particularly in view of promises which they considered to have been made to
them.

It was possible to gather precise data on the social mobility of 130
veterans. Temporarily unemployed veterans were not rated because their
unemployment was almost always transitional and sometimes deliberate.
Nine of the men, who were studying under the G. I. Bill of Rights or
obtaining benefits through the on-the-job training program, were rated as
upwardly mobile because they were expected to improve their status
through increased skills or learning. Table 4(IV) indicates that a third of
those for whom data were available were in the upward mobility group,
one-seventh in the downward, while the remainder, slightly more than
half, registered no change of status.

Aggressive attitudes, both spontaneous and elicited, were found to be
most highly concentrated in the downwardly mobile group, while the
pattern was *significantly* reversed for those who had advanced in social
status since the period of their previous civilian employment. Those who
had experienced no change presented a picture somewhat in the middle;
among them the number of tolerant persons was almost equal to that of
the men who held stereotyped anti-Semitic beliefs.

[6] The men were asked about their occupational status before the war and at the
time of the interview. These two data were compared with the Alba Edwards classification, described above. A shift upwards of one or more grades on this scale was
held to constitute upward social mobility; while a reverse shift was classified as downward social mobility.

TABLE 4(IV)

ANTI-SEMITISM AND SOCIAL MOBILITY

	Downward Mobility		No Mobility		Upward Mobility		Total	
	No.	Percentage	No.	Percentage	No.	Percentage	No.	Percentage
Tolerant	2	11	25	37	22	50	49	38
Stereotyped	3	17	26	38	8	18	37	28
Outspoken and Intense	13	72	17	25	14	32	44	34
Total	18		68		44		130	

While the previously discussed social and economic characteristics, viewed, as it were, in a static context, proved relatively unrelated to anti-Semitism, they were *significantly* related to the expression of intolerance when viewed in the dynamic context of the individual's social mobility.[7]

The no-mobility group showed the highest concentration of stereotyped opinions—that is, they were "middle-of-the-roaders" in the intolerance continuum. (Over 70 per cent of the stereotyped anti-Semites were found in this middle category.) This datum tends to highlight the relation between mobility and intolerance.

It should be realized that the stereotyped and the outspoken anti-Semites held many attitudes in common about the Jew. The difference between the stereotyped and the outspoken anti-Semites appeared to be the greater tendency of the stereotyped anti-Semite to control his hostile feelings so that they expressed themselves only in unfavorable opinions rather than in demands for action. The demand for action, and action itself, threatened the *status quo* which this middle group seemed to wish to preserve. It can also be assumed that self-discipline with regard to social attitudes is a result of the willingness to accede to society's demands for conformity. It then seems understandable that the individual who reacts to downward social mobility as to the consequence of an act of injustice by society would experience a weakening of the desire or the ability to conform to society's demands. Such conformity, in a society

[7] It might be argued that the relationship between anti-Semitism and mobility (as defined in this study) may have been the result of a third attribute: education. This however was not the case, for association of social mobility and tolerance remained present when educational level was held constant.

which deprives the individual, seems pointless to the person deprived.[8] The stereotyped anti-Semite therefore becomes a potentially outspoken anti-Semite, given conditions which may weaken his self-discipline. One such condition is likely to be downward social mobility.

It may be assumed that the wish to "play safe," on the part of the non-mobile group, prevented it from taking those social and economic risks which, while offering the chance to rise in status, also entailed all the risk which changes imply, among them that of declining in status. It was particularly true for this group, to whom the G. I. Bill offered easily accessible chances to raise their educational (and, by implication, their social and economic) status. As noted above, the men who availed themselves of this opportunity were classified as upwardly mobile.

The same lack of desire to assume even temporary risks on the chance of bettering oneself also prevented these men from taking an extreme view of ethnic problems. Holding stereotyped opinions on the Jews was the accepted pattern for the group, while both great tolerance or violent anti-Semitism, they felt, might expose them to the criticism or the ridicule of their peers. Such tactics seemed risky and to be avoided.

The German example may again be mentioned in this connection. The socially and economically downward-moving lower middle class groups (frequently referred to as the "squeezed-out groups") were the followers of Hitler, while the "respectable," relatively secure, and static middle classes (those who had not yet experienced downward mobility) held apart from this extreme form of nationalism (and anti-Semitism). Before Hitler, they were the followers of the *Stahlhelm*, of the conservative parties who embraced "stereotyped" and social anti-Semitism without being outspokenly intolerant. All this changed with the advent of Hitler. Then anti-Semitism became not only respectable, but the social norm. Moreover, these middle classes which had formerly enjoyed relative security now themselves became part of the squeezed-out group, squeezed out first by the new ruling group of National Socialists and then by the war mobilization economy. At this point, most of them became intensely hostile to the Jews, both because they were again following the accepted and successful pattern and also because they needed more vio-

---

[8] This is a process which can be observed in other situations in which the individual experiences frustrations. The typical nonconformist is the delinquent. With the exception of those cases in which delinquency is nothing but conformity to the mores of the delinquent's immediate environment, delinquency is almost always the consequence of the delinquent's conviction that he has not received his due, and has been cheated by those who to him represent society.

lent outlets for the hostility aroused by sudden and severe frustration.[9]

In view of the association between downward social mobility and intolerance, and upward social mobility and tolerance, the few cases (fourteen) who displayed both upward mobility and outspokenly intolerant attitudes warrant special attention. An analysis of the actual income gains associated with upward mobility reveals that these veterans who were both outspokenly anti-Semitic and upwardly mobile tended to be considerably more mobile than the others. Veterans with moderate increases in yearly income (up to $1,000) were more frequently tolerant than intolerant. However, among those veterans whose salaries increased $1,500 and more the number of outspoken anti-Semites equaled that of the tolerant veterans. This may tentatively be explained by the fact that sharp upward mobility is likely to be associated with marked aggressiveness in general. Sharp upward mobility implies changes in life patterns which produce great stress in the individuals involved. This was first observed by Durkheim in his study of suicides in Europe.[10] The data at hand indicate that while slow upward mobility is closely associated with tolerance, rapid mobility either upward or downward, is positively related to interethnic hostility.

In conclusion, it may be said that these data support the theory that intolerance becomes a more serious problem to the degree that large groups become downwardly mobile at a rapid pace owing to changes in the structure of society. The data also seem to indicate that to understand intolerance it is less important to concentrate on the social and economic background of the individual than to investigate the nature of his social mobility. The question which must be answered for each individual is whether or not he is being forced downwards or prevented from fulfilling his expectations of upward social mobility.[11]

[9] One of the authors of this study made a series of observations on the manner in which this group dealt with their frustrating experiences following the rapid loss of secure status. The vast majority reacted as described above. A small minority became even more tolerant than they had been, and rejected Hitler severely. But they paid a great price in increased anxiety, an anxiety which those avoided who accepted Hitler and found a discharge for their hostility in aggression against Jews and other outgroups.

[10] Durkheim, Emile: *Le Suicide*, F. Alcan, Paris, 1897.

[11] The same analysis was employed with respect to anti-Negro intolerance and revealed a pattern similar to that of anti-Semitism. For further discussion of this analysis, see Chapter VIII.

CHAPTER V

THE WAR EXPERIENCE[1]

Whatever the pattern of their life histories each of the men interviewed had had one common experience—the army. No matter how different their individual fate during the war may have been, it was something they had all shared to some degree. This shared experience permitted some objective evaluation of how reasonable they were in their attitudes toward their own experiences. A man who had been severely wounded had more obvious reason to complain than another whose worst experience was his separation from his family. The men were queried both as to their actual experiences in the army and their own evaluation of them. In this way, it was possible to determine whether tolerant and intolerant persons viewed comparable life experiences in the same way. The answer to this question was to provide evidence as to whether, in addition to the social and economic correlates (social mobility), there were also psychological correlates of intolerance, such as viewing one's experiences as deprivational, regardless of their objective character.

In setting up the questions, no effort was made to study the full impact of war experiences on a man's attitudes. The questions were designed to ascertain whether the reactions of veterans to wartime experiences were rather a reflection of their total personalities than of the actual content of their experiences. In particular, it was anticipated that the discussion and analysis of wartime experiences might produce data which could be used in testing the hypothesis that hostility toward out-groups is a function of the hostile individual's sense of past deprivation.[2] Therefore the veteran's war experiences were examined both in terms of the actual deprivations he experienced and of his feelings of deprivation.

[1] In this chapter no effort is made to study directly the impact of the war on inter-ethnic attitudes. The war experience is used solely as a means of analyzing the veterans' attitudes and outlooks on life.

[2] It was also anticipated that the analysis of wartime experiences would produce other pertinent data on attitudes toward the army. Some of them are discussed in Chapter VII.

On the other hand, it was also important to find which of the men reacted favorably to army life because they experienced it as a relief from the insecurities and routines of civilian life.

The different types of army experiences were classified on the basis of objective characteristics and the apparent deprivations associated with them, for example: (1) the objectively greater danger of combat service; (2) wounds and injuries; (3) length of service.

Nevertheless, the findings revealed that army experiences which seemed to involve objective deprivations were not related to differential degrees of interethnic intolerance.[3] Thus, as in the case of low economic status, where the objective deprivation which it implied was not positively related to intolerance, objective deprivations in the army were without relation to intolerance.

On the other hand, when a number of different approaches were employed to determine whether army life was subjectively experienced as deprivation, a *significant* association emerged between the expression of subjective feelings of deprivation and outspoken and intense anti-Semitic attitudes.

For example, the men were queried, "Do you feel that you got a bad break in your army career?"

Typical examples of responses by men who thought they had had a bad break were the following:

A twenty-seven year old private first-class said:

"Being in the infantry was a bad break—anything would have been better. You had no way to keep clean—we had the worst food of any."

Another twenty-seven year old private said he had had a bad break because:

"I wanted to get somewhere. But somebody else always got it. I deserved a rating and never got it. When they wanted somebody to repair something on a gun, I was always called because the other guy didn't know. That's why I never had no use for the army. They never gave a rating to a person who should get one."

On the other hand, some men felt it characteristic of the army to give men a good break. A twenty-nine year old private first-class said:

"I got a good break. I went to school and had the opportunity to be somebody. What I liked about the army is that they always give you a break."

A thirty year old staff sergeant had once been demoted; yet he bore no resentment and felt well satisfied with his lot. He said:

[3] For an analysis of these characteristics and their relationship to intolerance see Appendix Tables 9(A), 10(A), 11(A).

"In my army career I got a good break. I was made staff sergeant in 1942 only I was busted. But I made it back in another outfit. And I got to be mess sergeant, and mess sergeants eat good."

The responses revealed a sharp distinction between tolerant and intolerant veterans (Table 1(V)). Of those who claimed to have had a bad break in the army, almost five times as many were intolerant as tolerant. On the other hand, a considerable majority of those who claimed to have had a good break were tolerant.

TABLE 1(V)

"Do You Feel That You Got a Bad Break in
Your Army Career?"

	Tolerant		Stereotyped		Outspoken and Intense		Total	
	No.	Percentage	No.	Percentage	No.	Percentage	No.	Percentage
Good break	38	62	26	62	20	43	84	56
Bad break	3	5	5	12	16	34	24	16
"Normal"	13	21	5	12	3	6	21	14
Other	7	12	6	14	8	17	21	14
Total	61		42		47		150	

Below it will be shown that, by and large, both tolerant and intolerant persons had had the same type of army experience. Hence, the intolerant man's tendency to consider his fate as worse than it should have been was five times that of the tolerant man's. Equally interesting was the distribution of the opinion that one's fate was average; that one is (or was) not particularly "bad off" or the converse. Of those men who considered their fate in the army to have been "normal," over four times as many were tolerant as were intolerant.

Despite the clear association between subjective feelings of deprivation in the army and hostility toward ethnic minority groups such as the Jews, it should be noted that there was a small group of men who did not follow this pattern. Twenty expressed outspoken intolerance toward the Jews, but felt that they had had a good break in the army. On the other hand, three men who fell into the tolerant group claimed that they had had a bad break in the army.

Of course, the type of statistical analysis applied in this study reveals only the tendencies of attitudes to be related; almost never will there exist a perfect correlation. As a matter of fact, if a perfect correlation were to exist, it would probably mean that data on one and the same attitude were gathered under two different headings. Still, much could be learned about the relationship between attitudes from a study of deviant cases.

An examination of the interview records suggests interesting hypotheses which may partially explain why some of the men deviated from prevalent patterns. All three tolerant men who claimed that they had gotten a bad break in the army gave the same reason for their "bad break." In a general way they all resented the treatment they received from their officers. For example, a thirty-three year old air corps sergeant said:

"I wasn't treated right by those damn officers. There was no respect due to an enlisted man from an officer."

Thus, their feeling of having had a "bad break" was not due to an overall attitude toward the army but rather to a specific resentment of officers.

On the other hand, it is also striking that contrary grounds were offered by the intolerant men for their thinking they had gotten a good break in the army. Five of them, either in connection with this question or elsewhere in discussing army experiences, declared that they reacted favorably to the army because of the discipline of army life or because of the position of authority they held. For example, one intolerant man stated that what he liked most was:

"The discipline and the strong order. . . . If I were single I'd make a career out of it. I liked the physical culture, fitness."

A twenty-six year old sergeant said:

"I enjoyed every day of it. When you're home you have no steady routine, you do what you want when you want."

For three other intolerant men, army life was a "great adventure." For example, a twenty-six year old private first class said:

"It was a good experience; things happened that never would have happened. Going across, seeing some of the wonders of the world. Before that I never got farther than the north woods and never expected to go any farther. It's a good experience."

A thirty-one year old sergeant said:

"It's put more beef and muscle on me. . . . Panama was very beautiful and the Islands—they get you. I'd like to go back."

Clearly these eight of the twenty intolerant men felt that they had had a good break for reasons markedly different from the matter-of-fact attitude of having had a "good break" in the army which characterized tolerant veterans.

Another question designed to probe subjective feelings of deprivation, may also be discussed. Responses to: "Do you think the time you spent in the army set you back in any way?" revealed a statistically *significant* difference between tolerant and anti-Semitic veterans (Table 2(V)).

TABLE 2(V)

"Do You Think the Time You Spent in the Army Set You Back in Any Way?"

	Tolerant		Stereotyped		Outspoken and Intense		Total	
	No.	Percentage	No.	Percentage	No.	Percentage	No.	Percentage
Yes	29	47	19	45	36	77	84	56
No	26	43	15	36	9	19	50	33
Other	6	10	8	19	2	4	16	11
Total	61		42		47		150	

Here again, there was a greater tendency among intolerant persons to view their army experiences as deprivational. The tolerant men who expressed an opinion on this question were almost evenly divided as might well have been expected; but only a fifth of the anti-Semites saw their war experiences as having been no setback.

The tendency to "feel" that an experience was deprivational can coexist with the ability to objectively evaluate what has actually happened. The findings seem to suggest that intolerance is highly associated with feelings of deprivation and that such feelings persist despite the "knowledge" that one's fate was by no means particularly bad. If this is so, then it should be obvious that attempts to guide the individual to a rational view of past experiences must fail if emotional (and, one may add, unconscious) needs force the individual to view them as deprivational. Similarly, attempts to combat intolerance by means of rational arguments may fail for identical reasons.

In this connection, statements by certain veterans were striking in the degree to which they revealed the discrepancy between objective conditions and the individual's estimate of them. These veterans admitted frankly that frustrations suffered in the army were slight. Nevertheless, they expressed feelings of deep deprivation which revealed convictions of personal incompetence. For example, a twenty-five year old air corps mechanic who held the rank of corporal summarized his army career as follows:

"I did no fighting, I was never wounded, I was never hospitalized."

Yet, in answer to the question as to whether he had had a bad break in the army, he declared:

"I decided it was impossible to get ahead with the rules the army had and the way the game was being played. I couldn't do the things you had to do to get ahead. There's no use for one person to try to change things. If you want a rating, you let the sergeant make a loan that you know he won't repay."

Thus, for him, failure to rise in the ranks was a subjective frustration. His remarks revealed efforts to rationalize his real or felt incompetence in gaining promotion in the army, in exactly those terms which anti-Semites often use to rationalize their intolerance. He accused others of under-handed methods, against which it was useless to fight, and he considered the hated institution as so overpowering that it was impossible "for one person to try to change it."

A most convincing demonstration that objectively bad experiences do not necessarily lead to feelings of frustration and deprivation was found in the statement of a twenty-five year old ex-combat infantryman private first-class (not a corporal as in the case above), who fought in North Africa, Italy, and Germany, and who claimed, with some justification, that army life had ruined his health and set him back both in education and in the business world. He described his war experience as follows:

"I was a teletype operator in Africa for three or four months, and wasn't in combat then, but all the rest of the time I was laying wire in combat areas. We lost 80 per cent of our company. I never thought I had a chance to come out of it alive."

Yet when questioned about his "break" in the army, he declared:

"I came out lucky. I came out swell on money and passes. I didn't get any breaks, but to come back and be alive today is really swell."

It is not possible to say a priori that all combat soldiers experienced greater actual (as opposed to felt) deprivations, since a man might have experienced rough treatment while training in this country, and even have been maimed in the army without ever having seen the front. But, aside from these individual cases it may be assumed that, within a random sample, noncombat soldiers experienced the least actual hardship, combat soldiers the most, and combat-support troops something in between. The lack of any relationship between type of army service and subjective feelings of deprivation can be seen below, from Table 3(V). Whether the individual soldier felt he had had a bad break in the army proved independent of his war experience. In fact, the percentage of combat soldiers who felt they had had a bad break was somewhat lower than that of noncombat soldiers.

Thus, a man's evaluation of his army career in retrospect was largely independent of the actual deprivations experienced and depended mainly on his emotional attitude toward this experience in particular, and, one may add, to life experiences in general.

TABLE 3(V)

ARMY EXPERIENCE AND FEELINGS OF DEPRIVATION

	Combat		Combat Support		Noncombat	
	No.	Percentage	No.	Percentage	No.	Percentage
Good break	30	57	12	40	42	63
Bad break	7	13	4	13	13	19
Normal break; Other	16	30	14	47	12	18
Total	53		30		67	

Answers to specific interview questions on army experiences could be tabulated with exactness and statistically treated, but they did not encompass the totality of the war experience or the total reaction to it. Therefore, in an additional effort to study these reactions, the entire section of each interview dealing with wartime experiences was evaluated as a whole. In this evaluation an attempt was made to estimate the dominant feeling of the subject toward his army experience. It was found that the data permitted reliable judgments as to whether the veteran's responses indicated that he was either: (1) embittered about army life; (2) attached to it (gratified by it); (3) indifferent to it or had feelings about it which could not be clearly determined; or (4) accepted it in a matter-of-fact way. (See Appendix for reliability of coding procedures.)

When, on the basis of these categories of analysis, those men who accepted army life were contrasted with those who were embittered by it, a strikingly *significant* difference was found between the intolerant and tolerant veterans (Table 4(V)). The overwhelming majority of those who were tolerant had an attitude of acceptance toward army life. The outspokenly and intensely anti-Jewish veterans presented a completely reversed picture, in that they were overwhelmingly embittered toward it.[4]

TABLE 4(V)

ACCEPTANCE OF ARMY LIFE

	Tolerant		Stereotyped		Outspoken and Intense		Total	
	No.	Percentage	No.	Percentage	No.	Percentage	No.	Percentage
Accepted army life	44	81	21	64	6	17	71	50
Embittered about army life	6	11	7	21	20	56	33	35
Attached to, or gratified by Total	4	8	5	15	10	27	19	15
Total	54		33		36		123	

In evaluating the preceding table, it should be mentioned that mere "beefing" about the army was not evaluated as constituting embitterment. On the contrary, it was part of the mores of most enlisted men. Nor were statements about the army as being "O.K." considered as revealing attachment to army life.[5]

All sociopsychological investigations seem to indicate that attitudes toward the army are largely the result of experiences antedating enlistment. Thus, what these tables reveal about attitudes toward life, is largely independent of whether or not the individual was a soldier. Judging one's

[4] Similar patterns characterized the attitude of the veterans in respect to anti-Negro feeling. See Chapter VIII.

[5] Within a consensus society one would expect that in time of war such a central institution of society as the army would be accepted as "normal" in a matter-of-fact fashion. That fully 35 per cent of those who expressed their opinions in this type of interview should have revealed an essential embitterment toward army life, was therefore striking. To this figure of 35 per cent must be added the 15 per cent who were gratified by army life—again an attitude which in our society can hardly be considered a "normal" reaction to army experience. Thus, an underlying dissensus with one of the basic institutions of our society was found among 50 per cent of those who could be classified.

war experiences as either deprivational or not is a function of the individual's total personality or of the adequacy of his adjustive mechanisms in particular. The case material collected by Grinker and Spiegel[6] corroborates this observation for combat soldiers. Likewise, the fifth of the group who declared themselves attached to or gratified by the army experiences were disposed toward such a reaction because of long-standing factors. They displayed neither a general tendency to accept life experiences in a matter-of-fact fashion nor an ability to make the best of a given situation. These men liked army life because it offered gratifications not previously available to them in civilian life. An examination of their interview records indicates they were men who described their economic or social position before induction into the army as having been deprivational. They seemed to be men who were poorly adjusted to civilian society, and who found gratification and release in the particular adventure and comradeship of army life. They appreciated the "freedom" they experienced in the army from certain restrictions required by "nice" society. It was not surprising, therefore, that among this group there was a high concentration of intolerant men.

It is easier to understand why intolerance was much more frequent among those who rejected military life. The army—particularly during a time of war—is such a central institution of existing society that one cannot very well accept existing society and reject the army, or vice versa. Racial tolerance is the attitude officially favored by the spokesmen of existing society, although they themselves may follow customs condoning intolerance. But intolerance is not favored by the men who reject the army simply because official society condones it, though pretending to frown upon it. On the contrary, intolerance, like hating the army, is an expression of the same body of underlying tendencies, namely a dissatisfaction with existing society, which expresses itself through all channels available.

The thesis postulating an association between intolerance and rejection of existing society was such an important one that it had to be given further attention. When all has been said, the army as such is but one institution, and not the whole of existing society. To investigate this problem, the exclusively negative approach, namely the study of the rejection of institutions of existing society, would not do. There is hardly a man who does not disapprove of some aspect of existing society. And even if it were not so, according to the frame of reference within which this investigation proceeded, rejection of society, or the inability to form positive

[6] Grinker, R. R., and Spiegel, J. P.: *Men Under Stress*, The Blakiston Company, Philadelphia, 1945.

ties, was not considered an attitude basic to human nature, but rather an after-phenomenon, the consequence of not having formed positive attachments in infancy and childhood.[7] Therefore, it was considered equally important to study the individual's positive attachments in order to complete the picture of his attitudes toward existing society or any of its institutions. It was not enough to probe the individual's attitudes toward the army since this institution had certain features which might reasonably be rejected by the citizen who was unable to see beyond the petty annoyances of army life to the essential values at stake. The need thus arose to investigate the individual's positive ties to existing society and how their distribution related to intolerance. This was done chiefly in terms of national identification, for reasons outlined below.

The sample under investigation included many second generation Americans living in a metropolis and coming from a social and economic group which had inferior status within that city. They had all felt the impact of modern urban society with its high mobility and complicated division of labor, both of which tend to destroy the identification of the individual with primary and local groups. Instead, social identification and consensus among them was, in a measure, based on identification with functional organizations, and with more inclusive and national symbols of identification.

It is through these identifications that the individual gains a sense of belonging, a sense of personal security, and a sense of worth. It is obvious that the extent and strength of feelings of identification with more inclusive and national symbols of identification are not uniformly distributed throughout the community. For the purposes of this analysis, it seemed reasonable to assume that those sectors of the community where feelings of national identification are weak are made up of individuals whose personal disorganization, insecurity, and apprehension are relatively high.

Interviewing on army experiences presented an adequate opportunity to gather attitude data on identifications with the community at large— the nation. This section of the interview was chosen because in the context of reporting the hardships of wartime experiences, veterans seemed less likely to offer superficial verbalizations which fitted patriotic formulae.

Observers have pointed out that while the war was in progress, American soldiers were not apt to make spontaneous use of patriotic symbols in discussing the war, either among themselves, in conversations with Allied

[7] The valid assumption that rejection is due to an initial positive attachment which was frustrated may be disregarded here, since rejection as a reaction-formation following initial positive ties still signifies an absence of positive attachment at the present moment and a felt alienation from existing society.

troops and civilians in foreign countries, or for that matter, in conversations with the enemy during occupation. This same absence of a spontaneous use of patriotic symbols was encountered in the sample. It was
found that less than one-tenth of them referred favorably to such symbols during any part of the interview. (For example, "the United States,"
"the flag," "the nation," were considered as patriotic symbols or phrases.)
Three per cent referred negatively to such patriotic symbols, while the
bulk of the veterans (88 per cent) made no references to them whatsoever. The section of the interview dealing with wartime experiences
contained a wide range of questions, both direct and indirect, which
might well have supplied the opportunity for such responses.

However, these data throw little light on the actual extent of the men's
national identification. They merely indicate a pattern of speech according to which it is "silly" or in bad taste to express freely one's attitudes
in terms of traditional symbols of patriotism. This lack of a spontaneous
use of symbols, it should be noted, was typical for both intolerant and
tolerant veterans.

Since national and patriotic symbols were of no help in fixing the
degree to which a man felt he "belonged," other methods were used to
determine the character and extent of the veteran's identifications with
the nation, and his ability to identify with the objectives of the war. The
results of such probes indicated that, by and large, reasonably well
grounded identifications of such types were associated with significantly
greater intolerance.

For example, in an indirect attempt to probe identifications with the
war effort, the veterans were asked who gained through the success of
the war. The responses could be classified as to the presence or absence
of collective identifications. The men who employed collective symbols
which obviously included themselves, rather than specific symbols which
excluded them from the group who gained through victory, were *significantly* more tolerant. Collective identifications including the veteran
himself were such responses as: "we all gained," "the people," "our country," and the like (Table 5(V)).

As can be seen from the following table, only an approximate two-
thirds of the group used symbols which made it possible to determine
their attitudes.

Respondents who manifested their collective or national identifications,
as well as those who failed to manifest such identification, were not
characterized by any particular wartime experiences. Those who felt that

TABLE 5(V)

"WHO GAINED THROUGH THE WAR?"

	Tolerant		Stereotyped		Outspoken and Intense		Total	
	No.	Percentage	No.	Percentage	No.	Percentage	No.	Percentage
Collective symbols, including veteran	14	34	11	52	6	19	31	33
Nobody	19	46	5	24	4	12	28	30
Specific symbols, excluding veteran	8	20	5	24	22	69	35	37
Total	41		21		32		94	

they, too, were recipients of the benefits of the war, irrespective of the cost of the war to themselves, obviously had strong enough feelings of identification to believe that the results of their effort were beneficial to the country as a whole and thus also to themselves. They had a stronger sense of personal security, of "belonging," and these factors seemed intimately connected with a lesser need or desire to express hostile sentiments against particular groups—either functional or ethnic.

CHAPTER VI

ANXIETY AND INTOLERANCE

One of the basic problems on which this study has tried to throw light was the question of whether intolerance is a function of the hostile individual's anxiety. Those factors most popularly associated with intolerance —economic status and other social attributes—have already been examined in Chapter IV, where it was shown that for the group studied, low income was less related to intolerance than the decline of a person's socioeconomic status. In addition, the data in Chapter V have shown that actual hardships in the army were relatively unrelated to intolerance, while subjective feelings of deprivation were closely related to aggressive feelings against an outgroup. All these data suggest that contrary to prevalent belief, intolerance is less a function of the objective situation and more one of personal evaluation. Since anxiety originates in past experiences and attaches itself to what are considered dangers of the present or the future, the investigation then turned to an analysis of subjective attitudes about present and future tasks.

Here an important reservation must be made. A person may evaluate his position as precarious and still remain tolerant because he blames only himself for the circumstances of his life. Psychological studies of depressed individuals have shown that depression is due to critical and otherwise hostile feelings which have been turned inward against the self. If this interpretation of depression is accepted, then feelings of intolerance will, psychologically speaking, originate in a middle area between feelings of security and competence, and those of great self-criticism and depression.

There were seven men in the sample who evidenced considerably greater anxiety and pessimism than was characteristic of the majority of tolerant men (see also footnote page 120, Chapter VII). Some of these seven who were tolerant indicated tendencies towards severe self-criticism and toward a desire for greater punishment by their parents and/or more rigid discipline in the army. However, in the initial statistical treatment of the data on anxiety, all persons showing anxiety are grouped together in the following discussion, whether or not they directed their hostility toward an outgroup.

In studying the impact of anxiety on intolerance, it must be realized that although anxiety can be viewed as a psychological phenomenon, and as such is not directly related to events in the outside world, there are degrees of reasonableness in fear. Obviously a person whose position, experience, and special job-training make him relatively indispensable will have less reason to be anxious about a slight recession than a person without such security on the job. Therefore, an attempt to establish an unqualified association between intolerance and a fearful anticipation of what the future might have in store would have been erroneous. Persons who have valid reasons to be uneasy about the future, and who express such uneasiness freely, possess a different personality structure, and their apprehension is different in character, from those who are anxious about their future without valid reasons. Failure to discriminate between the two groups might have distorted the true picture of an association between anxiety and intolerance. The problem therefore arose of separating these groups, as it was possible to separate them in determining the actual deprivation they experienced in the army and their own evaluation of it (combat versus noncombat, wounded versus nonwounded men). The man who carefully evaluates his future and then correctly estimates it as bad is basically different from the man who is apprehensive without good reason.

Within the structure of this study it was relatively difficult to establish a reliable basis for evaluating how realistic a man's anticipation of his own future was. Therefore this was gauged by indirect methods. By asking the veteran to estimate future events, he was forced to base his answer on feelings of what the future had in store for everybody, rather than himself alone. In this way, his answers reflected his own feelings of optimism or pessimism rather than an evaluation of his personal life expectations. Such methods, moreover, had one great advantage—they eliminated to some degree the previously mentioned difficulty of isolating the person who is anxious about his future but finds it threatening because of his own shortcomings.

Questions about unemployment proved useful in learning about these anxieties. The depressive person who expected to experience failure because of his own incompetence was likely to begin with: "It won't be so bad, but as for me. . . ."

On the other hand, the person who tended to blame his failures on others rather than on himself was most likely to accept his fate not as something personal, for which he would have to carry responsibility, but as the common fate of his group. Such a man usually predicted that things would be "terrible for all."

Rather than attempt the impossible, namely to examine degrees of anxiety in all the major areas in which male adults must function (including their sexual role as husbands, their emotional tasks as fathers, or their economic duty to provide) as well as their fears about their health, or political change, it was preferred to make a careful analysis of the veterans' expectations in a few areas, particularly in economic and political matters where it was possible to infer the presence of underlying apprehensions.

For each man a discharge from the army meant facing anew the economic problems of civilian life. Before detailed questions were asked about specific insecurities and apprehensions, an effort was made to gauge a man's general level of optimism. During the initial portion of the interview, for example, the veterans were asked how they thought "things in general" would turn out.

The expression of optimism, regardless of the veteran's definition of "things in general," was *significantly* associated with tolerance toward Jews, as can be seen from Table 1(VI).

TABLE 1(VI)

OPTIMISM

	Tolerant		All Anti-Semites	
	No.	Percentage	No.	Percentage
Optimism	27	44	23	26
Pessimism	20	33	45	51
Other (including don't know)	14	23	21	23
Total	61		89	

This general question was followed by a number of related questions, one of which referred specifically to veterans. "Now that the veterans are back," they were asked, "how do you think they are going to get along?" This question allowed the veteran to project his own personal views on to the veteran public at large. The subjects who reported that veterans are (will be) getting along well, or very well, tended to be *significantly* more tolerant toward Jews than intolerant. Those who reported that the veterans are (will be) getting along badly or very dissatisfied, were more intolerant than tolerant (see Appendix Table A(12)).

The similarity of reaction to these quite similar questions speaks for the reliability of the instrument. Posing the question was also in line with the conversational character of the interview and led on to a discussion of specific complaints and circumstances interfering with the welfare of veterans. No correlation was found between intolerance and specific gripes such as the lack of housing and decent paying jobs, or difficulties in getting former jobs back.

While general feelings of optimism or pessimism—and their relation to intolerance—could be studied from the reactions to these questions, they permitted no estimates of the reasonableness of the men's expectations. A more specific study of attitudes underlying optimism and pessimism was made on the basis of reactions to the government program for veterans, in particular the G. I. Bill of Rights. Responses to questions about the bill revealed a tendency among some veterans to feel both cheated and deprived because "not enough is being done for the veteran," and also a tendency to fear the future, where the men felt that the Bill provided inadequate assistance. The government aid program was available to all veterans on an equal basis. Therefore to criticize it as inadequate indicated either a feeling of deprivation (not receiving enough) or fearful anticipation (not being provided for in the future), or both. The belief that enough was being done for the veterans was *significantly* related to tolerance toward the Jews. The reversed pattern was encountered among the outspoken and intense anti-Semites (see Table 2(VI) below).

TABLE 2(VI)

"Do You Think Enough Is Being Done for the Veterans Now?"

	Tolerant		Stereotyped		Outspoken and Intense		Total	
	No.	Percentage	No.	Percentage	No.	Percentage	No.	Percentage
Enough	36	59	16	38	12	26	64	43
Not enough	16	26	17	41	27	58	60	40
Other	7	12	6	14	5	10	18	12
Don't know	2	3	3	7	3	6	8	5
Total	61		42		47		150	

In spite of the foregoing it would be incorrect to evaluate reactions to the government aid program without considering the realities of the veteran's life situation. Certain provisions of the program added to the earning power and well-being of men who were well able to support themselves and their families without such aid. They were relatively less satisfactory for men without means of livelihood who had also to care for dependents. Therefore reactions to the bill had also to be analyzed in terms of the man's economic status.

Statements about the adequacy of the veterans' program were compared with the veterans' actual income at the time of the interview and the two were found to be entirely unrelated. The following table shows that in all income groups the men were evenly divided in their opinions.

TABLE 3(VI)

"DO YOU THINK ENOUGH IS BEING DONE FOR THE VETERANS NOW?"

Income at Time of Interview	Number	
	Yes	No
Up to $3,000	39	40
Over $3,000	14	12
Unemployed	3	4
Student	5	3
Total	61	59

Thus while anti-Semitism was associated with the feeling of deprivation (that not enough was being done) this feeling was *not* related to current income level and the higher degree of security and comfort which higher income levels imply.

Intolerant men who feared that veterans would find it hard to get along tended to mix their personal difficulties with their estimates of the situation in general. Usually, their remarks elaborated in great detail the many sources of difficulty which they claimed were beyond the control of the individual veteran. For example, a veteran who was intensely hostile to Jews and Negroes declared:

"There's little prosperity today. On the whole veterans won't get along too good. They're running into the housing shortage, lack of funds, poor physical health, and difficulty in free enterprise. He isn't able to advance himself. He's hampered by people refusing to help him. If he tries to get into business—look at the cab company. If he wants to open a tavern he can't get a license. They say they give him seniority, but they don't. If a man's been with a company for four years while the veteran was at war, he gets more money than the veterans. The company doesn't give the veteran seniority because he doesn't want to hurt the man who's been with him for these four years. The disabled veteran can't get hospitalization. There's a lack of sufficient hospitals. He can't get a physical checkup until his claim is settled. I was turned down at Hines (the local veteran's hospital). I filed my claim six months and haven't heard from it yet."

Complaints of intolerant veterans who felt that not enough was being done for them were frequently characterized by a sense of being cheated or defrauded through no fault of their own:

"They're just putting up a big front and it's colorful on paper only. They're doing a few good things for the veteran but they're certainly not living up to what they said they would do. They should have jobs with a pay scale according to ability. The employers aren't giving credit for what the veteran learned in the service. They won't hire if the veteran hasn't had civilian experience and the veteran doesn't get a chance to prove his ability. They should also do something about living costs and housing."

By contrast, tolerant men who thought veterans were getting along well, gave responses which were usually less personalized and they revealed a willingness and ability to make more objective estimates of the situation as a whole. For example, one tolerant man felt that veterans fared "very well," and added:

"Most have seen enough of travel and are willing to settle down. It may take a little while for them to settle down. They appreciate home. It may take a little while for them to tone down. They may be nervous for six months to a year, but he'll be better than if he'd never been overseas. They've seen enough of the rest of the world to appreciate this country. England and France haven't a thing compared to this country."

Another tolerant man said:

"The majority are doing fine. Most of them are glad to get home, settle down, marry and have families. Ultimately, they'll reach the objective."

The responses of tolerant men tended to emphasize, or at least to recognize, the possibilities for individual initiative in availing themselves of governmental aid; they appeared more self-reliant in this respect. Two typical examples were:

"It seems like it (that enough is being done for the veteran). The state's trying to put through a bonus and there's all kinds of schooling if the veteran wants to take advantage of it."

"They've given them most every opportunity. The Employment Service gives them preference on jobs and they've encouraged the G. I.'s to continue their education under the G. I. Bill."

FEAR OF UNEMPLOYMENT

In discussing whether they had had a good or bad break in the army, or whether the V.A. program was adequate, the men were talking about matters on which they had reasonably adequate evidence for forming a judgment. When speaking of how things were likely to turn out, they had to speculate about what the future held in store for them and such speculation was strongly colored by their personal outlook on life. In terms of the characteristics of the sample, the economic well-being of most of the men would depend on their ability to secure employment. Therefore, in order to secure data on the relationship between intolerance and feelings of personal insecurity, the interviewees' fears about being unemployed were investigated. Anxiety about their economic future was not fully revealed in response to any one single question. Statements indicating fear of unemployment, or the conviction that, come what may, a man would always be able to make a living, appeared not only on direct question, but also in response to such questions as whether enough was being done for the veterans, or who should be given priority on the job. It was necessary to analyze an entire section of the interview in order to secure adequate data on apprehensions about unemployment. Table 4(VI) presents the conclusions of two independent analysts, who classi-

TABLE 4(VI)

APPREHENSION ABOUT UNEMPLOYMENT

	Tolerant		Stereotyped		Outspoken and Intense		Total	
	No.	Percentage	No.	Percentage	No.	Percentage	No.	Percentage
Low apprehension	17	28	5	12	4	9	26	17
Moderate apprehension	29	47	22	52	25	53	76	51
Great apprehension	15	25	15	36	18	38	48	32
Total	61		42		47		150	

fied this portion of the interview into three categories of high, moderate, and low apprehension about unemployment.[1] Examination of the table reveals a *significant* relationship between economic apprehensions and intolerance.

One-half of the sample showed an attitude of moderate apprehension, which was about equidistant from exaggerated fear and uncritical optimism. This attitude may be considered a "normal" evaluation of the chances for unemployment as they existed at the time of the interviews. This attitude was characteristic for approximately the same group which accepted army life matter-of-factly, without either enjoying the experience or being overcritical about it. Thus, again, the same percentage took a more or less matter-of-fact attitude on a central economic problem of our society.[2] That half of the sample expressed moderate apprehension about the future at the time of the interview has other important implications for an understanding of intolerance.

Table 4(VI) also shows that only the low apprehension group was considerably more tolerant. The middle group and the very apprehensive group displayed a similar pattern as regarded tolerant, stereotyped and outspoken attitudes toward the Jews. Still, a fourth of the men who had great apprehension about their future were, nevertheless, tolerant. Thus, although there was an association between apprehension and intolerance, there was little basis for believing that a high degree of apprehension was characteristic of a high degree of intolerance. If one dared to predict on the basis of these data, one might say that any shift from low to even moderate apprehension would be likely to increase the frequency and intensity of anti-Semitic feelings, while a shift from moderate to great apprehension might produce less marked consequences in this respect, provided the degree of apprehension did not become extreme—our data permitted no generalizations on the possible consequences of extreme apprehension.

Since the fear of unemployment is, among other factors, a consequence of feeling unable to protect oneself against it, the veterans were questioned as to how well they felt able to cope with the problem of future unemployment. More than 40 per cent indicated that they had no resources with which to meet a depression. The few persons who claimed they need not fear a depression (22 per cent) were those who stressed

---

[1] The percentage error in classifying these data, as reported above, was 8.0 per cent.

[2] In terms of an ideal statistical distribution, it is significant that the curve, although normal in the middle area where half of the sample was located, was so obviously overweighted with respect to great apprehension. There, twice as many men were found as in the low apprehension group, indicating an imbalance toward fear.

that their current jobs were ones which offered security even in bad times. In the main, these were civil servants and public utility workers. Within this group the tolerant, stereotyped, and outspoken anti-Semites were evenly distributed. Apparently such "job security" had no direct effect on the degree of intolerance. Less than 5 per cent mentioned financial resources. Compared with such external security, only less than 5 per cent mentioned personal skill and social qualifications—the traditional bases for success and security in the United States.

By contrast, tolerant men who felt secure (low apprehension about unemployment) made relatively frequent reference to the fact that they were part of a family group which was so well knit that each member could rely on the support of the others.

"There are three of us working in my family. I don't think all of us would be out of work at one time. My sister works at the telephone company, and she works on pensions and if there were unemployment they would still have to have someone working in pensions. My other sister works in a hospital and she certainly wouldn't lose her job. People are always sick. I don't think it would hurt us very much."

In view of the fact that tendencies to react violently to frustrating experiences are by no means restricted to ethnic hostility, it may be mentioned that five of the seven men who predicted resort to violence in the event of another depression were also strongly intolerant toward Jews. All of them were also strongly intolerant of Negroes as well. A few examples may illustrate predictions of violence in the event of a depression. The last of them was most explosive and also provides an example of how violence in ethnic relations was spontaneously mentioned in response to the seemingly unrelated question of possible unemployment during a depression.

"The next depression will be pretty bad because you have a lot more children than you had in the last one, and a lot of these soldiers have been taught to use a gun and they'll use it. You know yourself, you're not going to see your children starve."

"My family will eat, and I will. I don't know how but I'll get it. I'm a believer in self-preservation."

"We'd better not have it. Chicago'll blow wide open. On South Park the niggers are gettin' so smart. We'll have a race riot that'll make Detroit look like a Sunday School picnic. So many are bitter about the part the Negro played in the war. They got all the soft jobs—in the quartermasters, engineers. They're no good for anything else. The white got his ass shot off. They're pretty bitter. If both whites and niggers get laid off, that'll be bad. I'm gonna eat. I know how to use a gun."

It was to be expected that recollections of the last depression would lead to fears about future depression, unemployment, and deprivation. Many answers indicated that the impact of the last depression was still keenly felt. Only seven veterans stated that they had no recollection of it because they had been too young. Only a fourth said that their families got along pretty well, while approximately 40 per cent stated that they and their families had suffered to some degree. The rest (nearly a third) said they had suffered very much.

When the men's recollections were classified on the basis of their anti-Semitic attitudes a *significant* difference in degree of intolerance was revealed as between those who claimed to have suffered to some degree and those who said that they got along pretty well (Table 5(VI) below). Those who got along well were the most tolerant.

Thus the individual's evaluation of his economic past and of his economic future were both shown to be statistically related to his inter-ethnic attitudes. Thus too, it seemed that the tendency to view things optimistically or pessimistically was more a function of the individual's personality—as was the degree of his intolerance—than of any particular

TABLE 5(VI)

RECOLLECTIONS OF THE DEPRESSION

	Tolerant		All Anti-Semites		Total	
	No.	Percentage	No.	Percentage	No.	Percentage
Suffered to some degree	38	64	69	82	107	75
Got along pretty well	21	36	15	18	36	25
Total	59		84		143	

past experience. Further confirmation was found in the fact that the tendency to recollect the last depression as having been deprivational was associated to some degree[3] with fear of unemployment in the future. However, it should be noted that this association was by no means as marked as the association between either form of pessimistic evaluation and anti-Semitism. In some measure it was to be expected that the link established between intolerance and subjective feelings of deprivation during the war would also hold true for recollections of the last depression.

[3] Significant at the 0.06 level.

188   DYNAMICS OF PREJUDICE

Typical of the responses of intolerant veterans recollecting deprivations during the last depression were the following:

"Very bad, hit us right between the eyes. It got so bad that we had to apply for relief until my brother and I were old enough to go to work. I had to go to sea for six months, because I wasn't old enough to work, and then came back and started working. That's why I didn't get to finish high school."

"Well, my old man worked until 1930. I was about ten or eleven when things got really bad, and the humiliations and insults are hard to take. I've seen so many of these relief workers they make you antisocial. This one bitch, a Polack, wanted to slap me on W.P.A. I got fired for nonsupport, so I got a private job at $15.00 a week and that was pretty good. My family had to send me to live with another family because they couldn't afford to have me live with them."

Almost every member of our society is at least occasionally subject to feelings of uneasiness about his economic future. The men in the sample seemed particularly exposed to economic set-backs such as unemployment. The association between apprehension about unemployment and intolerance has already been established. The next question to be investigated was why the tolerant men were less fearful of unemployment and what gave them the security to look to the future with relative calm.

During the last depression, the assurance of at least the bare necessities of life depended, for many people, either directly or indirectly on governmental or other forms of public support. Since then, social security legislation has broadened that minimal basis still further. Moreover, the lessons of the last depression have not been forgotten and the nation is more prepared to combat a depression—particularly in its deprivational consequences for the individual. None of the men doubted that the government would have to supply relief in the event of large scale unemployment. Most of them were convinced that the machinery of unemployment compensation, works programs and so on would be more adequate than in the last depression. They were also more or less convinced that, as they put it, they "wouldn't starve." Why, then, were the majority of the intolerant men fearful in anticipation of future depressions, and the majority of the tolerant men much more secure in this respect? It may well have been that only those men could find security in the conviction that governmental help would be forthcoming, who were not only convinced they would get relief when they needed it but also felt themselves part of that large social community, the nation.

The history of the German republic provides some confirmation of this hypothesis. After the first World War, the socialistic and democratic parties instituted a social security program. When large scale unemployment set in, unemployment relief aroused little resentment at first and then, only because it was inadequate. In general, it was accepted as a source of relative security, and was not regarded as a stigma on the individual. As a matter of fact, many workers took pride in the program as something they had fought for which was now helping the entire community. Moreover, it was administered by agencies of what those on relief still considered "their" government. At the same time, it was even then regarded as degrading by the small nondemocratic minority of workers who hated the government and who felt it degrading to accept money from a regime which stood for everything they detested. Similar reasons accounted for the hatred of the conservative officers' caste for the democratic government which nevertheless provided them with jobs and pensions. In terms of their caste mores, they felt it particularly degrading to have to accept money from persons and parties whom they despised. The fate of the German republic might have been different if these conservative circles had considered the democratic government "their" government and could therefore have been able to accept pensions without feeling degraded, or guilty for accepting money from a government against the very existence of which they conspired.

When German party coalitions changed and the conservative element held the balance of power, the attitude of nearly all recipients of unemployment relief seemed to change with it. Accepting relief from a hated government which was opposed to the relief program and distributed benefits only unwillingly no longer provided security but only a livelihood —if that—and added to the feeling of deprivation.

It might be assumed that those who feel part of the government can derive emotional security from being an integral part of it, while those who feel themselves outsiders, rejecting or feeling rejected by the government, will feel even more insecure just because of these factors.

The following analysis of political attitudes investigates the data assembled in this study on the validity of the proposition that economic security (and therefore intolerance) is related to a feeling of political identification with the nation.

POLITICAL ATTITUDES

It was of prime interest to learn whether the men felt that they had a real stake in the nation as a whole, whether they felt part of it, and how such feelings related to intolerance. How did the individual view our political system? Did he feel overpowered by the system in general and the existing party system in particular? Did he believe that he as an individual could look toward political action in general, and his own in particular, as means which would help him to achieve his personal goals?

A study of political attitudes with objectives such as those of this investigation could not assume the veteran's ability or inclination to verbalize an explicit system of political opinions. Even the absence of such an articulate system of political opinions and values could hardly be accepted as evidence that they were nonexistent and that the individual was politically disinterested, or that he did not feel that politics affected him. The high percentage of "don't know" responses to political questions on many opinion polls is misleading in this respect. They may reveal something about the individual's attitudes toward existing parties and the limited alternatives they offer at the moment, but they prove little about the personal political opinions of the subject. There are many people who do not seem to view political problems merely as alternative collective actions with which the individual may or may not concur. A "political problem" frequently centers around an individual's personal concerns and the way in which collective action would affect himself, his income and his family. Therefore, in dealing with political problems, questions were asked which would encourage the men to state their political views as if they were dealing with personal problems. It was left to them to decide whether they wished to conceive of a problem, so introduced, as one which required personal action on their own part, or collective and political action on the part of a group.

Probing for the men's conception of positive goals in national affairs was revealing only in so far as it showed that most veterans had given little thought to such problems. In response to such questions as "What do you think can be done to insure a decent life for us?" there was a marked absence of positive recommendations; almost nothing was evoked save criticism of existing conditions. The men were much more articulate about the obstacles which, in all likelihood, would prevent them from achieving their own individual ends. Then they repeated their gripes, but in more specific and elaborate form. The question which introduced this discussion was: "What will interfere with our having a decent life?"

The majority of the answers tended to be concerned with personal problems of an immediate economic character. Fear of inflation was mentioned most frequently, that is by almost a fourth of the group (24 per cent). Next most frequently came complaints about the greediness of people (21 per cent). It should be mentioned that at the time of the interview most men found themselves buyers in a seller's market. Moreover, the two things many of them needed most, dwelling quarters and a car, were accessible only by catering to a group of people of whom many were profiteering. This may explain why greediness was so high up on the list. Disgust with politicians and political parties was also quite high (19 per cent), but again local conditions may have exercised some influence. Dissatisfaction with the local Kelly-Nash (Democratic) machine, which had dominated the city for many years, was widespread, and its deficiencies were well advertised. There was also considerable dissatisfaction with the Republican state government. Compared with these dissatisfactions, the conviction that another war would interfere with the enjoyment of life was not frequently mentioned (13 per cent), although another 10 per cent decried our too international foreign policy which might involve us in another war. Thirteen per cent mentioned big business and monopolies. In view of the widespread fear of unemployment, which emerged later in the interview, it should be noted that depression and unemployment were spontaneously mentioned by only 9 per cent of the group as factors which were likely to interfere with the prospect of a decent life.

The selection of a particular obstacle as interfering with a decent life bore no correlation to tolerance or intolerance toward Jews.

None of these dissatisfactions seemed to reveal underlying attitudes. They seemed to be repetitions of current slogans, although each man emphasized different gripes. Reflective of what seemed more persistent attitudes were answers to the question: "Do you think that what the government has been doing these days is affecting the liberties of the ordinary people?" A third of the veterans thought that their liberties were impaired by governmental interference. They were *significantly* more tolerant than those who felt either that government action was not affecting their liberties, or that it was necessary or helpful.

Attitudes toward governmental actions which might be characterized as interfering with the liberties of the ordinary people may, in parts, have been influenced by the men's attitudes toward the party in power. In order to be certain that the relationship between tolerance and identification with the nation was not due to an equation of the government in power with the nation as a whole, another measure was employed to gauge acceptance of the existing political system. A man might violently reject the party in power and still feel himself identified with the nation's political institutions, if he assumed for instance, that at some future date his party would be able to exercise an important influence on the state.

TABLE 6(VI)

"Do You Think That What the Government Has Been Doing These Days Is Affecting the Liberties of the Ordinary People?"[a]

	Tolerant		Stereotyped		Outspoken and Intense		Total	
	No.	Percentage	No.	Percentage	No.	Percentage	No.	Percentage
Gov. is affecting liberties	20	33	14	33	22	47	56	37
Gov. is not affecting liberties to any great extent	24	39	12	29	15	32	51	34
These restrictions are necessary; are helpful	11	18	11	26	3	6	25	17
Some Americans have too much freedom	0	0	1	2	1	2	2	1
Don't know	6	10	4	10	6	13	16	11
Total	61		42		47		150	

[a] The level of significance in this table is .05.

TABLE 7(VI)

Attitude Toward Parties in General

	Tolerant		Stereotyped		Outspoken and Intense		Total	
	No.	Percentage	No.	Percentage	No.	Percentage	No.	Percentage
Rejected the major political parties	17	28	14	33	22	47	53	35
Accepted major political parties	24	39	10	24	14	30	48	32
No opinion or indeterminate	20	33	18	43	11	23	49	33
Total	61		42		47		150	

Thus another estimate of a person's identification with our political system, and hence the nation, could be found in his acceptance or rejection of the party system which characterizes the political life of this nation.

In Chapter IV it was reported that no significant association was encountered between intolerance and nominal political party affiliation. Table 7(VI) above shows that a *significant* relationship exists between ethnic intolerance and attitudes toward the existing major political parties in general. Those veterans who rejected or condemned the political party system, regardless of whether they declared in favor of one of the two major parties or claimed to vote for it, were *significantly* more intolerant than those who accepted or approved of political parties as they were currently set up.[4]

Despite this rejection of the two major parties and of the existing political system, there emerged no tendency on the part of the intolerant veteran to display a sense of genuine individualism. The contrary, in fact, appeared to be true. Among the men who rejected the existing political party system were those who threatened violent action in the event of serious economic difficulties. They expressed a desire for action which could be characterized as explosive and chaotic, but without stable direction. Nevertheless, these men did not conceive of their actions as leading to a change in the structure of society.

The absence of any sense of genuine individualism emerged most clearly from the responses to the question of who should be the agent to take action in their behalf. The particular suggestions as to what should be done to assist the veteran in adjusting to civilian life were closely connected with specific gripes. Of those who had specific suggestions to make, more than 40 per cent designated the government as the proper agent to implement them. The veterans themselves were mentioned by only 9 per cent of the group, while another 5 per cent invoked the symbol of "the people."

The selection of the agent who should undertake the reforms or provide the assistance suggested by the veteran was *significantly* related to their depth of intolerance. The intolerant group (whose tendency to reject the existing political system and to think government interfered too much was mentioned above) was most prone to call upon the government to aid the veterans. Fifty-eight per cent of the outspoken and intense anti-Semites thought the government should take care of the

---

[4] The analytical categories of acceptance, rejection, or indeterminate were applied to the entire section of the interview dealing with political parties, since no single question was adequate.

veterans, or should at least assist them considerably more than it was doing. Only 38 per cent of the tolerant men expressed similar views. While such demands may seem reasonable for the tolerant veterans, whose tendency to accept the existing political system has been established, it certainly reveals an apparent contradiction in attitudes among the intolerant group. This may be exemplified by the statements of two intensely anti-Semitic men.

One of them made disparaging statements about both political parties throughout the interview. He could not "see either one of them in power." His notion of the working of the two-party system was confused, and his hatred for both parties was so great, that he felt "we should have a split ticket and let them fight it out. We shouldn't have more than half of each in power." He was very critical of governmental efforts in behalf of the veterans; as a matter of fact, he was most critical of anything the government did, or might do. Nevertheless when asked who should provide the abundant assistance for the veterans which he considered the required minimum, he answered: "The War Department, since it put him (the veteran) in the position he's in."

The other man was also highly dissatisfied with both parties, and felt that aid to veterans was a far cry from being adequate. But when asked who should better things, he replied: "The veterans will never do anything for themselves. The government will give them the benefits coming to them."

Thus, while many tolerant men felt either that enough was being done for them and thus approved of governmental actions in their behalf (or felt able to take care of themselves without added assistance), the intolerant men tended to reject the political system on which the government rested but to call on it for the help which they felt otherwise unable to secure. It should not be overlooked that statements such as those quoted above, which were quite characteristic for men who rejected the government, nevertheless showed a certain expectation that the government would "give them the benefits coming to them."

Some insight into this attitude may be found in the collective findings of this study on tendencies which prevailed among the intolerant group: They rejected the government, they felt that not enough was being done for the veteran, they were apprehensive about their economic future, and they showed a lack of identification with national symbols. It seems altogether likely that these attributes were closely connected with one another in the intolerant men's personalities. Perhaps their feelings that not enough was being done for them originated in their insecurity about governmental help, which was due in turn to their rejection of the existing political system which again therefore, could not provide them with a feeling of security. Perhaps, on the other hand, those who felt that ours is a workable system of government and a true provider for the needs of the people, derived considerable comfort from the conviction that the government would fulfill its role in providing at least a minimum standard of living.

If this analysis were valid, then the reason for the intolerant men's inability to find security in the thought that the nation would carry the burden for their well-being in times of need may well have been psychological rather than economic. Why did the intolerant men's conviction that they would be cared for by the government to some degree fail to provide them with security? Very possibly the prospect of receiving economic help from that large family, the nation, offered security only to those who felt themselves emotionally part of the social community. To those who rejected their community and its representation, the government, accepting help took on a degrading character. Such help, therefore, could offer only physical comfort but not emotional security, for that requires the feeling that one's self-respect, if not one's status, be protected. By contrast, it should be recalled that some tolerant men found security as regarded their future in the fact that they could rely on receiving help from other members of their family.

This hypothesis found support in clinical observations of persons who had fallen out with their families, who rejected their relatives and felt rejected by them. When in need, the majority of them would accept help from the hated members of the family. But little security was derived from such help because it was detrimental to their self-respect. They looked forward to receiving it as just one more emotional (though not economic) deprivation which was being forced upon them.

Yet in spite of the foregoing, anxiety cannot be inferred solely from a man's economic apprehension and his estimate of governmental assistance in that regard. In the modern world—torn by national rivalries and the actuality of their eruptions—the individual's reactions to the threat of war are also a measure of his anxiety. Economic security is by no means the only protection which a well-functioning government provides for the people. The government is also looked upon as a securer of external and internal peace. If the previous assumptions were valid, it was to be expected that those tolerant men who showed their tendency to accept the government would derive relative security from the thought that it would also be able to fulfill its protective functions. On the other hand, men who rejected the government would feel insecure about the government's ability to provide security in these respects.

Intolerant men did in fact reveal a tendency to feel threatened by future events which were in many ways related to security. Such feelings were often coupled with feelings of despair about the chance of altering the course of events. Feelings of political inevitability and vague anxiety about the future characterized the intolerant veterans.

Opinion on the chances for a long peace, for example, was divided about evenly among those who thought the chances were good, those who thought they were poor, and those who thought it depended on circumstances. Those who felt the chances were good were *significantly* more tolerant than those who felt they were poor (Table 8(VI)).

TABLE 8(VI)

"WHAT DO YOU THINK ARE THE CHANCES FOR A LONG PEACE?"

	Tolerant		Stereotyped		Outspoken and Intense		Total	
	No.	Percentage	No.	Percentage	No.	Percentage	No.	Percentage
Good	23	38	15	36	11	23	49	33
Poor, slim	19	31	10	24	20	43	49	33
Depends	19	31	17	40	16	34	52	34
Total	61		42		47		150	

The relation between intolerance and a general inclination to feel threatened was also encountered in other respects. For example, when asked, "Do you think there are any threats to peace inside the country?" about 40 per cent of the sample declared, in effect, "There aren't any at the moment." This response, was found to be *significantly* concentrated among those veterans who had the least amount of intolerance. The number of responses were too small to differentiate statistically among other frequently employed symbols of threat on the part of the intolerant veterans. The latter tended to refer to labor disputes, foreign diplomats, and "spies." Ten veterans mentioned race riots or racial problems, and eight of them were either outspokenly or intensely intolerant.

The most frequently attributed threat coming from outside the United States was Russia (59 per cent). The next most frequently alleged was England (10 per cent); while only a small minority (16 per cent) felt secure enough to declare that there were no external threats to the

United States. When these responses were classified by anti-Semitic attitudes, there was a tendency—although not statistically significant—for Russia to be labeled as a threat more often by the intolerant veterans.

As an index of the individual's attitude toward politics, the veterans' use of the symbol "common man" when referring to themselves in the context of political problems was tabulated and analyzed. The contextual use of the phrase leaves little doubt as to what meaning it implied for the individual, or what purpose it served him. It was an expression of his rejection of personal involvement in politics. It bore none of the equality or self-assertiveness associated with earlier democratic ideology. On the contrary, it represented an inability to cope with politics as well as a lack of personal self-reliance. It gave expression to the individual's desire to abandon political decisions to other men and may well have been expressive of feelings of inferiority.

TABLE 9(VI)

REFERENCE TO THE COMMON MAN

	Tolerant		Stereotyped		Outspoken and Intense		Total	
	No.	Percentage	No.	Percentage	No.	Percentage	No.	Percentage
References to the common man	19	31	16	38	25	53	60	40
Absence of such symbols	42	69	26	62	22	47	90	60
Total	61		42		47		150	

The use of this symbol[5] was *significantly* related to the expression of ethnic intolerance (see Table 9(VI)). Of the sixty veterans who made use of the phrase, about one-half made repeated use of it. Not only was intolerance related to use of the symbol, but there also appeared to be a rough association between the *amount* of intolerance and the frequency of using this stereotype. This was particularly the case among those who employed the phrase more than four times in the course of the interview. Thus ethnic intolerance was found to be positively associated with this symbol of personal and political insecurity.

[5] The symbol "common man" was defined to include "little man" and "ordinary man."

CHAPTER VII

TOLERANCE: A FUNCTION OF CONTROL

The significance of anxiety as a factor contributing to ethnic hostility has been demonstrated in the previous chapter. It would be incomplete, however, merely to predicate that experiences which produce anxiety in the individual will necessarily contribute to overt hostility—either ethnic or otherwise. The fact that individuals experience anxiety without manifesting hostility in their actions, as well as the fact that they may behave aggressively without being intolerant in ethnic matters, shows that the relationship between ethnic intolerance and anxiety needs further elaboration. In terms of dynamic psychology, anxiety is experienced when the organism is flooded with excitation which cannot be mastered or manipulated. Vernacular speech has long recognized the relationship between explosive or hostile discharge and the inability to master emotions, by describing a person as having "lost control" of himself. Control, or more technically speaking, the ability to store tension internally, or to discharge it in socially constructive action rather than unwarranted hostile action, thus becomes a central problem in the study of intolerance.

Each individual who is not plainly psychotic is able to exercise some control over his discharge of tension. The predominant mechanisms of control which a person uses for dealing with inner tensions are among the most important elements characterizing his personality. Each of these mechanisms is more or less adequate for containing a particular type of aggression generated in the individual by anxiety. These controls or restraints remain adequate only if the level of tension does not become overpowering and thereby create unmasterable anxiety. At some level, for each individual, tension becomes disruptive of whatever controls the individual has learned to develop.

The problem which confronts the student of intolerance is not one of a total or long term (psychotic) breakdown of controls. Temporary breakdowns of control, including panic, such as may occur in race riots or other explosive outbursts of violence, are of major importance in the analysis of intolerance, but these remained outside the scope of this

study. Hitler's anti-Semitism, for example, was so devastating because—
although irrational in origin as is all interethnic hostility—it was controlled enough to permit an effective anti-Semitic policy to be carried out
step by step rather than in one big explosive action.[1]

On the contrary, it may be said that interethnic hostility is a symptom
of the individual's effort to maintain balance in his psychic economy by
discharging tension through the channel of ethnic intolerance. Obviously,
excess tension can be readily discharged when socially acceptable channels
for such discharge are available. When no such channels are available, the
capacity to discharge tension aggressively depends on the structure of
individual controls opposing such asocial behavior. The problem which
presents itself is thus at least twofold: (1) Why are some persons subject to controls strong enough to prevent them from discharging tension
aggressively against outsiders; (2) Why, of all available channels, do
other persons find it most expedient to discharge tension in interethnic
hostility.

The foregoing chapter has established the positive relation between
degree of intolerance and intensity of apprehension; in this chapter an
effort is made to analyze the relationship between controls and intolerance.

The source of the individual's control lies in the impact which societal
authority makes on his developing personality. The strength of his controls rests on the success he achieves in integrating these requirements
into his personality. Clinical observations suggest the manner in which
early childhood experiences determine the patterns by which the individual incorporates the demands of society. Short of the psychoanalytical
investigation of every individual, it would have been impossible to reconstruct this process for each member of the sample. Nevertheless, and in
terms of this study, an effort was made to isolate a number of important
authority constellations in the lives of the subjects and to evaluate the
individual's reactions to these institutions as a measure of the adequacy
of his controls. This made it possible to examine the relationship between
the individual's controls and his manifestations of ethnic intolerance.

At this point it should be stated that the *acceptance* of an authority in
the shaping of which the individual exercises a relatively high degree of
autonomy, (such as when changing party affiliation on purely ration-

[1] Dr. Kelley, in his psychiatric study of the twenty-two main defendants at the
Nuremberg trials, all of whom were anti-Semites, found only one of them to be psychotic in the clinical sense of the term. (Kelley, Douglas McG.: *22 Cells in Nuremberg*, London, W. H. Allen, 1947.)

alistic grounds), is radically different from *submission* to authority. As varied as religious and political institutions are and as varied as the men's reactions to them were, most of the men viewed them as relatively immutable. Only a very small minority felt that they could influence existing political parties to any extent or that their vote would make much difference. Although some men felt that they could protect themselves against the impact of another depression, none believed that their efforts (either alone or combined) could prevent its arrival. Political and economic systems, in themselves, seemed to them overpowering.

Because religious attitudes and religion as an institution have been more thoroughly analyzed, in dynamic terms, religion may serve as a prototype of an institution, the acceptance of or submission to which was to be related to tolerance. It may be said that unquestioning acceptance of religious values as taught by minister or priest indicates that the individual, in exercising restraint, tends to rely on a type of control in which conscious attitudes and actions are controlled by traditional and nonrational external forces. In contrast to such relatively external control, is a control exercised neither by minister nor priest but originating within the person although such inner control may originally have been achieved through their teachings. If the moral teachings of the church are accepted by the individual, not through fear of damnation or of societal disapproval, but because he considers them absolute standards of behavior independent of external threats or approval, then we say that the individual has internalized these moral precepts. They have become an internal control, but a control which is still only partially conscious and only partly rational. Such control is exercised over the individual by his "conscience," or, technically speaking, by his superego.

Markedly different from *external* control through outside institutions and from *superego* control which also depends for its effectiveness on props in the external world (such as parental images or institutionalized religion) is the rational control of irrational tendencies which forces them into consciousness and then deals with them along purely rational lines. The latter may be termed *ego* control. In actuality, the three types of control are nearly always coexistent, and in each individual case, control will depend in varying degrees on all three—external, superego, and ego control.

Therefore, it will not suffice to investigate the association between control and tolerance in general; it is equally necessary to discriminate between tolerance as related to external control, superego control, and to ego control over hostile tendencies.

Partial evidence of the relation between authority symbols and tolerance has been presented in the analysis of religious attitudes which indicated that veterans who had persistent religious convictions tended to be more tolerant. If the political party system is viewed as a norm-setting institution, then a similar relationship of at least partial acceptance or consensus with this basic institution was found to be associated with tolerance. Such stability of attitudes signifies an ability to store tensions, because acceptance of these institutions indicates the individual's reliance on them to solve his conflicts or at least to assist him in coping with those conflicts which created the tension. Frequent and sudden changes in attitudes are characteristic of persons who have inadequate control over their instinctual tendencies and who are unable to rely on existing societal institutions for providing stability.

Thus it becomes understandable that greater stability in societal status as well as in religious and political affiliations proved to be correlated with tolerance, since they were all phenomena closely related to the individual's relatively greater control over his instinctual tendencies, controls which were strong enough to prohibit immediate discharge in asocial action. Such delay in the discharge of tension permits its channelization into more socially acceptable outlets.

It was to be expected that attitudes toward symbols of army authority would follow the pattern of attitudes toward other representations of society. Army discipline was the specific representation of control within this particular institution and if tolerance was a function of control, then acceptance of army discipline had also to show a statistically *significant* relation to tolerance. This proved to be the case. About a fifth of the tolerant men thought army discipline was too strict while a third of the outspoken and intensely anti-Semitic men held that opinion. (Table 1(VII)).

Controls, it should be said, are not internalized by merely accepting society. On the contrary, general attitudes of acceptance toward existing society and its institutions are the result of previous internalization of societal values as personally transmitted by parents, teachers, and peers. Hence the acceptance of individuals who are representatives of societal values should be more closely related to internal control than the acceptance of discipline in general, which is more characteristic of external control.

Even an individual whose ego is deprived of adequate powers of control can submit to control; in fact, he often seeks conditions which will help to protect him from being overpowered by dangerous instinctual or hostile tendencies. He then seeks external discipline or superego control to compensate for the weakness of his ego. Ego strength, on the other hand, is characteristic of the ability to master a task along rationalistic lines. In actuality, this means that the individual is able to come to terms with society and "get along" in it without giving up more of his rights to unique individual existence than is required by society.

TABLE 1(VII)

OPINIONS ABOUT ARMY DISCIPLINE

	Tolerant		Stereotyped		Outspoken and Intense		Total	
	No.	Percentage	No.	Percentage	No.	Percentage	No.	Percentage
Was too strict	14	23	6	14	16	34	36	24
Was not too strict[a]	47	77	36	86	31	66	114	76
Total	61		42		47		150	

[a] Includes respondents who declared army discipline was too strict on rare occasions but not generally.

It is the duty of army officers, for instance, to enforce such requirements as orderliness and regularity. This in itself would only constitute external control. But in their power to enforce obedience officers closely resemble parental figures whose actions and examples force the child to develop a superego. The child must internalize parts of the parental requirements in order to get along with them on a long-term basis. The soldier who remained unable to come to some terms with his officers more or less permanently (i.e., by internalizing some of their demands), was unable to behave in a soldierly fashion, except in the presence of officers or M.P.'s. He remained a "bad" soldier, though he may have behaved heroically in battle. Therefore, attitudes toward officers seemed suitable gauges of the individual's attitudes toward control. On the other hand, a democratic army expects an officer to induce soldiers to do their duty not merely by brandishing his punitive powers, but by setting, in the first instance, an individual example. He is indoctrinated to get his men to do their duties out of liking and respect. Most soldiers, in fact, evaluated their officers on exactly this basis of personal quality.

The tolerant veteran seemed able to make the better adjustment and to maintain better relations with his officers; he was more willing to accept the authority and discipline of the army as represented by its officers. In general, his attitude was one of general reasonableness. When queried as to how the fellows in their outfits got along with the officers, veterans tolerant of Jews were *significantly* more prone to claim they got along well than were the anti-Semites (Table 2(VII)).

TABLE 2(VII)

"How Did the Fellows in Your Outfit Get Along with the Officers?"

	Tolerant		Stereotyped		Outspoken and Intense		Total	
	No.	Percentage	No.	Percentage	No.	Percentage	No.	Percentage
Well	21	34	4	10	11	23	36	24
Some were good, and some were bad	34	56	26	62	27	58	87	59
Bad	6	10	12	28	9	19	27	17
Total	61		42		47		150	

It was assumed that men who claimed the fellows got along well with the officers were most probably projecting their own attitudes onto those of the men in their outfits. It might be argued that in interpreting these data, cognizance must be taken of the objective character of the officers, namely, that some were better than others. However, it is most likely that good and bad officers were randomly distributed. Moreover, the results of the Hawthorne research study of industrial relations,[2] as well as similar studies, indicate rather conclusively that human judgments about supervisory personnel are not objectively reliable, but reflect the individual's point of view. Therefore, the relation between getting along with officers and tolerance toward minority groups remained significant for this study.

It was not assumed, however, that the acceptance of army discipline is identical with submission to external control or to superego requirements, nor that getting along with the officers as individual human beings is indicative of ego strength. Such a clear-cut relation does not exist. But the data permit another interesting comparison. The two preceding tables

[2] Mayo, Elton: *The Human Problems of an Industrial Civilization*, Division of Research, Graduate School, Harvard University, Boston, 1933.

show that the same number of intolerant men rejected each type of control, the impersonal discipline and the interpersonal contact with individual officers (twenty-two and twenty-one respectively). The data for the tolerant men, on the other hand, show that in their case a distinction was made between the two types of control. (Fourteen thought the discipline was too strict, but only six got along badly with their officers.) Thus, among tolerant men, there was a greater acceptance of personalized control originating in individual officers than of the distant, immutable control of discipline. In summary, an analysis of the men's attitudes toward army discipline indicated that the individual's ability to deal with institutional demands by self-control or submission is associated with tolerance.

To more fully explore this relationship between tolerance and control, the responses of the individual to symbols of societal authority which signified external control were also studied.

Before that could be done, some relatively precise definitions were needed which would lend themselves to quantitative analysis. In modern society many of the individual's life activities are regulated by a variety of institutions, each of which may command a degree of authority and thus exercise control. A comprehensive index of the individual's relation to institutionalized, external control would have had to be based on his attitudes toward all of them. In this study two groups of institutions were analyzed separately. The first group, that of army control by means of discipline and officers' authority, has already been discussed. The second group is analyzed below. It is composed of significant representatives of civilian authority to which the men were relatively subject at the time of the interview.

The four institutions singled out as being most relevant were: (1) the administration of veterans' affairs; (2) the political party system; (3) the federal government; and (4) the economic system, as defined by the subjects themselves.

The veterans' views of each of these institutions were quite complex, and in some respects, ambivalent. Nevertheless, it was possible to analyze attitudes toward them on a continuum from complete rejection to complete acceptance. To prepare an overall measure of attitudes toward such representatives of external control, each of the statements about these institutions was classified either as acceptance, rejection, or intermediate.

Employing these categories the distribution of acceptance and rejection of controlling institutions that was encountered is shown in the following table:

TABLE 3(VII)

ATTITUDES TOWARD CONTROLLING INSTITUTIONS

	Tolerant		Stereotyped		Outspoken and Intense		Total	
	No.	Percentage	No.	Percentage	No.	Percentage	No.	Percentage
Acceptance	41	67	20	48	11	23	72	48
Intermediate	15	25	17	40	13	28	45	30
Rejection	5	8	5	12	23	49	33	22
Total	61		42		47		150	

More than three-fourths of the group was at least enough in accord with existing society to accept the control exercised on their lives by some of its societal institutions. Characteristic for the degree of dissensus was that more than a fifth of these men (who were predominantly of the lower middle and lower classes) rejected three or all four of the institutions.

If acceptance or rejection of the four representative institutions is compared with the degree of anti-Semitism, it appears that only an insignificant percentage of the tolerant men rejected them. On the other hand, nearly half of the outspoken and intense anti-Semites fell into the group who rejected these institutions.

Thus the relationship between acceptance of controlling institutions and tolerance was very marked. It was quite revealing to compare the attitudes of the men toward the political party system with their attitudes toward all four institutions of control combined (one of which was the political party system). This comparison is presented in the following table which compares data reported separately in Tables 7(VI) and 3(VII).

Among the outspoken and intense anti-Semites there was no marked difference between attitudes toward the political system alone and the four controlling institutions taken together. The attitudes among stereotyped and tolerant men, however, were markedly different. The more tolerant the men were, the greater was the difference between acceptance of controlling institutions as compared with acceptance of the political party system. A little more than a third of the tolerant men accepted the party system, but two-thirds of them accepted the four controlling institutions. On the other hand, only a twelfth of the tolerant men rejected the four controlling institutions, but a little more than a fourth of them rejected the political party system.

TABLE 4(VII)

COMPARISON OF ATTITUDES TOWARD POLITICAL PARTIES
AND CONTROLLING INSTITUTIONS

	Tolerant		Stereotyped		Outspoken and Intense	
	%		%		%	
	Party System	% Institutions	Party System	% Institutions	Party System	% Institutions
Acceptance	39	67	24	48	30	23
Intermediate	33	25	43	40	23	28
Rejection	28	8	33	12	47	49

The question might be raised as to why the two-party system,[3] which offers the men some choice, was less acceptable than the other institutions which permit no choice at all. It seems that while acceptance of existing institutions in general was positively related to tolerance, acceptance of those institutions which relieved the individual of having to make choices was more related to ethnic tolerance. On the other hand, no such marked difference could be seen in the attitudes of the outspoken and intense anti-Semites; the degree of their rejection did not seem materially influenced by the fact that the party system offered them relatively greater freedom of decision.

Compared with this relationship between acceptance of external and superego controls on the one hand and tolerance on the other, efforts to probe for statistically significant relationships between degree of tolerance and relative ego strength came to naught. Various questions were asked in an effort to determine the degree to which the individual felt able to master those problems of everyday living which confronted him. He was asked, for example, whether he felt he could insure his economic well-being within the existing economic system. The responses to this question have been summarized in Chapter VI, where it was reported that less than 5 per cent of the group felt they could count on their own

[3] Almost none of the men were considering anything but a two-party system at the time of the interview.

abilities to protect them in an economic crisis, although another 5 per cent felt that their financial resources provided security. The rest of those who felt secure in their jobs also relied on external factors for their security in this area, such as being in civil service.

Lack of ego strength was further indicated by the men's responses to the problem of insuring a decent life for everybody. When asking about desired social and political action, particular courses of action were deliberately not suggested by the interviewer; instead, the individual was left to volunteer his preferred course of action and was then asked who ought to undertake such action. A similar procedure was applied to the problem of what might interfere with "our having a decent life." In both cases, the absence of references to individual action or to individual participation in group action was striking. Suggestions of group action by others seldom went beyond a reference to the vote, and even when voting as a means of improving conditions was mentioned, it implied no positive action by the individual, such as getting out the vote.

It has been mentioned above that the political party system was the one least accepted when compared with acceptance of other institutions of control. But despite this degree of nonacceptance of the party system, there was no desire to take action. When the men were asked whether they thought the ordinary individual had a chance to influence politics, the vast majority answered "No." These data are reported below in Table 5(VII). They indicate that no significant difference existed between tolerant and intolerant men in their hopelessness about the chance to influence political events.

The marked lack of feelings of competence in mastering anything but the most private events of one's life, as well as the tolerant men's willing-

TABLE 5(VII)

"DO YOU THINK THE ORDINARY INDIVIDUAL HAS ANY
CHANCE TO INFLUENCE POLITICS NOWADAYS?"

	Tolerant		Stereotyped		Outspoken and Intense		Total	
	No.	Percentage	No.	Percentage	No.	Percentage	No.	Percentage
Yes	13	22	6	14	6	13	25	17
No	45	74	33	79	37	79	115	77
Don't know	3	4	3	7	4	8	10	6
Total	61		42		47		150	

ness to accept external control as regulating their lives, can be related to the characteristics of this group. True, the selection of the sample tended to produce a group of men of whom many were lacking in ego strength. That is, the system of selective service actually permitted the men some freedom of choice, particularly when they were willing to take the initiative. Those who took advantage of the chance to influence their fate within the selective service system were those least likely to be found among enlisted men in the army, although they were not absent there. Men of independence, whose ego strength permitted them to shape their own fate to some degree, were those, for example, who enlisted in the merchant marine, or tried to enter the navy while it remained a volunteer service. Others who had initiative may have succeeded in earning commissions as officers. Thus, men with sufficient ego strength to influence their lot even within the controlled situation of a wartime emergency were least likely to appear in the sample. On the other hand, these selective factors made the group more important for this study, which sought to determine the degree to which tolerance is related to acceptance of external controls. This sample, in fact, represented the most numerous group of our male urban population.

The ability to submit to external controls, as much as the internalization of a superego, or the development of a strong ego, depends to a large degree on childhood experiences. Therefore a discussion of relative ego strength, the absence of superego control, and frequency of control by external institutions would be incomplete without some reflection on childhood experiences. This study, however, was not a genetic study. Even when questions about the individual's past were asked, the intention was not to gain correct information, but rather to learn about the individual's present evaluation of past experiences. In the case of recollections of experiences during the depression (see Chapter VI) no effort was made to assess whether the individual had actually been exposed to deprivation during the depression, but only to learn how he viewed his own and his family's economic experience at that time. Similarly, questions about the individual's childhood were designed not to reconstruct the development of his personality structure, but to see how he now evaluated parental attitudes. Evidence from psychiatric sources abounds to show that recollections of childhood experiences as given in a first interview are very different indeed from those which slowly emerge during psychoanalytical treatment. Hence such first statements about the central experience in any individual's life, namely, his relationship to his parents, have symptomatic significance alone. They are revealing of the man's present and conscious evaluation, different as that may be from the reality of his past. However, it may still be said that, by and large, an individual is more likely to recall his parents as kind when they were relatively "good" parents, while recollections of an absolute lack of parental love are reasonable indications that the relationship between parent and child was full of conflict.

Indirectly the men were led to recollect and to associate on childhood experiences in a section of the interview dealing with marital plans and problems. No direct questions were asked, but the men were queried on the number of children they would like to have, what they thought was the best way to bring up their children, whether they thought that ways of bringing children up had changed since their parents' time, how they would try to get children to behave, and whether they would bring their children up the way their mothers and fathers had. In seven cases, responses were not adequate enough to permit analysis. In all other cases, responses were classified into the two categories: affectionate parents and lack of parental love. A *significant* association was found between tolerance toward minority groups and the recollection of love and affection on the part of the parents, while intolerance toward minority groups was associated with the recall of lack of parental love and harsh discipline.

TABLE 6(VII)

RECOLLECTION OF PARENTAL ATTITUDES

	Tolerant		Stereotyped		Outspoken and Intense		Total	
	No.	Percentage	No.	Percentage	No.	Percentage	No.	Percentage
Affectionate parents	40	68	18	47	21	46	79	55
Lack of parental love	19	32	20	53	25	54	64	45
Total	59		38		46		143	

The most interesting aspect of the association between intolerance and recollections of parental strictness is that there was virtually no difference (1 per cent) between stereotyped and outspoken anti-Semites. Therefore, it may be assumed that having had affectionate parents (or at least believing so) is definitely related to tolerant attitudes, while the reverse, though having some influence on intolerance, hardly influences the degree of tolerance. If this should be so (and the data permit of little more than speculation) then one might think that adverse childhood experiences, particularly lack of parental love, have much to do with the need to discharge hostility in later life, but relatively little to do with the intensity with which such hostility will be discharged. This seems to corroborate the findings of other research workers which indicate that ethnic intolerance is acquired relatively late as compared with the development of a general need for hostile discharge.

In view of the particular characteristics of the sample and of the role of external control in shaping their attitudes—particularly toward the ethnic minorities—it may be inferred that this was a group which had not succeeded in internalizing moral standards on tolerance. It was a group which relied on external motivation for most of its life activities and opinions, including its attitudes of tolerance or intolerance. For instance, only a very small percentage based their job choices and aspirations on motives originating in their own personalities or talents, or the assumed social importance of a job. Not only were their current choices of jobs due largely to external factors, but their future aspirations, too, were based mainly on considerations of income or job security.

CORRELATES OF CONTROL

Generalizations from statistical data become more hazardous as consequent analysis deals less with delimitable traits or attitudes than with such complex phenomena as psychological structure and its inner contradictions. In itself, statistical analysis of the relation between tolerance and specific opinions, fears, and expectations is justified. But present day statistical methods seem, as yet, too inadequate to permit refined discrimination as to whether tolerance is related to external or internal controls—and if the latter, whether it is related more to superego than to ego control or a combination of all these factors. In these areas of investigation statistical data can provide approximations which must nevertheless be elaborated by an individual study of each case. The cases were therefore analyzed in these terms and the findings reported below are summarized in Tables 7(VII) and 8(VII). A study of characteristic cases is also presented later in the chapter to support the propositions based on statistical analysis.

The analysis of individual cases proceeded differently from the content analysis yielding the data in the foregoing portion of this study. Instead of evaluating responses to individual questions, or groups of questions, an independent rating of each interview as a whole was made on the basis of a variety of psychological attributes. It was felt, for example, that in addition to separately evaluating a man's hostility toward Jews, Negroes, officers, fellow soldiers,'political parties, and foreign countries, his hostility as revealed by the whole interview record should also be evaluated and correlated with other factors studied. This overall evaluation covered such aspects as controls (external and internal), security, ego strength, hostility, frustration, isolation, and so on. This evaluation may be considered as lying midway between the reliably determined statistical analysis of factors which could be studied separately, and the examination of individual cases presented in the second half of this chapter.

It was evident that in rating the interviews, no norms external to this group could be applied to define low, average, or high degrees of control, hostility, frustration, and so on. The interviews themselves provided the measure of what, for this particular group, was an average, or greater, or lower degree of these attributes. It was intended, if possible, that the average group should contain approximately half of the total number of cases. With this average group as a gauge, deviate interviews could then be rated as higher or lower than the group as a whole. The category of isolation may serve as an example of this procedure. Each interview was read for the frequency with which the incidence or desirability of contacts with others, was mentioned. But the number of such associations was not the only factor taken into consideration; the frequency and relative importance of any one set of contacts were considered equally important.

Inspection of Tables 7(VII) and 8(VII) shows that the method was fairly successful since approximately half of the men fell into the middle group for the categories: security, ego strength, frustration, and isolation. This was not true for the two categories, hostility and controls. Since almost half of the interviews contained little or no indications of hostility, it was not possible to rate them as average for this category. Instead, they were classified as low in hostility, and the rest of the interviews were then divided into two approximately equal groups. A somewhat different procedure was used for controls since it was found possible to divide the men into three groups of approximately equal size.

Of the six psychological attributes, three (controls, security, and ego strength) were positively associated with tolerance toward Jews. Three others (hostility, frustration, and isolation) were negatively associated

TABLE 7(VII)

OVERALL EVALUATIONS—FACTORS POSITIVELY RELATED TO TOLERANCE

Total Cases	61		42		47		150	
	Tolerant		Stereotyped		Outspoken and Intense		Total	
	No.	Percentage	No.	Percentage	No.	Percentage	No.	Percentage
Controls								
Adequate	32	52	9	21	2	4	43	29
Intermediate	22	36	18	43	15	32	55	36
Inadequate	7	12	15	36	30	64	52	35
Security								
High	22	36	5	12	4	9	31	21
Medium	26	43	23	55	17	36	66	44
Low	13	21	14	33	26	55	53	35
Ego strength								
High	14	23	3	7	5	11	22	15
Medium	39	64	28	67	24	51	91	61
Low	8	13	11	26	18	38	37	24

TABLE 8(VII)

OVERALL EVALUATIONS—FACTORS NEGATIVELY RELATED TO TOLERANCE

Total Cases	61		42		47		150	
	Tolerant		Stereotyped		Outspoken and Intense		Total	
	No.	Percentage	No.	Percentage	No.	Percentage	No.	Percentage
Hostility								
High	2	3	8	19	30	64	40	26
Medium	10	16	18	43	12	25	40	26
Low	49	81	16	38	5	11	70	48
Frustration								
High	3	5	7	17	19	40	29	19
Medium	24	39	25	59	24	51	73	49
Low	34	56	10	24	4	9	48	32
Isolation								
High	12	20	12	29	16	34	40	26
Medium	27	44	23	54	27	57	77	52
Low	22	36	7	17	4	9	33	22

with tolerance toward the Jews. The negative association between frustration and tolerance supports, and in some respects amplifies, the basic hypothesis linking intolerance with anxiety. The correlation of generalized hostility with the particular outlet, ethnic intolerance, was to be expected. The link between isolation and intolerance which these data reveal is also in accord with the data reported on childhood recollections. Affectionate relations with parents apparently set the path for good interpersonal relationships later in life; liking people in general (and being liked by them) enhanced tolerance. The association between security and tolerance is also compatible with the findings on social mobility, economic security, and general optimism.

Of all these psychological attributes, the association between control and tolerance was the most important in terms of the problem of this chapter. It was, therefore, the category with which all others were compared.

An analysis of these tables shows that important generalizations can be made if persons showing each type of ethnic attitude are classified in terms of the structure of their controls.

TABLE 9(VII)

TOLERANT MEN WHOSE CONTROLS WERE ADEQUATE
(32 Men)

	Security		Ego Strength		Hostility		Frustration		Isolation	
	No.	Per-centage	No.	Per-centage	No.	Per-centage	No.	Per-centage	No.	Per-centage
High	12	37	13	41	0	0	0	0	4	12
Medium	15	47	17	53	3	9	9	28	13	41
Low	5	16	2	6	29	91	23	72	15	47
Total	32		32		32		32		32	

The *tolerant* men may thus be seen in their majority as relatively strong in controls, markedly low in hostility and frustration, and high in security. Nevertheless the impression received is that for many of them their controls were only adequate in a relative sense—mainly because they were low in hostility and frustration so that even relatively weak controls were adequate.

This overall evaluation also permits dividing the tolerant men into two types—those of a majority and a minority—on the basis of each man's adequacy of controls. Tables 9(VII) and 10(VII) show the distribution of men with adequate and inadequate controls in relation to the other five categories. Those men whose controls were adjudged intermediate more closely resembled the majority.

These tables highlight the fact that the tolerant men who had adequate controls were also characterized by an absence of hostility and frustration. They also support the conclusion that adequacy of control for these men was relative, depending on the absence of strong feelings driving for discharge.

By contrast, the minority of seven tolerant men whose controls were classified as inadequate presented no consistent picture, as far as their psychological attributes were concerned, although the smallness of their number may have accounted for this. While the majority of the tolerant men showed common features, the minority consisted of men whose tolerance was associated with highly personal factors, differing from case to case, as can be seen from the case material.

In terms of these psychological attributes, no overall characterization

TABLE 10(VII)

TOLERANT MEN WHOSE CONTROLS WERE INADEQUATE
(7 Men)

	Security		Ego Strength		Hostility		Frustration		Isolation	
	No.	Per-centage	No.	Per-centage	No.	Per-centage	No.	Per-centage	No.	Per-centage
High	2	29	0	0	2	29	2	29	2	29
Medium	3	42	5	71	3	42	2	29	3	42
Low	2	29	2	29	2	29	3	42	2	29
Total	7		7		7		7		7	

of a positive nature was possible for the *stereotyped* anti-Semites. Their characterization was more of a negative nature; they were the "neither-nors." Their controls were predominantly intermediate and they were neither high nor low in security, ego strength, or hostility. They were moderately frustrated and isolated. On the basis of their strength of controls, they could not readily be classified into distinct groups. Their middle position, as well as the diffuse nature of their characteristics, permitted no such separation. In all six categories they stood midway between the tolerant and the outspoken anti-Semites.

As a group, the *outspoken and intense* anti-Semites were characterized by the inadequacy of their controls. Their hostility was as high as their controls were inadequate to contain so high a degree of hostility. The majority of them were low in security, which tallied with their pessimistic outlook as reported in Chapter VI.

They could be subdivided into two groups on the basis of control. The two following tables (Tables 11(VII) and 12(VII)) compare the majority of this group, namely, those men who had inadequate controls, with the minority, namely, those who had some measure of control over their emotions.

TABLE 11(VII)

INTOLERANT MEN WHOSE CONTROLS WERE INADEQUATE
(26 Outspoken and 4 Intense Anti-Semites)

	Security		Ego Strength		Hostility		Frustration		Isolation	
	No.	Per-centage	No.	Per-centage	No.	Per-centage	No.	Per-centage	No.	Per-centage
High	1	3	1	3	22	73	15	50	13	43
Medium	10	33	15	50	8	27	14	47	15	50
Low	19	64	14	47	0	0	1	3	2	7
Total	30		30		30		30		30	

In comparing the two types of outspoken and intense anti-Semites, the outstanding difference was that one-half of the minority group had only low or medium hostility so that some measure of control was possible.

TABLE 12(VII)

INTOLERANT MEN WHOSE CONTROLS WERE INTERMEDIATE OR ADEQUATE
(15 Outspoken and Intense Anti-Semites Had Intermediate Controls
and 2 Outspoken Anti-Semites Had Adequate Controls)

	Security		Ego Strength		Hostility		Frustration		Isolation	
	No.	Per-centage	No.	Per-centage	No.	Per-centage	No.	Per-centage	No.	Per-centage
High	3	18	4	24	8	47	4	24	3	18
Medium	7	41	9	52	4	24	10	58	12	70
Low	7	41	4	24	5	29	3	18	2	12
Total	17		17		17		17		17	

In the majority group, on the other hand, there was not a single man whose hostility could be classified as low, while three-fourths of them showed a high degree of hostility. Data on frustration and isolation followed the same pattern.

These overall judgments about majority and minority types of tolerant and intolerant men, and about typical characteristics of the stereotyped anti-Semites may be exemplified (and corroborated) by excerpts from individual interviews. For each of these groups typical cases were selected for further discussion below.

CASE MATERIAL

1. TOLERANT MEN WHOSE CONTROLS WERE ADEQUATE. The first characteristic case to be discussed will be that of a *tolerant* man whose tolerance seemed to be the function of rigid control.

This veteran was twenty-three years old and had had one year of business college. He grew up in a lower class Catholic-Polish neighborhood in Chicago and both his parents had been born in Poland. The interviewer described him as being of medium height and stocky build; he was friendly but slow thinking.

His outlook on life was optimistic and accepting. In attitude he was consistently tolerant and of very reasonable character. Toward the end of the interview, for example, he spontaneously said:

"Why are there so many questions against the Jews? I've never had any trouble with them. I go out with them and never think about their being Jews. There may be bad Jews, but there are also bad Italians, bad Polacks and so on."

He was also relatively tolerant of Negroes. As regarded working with them, he said:

"As a matter of fact, I do. I work in a large office and the niggers are all very pleasant. Not being in real close contact with them, it's O.K. True, with some, I'd rather quit than work alongside of them, but there are many others who're all right."

A reliance on external control for shaping his life was most strikingly evident in remarks about his army career which included thirty-seven months overseas and participation in the amphibious landings at Salerno and at Anzio. Despite this prolonged combat experience, he felt he had had a good break in the army. About army discipline, he said:

"It was too lax. That might sound funny. The army with all of its discipline —but I still think they were too lax."

Originally, he had hated having to join the army.

"I was fancy free and when they wanted to put me under discipline, I wasn't sure that I was the type that could be bossed around. I could have resented it like the others did, but I didn't. I was a good boy.

"Before I went into the army, I was babied and pampered but I came out of it self-reliant. I'm now getting more independent about myself. It knocked more sense into me. It made me more serious. It made me think more seriously than before and it made me conscious of how I dressed and of my general appearance . . . I didn't think I would like the army but it did me a lot of good. The army made a man out of me."

Thus, the army taught him what parents are expected to teach their children: how to dress, to think seriously and, out of choice, to submit to discipline. His need for being controlled was also revealed by the way he criticized his upbringing. He felt he had been spoiled too much and thought the best way to bring children up was for parents

"to agree on religion, the Catholic religion. They shouldn't baby the child. It makes them too soft. You should make them self-reliant. Children nowadays lose respect for their parents far too much. The old ways were better. Then they used the whip, and that seemed to have a better effect than the modern way of bringing up a child."

He continued:

"Use the whip if they do something they shouldn't have done instead of bawling them out, which goes in one ear and out the other. One should use the whip where it hurts most."

His parents "used the whip moderately"; off-hand, he thought not enough. Then he added:

"If they had used the whip more I'd be more impressed with the necessity of doing the right thing instead of doing the wrong thing."

He fully accepted control by societal institutions and it was his opinion that veterans were being reasonably well cared for. He also felt that the existing economic system, as well as the government, functioned adequately. Nevertheless, he asserted that the individual had no chance to influence the institutions of society; nor could he, by himself, do anything to influence politics or the government. There was nothing, he felt, that could or should be done about depressions, which were "inevitable." For his economic security he relied on his civil service job with the post office.

In summary it may be said that this man's attitudes were representative of a group of eleven tolerant men whose tolerance was closely related to strong tendencies to submit to external control. Most of them felt relatively secure within the circle of their families and at their jobs. In a matter-of-fact way and without complaining, they accepted their inability to influence the larger events of their lives which they saw as entirely controlled by societal institutions. They felt the need to be controlled and they accepted such control, even when it was quite stringent. Without such control, they feared that the functioning of society would be impaired.

In general, they were men who had experienced adequate love but inadequate control in childhood. They were, therefore, unable to internalize control through identification with their parents. But since they had experienced parental love and had achieved a measure of economic security, no excess hostility pressed for discharge through intolerance toward Jews. Life experiences after they had left the family circle showed many of them the need for controls which they now sought in externally enforced discipline. Experiencing discipline led these men to submission, and also to belated partial internalization in the form of superego control. Basically, their controls remained a combination of external and superego control. This is what many of them meant who said: "the army made a man of me." Since they were submitting to control rather than exercising it, they could not conceive of the possibility of exercising a measure of rational mastery over their fate—of exercising ego control. They were convinced that the whip was needed to teach people to conform.

Quite different in origin and functioning of controls was the tolerance of a twenty-seven year old veteran of Irish-French extraction with high school education. He was born and raised in Chicago. The interviewer described him as of medium height and weight; his manner was friendly, informal, and completely at ease.

His outlook on life was optimistic and accepting. Of the Jews in the army he said:

"They were treated all right. I wouldn't say that they had a lot of friends. In my outfit everyone got along. We had one Jew. He was a good Jew. I liked him."

He also felt that:

"The Jews are in the same class of people as we are."

This man, too, felt that discipline was essential and that nowadays, in bringing children up, discipline was too lax; but his conception of discipline differed materially from that of the man cited above. It was of the nature of internalized control, and to some measure, of ego control; it was, therefore, quite different from the external control advocated by the first veteran discussed. His parents brought him up well although his father died when he was eleven years old. They educated him, he stated,

"by treating me as a person who had ideas, and although they were childish, they weren't necessarily wrong. Mother started early talking to me and I just behaved."

Consequently he felt that the best way to rear children was

"to treat them as persons who have their own viewpoints. Children have intelligent minds. They see a lot more than they talk about."

Religion was very important in his life. He and his parents were Catholics.

"My mother's parents were very devout Catholics, and Mother taught me to believe along the same lines; that if you're in earnest and if what you want is good, then proper prayer will help you in getting it."

Throughout the interview he revealed great love and respect for his parents, particularly for his mother. Yet despite his great appreciation of his mother and his happy childhood relationship to her, he was now quite independent.

"I like living alone and being my own boss, and I like that. I don't have to explain what I do. My mother lives on the North Side and that's why I don't get to see her too often."

His reaction to the army was most revealing of the dynamics by which he developed some internal control of his own life activities. He felt he had had a good break in the army, in which he spent five years, including twenty-seven months in the Pacific as a rifleman. As in the former case, he praised the army because it had forced him to develop independence:

"It made a man of me. I want to repeat that, it made a man out of me. It also taught me to think for myself, and it taught me not to rely on other people."

But in contrast to the attitudes toward discipline expressed by the tolerant man discussed above, this man showed an independence from and even resentment of external control in his statements about army discipline. He particularly resented

"the unnecessary regimentation. At times it was too strict, and at times they didn't treat you as if you were even human, but treated you like machines with their 'do this and do that.'"

Although this man seemed rather self-reliant, with well-developed superego controls and some measure of ego strength, the dependency gratification offered him by the army still seemed exceedingly important to him.

"The biggest thing about the army was that I didn't have any worries about my next meal, and I knew that I'd be taken care of as far as all my needs were concerned."

He accepted governmental institutions and felt that those organizations were most dangerous to society which "defy the government." The economic and political systems were working very well in his estimation, yet he did not feel the individual could influence them one way or the other.

As far as his job was concerned, he was very happy: "I don't have any gripes." By occupation he was a crash fireman at an airport, which he considered a very soft job. He did not even mention its dangerousness.

In summary it may be said that his case was characteristic of the group of fourteen tolerant men who showed some measure of ego strength, although their tolerance was closely related to acceptance of external authority—an acceptance which was combined in their cases with some internalization of controls. However, in contrast to the externally controlled group first described, these men possessed a measure of ego strength.

The reaction of both types of tolerant men showed their need to experience external control as a support before their latent tendencies to develop internalized controls could become manifest. One may speculate as to why these men were able to develop some measure of internalized control and even ego strength, while the first group was unable to do so. Perhaps, it was a result of happy childhood experiences, particularly their good relationships to their parents, combined with the fact that, as children, they had been treated as human beings, able to make decisions for themselves.

For these men it was not enough, apparently, to have had loving parents in order for them to develop adequate internal controls, not to speak of ego strength. It may well have been that their social and economic situation subjected them to overpowering, though ill-defined, political and economic controls which prevented them from developing that feeling of mastery over their own fate which is required for ego strength. To such men the army with its comparatively clear-cut regulations limiting the number of ways of action and regulating nearly all life activities was a haven of security. For some of them, successful testing of ego strength became possible for the first time. Moreover, their equipment, their personal tasks, and their responsibilities gave many of them a sense of power and accomplishment which civilian life could hardly afford. One man, for example, reports the great feeling of power he experienced in combat when swinging around the turret and firing the gun of a medium tank.

It must have been tremendously gratifying to these men to realize that they bore themselves well under difficult conditions which also allowed them to compare themselves with others in terms of their own most significant values. For example, one man's opinion of himself was materially enhanced when, during a critical battle situation, repairs on his tank became necessary. Without much ado four of the five crew members (including himself) jumped out in the face of enemy fire. The fifth did not follow but remained inside the tank even after he was ordered out. The veteran recounting the experience derived self-respect from the fact that even without having been told, he showed more courage and resourcefulness than the fifth man who, incidentally, was the athlete of the company. For these, and similar reasons, some men said the army made "a man" of them. In like manner, the army permitted them to use such experiences for developing ego strength under conditions where army control no longer seemed entirely externally imposed, but to some degree self-chosen.

Development of ego strength was also aided by the fact that reliable and predictable gratification of the most pervasive biological needs was assured. As psychoanalytic studies of the development of ego strength point out, dependable and ample gratification of physiological needs is necessary in developing internalized controls.

Love alone is not sufficient for a child to develop adequate internal controls, and what has here been designated as ego strength. Parental love may result in an optimistic outlook on life, may promote the conviction that the individual is lovable and will be loved. It may also permit the formation of satisfactory interpersonal relationships. But love alone will not give the individual a sense of permanent security and the feeling that he is able to master successfully the situations he must meet. For that, love must be combined with a conviction that adequate gratification of biological needs such as intake and elimination, rest, motility, warmth, and shelter will always be available. The example given above seems to indicate that parental love prepared the basis for the development of independence and those self-controls on which it rests. But the controls only reached mature development in the army where gratification of the most primitive needs was assured and where success was experienced under conditions which allowed for comparison with adult peers.

Examples of the intolerant men, on the other hand, show that in their case the personalities they had developed long before entering the army prevented them from internalizing controls. They violently resented the external controls of the army and also tended to run into actual disciplinary difficulties because of their rejection of all controls.[4] The conclusion may be that only a personality which is so structured by early experiences that internalization of controls is possible can permit the individual to accept external control. The men whose personalities were better integrated were also better able to use the army experience for internalizing controls.

Harsh discipline by parents does not necessarily lead to intolerance if other factors, such as good interpersonal relationships and actual success in life experiences, compensate for it. This may be illustrated by the case of a twenty-eight year old veteran with one year of college education. Both of his parents were born in Italy, but he had been born and brought up in Chicago. The interviewer described him as stocky and of average height; he was very responsive and patient.

He too had an optimistic outlook on life. At the time of the interview, he was tending his own bar, an occupation which he enjoyed because he "liked to meet the crowds" as they came in for drinks.

His upbringing had been strict and submarginal, partly because his parents knew no better and partly because they were poor—but not because they were not fond of him. As he put it, they educated him "with a big stick over my head." Nevertheless, he felt that their disciplinary efforts could not have been too bad, since he and his siblings turned out well enough. He planned, however, to bring up his children quite differently. He intended, he said, to

"give them everything I didn't have. A good education, and I'll see that they have everything that they need. I'll treat them decently. One shouldn't make the child feel that you are the big boss, with a big stick. You have to meet them half-way and use reason."

In this man's family the Catholic religion was quite important and he planned to make it so for his children.

---

[4] All of these observations hold true only for the middle, and by far the most common, area of experience. Implementation of army discipline by deviant officers may, of course, have resulted in counterreaction.

While he felt competent on his job and enjoyed it, he felt that reliance on the government, and particularly on the President as a person, was the only way a person could derive security in view of the very difficult political and economic situation. In general, he thought things looked pretty well and that all that was needed was for everybody to

"get behind the President 100 per cent, then everything should be O.K. He knows what he's doing. One person has to think for the country, for the majority at least."

When asked who ought to instigate and execute necessary actions, he replied emphatically, "the President!" When asked who should protect our liberties, and who could do it, he asserted "only the government."

For those who complained, he had no compassion: "They're a pretty poor bunch, these gripers." When asked if the individual had any influence on politics, he answered: "That's not for me to say." On being pressed, he repeated:

"No, I don't think so. The individual can't do anything by himself. It used to be the people, but now it's a clique."

His attitude toward the Jews was consistently tolerant. About the Jews in the army, he said:

"They were O.K. They got along all right. There was no trouble."

When asked if the Jews made good soldiers, he answered:

"These are ticklish questions. They were just as good as any. They were swell fellows, the ones I knew. We had one Jewish officer who used to take my place on Sunday mornings so I could go to Mass."

Then he added:

"You hear so much and as far as I'm concerned, nothing should be done about the Jews. It's all right as it is, they all get the same chance. This country was formed for all."

In summary, it may be said that this man, and five others whose life history and attitudes were similar, managed despite harsh upbringing to develop into citizens who were competent, self-reliant, and independent in their own private spheres. They felt they could control their personal and private affairs, but lacked the confidence to think they could influence the broader aspects of their lives or of society. Control they could accept, and to some measure exercise, because they had been brought up under the control of accepting parents and of the church. The relative satisfaction they found in their own family lives (the man described was happily married and had a daughter of whom he was very fond), together with the pleasurable contacts they enjoyed with others, more than balanced the frustrations they experienced because of their inability to influence larger social issues, in which, moreover, they were not too interested.

This case was fairly typical for a small group of men who held to the ideals of the lower middle-class businessman. They got along with everyone and found gratification both in their jobs and in their families. To the larger societal issues they were indifferent. But this type of man was comparatively infrequent among the sample.

2. TOLERANT MEN WHOSE CONTROLS WERE INADEQUATE. While the three types described above represent the majority of the tolerant men, there were a few more or less specific constellations of individual reasons for tolerance. All of the seven men in this category shared a pessimistic outlook on life.[5] Their tolerance may be characterized by the fact that it did not preclude their holding to some unfavorable stereotypes about the Jews.

Among the particular reasons for being tolerant and understanding of an ethnic minority group was, for example, the feeling of having been subject to discrimination by the majority of one's own family, that is, of having oneself been treated as an outcast.

One more or less typical case was that of a twenty-five year old Protestant veteran of high school education who was raised in Chicago. Both parents were born in Lithuania. The interviewer described him as goodlooking and friendly, verbose and vague.

His outlook on life was rather pessimistic, thus setting him apart from the majority of the tolerant men. The pervading feature of his attitude toward life was that "everything's all wrong." He complained continuously of the "big shots" who were "running everything" and "didn't give the

[5] As indicated briefly in Chapter VI, depressive attitudes may be viewed as hostility turned into self criticism (or feelings of guilt), and as such may form another basis for tolerance. That is, with aggressions turned inward, there is no need for the persecution of an outgroup, and the mechanism of projection need not take place; integration is maintained as the ego accepts persecution by the superego instead of fighting it. Frequently too, the guilt feelings of the depressive will look to the outside for additional "punishment." In this sense, some of the men were probably voicing their own needs when they cautioned against sparing the rod in child rearing. Furthermore, to the extent that tolerant men enjoyed (approved) of the rigid if not punitive discipline meted out by parents or other institutions of authority, to that extent they could afford to be tolerant since part of their hostility was directly or vicariously discharged on their own persons. Their hostility was gratified in a way typical for the sadomasochistic personality: by identifying temporarily with the aggressor, in our case the punitive parent or the strict officer.

little guy a chance." If you wanted to get ahead in life, he said "it's like bucking a brick wall." He had great anxiety about the future.

"It's going to be pretty bad. Yes, I think there's going to be another depression. Maybe I'm wrong, but it will be a miracle if we don't. People will be sorry for what they believe. It's a hell of a mess."

Emotionally he was quite unstable, and particularly so since his discharge from the army.

"I'm nervous a lot, now that I'm out of the army. I don't know what it is exactly, but I just feel nervous a lot, and a lot of times I break out in a cold sweat. Like the other night, my wife got real scared because I started perspiring like everything. The pillow and the bed got all wet."

His attitude toward Jews was characterized by statements such as:

"I tell you, there's nothing wrong with the Jews. Naturally, they control a lot of business. On the other hand, a lot of them don't. It's not right to have one nationality that you're against. They're just trying to make a living like anyone else."

He accepted the stereotype of Jewish control of business, an opinion which must have made them obnoxious to him since he hated the "big shots who didn't give the little guy like me a chance." But he controlled himself and qualified his stereotyped statement by saying it was not true for all Jews.

Suggestive of the sources of his controls were his ideas about educating children:

"Well, some people say, always talk to the child and he'll listen, but that doesn't work for most, from what I see. I don't mean that you have to break all the bones in the little child's body, but spank him a little bit and don't forgive the child right away. Like some people spank the child a little, and right away hold him close and say, 'I forgive you.' So the child goes right ahead and does it again. But if you spank him and don't forgive him right then, well, he'll hate you for a little while but he'll get over it. And then he'll mind after that. You do have to use the hand to rule your child, I think."

The main problem of his life was his hatred for and jealousy of his older brother.

"Well, I'll tell you. I had an older brother and when he wanted something, he always got it, but I didn't. They never gave me what I wanted, never gave me the things they gave him. It was always like I was in bad, not exactly neglected, but not handled as good. If I wanted anything, I would have to get it myself. For example, he got a car when he was very young. But when I wanted a car, I had to go to work to get the money for a car. I don't think that's fair, to do everything for one and nothing for the other. If they're your own, why, treat them equally. Even if one is worse, treat them the same, on an equal basis. If you neglect one, he might turn out better than the other one, anyway, so you can't tell. On the other hand, it might be very bad for the child to be neglected that way. I don't know. But I do know you should treat them equally and fairly."

Thus this man's desire for equal treatment for all originated in the particular set of interpersonal relationships which prevailed in his family and forced him into the position of the helpless and the oppressed. It is possible that he was able to contain his hostility against the Jews, despite his opinion that they control business, because of his hatred for his brother. This hatred was so all-pervasive that all his tensions were discharged into private feud, and no other channel for discharge of hostility, such as minority discrimination, was necessary for him. Of course, this feeling of being an underdog supported his efforts at being objective about a minority, since he felt so strongly that he had been discriminated against as a minority at home. Moreover, his opinions about child rearing, while indicative of his hostility, were also revealing of his general need to control—be it his child, or himself.

Quite different was the pattern of tolerance in a twenty-nine year old veteran of French-Italian parentage who grew up in a small community in Illinois. The interviewer described him as a short man, of pleasing appearance who responded in a patronizing manner. His education had ended after two and a half years of high school.

His outlook, too, was very pessimistic. Everything, he thought, was going to

"turn out bad. I can see the handwriting on the wall. Things are going to turn out worse than we expect. Maybe even you can see the handwriting on the wall."

At another point, he suddenly exclaimed, "But Jesus, I hope we don't have another depression."

About his own children, he declared:

"I'd like to have good, healthy kids. Fight a little, steal a little—I did. No incubator kids for me. If I had a kid and he was thirsty and asked for a drink and he was standing there with his tongue hanging out I wouldn't get one. Too much trouble."

He had always been isolated:

"I've always been a lone wolf, you might say. Familiarity only breeds contempt."

He was very strict with and critical of himself and thought poorly of his own abilities. His attitude toward his father was revealed by the following statement.

"He and Mother were divorced. The family visited him once a week, but not me. My mother still can't understand why I didn't go out to see him, even when he was dying. She and my sisters visited him when he was in the hospital, and often before that time. I didn't see him for five years. My mother said that I'm hard. Well, I am, but that's not the reason. I didn't want to go to see him. It's too much trouble to explain."

His attitude toward the Jews was characterized by statements such as the following:

"I don't have any feeling about Jews. When they're smart, they're smart. Most of them are. They'll do things a white man seldom does—and they get ahead."

One may assume that the "too much trouble to explain" and "Mother said I'm hard, but that's not the reason" show that there were certain strong emotions underlying the man's attitudes. He may have been afraid of being overwhelmed by them and may therefore have had to protect himself by attitudes of coldness and indifference. Thus he must have been a man who possessed strong controls over his emotions. If he had not been so controlled, his feeling about the "smartness of the Jews" combined with his conviction that he was unable to take care of himself might have led to open hostility which would then have placed him in the anti-Semitic group.

If one wished to generalize about the group of men who were tolerant although pessimistic, one might say that, as in the last two examples, their tolerance (as opposed to that of the majority group) was not due to the absence of tension or hostility. They were men who were rather high in hostility, frustration, and isolation, and low in security and ego strength. But they were able to restrain themselves from interethnic hostility although such restraint did not usually originate in ego strength or super-ego control but rather in a particular life history or family constellation.

Within the psychoanalytical frame of reference it may be said that most of the tolerant men with adequate controls succeeded in integrating their hostility. The controls of other tolerant men succeeded in directing the discharge of tensions into other than anti-Semitic channels, such as successful competition in their occupations. The "deviate" tolerant men were not quite so successful in restraining their hostility. It broke through the dams of their controls and revealed itself in occasional stereotyped statements about the Jews. But as such discharge of hostility became conscious, the controls asserted themselves and intolerant remarks were immediately qualified or retracted.

3. THE STEREOTYPED MEN. The *stereotyped* anti-Semites showed less ability to integrate their hostilities. For most of them, controls were relatively effective in exercising some restraints, or their stereotyped opinions would have led them to develop a higher intensity of intolerance. But they had failed to integrate them. Although stereotyped opinions which should have led to a demand for action were not restrained by controls, no demand for action ensued. The reason for this may either have been that the controls were not strong enough to contain the hostility, or that the tension generating the hostility was too great. Examples may illustrate this analysis.

A typical example of a stereotyped veteran, whose controls were strong enough to block the logical consequence of his opinions was that of a thirty-three year old veteran of Czechoslovakian parentage. He was born and raised in Chicago and had completed two years of high school. The interviewer described him as a handsome, well-built man, quite self-conscious of his own "bad tendencies" but generally secure.

When asked who the "goldbrickers" in the army had been, he replied spontaneously:

"The Jews. A known fact. They used excuses, pain, lies, combat claims, physical disability, everything. Lack of energy and stability, too, so they usually failed on the job. They took all the soft jobs they could get, too. I knew one in Salt Lake City. It didn't bother him. He was proud of getting out into a soft job. They got the soft desk jobs, all of them."

When asked what should be done about them, he said:

"Why do anything? We haven't before. Why should we now? Just let them live like anybody else."

This man continually depreciated himself; he saw himself as the black sheep of the family. Whenever he made critical remarks about people in general, he always included himself.

"Greed is what interferes with our having a decent life. Everybody's greedy. That's too bad. We're all greedy; that's the problem."

Of the veterans, he said: "We all expect too much now," and he repeated several times that the veterans, including himself, made unreasonable demands and should not be given special consideration. He did not feel that the individual could influence politics or the economic system. ("He has no influence, none whatever.")

All of his conscious life he had felt very guilty. As a child he had been "a very bad boy." At five, he set fire to his parents' home and he connected his misdeed with their death which was unrelated to it, but occurred a short time later. After their death he was brought up in a Catholic orphanage where he formed his notions of education.

"The right way to bring up children is to bring them up in the fear of God. I was the black sheep of my family; that's why I would be sure to trip up any kid of mine that was like me. Education isn't as strict these days as it should be. Parents aren't as good as our parents were. They followed the rules more strictly. They used more discipline and you have to use it, too. It's a good idea. After my parents died, I knew the discipline of the orphanage. This discipline was very good for me. In order to make children behave, stop them off the bat. I mean, correct it right away. Discipline them. My parents didn't spare the rod and I think that I won't either."

He approved strongly of the moral teachings of the Catholic religion. "Religion was life itself in our family." He also described army discipline as necessary and good.

In order to understand the general pessimistic attitude of most of the anti-Semites, their frustrations, their hopes, and the gratifications they desired, this man's statement may be quoted for its evidence of the craving for primitive gratification. He was asked whether there was anything about army life which he now missed and his answer was:

"The food. We got the best food out there. We could sleep late, we always knew we'd be taken care of, no matter what you did. Your room and board was free and you had no worries. You had security and relaxation because when your work was finished, you were free. There was no clock to punch."

Here, a potentially outspoken anti-Semite (as indicated by his derogation of Jews in the army) restrained himself to a milder form of anti-Semitism because his guilt prevented him from demanding discriminatory action. Since childhood it had been impressed on him that hostile impulses are dangerous if they are permitted to express themselves in hostile actions. Therefore he submitted to rigid control, as may be seen from his statements about discipline.

The strength of their controls prevented most stereotyped anti-Semites from asking for discriminatory actions against the Jews. This is further illustrated by the statements of a twenty-one year old veteran of German-

Scotch parentage who was born and raised in Chicago. His denomination was Presbyterian but religion was not very important in the family.

The interviewer described him as a slight, boyish, and pleasant-looking man who was very obliging. His remarks showed a clear ambivalence toward the Jews. They also demonstrated that his hostility pressed for discharge but was contained by his controls as soon as his aggressive feelings become conscious.

"The Jews always seem to have a name for going somewhere, they're go-getters. I don't know how, but they get there. In a lot of cases, the Jews use a lot of underhanded methods. They're always blamed for it, then I feel sorry for that. The Jews don't get along with anybody but themselves. Well, the way they have of getting places irks me most. I wouldn't care to have them use underhanded ways to push me out. As individuals, they have a right to take a job."

With each derogatory statement about Jews, his controls forced him to protest the accusations as somehow unjust.

The role which discipline played in his upbringing may be indicated by his statement about his own education and by his ideas about child rearing.

"Well, my father never spared the rod but I don't know if this new modern way would work. I think I'd bring up my children the way my parents brought me up. Definitely not by bribing. I think it best to make them pay for wrongs they've done. That's probably against modern methods, but I think the old ways worked. There are many spoiled brats from families where the mothers have read too many books on modern methods. Well, we at home had a stick about four inches wide and half an inch thick, that hung on a nail on the back door. When one of us stepped out of line we had to go and get the stick and take a licking with my two brothers present. It scared us pretty much. It really worked. I think it was the right way. I don't regret it now. I like my folks just as well as if they hadn't punished me this way. When I was young, I thought it was wrong, but I'm pleased now. My brothers are, too."

He was able to accept this harsh parental discipline and also to internalize it in some measure because mutual love was an important feature of his relationship to the disciplining parent; this permitted identification with the parent and acceptance of his discipline.

"My father was never mean. He was the harsh disciplinarian but he was a pretty happy-go-lucky man. You realize things like that when you're older."

The manner in which superego control prevented a man from advocating discriminatory action despite his stereotyped opinions about the Jews was further illustrated by a thirty-three year old man of British descent, who was brought up in Chicago. The interviewer described him as a short, slender man who spoke in a compulsive and almost oratorical fashion.

Although he had only had a high school education he was very ambitious, intellectually—one of the few men who had decided on a career. He wanted to become an artist. This desire led him to embrace opinions and to develop attitudes which he considered to be those of the well-educated person.

His open ambivalence, indicative of underlying hostility against the Jews, was barely contained by his rational efforts as may be seen from the following quotation:

"There should be no discrimination just because a man is a Jew. He's a member of the white race. He's of the Semitic branch and we're the Caucasians. But I don't want any business dealings with a Jew. He has an inherent something in him that will always cause him to win, but I have no prejudice because of that. Much of the problem is due to the individual Jew. The cultured, refined Jew doesn't see what the kike is doing for his race. The kikes do a great deal of harm. They're overdressed, noisy, and loud."

About the Jews in the army, he said:

"The Jewish boys were all right. We didn't say a lot to their face unless they were ignorant fellows without manners. They're peculiar people. Some have bad traits that came out in different ways. One of the Jewish soldiers was a kike but I don't care for the kike part in Gentiles either; some of them may also be loud-mouthed and overassertive. Some Jews can't help their gestures and the way they talk. Lot of them tried to get out of combat outfits and tried to stay in the States. They call quartermasters the Jewish infantry but if he'd been in the clothing business before, he was better in the quartermaster than he would be any other place, and probably better than someone who hadn't been in that business."

He felt that the Jews should be let alone, although

"they control a lot of business but I don't think we'll have a Jewish ascendancy."

When asked how the Jews should be dealt with, he summed up his attitude:

"If we discriminate against different groups, then we'll have to change what's at the foot of the Statue of Liberty."

His upbringing had been relatively strict:

"I was raised strictly enough. Discipline was important in my family. Mother taught me to divide my toys and also to have respect for my elders. I was taught how to eat properly. Mother didn't want to have oranges every morning, but we did so I would learn to use an orange spoon. Supper was extremely formal with a complete set of silver, different forks and spoons so I would learn how to use them. I thought everybody had been trained the same way until I was about seventeen or eighteen years old. I was very carefully trained to read because Mother had been a school teacher. If children aren't trained more properly, they'll become delinquent morally and it'll be the downfall of the country."

Another example may illustrate the degree to which the strength of his controls prevented even a bold and adventurous veteran who held many stereotyped anti-Semitic views from expressing himself with outspoken or intense hostility. He was nineteen years old, of Polish descent, had been born and raised in Chicago, and had just reenlisted in the army. In response to the question of whether Gentiles should receive job preference, he replied:

"No. If the job has anything to do with business, the Gentiles aren't as gifted as the Jewish."

Then he burst out:

"That's a peculiar question to ask, and I refuse to give an answer."

When asked why, he said

"I refuse to give an answer to that one also. About two weeks ago, in all the theaters in the neighborhood, they had something called Brotherhood Week. It actually made me sick."

At another point, he said: "The Jews own most of the country. State Street anyway." Nevertheless, at no point in the interview did he ask for any restrictions of Jews.

His view of civilian life was very negativistic. His experiences in the service he had enjoyed very much. There he "found something very exciting, terrifying." At the time of discharge he had planned to go to school.

"I got out some of my old school books but then I knew I could never stand it. I want something more exciting. I like nothing about civilian life. That's the reason I decided to reenlist in the army. I couldn't stand just working and going to bed at night. It was deadly. I nearly went crazy before I reenlisted. What this country needs is more discipline, like the discipline in the army. But even in the army discipline wasn't strict enough."

Generally, he complained about lack of discipline:

"Here, it's disgraceful, the way things are done in Chicago. There's no discipline whatsoever. They're far too lax and it's a disgrace. I like the English army much better because it's much stricter. I sometimes felt that Germany was progressive in a way and on the right way, and was building up a beautiful country. They only went too far."

It seemed to him that

"the children back here are disgusting. They're softies and they're given entirely too much freedom. They're not brought up right. I was also not brought up the right way. Mother babied me too much. I wouldn't want my wife to do that to my child. My mother was good to me, but she did everything for me and that spoiled me. It made me too dependent. I got out of it. The army's good for that, as long as one doesn't yield to its sordid atmosphere. You should be fair to your child but you should make him obey. I always did what I was told."

He was also full of suspicions:

"There are a lot of very harmful organizations. Our enemy had a network of spies in 1939 and 1940 and the same is true now. You probably read about the young lieutenant who was caught stealing the details of the atomic bomb. We're too lenient with the Russians."

In more than one way, this man had the leanings of a fascist follower. But his desire for discipline kept his anti-Semitism within the limits of stereotyped opinions. It was as if he sensed that his desire for excitement and adventure might easily land him in difficulties, and from these the rigid external control of the army seemed to offer protection. It is not difficult to speculate about what the attitude of such a man might be if external controls, instead of quietly condoning and officially disapproving of anti-Semitism, should openly approve.

In general, it may be said of the stereotyped anti-Semites that it was the relative presence of their controls more than anything else which prevented them from taking a more outspoken and discriminatory stand on what they considered the Jewish problem.

4. THE OUTSPOKEN ANTI-SEMITES WHO POSSESSED SOME MEASURE OF CONTROL. The stereotyped anti-Semites stood midway between the tolerant men and the *outspoken anti-Semites,* because their controls were less adequate for containing anti-Semitism than those of the tolerant men, but more adequate than those of the outspoken anti-Semites. Similarly it might be said that the minority of the outspoken anti-Semites (seventeen men), who possessed some measure of control, formed a group whose position on anti-Semitism was somewhere between that of the stereotyped and that of the majority of the outspoken anti-Semites who were more markedly characterized by the inadequacy of their controls.

The two outspoken anti-Semites whose controls were adequate were both unique cases. One of the two, for example, was a very recent immigrant to the United States. He came to America after the start of the war in Europe and transferred to this new country attitudes which really belonged to his previous environment. His controls seemed in process of adaptation to the new setting, and it was probable that as he grew into the pattern of this country they would become more effective; eventually, they might become strong enough to restrain his anti-Semitism to such a degree that he would then fall into the category of stereotyped anti-Semites. Equally unusual reasons accounted for the second case of this type, so that neither of them seem in need of further discussion in a study not mainly concerned with the behavior of exceptional cases.

The following excerpts from one of the interviews may illustrate those characteristics which were typical of men who, in spite of intermediate controls, were nevertheless outspoken in their anti-Semitism.

It is the case of a twenty-three year old man whose father was of American stock, and whose mother had been born in Austria. He himself was born and raised in Chicago where he went through grade school and high school. The interviewer described him as a tall, thin, well-built man; his personality was pleasant and he seemed friendly and humorous.

In his demands for restrictions against Jews he was quite outspoken. Gentiles, he felt should be given preference on jobs:

"Take the Jewish race. Financially they're better off than the Gentiles. I believe that we should let the Gentiles get to where the Jewish is today, and in that way we'll be on an equal basis. The Jews made good soldiers, as good a soldier as the Gentile, but only when there wasn't a group of them together, or not too many in one group. Four or five in a company was all right, but if there was twenty in a company they'd stay together and not mingle with the other men. Nevertheless, we got along all right. We had no trouble, but I do think that the Jews should be held down and not given too much power. The biggest percentage of merchants are Jews, and that's why prices should be held down, so they won't get an abundance of money."

On the other hand:

"I don't think that the Jews should be forced to leave the country. After all, most of them have established themselves as citizens, and as long as they stick to the law and have their citizenship papers, they shouldn't be forced to leave."

He was also unopposed to intermarriage, nor did he object to working with Jews. He did, however, object to the idea that a Jew might live next door to him:

"They more or less have their own sections. I'm from an Irish neighborhood. I'm Irish and I'm used to Irish neighbors."

Thus, although he was quite outspoken in his discriminatory statements about the Jews, a modicum of rational control was still operative.

His outlook on life was rather optimistic. The future, he thought, looked bright, at least for him. "The condition in this country is a lot better than it was before the war." As he saw it, the individual could exercise some influence on politics.

"I guess that most everyone has an influence on politics, down to the last person. Of course one person can influence things only a little bit."

His general acceptance of existing society was epitomized by his statement that the government was run by "intelligent people."

"They had to be, by the way they handled the country and the situation we've just been through."

His upbringing had been strict on the part of his father, affectionate on the part of his mother:

"My dad used the cat o' nine tails. Yes, he really did. But I believe that reasoning with children is lots better than getting rough with them. Mother reasoned with us, and through that way she could teach us things. You always have respect for your mother, and whatever she tells you, you listen to her. Father used force, and then mother would reason with us and tell us what was wrong. I didn't like my father using force, but today I can appreciate that what he did has probably had a good effect.

"I believe I was brought up the right way—just don't go too far in using force—then it's all right. A good crack won't hurt any kid. After I got a good one, it put me in line for about a week."

His attitude toward discipline was ambivalent. He rejected as too harsh the discipline of his father, but admitted that some discipline might be needed and have beneficial effects. His position on army discipline was halfway between rejection and acceptance. Army discipline was "in some cases too strict, but only in some cases."

Here was a man whose hostility was not too intense. He could, moreover, accept some external control and his upbringing had probably led him to integrate some of it. Therefore, although he readily permitted himself to voice stereotyped criticism of the Jews and although he even asked for some discriminatory legislation, his anti-Semitism was, nevertheless, tempered by controls.

5. The Outspoken Anti-Semites Whose Controls Were Inadequate. The controls of twenty-four of the outspoken anti-Semites were quite in-

adequate for restraining anti-Semitism, and the interview records showed no attempt on their part to qualify derogatory statements about the Jews. On the contrary, their remarks often became more violent, the longer they talked. It was as if their inadequate controls, once pierced by unfavorable statements about Jews, led to more unfavorable associative material and finally gave way under the added pressure of hostility aroused by such associations.

Typical for the attitudes of this group were those of a twenty-five year old Protestant, of native-born parentage who had been born and raised in Chicago. This man had had two years of high school education and was described by the interviewer as a short, heavy-set man of flashy appearance. His behavior during the interview revealed his aggressiveness. Looking through a book which the interviewer left lying on the table, he found a personal letter, which he provocatively started to read, obviously testing the interviewer's patience. When she failed to react, he dropped this tactic.

His attitude toward the Jews was characterized by statements such as the following:

"As for the Jews, run them out of business because they already control most of the business in the United States. Or make them work as anybody else. In the army there were no Jews in our outfit, but when we were inducted I know the Jews angled around and got out of it. When they were in, they always got the best jobs. Send the Jews back where they came from because they don't get along over here. All the people are against them because of how they do business and control most business."

He objected to a Jew moving in next door to his residence:

"They aren't liked, the way they act and do business. They lower neighborhoods, keep things pretty dirty."

He was unwilling to have a Jew work on the same job "because they would probably knock me out of my job."

It was obvious that his attitude toward the Jews was closely connected with his great insecurity about his abilities and with his anxiety about his future. He felt sure that things

"are going to turn out pretty lousy. Everything's going to be bad, and going to be worse. Nothing is being done for the veteran beside all the talking. The ordinary individual has no influence on politics, none at all. If a depression should come it would hit me hard, harder than most others, I guess. It'll be very bad."

He had been brought up "the old-fashioned way." But contrary to the reaction of most tolerant men, he resented his childhood experiences as having been "far too strict." He felt that his parents punished him far too often, though he later admitted that he was punished only rarely. Although religion had been very important in his home, he had little use for it; even in the army he went to church less frequently than he had before that time.

Both the high degree of his hostility and the absence of any desire or ability to control it were revealed by statements such as the following which he made spontaneously when discussing the Negroes in the army. He had been speaking of Negroes dancing with white girls in Europe and related that on one occasion this had led to an argument between a white and a Negro soldier. The Negro made some disparaging remarks without threatening the other physically. At that:

"The white guy shot the Negro right there—killed him. He didn't even get court-martialed for it. He got off clean, and that's O.K. That's how it should be all over the place."

He liked his life in the army, although he disliked army discipline. Since his discharge he particularly missed his "jeep and all the girls." When asked who gained because of the war, he answered, with a broad smile:

"Hum, the French girls gained a lot. I like the girls over there in France and those in Germany. I like them all. Girls are girls."

This man hated army discipline (and all other types of discipline, including parental and governmental control) but liked his army experience for the sexual freedom and the outlet for aggressions which it provided. His strong hostilities were barely controlled and he harbored great anxieties about his economic future and private affairs. Moreover, he felt that the government provided no security since it consisted of "nothing but crooks."

Another outspoken anti-Semite who showed more or less the same pattern of psychological attributes was a thirty year old man of Bulgarian extraction. He was born on a farm in Ohio. This man was described by the interviewer as a short, very thin man who was shabbily clothed. He felt insecure about everything, including his relationship to the interviewer, whom he accused of wanting to put something over on him. When she reassured him, he said: "It's always the smoothest talkers that take you in." His opinions about the Jews were:

"They don't work or fight. I'd always give preference to a non-Jew. In the army the Jews weren't treated very nice. There was always a grudge, the Jews against the Gentiles. There was a grudge against the Jew because of his being intelligent and getting ahead faster. The Jews always held down good jobs and good ratings, and the boys disliked them for that. They made good clerks. As field soldiers, no. They don't fall into the routine, they were bad combat soldiers because they'd never stick. To their face we seemed to get along with them, but behind their backs we raised cain. There are too many of the Jews around here now. They should never have allowed so many in here. Their population is too great. You can't chase them out—then we'd be another Hitler. We should close immigration to them. They're producing so fast that we'll have trouble with them here, a great deal. There's no place to send them. They're not even wanted in Palestine."

When asked about questions of policy toward Jews he answered:

"I'd object against a Jew moving next door. They raise too much stink and too much commotion. The low Jews are filthy, and the higher class always think that you're doing wrong. Those who own stores on Milwaukee Avenue are filthy, and you should see the alleys behind the stores—they're terrible. I wouldn't want to work with a Jew because he wouldn't want to do the manual labor. He wouldn't share the work. I just can't get along with them. I can't get accustomed to the way they do things—they always want to take advantage."

His insecurity about his own future and that of the country was revealed by remarks such as the following:

"People are too unsettled. Everything in general is unsettled. Things will slide downhill right into a depression. As a matter of fact we have a depression right now. Thirty-three per cent of the people in Chicago aren't employed, including the veterans.[6]

"People like me will starve. We don't have the education or the money to exist."

Not enough was being done for the veterans, in his opinion; there, too, he felt that everybody was taking advantage of him and other veterans.

"There are a million in Chicago that have made a million off the veterans. Look at me, for example. I wanted to go to school, and a high-pressured sales-man came by the house here one evening and sold me a course on electricity, which isn't in my line at all, and now I'm stuck. That's how you get gypped on anything."

He was as dissatisfied with the world as he was dissatisfied with himself:

"No party is any good now. The ordinary people don't have a chance. There are too many ways of holding them down."

and:

[6] This statement was made at a time when unemployment in Chicago was extremely low.

"Just now I'm taking a course in electricity. The course is no good. They push you through too fast and the person with a low education like me can't understand what it's all about. They have one teacher for about forty people. They don't explain things to you, just tell you to figure out the problem yourself. I spent about five hours last night trying to figure the problems out and I can't. I'm on problem four and the class is on problem eleven, so you can see how I'm getting along. When I ask for help they tell me to figure it out myself. If I were out on a job I wouldn't be able to ask people how to do things. I get very discouraged."

All he hoped for in the future was that he might eventually earn $3,000 a year, but he felt that the chances for that were slim:

"I don't think I'll ever work on a job that pays that much I don't have much education and I don't know the right people."

His childhood recollections were unpleasant:

"I had to work too much and that was a hindrance to my education. My parents were too strict. I got shoved in a corner; I had hard discipline, and got hit around. I lost faith in my parents because they didn't treat me right, although I admit I deserved most of it."

About religion he said: "There are foxhole atheists. In fact, I'm sitting here." The only thing about the army he liked was "the uniform and the discipline."

One of his biggest gripes was that most of his friends had married and were being prevented by their wives from spending time with him.

The asocial attitudes of some of the outspoken anti-Semites may be indicated by the statements of a twenty-four year old man whose father was of American stock and his mother, German-born. He had had two and a half years of high school education and was described by the interviewer as a handsome young man, about six feet tall. He sneered throughout most of the interview, and seldom gave precise answers.

Characteristic of the explosiveness of his reactions were statements such as the following:

"If they don't do enough for the veterans, they're going to start shooting. They've put up with enough. They better see to it that the veterans get along all right or there'll be plenty of trouble."

He was not only afraid of the Communists, but also of the British:

"People would like to have us fight for the British. If people start shooting the Jews, the Jews will have us in another war."

When speaking of army officers, he said:

"The soldiers didn't have no use for them. They'd just as soon shoot them as the Japs."

In referring to the Jews he was one of the very few who used the term "Yid." But anti-Semitic though he was, he still made occasional qualifying remarks which showed that a minimum of control was exercising some restraint and was pressing for rational elaboration of hostile statements.

"There are different kinds of Jews. There were some who were obnoxious, but there were some who got along as one of the crowd. It's hard to say what the Jew really is."

The best way to influence politics, he said, is to "get a gun." His outlook on life was very pessimistic and asocial:

"Things are bad and are going to be worse. Me? All I ask is to be left strictly alone."

When talking about a depression and unemployment, he was certain that it would come, and with it, an outbreak of violence.

He was unwilling to discuss his own childhood recollections or how children should be brought up. This was probably indicative of his hostility against his parents, as was his desire for isolation.

"Kids? No one in his right mind would have any. I can't understand how anybody would like to have any of them."

He had always been lonely, never associated with others, never went around with the gang.

"I sure am a lone wolf. All I want is to live in a cabin in the woods, all by myself, and see nobody all year long."

His hostility and isolation were epitomized by his recollection of his own outfit as a place where "everybody hated everybody."

Nevertheless, this man had some insight into the mechanisms which accounted for his own ethnic hostility, although the pressure of his hostility was so great that he could not act in terms of this insight. When speaking of the Japanese-Americans, he said:

"The Japanese will never get rid of their slant eyes. That makes them stand out. It makes them a target for all kinds of prejudice. Everyone has prejudices. *You just have to have something to aim at.*"

These examples of outspoken anti-Semites, even the last one, show that they possessed some, even if inadequate, controls.

A final case may illustrate those few extreme outspoken anti-Semites who rejected almost all discipline and authority. A thirty-five year old man of Italian parentage, born and raised in Chicago, exemplified the type of outspoken anti-Semite whose controls were entirely inadequate. In addition to those psychological attributes which he had in common with other outspoken anti-Semites, he was also characterized by strong feelings of persecution.

The interviewer described him as a stout man who became very angry and shouted during the interview; so much so at one point, that he stopped himself for fear the neighbors would think there was "a madman in the house and call the police." His case was of additional interest because he was one of the few men who specifically asked for a third political party. His attitudes toward Jews were characterized by such statements as:

"Jews have all the money and they all stick together. They'll never work in a factory.

"The Jews in the army got away with everything. They all had jobs in the rear. The Gentiles did all the fighting.

"Send them all back to Palestine. All they're after is money. The Jews should be forced to leave the country."

He was afraid things were going to turn out very badly for the country in general and for the veterans in particular.

"Nothing's being done for the veterans. Employers don't give a rap for them. From the White House down to the greedy capitalists, everybody's against the veterans. They were all right when they were in uniform but now nobody cares. Nobody's fair to the veterans, though they enlisted to help the country. A friend of mine told me the other day that the people in Germany treated him better than he's been treated since he came back to this country. The people don't have any influence on politics. Nothing is done by the people or for the people. All is done for the politician. Roosevelt should have been impeached before Pearl Harbor. There are nothing but crooks in Washington."

He was against both parties and all in favor of a third party.

"Put the whole old parties in a washing machine and run the whole thing through the wringer. I don't think there's an American in the White House. Even the English imperialists run the F.B.I. The country's going to the dogs. What we need is to get some real Americans in the White House. Everyone seems to want to give our country away. Only if the English and the Communists would get out of the White House and let old-fashioned Americans in there, then somebody could get in who'll be for the American people, people that'll pull for this country. We haven't had such for a long time. And I don't mean the Republicans, either. But chances for that are very slim. When I was in contact with the Italians I heard the story of Mussolini. Roosevelt and Churchill are just the same as he was. We need a third party. The third party is the only solution."

His fears about his own future were great, particularly that unemployment would hit him very hard. He felt sure he would have to go on relief. All his life he had had nothing but bad breaks: "The international bankers are the reason for our miseries."

All he wanted was to make $3,000 a year, but he felt that the chances for even this were very bad, unless, for once, he got "a lucky break."

In his opinion, army discipline had been unreasonably strict:

"The higher-ups had far too much authority. They could railroad a fellow like nobody's business, if they didn't like him."

At this point it may be stressed that a steady increase in hostility and a steady decline in the adequacy of controls could be observed as one moved from the least intolerant to the most intolerant men. But all were subject to some controls. These controls formed a continuum from adequate to inadequate as the degree of anti-Semitism increased. But they also formed another continuum, although it was not quite so clearcut. It was the continuum from internalized to external control; from ego control, to superego control, to willingly accepted external control, to external control under grudging submission, and finally to controls which were so inadequate that they could only assert themselves occasionally and ineffectually.

The last group in the continuum of tolerance to intolerance, that is, the intense anti-Semites, fell beyond this continuum of controls. Their controls were not so much inadequate or external, as they were absent, so far as the restraining of interethnic hostility was concerned.

6. THE INTENSE ANTI-SEMITE. The group of six *intense anti-Semites* was characterized by low security, high hostility, high frustration, and social isolation. Nowhere in the interview could an assertion of control over interethnic hostility be observed.

In addition, these men were all characterized by strong feelings of persecution as in the case of those outspoken anti-Semites whose controls seemed entirely inadequate.

However, as irrational as were some of the statements made by intense anti-Semites, the men were not totally without control, or they could never have maintained themselves in society. The question then arose of why control was so lacking in the case of ethnic hostility. The following hypothesis may account for this phenomenon, with the feeling of persecution by an ethnic minority as a necessary clue.

As regarded ethnic hostility (and perhaps other areas of interpersonal contacts) the intense anti-Semite had externalized controls by the mechanism of projection.[7] The price he paid for thus freeing himself of restraint by his own controls was to feel persecuted by the minority and this minority was now the vicarous carrier of his control over ethnic hostility. But while he felt controlled by the members of the hated outgroup, he could now give free reign to ethnic hostility which was no longer held in check.

A twenty-six year old veteran may serve as an example for the group of six intense anti-Semites. He completed two years of high school education, was of Czechoslovakian parentage and had been born and reared in Chicago. The interviewer described him as a good-looking, well-built man who spoke with a decided lisp. Throughout the interview he maintained a flippant but suspicious attitude.

His hostility against the Jews may be characterized by the many spontaneous statements he made about them. For instance, when asked whether there were any groups of people who might be harmful to the country, he replied:

"Well, the nigger. They're getting a lot out of hand. And then the Jews. They should run all the Jews out of the country. On jobs, Gentiles should always get preference. Well, most of the Jewish people have all the factories, so the white people are working for them. You don't see Jews working. Another thing, how about this Jewish boat that came across—what was it?—with fifty thousand of them. Why are they bringing them in here? They just persecute us Gentiles."

When asked what he hated about the army he said:

"What I hated most?—the officers, especially the Jewish ones. I just love the Jews—I'd like to hang them all up."

Referring specifically to the Jews in the army he said:

"They were treated like kings. They got away with more stuff than we did. They were poor soldiers. They haven't got the fighting ability. The best thing would be to get rid of them, export them. Well, if they'd move all the Jews out, I've reasoned it out—if they moved them all out, there'd be no more wars."

[7] For a detailed discussion of this mechanism, see Chapter VIII.

His animosity against other ethnic groups was equally strong. For instance he felt that the best thing to do with Japan would be to sink the islands and thus kill all Japanese.

He was extremely fearful about the future and felt certain that things would turn out very badly. His anticipation of unemployment was full of aggression and anxiety. He was sure he would "starve to death."

"We'll have a lot of unemployment and a lot of crime. Why shouldn't there be? We learned a lot of tricks, how to handle a gun, and we'll use them."

He was convinced that all political parties consisted only of crooks. One should "do away with all of them." The government was "all against the people."

Recollections of his childhood were pleasant but he planned to bring children up much more harshly.

"Children nowadays get away with too much. Well, if you can't talk to them, then tan their hides for them. Of course, I'm going to do that.

"My parents were too good, but I never have done much wrong. I was just naturally a good kid. My parents never had any trouble with me. Well, my next to the youngest brother, he wasn't so good, he always got the spanking, but it sure was good for him."

In summarizing the impression received from all interviews, and not solely from the excerpts above, it may be said that no final understanding of the group is possible on the basis of the association between relative strength of controls, relative degree of hostility, and anti-Semitism. The intention was primarily to show the general relationship between these psychological attributes. This underlying relationship remained the same when the anti-Negro attitudes of the group were examined, but in that case the group as a whole appeared much more hostile and far more intolerant. In the case of the Negroes, controls gave way much more readily, as will be shown in the following chapter.

It has already been stated that the analysis of controls as it relates to interethnic hostility is twofold. The adequacy of controls of some individuals for restraining interethnic hostility has now been discussed. The reasons for which some individuals select interethnic hostility as a channel for discharging hostility remains to be analyzed. This question may be discussed in connection with the related problem of why controls asserted themselves so much less vigorously with regard to one type of interethnic hostility, anti-Negro feeling, as compared with another type of interethnic hostility, anti-Semitism.

CHAPTER VIII

CONDONING INTOLERANCE:
ANTI-NEGRO ATTITUDES

The relationship between control and tolerance was established in the preceding chapter. There, analysis indicated that, for the majority of those studied, tolerance was coexistent with an acceptance of external control; tolerance as a consequence of strong internalized controls was the rare exception. To further test the validity of these findings, anti-Negro attitudes were analyzed in a similar manner. Such analysis was particularly relevant in view of the fact that anti-Negro attitudes enjoy greater acceptance, both socially and legally, than almost any other form of ethnic intolerance.

Here it should be emphasized that controls are internalized only if the individual has erected barriers *within himself* against discharging tension in aggressive behavior—barriers which function adequately under almost all circumstances except those of self-defense. Such controls, once established, are relatively independent of prevailing mores and of who the object of aggression may be.

As pointed out in Chapter VII, the adequacy of a person's controls not only reflects the impact of controlling institutions, but also determines the degree of his hostilities. Thus a man may have developed strong and internalized controls precisely because his hostilities are over-powerful. Such a person may be tolerant, but he is not the most desirable member of a society striving for greater tolerance. He remains a deviate whose vital energies are spent not in constructive social action but in a personal battle with his own unintegrated hostility.[1]

---

[1] The example of the extreme pacifist seems to support this contention. The conscientious objector is a man whose conscience objects even to socially approved hostility. He obviously fears disapproval by his own controls more than condemnation by the rest of the citizenry, because the power of his own controls is stronger motivating forces than those exercised by society. In his case, temporary or even permanent societal attitudes toward aggression cannot influence his personal behavior. Conscientious objectors are usually characterized not only by their rejection of wartime aggression, but also by a consistent rejection of ethnic intolerance. Since aggression itself is prohibited by their controls, their attitudes of tolerance do not falter or

While fully internalized controls function relatively independent of the changing social picture, persons whose tolerance is due less to internal than to external controls, show significant differences in their attitudes. These differences depend chiefly on whether the external controlling institutions prohibit, disapprove, condone, or even approve of intolerance against a particular group. It is common knowledge that the institutional patterns and the informal mores of the community differ sharply for the Negro and the Jew. Imputed racial differences also affect the status and treatment of the Negro to a greater extent than they do those of the Jew. This was particularly true among members of the sample, as was indicated by many statements to the effect that the Jew was "white after all," or that there was "no racial difference" between Jew and Gentile. Social scientists may agree on the fallacy of thinking in racial terms. But a scientific study of interethnic hostility cannot overlook present day thinking in terms of "race" because of its widespread influence on attitudes and behavior.

Popular attitudes toward ethnic groups are based on a type of thinking which can neither be understood nor analyzed when it is conceived as being similar to that of the social scientist. For instance, the concept of

---

vary when confronted with different ethnic groups, even if society directs various degrees, or types, of hostility against one or the other of these groups.

Psychoanalytical study of some conscientious objectors has revealed that the unusual strength of controls which prohibited them from any discharge of hostility against other human beings was not a matter of rational conviction but a vitally needed defense against the fear of total disintegration. Their unconscious hatred of man originated in their hatred of some of the most significant figures of their family and was so overwhelming that they dreaded the consequences of discharging even the smallest amount of hostility against anyone. They behaved as though any lapse in control might lead to a total and uncontrollable discharge of hostility, including discharge against the original source and object of hatred—their parents or siblings. In one case, conscientious objection was traced to the fear that bearing arms on a home visit might accidentally lead to the killing of a particular member of the family. The only way to avoid such danger, this C.O. felt, was under no circumstances to touch any weapon, even if such behavior led to the most far-reaching consequences. One might add, of course, that no imagined consequences could possibly have been as far-reaching as the feared patricide.

Frequently it is the argument of the brotherhood of men which is put forward by pacifists. They feel they must avoid wartime service because to them it implies not only the killing of human beings, but fratricide. This fear of doing violence to a brother figure is likely to be a reaction-formation born of an animosity toward close relations.

Individuals who find no basis in their own feelings for fearing potential fratricide can more readily permit themselves to discharge aggression into socially approved outlets. They have fewer doubts about their ability to control aggressive tendencies. They can view the opposing soldier either as an enemy, or as a potentially lovable human being who is as unfortunate as they are in having to bear arms and to fight a war.

"race" has to the unsophisticated person a wealth of emotional connotations which relate it far more closely to mythical (magical) thinking than to reason. The "inscrutable" Chinese seems so uncanny, so alien, that the feeling of foreignness blocks most attempts at the real contacts differentiated from mere propinquity,—which might reduce differences to a comparable and an understandable level.

Similarly, it appears that German propagandists, in order to make the German people (or a sizable segment of it) accept genocide, had to employ the notion of racial differences, of the inferiority of the Jewish "race" and the danger that it might contaminate the "superior" German race. That genocide, where it was accepted, was approved of only on racial grounds is indicated by the fact that before the large-scale extermination of Polish and Russian people was launched, the idea of their racial difference and inferiority had first to be propagated with great vigor.

Why, in the twentieth century, the racial idea was selected by various authoritarian governments as a central idea for arousing masses is a critical question. Recently, progressively larger groups have come to constitute ingroups. Historical development in the western world from the tribe, to the city-state, to the small country, and finally to the national state has led in the last century to the consolidation of empires on a national and multinational basis. Under the impact of modern technology which required larger and larger areas for effective economic organization as well as the earlier spread of common cultural and religious values, the recognition of "sameness" was gradually extended beyond national barriers. In most recent times there have developed alongside of nationalistic attitudes a number of ideological identifications which have further loosened national boundaries and are being used to extend the power of major nations—for example, communism and aryanism. If this process were to continue, extranational units based on common ideologies would eventually replace nations as the ingroups.[2]

One of the tests which permits one to determine who is a member of the ingroup is that of marital custom. If, for instance, one tries to understand "race" as it is generally conceived, no other single criterion seems equally as suitable as the taboo on intermarriage. Both in the law and in the mores some of the strongest taboos have been those against intermarriage between "races." In questions of exogamy it is

[2] The current and violent revival of nationalism in certain European countries may frequently be viewed as a defensive reaction against the explicit threat of outside aggression and the implicit realization of the passing of national identity.

consensus alone which determines who belongs to a different race. To the
Germans, the Jews were exogamous—a dangerous alien "race" with
whom one ought not to cohabit. (The first and most far-reaching anti-
Jewish laws in Germany had for their central topic the problem of intermarriage.) In the United States, the Jews, though not particularly
sought after as marriage partners, are nevertheless in the main accepted
as "endogamous," while intermarriage between whites and Negroes is
still rejected as "exogamous."[3]

In view of the prevalence of anti-Negro attitudes it was expected
that those men whose control of aggression depended on the influence
of external factors would follow the patterns set by controlling institutions with regard to their own attitudes toward Negroes, and hence be
intolerant. On the other hand it was assumed that those subjects whose
controls against aggression were truly internalized would be tolerant
regardless of the mores of the community. But the nature of his controls
is not the only determining factor of an individual's intolerance. It was
also expected that whether or not a person's anti-Negro feelings tran-
scended those of his community would depend on the degree of his
personal feelings of deprivation and anxiety. In view of the prevailing
attitude towards Negroes among the group from which the sample was
selected, only those men, generally speaking, whose controls were fully
internalized should have been tolerant of all interethnic groups. In all
other cases, ethnic attitudes were likely to be influenced by the following factors: (1) the norms established by the controlling institutions
toward the particular ethnic group; (2) the degree to which the individual
accepted (or submitted to) external control; and (3) the intensity of
feelings of deprivation and anxiety.

It should again be emphasized that the acceptance or rejection, the
adequacy or inadequacy of controls mentioned in these pages are relative
quantities, describing only differences in degree. As a whole, the persons
studied were a group of law-abiding citizens. Hence they submitted to or
accepted some measure of external control, or at least as much of it as
was institutionalized in the law and its agencies. The acceptance of controls seemed to indicate a relatively high degree of conformity to social
institutions and mores and was therefore expected to be paralleled by a
tendency to adopt society's discrimination of Negroes, at least as long as
they remained within legal bounds.

[3] Lately another subdivision seems to have been created, with all mankind separated
into two "exogamous" classes with respect to marriage—communist and noncommu-
nist. In 1948, the Supreme Soviet approved a ban on all marriages between Russians
and foreigners.

A study of the correlates of anti-Negro attitudes, and their comparison with anti-Semitic attitudes, seemed to corroborate these propositions.

Data in the previous chapter indicate that among the sixty-one men who were tolerant toward Jews there were only fourteen whose tolerance seemed due to fully or partly internalized controls, while the tolerance of the remainder seemed due rather to the external control of hostile tendencies. By contrast, half of those who were tolerant to the Negro (seven out of twelve) had internalized controls. It may be added that although twelve of the 150 men forming the sample were tolerant of Negroes, only nine were tolerant of both Jews and Negroes. Of these nine men whose tolerance embraced both Jews and Negroes, seven had fully or partly internalized controls. Only two of the men who were tolerant of both groups seemed to be motivated by external controls. Apparently, internal controls are necessary in order to remain free of accepted prejudice.[4]

Thus while disinterestedness was not uncommon, actual acceptance of an outgroup was relatively rare among members of the sample—as rare as truly internalized controls. The majority of the men tended to follow the dominant cultural patterns of the groups to which they belonged so long as they were not subject to the additional pressure of deprivation or anxiety.

Hostility, it may be said, is displaced not only from the particular object in relation to which it originated, but also from the incomprehensible and often intangible sequence of events which gives rise to frustration and anxiety. Such displaced hostility is often increased by hostility initially originating not only in the social but also in the most private sphere, such as a man's relations to his boss, or to his marriage partner.[5]

In general, such displaced hostility tends to be discharged against a weak group which cannot retaliate with threatening counteraggression, and hence creates no additional anxiety.

In the main, the life circumstances of the veterans were not too favorable for the development of independent ethnic attitudes. Most of them

[4] This distribution of tolerance among both groups is in line with Freud's analysis according to which all social feelings which embrace individuals outside the primary group are based on internalization—that is, they are due to superego control: "Social feelings arise in the individual as a superstructure founded upon impulses of jealousy and rivalry against his brothers and sisters. Since the enmity cannot be gratified, there develops an identification with the former rival . . . the identification is a substitute for an affectionate object-choice which has succeeded the hostile aggressive attitude." Freud, S.: *The Ego and the Id*, London, Hogarth Press, 1947, p. 50.

[5] The role of displacement originating in poor sex relations, as evidenced by accusations against Negroes here, and Jews in Germany, should be mentioned in this connection.

had parents whose life histories and cultural levels were such that, excepting for events within their own family circle, they had no need to develop an independent code of interethnic behavior. There was no motive for disregarding the mores of the surrounding community in this regard. Thus the parents transmitted to their children their own viewpoints on larger social issues—opinions which were in accord with the values and standards of behavior which the controlling institutions of society also represented.

Independent opinions on social issues are often the consequence of either rebellion against parent and community, or of the child's having first internalized parental values only to find, later on, that they do not accord with the mores of the community. If this sort of conflict is successfully resolved through integration, ego strength may result, and, in the area of ethnic relations, a high degree of tolerance.[6]

Most members of the group studied experienced no inner conflicts about ethnic issues. The mores of their parents in this regard were those of the surrounding community. When a child rebels against his parents he needs the support of his own age-mates, and selects issues on which he is experiencing such support. These controversial issues confront the individual with the important task of finding solutions independent of parental mores. However, no such pressure for the integration of conflicting values about ethnic relations was experienced. Since parental behavior and external authority were in accord, the individual tended to follow the interethnic pattern already prepared for him. In the case of the sample, the selection of targets for ethnic aggression was relatively predetermined: they selected those of whom not only they, but also their parents, and their community disapproved.[7]

The validity of this observation was demonstrated by the anti-Semite of Chapter VII, who said: "Everyone has prejudices. You just have to have

[6] Southerners have sometimes become fighters for tolerance. Their tolerance is not infrequently the result of rebellion against parental values, or those of the community in general. But those who do not solve their conflicts through integration remain eternal rebels and are not effective in their struggle for tolerance. For them, the tolerance movement is mainly an outlet for unintegrated hostility and is recognized as such by their opponents. Those who succeed in solving their conflicts emerge with a much stronger ego, and then their efforts, which are the consequence of effective sublimation, are of value to the community at large. They can succeed because they no longer hate their opponents and their opponents recognize that they are not merely being attacked.

[7] Such attitudes are in marked contrast to those of certain types of college students who are all too frequently made the subject of interethnic attitude research, although few inferences can be drawn from such studies to the population at large. These students, often only in temporary revolt against parental authority, frequently embrace the liberal attitudes of the college community without lasting effect.

something to aim at." Apparently, if there are various groups available against whom to discriminate, that group is selected against whom discrimination is relatively least contrary to an individual's controls.

While "everyone has prejudices," the very intolerant men "hated everybody," as one of them put it. But one cannot live in society and hate everybody. Therefore some psychological methods must be used for dealing with these emotions and one such method is to displace all hatred onto persons or groups who are more suitable for the purpose.

It has been noted that the social mores select the particular groups against whom more or less hostility is discharged. It was therefore expected that those phenomena which were significantly related to anti-Semitism would be analogously associated with intolerance toward the Negro. It was also anticipated that since American society in general, and the group to which these men belonged in particular, is more apt to condone intolerance toward the Negro, these correlates would prove less selective. Therefore, for example, relatively small differences in anxiety might be expected to be associated with different degrees of intolerance toward the Jews, while such differences in anxiety would be associated with intolerance toward Negroes, although the instrument would not permit ascertaining the difference. Conversely, the nature or degree of control which seemed adequate enough to restrain hostile tendencies from finding overt anti-Semitic expression might not be strong enough to restrain an individual from making anti-Negro statements.

It must not be overlooked that, to the men studied, Jew and Negro appeared in quite different relations to themselves. To the men who aspired to higher social status the Jews often seemed to have been successful in this regard, while the Negro almost always seemed an inferior who should be prevented from threatening the individual's superiority. The analysis of the stereotyped pictures of Jews and Negroes showed that the Jew was predominantly seen as the person who should be reduced in status (who "should not own so much"), while the Negro was the person who should not aspire to or be permitted to gain equal status with the men. The desire to achieve the symbols of higher status with which the Jew was invested counteracted hostility to some degree, since the attitudes ascribed to the Jew were at least partially accepted by the individual as features of his ego ideal.

High degrees of ethnic intolerance are seemingly incompatible with the desire to match the status of the discriminated person. Actually total rejection and extreme hostility cannot be maintained if the feeling of envy toward the discriminated person comes to consciousness. To the intolerant the superiority of his own group must always be assumed. In the sample, the intolerant men wished the Jews to have "less" than they themselves possessed, while tolerant men could admit they would like to have as much as they felt the Jews had. Partial identification which is implied in any wish to have as much as (be like) the other person is incompatible with high degrees of intolerance, and appeared to be wholly absent in the case of the Negro. In effect, the intolerant men wished the Jews not to be more successful than they were, and wished the Negro to remain definitely below their own standards. The last sentiment was only very rarely expressed in connection with the Jews, and then only by extreme anti-Semites.

A comparative analysis of the data gathered in this study bore out expected findings with regard to the Negro: the correlates of intolerance proved more selective for anti-Semitism than for anti-Negro attitudes. A higher degree of association was found between attributes of intolerance and anti-Semitism than anti-Negro attitudes although the degree of hostility against the Negro was much higher. Otherwise the data presented a pattern of similarity between the correlates of anti-Semitism and anti-Negro attitudes, with some few exceptions.

The five attributes most highly associated with anti-Semitism were the same as those for anti-Negro attitudes. When ranked in order they showed only a slight deviation for Jews and Negroes as may be seen below.

Anti-Semitism	*Anti-Negro Attitudes*
Feeling of deprivation	Feeling of deprivation
Social mobility	Social mobility
Rejection of controlling institutions	Rejection of controlling institutions
Economic apprehensions	General optimism
General optimism	Economic apprehensions

The greater selectivity of these attributes for indicating anti-Semitism than for indicating anti-Negro attitudes can be seen from their comparison.

The similarity between anti-Negro feelings and anti-Semitism was further corroborated by the fact that of the various other attributes for which the interview probed nearly all those which proved unrelated to anti-Semitism were also unrelated to the degree of intolerance toward Negroes.

Both age and education were statistically unrelated to anti-Negro attitudes, although, as in the case of anti-Semitism, those veterans who were older or less educated tended to be more intolerant. Political party affiliations and religious denominations were also unrelated to intolerance toward Negroes. (See Appendix, Tables 14(A), 15(A), 16(A), 17(A).)

TABLE 1(VIII)

ATTRIBUTES OF INTOLERANCE

| Attitude | Coefficient of Contingency | |
	Anti-Semitism	Anti-Negro Feeling
Feeling of deprivation	.249	.107
Social Mobility	.114	.098
Rejection of controlling institutions	.112	.072
Economic apprehension	.082	.030
General optimism	.049	.084

On the whole, newspaper reading habits among veterans of all attitudes toward Negroes did not differ significantly. (See Appendix Table 19(A).) However, as far as individual newspapers were concerned, the *Daily News* and the *Sun* had the most tolerant readers.[8] The tabloid *Times* had a largely intolerant readership among the sample. It was the only paper significantly different from the others in this respect. It should be observed that the *Tribune*, as in the case of anti-Semitism, did not attract a more intolerant readership.

Family composition, as in the case of anti-Semitism, was not associated with anti-Negro attitudes. An exception was the *significantly* greater percentage of divorce found in the families of the outspokenly and intensely anti-Negro veterans. (Appendix Table 19(A).) In Chapter IV it was reported that a greater tendency toward both anti-Semitic and anti-Negro attitudes could be found in those families in which one parent was foreign-born as contrasted with families in which both parents were either born abroad or were native-born. (See also Table 13(A) in the Appendix.) Both of these indices of the absence of family cohesion—divorce and mixed nativity of parents—seem to emphasize that family disorganization may be an important source of intolerance, at least for the group studied.[9] This observation is in line with findings reported in

[8] As noted in Chapter IV, the *Sun* and the *Times* were New Deal papers as opposed to the *Herald-American* (Hearst) and the *Tribune*, with the *Daily News* falling somewhere between.

[9] The absence of a significant relation between divorce and degree of anti-Semitism may be due to the fact that many more men were outspokenly and intensely anti-Negro than anti-Semitic and since only a small percentage of the sample came from broken homes the number of outspoken and intense anti-Semites whose parents were divorced was too small to make the relationship statistically significant.

Chapter VII that those men who
were *significantly* more intolera
more intolerant of the Negroes.

A pattern similar to that of anti-S
to social mobility. Outspoken and
were found most highly concentrated
while the pattern was significantly reverse.
upward mobility (see Table 2(VIII)).

Those who had experienced no change in social mo.
picture midway on the continuum of anti-Negro attitudes.
mobility group as a whole was *significantly* different from both the u.
ward mobility and from the upward mobility categories. This stands
somewhat in contrast to correlates of anti-Semitism where the no-mobility
group more closely resembled the attitudes of the upwardly mobile
group.)

While the no-mobility group was most generally in the outspokenly
anti-Negro category, anti-Semitism in this group was milder in that it was

TABLE 2(VIII)

ANTI-NEGRO ATTITUDES AND SOCIAL MOBILITY

	Downward Mobility		No Mobility		Upward Mobility		Total	
	No.	Percentage	No.	Percentage	No.	Percentage	No.	Percentage
Tolerant and Stereotyped	5	28	18	26	22	50	45	34
Outspoken	5	28	40	59	17	39	62	48
Intense	8	44	10	15	5	11	23	18
Total	18		68		44		130	

most generally in the stereotyped category. These data supply another
crude index of the limits of intolerance toward minority groups in a
northern urban industrial community. In the case of the Jew, the social
norms were most likely to produce merely stereotyped thinking, while it
was "normal" to be outspoken in one's restrictive hostility toward the
Negro.

It has been argued above that stereotyped anti-Semites are potential
outspoken and intense anti-Semites, should conditions of social mobility

be altered. The same reasoning appears applicable to anti-Negro atti-tudes, with the observation that downward mobility is likely to produce the extreme and unbridled hostilities.

As in the case of anti-Semitism, there was a small group of veterans who were upwardly mobile but intensely anti-Negro. Many more mem-bers of the upwardly mobile group revealed strongly anti-Semitic atti-tudes than revealed strongly anti-Negro attitudes; a comparison of Tables 4(IV) and 2(VIII) shows a difference of 32 per cent versus 11 per cent. It is suggestive to assume that this difference may be due to the fact that some members of this upwardly mobile group had reached the status of upper middle class, while their majority were still lower middle class despite their successful movement upward. As a group, they would now be in status competition with a group according to popular opinion more closely identified with Jews. On the other hand it is likely that as indi-viduals they would be less likely to feel the impact of Negro competition.

While these observations seem to stress the socioeconomic factor in ethnic prejudice (but also the psychological factor of fear of failure in competition) it should be repeated that the majority of this upwardly mobile group was on the tolerant end of the continuum. An identical number (exactly half the group) had the most tolerant attitude on the three-point continuum both toward Jews and toward Negroes. Thus it seems that the generally optimistic outlook on life which one might expect in a relatively successful group, combined with the relative ego strength which goes with success, is considerably more important in con-ditioning attitudes of tolerance than the social and economic factor of competition.

Further insight into the difference between anti-Semitic and anti-Negro attitudes was provided by the socioeconomic correlates of anti-Negro attitudes. Here, in contrast to anti-Semitism, anti-Negro attitudes bore an association to certain of the indices of socioeconomic status.

The current salary range of the veterans as well as their rank at the time of discharge produced no statistically significant differences when related to anti-Negro attitudes, as in the case of anti-Semitism. (Compare Tables 3(IV) and 20(A).)

However, socioeconomic status, as measured by the Alba Edwards scale (see Chapter IV) was found to reveal *significant* differences in anti-Negro attitudes. (See Table 21(A) in the Appendix.) Semi-skilled workers were found to be more outspokenly or intensely anti-Negro. Other levels of socioeconomic status were not signficantly related to intolerance. Among the clerks and kindred worker categories there was no concentration of outspoken or intense attitudes against the Negro. Within the age group studied the white-collar workers, often accused of being particularly prejudiced, proved to be no more anti-Semitic or anti-Negro than any other group. The study of attitudes prevalent among semi-skilled workers, however, suggests that the group which is directly threatened in its economic (job) security is likely to be more intolerant of the group with which it feels it is in competition.

This observation was borne out by the higher concentration of anti-Negro attitudes in the semi-skilled category which accounts in substantial measure for the association between anti-Negro attitude and socioeconomic stratification, an association which was absent as regarded anti-Semitism. This distribution of anti-Negro attitudes is compatible with the positive relation between tolerance and social mobility. A relatively high proportion of the sample was concentrated in the semi-skilled category. There the pressure for upward social mobility meets with a minimum amount of success as a result of increasingly rigid class stratification. In particular, this group is directly subject to economic competition from the Negro in the mass production and construction industries. This may explain why apprehension about unemployment was *significantly* associated with anti-Negro attitudes.

All of the foregoing also seems applicable to the association between anti-Negro attitudes and the veteran's job aspiration. Dubious feelings or outright doubt that he would be able to achieve his occupational ambitions were *significantly* associated with the degree of a man's anti-Negro attitudes. On the other hand those veterans who felt they would succeed in achieving their occupational and economic aspirations were *significantly* more tolerant of the Negro. Such associations were not found in the case of anti-Semitism.

Reactions to war experiences and their relation to expressions of anti-Negro feelings followed closely the pattern of anti-Semitism discussed in Chapter V. In both cases, subjective feelings of deprivation were significantly associated with intolerance. The more objective criteria of conditions of army service (such as combat vs. noncombat, injuries sustained, length of service, and the like) proved unrelated to intolerance. While the men's overall statements about army experiences demonstrated that *significantly* more of those who felt subjectively deprived by army life held anti-Negro attitudes, definite convictions of having had a bad break in the army, or that time spent in the army was a serious setback, tended to be concentrated among those men who were outspokenly and intensely anti-Negro, although this pattern was not definite enough to be statistically significant.

Remarks about army experiences which indicated the individual's tendency to identify with national goals were found to be associated with tolerance toward Negroes, as was the case with tolerance toward Jews.

During the discussion of army experiences the veterans were asked, "How did the fellows in your outfit get along with the Negroes?" Responses offered an indirect method of gauging the association between intolerance and personal contact with Negroes in the army. Almost 40 per cent of the men claimed to have had no contact with Negroes while in service (that is, close or sustained contact). Claiming to have had no contact with Negroes in the army was *significantly* associated with outspoken and intense intolerance toward the Negro. Of course, contact with Negroes in the army is not necessarily associated with decreased hostility toward them. However it is quite possible that outspoken and intense hostility toward Negroes may have been associated not only with a tendency to avoid contact, but also to deny having had such contact. (The percentage who claimed to have had no contact with Jews was too small to permit statistical breakdowns in terms of degree of anti-Semitism, so that no comparison with anti-Semitism was possible.)[10]

When the pattern of anti-Negro attitudes was viewed in terms of the structure of the men's controls, the hypothesis of intolerance as a function of inadequate controls tended to be confirmed. But while the thesis was qualitatively confirmed, its application in the case of the Negro shows that even relatively adequate controls were not strong enough to permit tolerance toward the Negro.

In general only those who possessed truly internalized controls seemed to have genuinely tolerant attitudes toward Negroes. In the case of anti-Semitism, the acceptance of or submission to external control seemed enough to support a relative tolerance. But where the Negro was concerned, the same degree of acceptance was accompanied by attitudes

[10] In contrast to the type of random contacts with Negro troops for which the interview questions probed, a study by the Information and Education Division, U. S. War Department, reports that more favorable attitudes toward Negro troops were encountered in white soldiers who had direct combat experiences with Negroes. Some Negro platoons of infantry volunteers were employed with white infantry platoons in combat conditions in Europe. But although the use of Negro platoons alongside of white platoons represented relatively close contact between white and Negro troops, it was still a form of segregation since, both under actual combat conditions and while in reserve, the men were organized into color-line platoons and not completely intermixed. (*Report No. B-17*, Washington: Information and Education Division, Army Service Forces, U. S. War Department, 1945.)

which were largely stereotyped and outspoken rather than tolerant—for those were the corresponding norms of our society.[11]

In the case of the Negro, societal controls exercise a regulating and restraining influence only on what would be classified as "intense" intolerance, or open expressions of the desire for violence. Such violence is generally disapproved of by the controlling institutions—while they approve, if not enforce, stereotyped and outspoken attitudes. Therefore, those men who were strongly influenced by external controls were, in the majority, stereotyped and outspoken but not intense in their expressions of intolerance toward Negroes.

This emerged quite clearly when the comprehensive index of attitudes toward institutions of external authority (see Table 3(VII) was related to anti-Negro attitudes (see Table 3(VIII)).

TABLE 3(VIII)

ATTITUDES TOWARD THE NEGRO AND TOWARD CONTROLLING INSTITUTIONS

	Tolerant		Stereotyped		Outspoken		Intense		Total	
	No.	Per-centage	No.	Per-centage	No.	Per-centage	No.	Per-centage	No.	Per-centage
Acceptance	9	75	19	48	38	51	6	25	72	48
Intermediate	2	17	16	40	23	31	4	17	45	30
Rejection	1	8	5	12	13	18	14	58	33	22
Total	12		40		74		24		150	

The division between those who rejected and those who accepted external control came between outspoken and intense attitudes toward Negroes. To score "high" on the index of rejection for the four controlling institutions meant that an individual was likely to fall in the intensely

[11] The legal sanctioning of segregation, such as in restrictive covenants, does much to develop and maintain stereotyped opinions about Negroes. Not only do the consequences of segregation breed "dirtiness" and "negligence," they also lend support to the rationalization of such covenants by creating tangible evidence that the presence of Negroes devaluates property. Such regulations also tend to increase the habit of stereotyped thinking about Negroes. Real-estate values may decline due to the influx of Negroes, but while this is commonly stressed, the increase in return which the property often yields due to higher rents is usually neglected. The correlation which psychoanalysis has revealed to exist in nearly every instance, between anal preoccupation on the one hand and an interest in cleanliness and money (property) on the other, is highly suggestive. The common reaction-formation against anality, in our society, is wealth and "property." Therefore the rejection of dirt must, psychologically speaking, coexist with the accusation that such "dirtiness" rules out the maintenance of wealth and property.

anti-Negro category. Acceptance of external controls was not only inadequate in conditioning men to be tolerant of the Negroes, it was not even enough to prevent them from holding outspoken views in that regard. It served only to restrain demands for open violence.

These observations are further corroborated by a more detailed analysis of the relationship between attitudes towards the Negro and those toward specific symbols of authority. No significant association between tolerance toward the Negro and acceptance of those authority symbols selected for investigation could be established. The number of persons who were tolerant toward the Negro was so small in the sample that it may have influenced the findings to some degree. But the number of men who held merely stereotyped opinions—and were thus relatively more tolerant—was large enough to indicate a significant tendency had it been present.

Of all the social institutions which represent symbols or systems of authority, one stands alone at the top of the ethical scale: religion. Problems of expedience or momentary dissatisfaction may influence a man's attitude toward any one of the four symbols of social authority which were used in constructing the index. Therefore religion and religious attitudes were deliberately not included because religious authority seemed to rank on a different plane. In studying the association between religious attitudes and anti-Semitism it was found that stability of religious convictions was *significantly* associated with tolerance toward Jews. Such association was *not* encountered in the case of the Negro, thus demonstrating an apparent weakness of religious authority in this respect.[12] The fact that nearly all correlates of tolerance toward the Jews proved less discriminating for the Negro seems to offer a convenient explanation. Nevertheless, this seems a rather flimsy explanation for so strong an influence as the precept of brotherly love.

Historically speaking, one might have expected that Christian animosity toward the unbeliever would have induced men with stable religious convictions to feel more strongly about non-Christians (Jews) than about fellow Christians (Negroes). True, while medieval religious fervor often led to religious persecution, the modern American-Protestant interpretation of Christianity has tended towards greater tolerance. But tolerance of the Jews out of religious conviction cannot explain why no similar

---

[12] True, there are regions in the U.S. where segregation in church attendance is upheld and condoned. In such instances, the church performs the same function in attitude formation that the law does when it supports restrictive covenants in secular life. However, this was not true in Chicago where the study was made, and where on the whole the church has preached tolerance and has practiced it.

association could be found between stability of religious convictions and relatively greater tolerance toward the Christian Negro.

In the discussion of stereotypes in Chapter III it was mentioned that prejudice against Jews is rationalized differently from prejudice against the Negro. It was pointed out that according to psychoanalytic theory the psychological mechanisms underlying prejudice are those of projection and displacement—both of them efforts to retain or to reestablish a threatened intrapsychic balance. While various inacceptable tendencies can be dealt with in this way, the projections themselves, in order to remain within the limits of "normal" behavior, must withstand a minimum of reality testing. This means that there must be a nucleus of reality around which they must be built up (see p. 32 f) and it must be possible to rationalize them by means which are satisfactory to the individual's controlling institutions and to the group to which he belongs. Reality is not tested out of context, nor are rationalizations developed independent of the prevailing frame of reference. Hence rationalizations which would frequently have to be reexamined or challenged for their compatibility with the individual's life experiences would finally prove useless either to the individual's superego, or to his ego. However such challenges would have to originate with members of his own group. Only if the ingroup challenges the rationalization does it become inadequate for protecting the projection or displacement which would thus lose its value in securing the individual's integration, devious as that might be.

But the rationalization of prejudice does more than just allow for displacements. It also serves more important and more devious purposes. Initially the superego objects to a tendency which must therefore be displaced. But for the same reason that the superego initially rejected the tendency, it not only comes to approve of the persecution of the individual onto whom the tendency was displaced, it even demands it. As a matter of fact, persecution on the grounds of morality has had superego sanction throughout history. This was particularly clear in cases of religious persecution where the pagan's destruction was not only permitted, but demanded by the superego. Such persecution is one of the instances in which the superego permits gratification of hostile and sadistic tendencies which must otherwise be warded off. Thus the usually restraining function of the superego over instinctual (id) tendencies is for all practical purposes perverted into its opposite. A major function of the superego is to demand—or so at least one would hope in our society—that the weaker group, the minority, should not be persecuted. But because of the rationalization it has invented to justify the persecution, and because of the inacceptable tendency it has displaced onto the minority, the super-ego now demands the minority's persecution.

In a way, this form of behavior is no more than a continued "persecution" of the self for its own objectionable tendencies and would, if it came to consciousness, be experienced as guilt. Therefore the ego in its defensive function rids itself of the guilt by externalizing it and displacing it on persons who thus become "guilty" instead, so that the ego itself can go free. In its synthesizing function the ego tries to eliminate all conflicts between id and superego by externalizing tendencies originating in one or the other and displacing them onto other persons. If such displacement is directed at members of an ethnic outgroup, the phenomenon of ethnic intolerance ensues. Once id tendencies are thus dealt with, for instance, the outgroup may then be experienced vicariously as enjoying filth. If superego tendencies are dealt with in the same way, the outgroup is experienced as persecuting the ingroup. The feeling of guilt which originally "persecuted" the self within its structure is now gone, for the persecution has been externalized. Thus, in a way, no persecution of a minority group takes place where the majority group does not feel "persecuted" by the minority.[13]

Eissler has pointed out that in those cases where tendencies rejected by the superego are displaced on members of an outgroup, the rationalizations for persecution of the outgroup induce the superego to join its energy to the id's asocial impulses. In this way the instincts are supplemented by seemingly moral convictions and support the ego's attempt to satisfy the tendencies of both id and superego.[14] If this analysis should be valid, it would follow that the fury with which an outgroup is persecuted, and the degree of guilt which such aggressive behavior entails, would depend to a large degree on whether the externalized conflict as well as the rationalizations applied to justify the persecution were of such a

[13] This projection of guilt, which makes individual members of the group projecting the guilt feel persecuted, is by no means restricted to phenomena of ethnic intolerance. In most wars known to history each warring group has accused the other of having "started" the war, i.e., of having persecuted the other group. This was usually explained as "hypocrisy" on the part of one or both warring parties. The view that this phenomenon is a rationalization by means of which each group tries to justify its case offers only a partial explanation. The justification of aggression by rationalization is only an addition to the primary phenomenon of guilt projection. Most members of the warring groups simply feel guilty about their own aggressions set loose. They project this persecution by their own superegos onto members of the other group, who thus become, psychologically speaking, the true persecutors. The fight against them then becomes true "self-defense," i.e., defense of the self against tendencies which threaten its integration.

[14] Eissler, K. R.: "Incidental Observations During Psychiatric Surveys on Seven German Prisoners of War," *American Journal of Psychotherapy* II:53, 1948.

nature that the superego could join forces with the id. If rejected id tendencies are externalized and if rationalizations used are in line with the superego's moral demands (as for instance when an outgroup is accused of disorderliness or laziness) then id and superego join energies in the persecution. If, on the other hand, superego demands are displaced, because they are too overwhelming or too contrary to the pleasure drives, then tendencies are externalized, which are still basically in line with the superego demands, although rationalizations may be used which are inacceptable to the superego. Therefore such "persecution" will never be quite free of guilt feelings, and never be as vicious as the persecution of amorality.[15]

In present-day U. S. society, inacceptable id tendencies are mainly displaced onto Negroes (sex libertinism, dirtiness, laziness). Therefore, the superego can lend full support to their discrimination, since these are tendencies against which it fights continuously. Religion, the representation of superego demands, is thus much weaker as a mitigating influence on intolerance of the Negro than on intolerance of the Jew. This may explain why stability of religious convictions was so markedly associated with tolerance toward the Jew but failed to be associated with tolerance toward the Negro.

This theoretical analysis seems to be borne out by the data on stereotypes (see Tables 2(III) and 3(III)). In terms of frequency, the two stereotypes most often applied to the Negro were that they are dirty and that they depreciate property. Both of them are related to id demands, and both contain symbols which are closely connected with anal preoccupation; the first directly, the second as the accusation that the Negro destroys what is the frequent, and in our society, the most highly esteemed reaction-formation against anality: wealth. The acceptance of dirt and the interference with a reaction formation against it are therefore most obnoxious to a culture which maintains that "cleanliness is next to godliness."

The two stereotypes most often applied to the Jews were that they are clannish and help one another, and that they have the money. Helping one another is certainly a superego demand. (True, this stereotype

[15] This can be observed, for instance, in a classroom situation where the mediocre students may sneer at intellectual achievements in others—a reaction which is not free of guilt and therefore relatively mild. On the other hand, if such a classroom group attacks one of its members because of dirtiness or bad smell, the persecution will be much more vicious, and free of guilt. In this case, the students feel their own balance threatened by the example of someone who is getting away with undesirable behavior. Against such a threat, the students who discriminate against the "dirty" one will be restrained in their actions only by societal sanctions.

is frequently combined with the depreciatory one of clannishness. But basically the accusation of clannishness implies nothing but a restatement of the otherness of this different "clan" and as such is without ethical connotation. It acquires its depreciatory flavor only through fear of the strange outgroup, and through envy—as discussed on p. 39.) Interest in the possession of money—quite apart from the high status it provides in our society—is certainly a reaction-formation, developed under societal and superego pressure, against the primitive interest in dirt. Thus the rationalizations used for justifying anti-Semitism are closely related to superego demands.

It now becomes understandable why external controls, as the creations, representations, or symbols of superego demands, lend support to the discrimination of those groups on whom id tendencies are displaced, while they mitigate the discrimination of groups on whom reaction-formations against id tendencies are displaced. In view of these observations it was to be expected that the lack of association between tolerance toward the Negro, on the one hand, and acceptance of the four societal institutions or stability of religious convictions, on the other, would also hold true for the other symbols of authority which were studied. The acceptance of or submission to army authority, for example, proved unrelated to tolerance toward the Negroes. Those who got along with their officers and those who felt that army discipline was "all right" were neither more nor less tolerant toward Negroes than the rest of the group.

In summary, a study of attitudes toward symbols of external control supports the impression received from the earlier evaluation of individual interviews: only integrated attitudes make for true tolerance. Only a strong ego is able to synthesize the opposing tendencies of pleasure and reality in line with the pressures of the environment. Only a strong ego manages to gratify instinctual tendencies without having to resort to "persecution" and only such a strong ego is able to maintain balance without projecting or displacing those strivings which in a weak ego lead to unmanageable inner conflicts.

While the study of anti-Semitism indicates that, other things being equal, the acceptance of or submission to external controls seemed sufficient to assure a moderate, if not tolerant attitude, the study of anti-Negro attitudes suggests that such moderation in feelings about Jews is of a rather tenuous nature. It will perhaps be maintained so long as another outgroup provides objects for the displacement and persecution of instinctual tendencies which threaten the person's integration, and so long as external controls favor a tolerant attitude toward Jews.

The study has revealed a few deviant cases in which men displayed tolerant attitudes toward both Negroes and Jews despite the absence of strong egos, but each of them was due to unusual combinations of circumstances. One man, for example, was tolerant of Jews and Negroes although he had the characteristics of those men whose egos were weak, and applied the same mechanisms for maintaining his integration which characterized the intolerant men. The fact was that he had displaced almost all of his unacceptable and externalized id tendencies on Russia and communism (and in turn felt persecuted by them) so that he needed no other "scapegoat."

Men who relied on nonintegrated controls—whether in the form of external authority or nonintegrated superego pressures[16]—for maintaining their defense against asocial instinctual pressures could not function without discriminating against some minority group or other. Their tolerance of the Jews was due mainly to the fact that Negroes presented more "suitable" objects for discrimination. This suggests that the specific problem of anti-Semitism, as opposed to intolerance in general, can never be viewed as isolated but must always be analyzed within the context of the societal structure in which it occurs. The same must also hold true for discrimination of the Negro, or of any other ethnic minority. If two or more such minorities are available for the displacement of internal conflicts, and if their position in society makes one more "logical" for displacement of id tendencies, while the other seems more suitable for displacement of reaction-formations against id tendencies, then the first of the two groups will usually experience more serious discrimination.[17]

Personality structure alone, then, cannot entirely explain why people set out to discriminate against particular ethnic groups, or why they are more discriminating of one group than another. The defensive needs of the individual, the economic and social structure of the community, and the ethnic realities of the moment must also be taken into account. From

---

[16] One veteran who held stereotyped opinions about minorities made statements which revealed considerable anxiety about his economic future and also displayed other attitudes characteristic of an intensely intolerant personality make-up. However, his ethnic aggressions were restrained by an overstrict, unintegrated super-ego. This was indicated by his remarks about the importance of strict upbringing, when he said:

"Nowadays children are too free. There's not enough discipline. I was ruled with an iron hand and it sure served a good purpose. The good old tanning system is best."

[17] This is why it would be erroneous to apply lessons learned from German anti-Semitism, for example, to settings such as the United States, without making ample allowance for differences in the social structure of the two countries.

the preceding discussion it appears that in the United States and in a northern metropolis, the stereotyping and discrimination of Jews is currently fulfilling certain defensive personality needs, while the stereotyping and discrimination of the Negro fulfills others. It might well be that in the absence of one of these two ethnic minority groups, all or most of these defensive needs would be satisfied by "persecution" of the remaining one, or so at least might be inferred from the German example. But in the city studied—and in most other important United States centers of culture and policy formation—these two ethnic minorities exist, occupy differing positions in the community, and are made use of accordingly.

CHAPTER IX

REFLECTIONS, AND APPLICATIONS FOR
SOCIAL ACTION

In this report, the authors have sought to isolate the main psychological and sociological attributes which might explain the intolerance manifested by the veterans. Our conclusions have led toward emphasizing the factors of subjective deprivation, downward social mobility, anxiety, and the absence of adequate control of hostile discharge against ethnic minorities. An approach such as that of this study has its limitations and leaves certain areas untouched which as yet cannot be fully investigated by means of the scientific methods (such as statistical analysis) that were applied throughout the study. This chapter attempts to round out the report through further speculation based on the data collected in the study.

All generalizations which have appeared in previous chapters must be evaluated as deriving from a particular though significant sample of men living within a particular social structure. In this chapter, the authors wish to do more than simply evaluate their findings in terms of social scientific standards. The point has been reached where some suggestion must be made as to the application of those findings to social action.

In the planning and analysis of this study the authors have utilized the theory and observations of dynamic psychology and of sociological analysis. There is little point in raising the question of which system is most adequate for explaining ethnic intolerance. It is clear enough from the findings that either system alone would have been inadequate. It is hoped that the present study—among others—may perhaps supply the basis for further theoretical developments in the integration of these now separate bodies of theory.

The personality structures of the men in the sample were to a large degree formed under the impact of existing society. If ethnic intolerance is rooted in the intolerant individual's personality, then we must ask ourselves what in this society shapes personality in such a way that ethnic intolerance seems a frequent, if not a favorite outlet for hostility. While it is not true, as the Marxist maintains, that ethnic intolerance is a consequence of the capitalist system, ethnic intolerance occurring within a capitalist society will nevertheless be deeply influenced in character by that society.

It may once more be stressed that intolerance is always an outlet for hostility, but that it depends for its intensity on the degree of hostility accumulated, and on the strength of the controls which restrain it. While hostility against outgroups is probably as old as society, the particular form in which hostility occurs is particular to the society in which it appears. Although anti-Semitism has been present in slave societies, feudal societies, capitalist societies, and recently too in communist society, it appears in each case to have been a different social phenomenon. What is historically permanent in anti-Semitism, for example, is only that members of a particular religious or ethnic group have been persecuted. The German-Jewish scientist, banker, physician, or laborer whom Hitler persecuted was as different from the medieval Jewish ghetto pawnbroker as was the German SS man from the German peasant or master craftsman who persecuted Jews in the Middle Ages. And as different as they were from one another, so also were their persecutions. Their differences originated in the different forms of society in which they lived—societies which shaped their personalities, outlooks, motives, and actions, which aroused their hostility, created frustration, and controlled its discharge. Hence their motives in persecuting the Jews were equally different, and equally rooted in the structure of their society.

In this book only that type of ethnic intolerance is analyzed which is prevalent in the urban centers of modern western society. Since the particular form in which it appears is an outgrowth of that society, it must be intimately connected with it, although it may still originate in each individual's personal frustrations, anxieties, hostilities, and so on. Two examples may serve to illustrate.

In a slave society in which one ethnic group rules another, the ruling group does more than simply tolerate the life—and even to some degree the well-being—of the discriminated group. The presence of this group is not only desired, it is vital to the working of society, and the latter, in case of need, must assure itself by warfare of securing new slaves. Some remnants of the attitudes originating in the needs of a slave society might account in part for observations made in the second chapter of this book. In that chapter it was mentioned that while the very intolerant men asked for the deportation of Jews, almost none of them requested deportation of Negroes, but requested instead that they be kept in their "place." The reason may well be that the Negro, although discriminated against, is nevertheless experienced as an important member of society, or at least as a person who serves a useful function. If the Negro were to leave, it would be left to the white man to perform those less desirable tasks which are now relegated to the Negro. Thus ethnic intolerance in its modern form was unthinkable in a society whose ethnic outgroups actually provided the economic base, as in a slave society. As a matter of fact, there are many ways in which modern ethnic intolerance tends to reestablish settings which were characteristic of slave society—the Negro must know and keep in his "place"; the Jew and members of other inferior races must labor in the concentration camp.

Ethnic intolerance as a social phenomenon takes on markedly different aspects depending on the social structure in which it occurs, and can be comprehended only when viewed in the context of that society. The example of medieval anti-Semitism may serve as an additional illustration. Jewish persecution in the Middle Ages charged the Jews with enjoying ill-begotten wealth—and the desire to gain, through plundering their riches, was an important incentive. But in medieval anti-Semitism these seemed only random phenomena. What seemed to excite real ire in the populace was that the Jews refused to be saved, thus reviving and enforcing in the Christians repressed doubts about their own salvation. (Without firsthand knowledge, all statements about the inner psychological processes of individuals who lived during the medieval period must remain conjecture. Still it might be reasonable to assume that his id, superego, and ego served similar functions in the psychological apparatus, but were differently constituted than those of modern man. Cleanliness was considered vain, if not unhealthy; the content of the superego was ordained by the Church; and the priest and the Church provided the most powerful superego representation. The superego had no need to evoke symbols of self-respect or individual conscience for restraining ego and id—the fear of hell and damnation were much more powerful incentives. Moreover, the ego was not confronted with an abundance of choices, and a relatively weak ego sufficed for mastering the tasks of life. Life activities were more rigidly organized and less subject to freedom of choice than they are today and the ego was less taxed in its need to synthesize opposing tendencies. Which of these tendencies, and in which ways they might be satisfied was more or less ordered by rules and tradition.)

It seems reasonable to assume that the ego of medieval man was at least as much concerned with saving his immortal soul as it was with making his temporal life successful. It is difficult to decide where his individual superego began, and where the Church and its teaching served him in its stead. Even the true medieval heretics (St. John of the Cross, etc.) bowed to the authority of popes, of whose individual shortcomings they were not unaware.[1]

What the individual during the Middle Ages appears to have feared most was not loss in status or economic security, but loss of grace. Much as he might have cherished the former, it was far more important, and a much greater threat, to fear damnation and the loss of eternal life. But it was not always easy to live by the rules of the superego-Church. (That the Church permitted considerable id gratification may be disregarded for the purpose of this discussion.) The id pressed for a gratification that was not always sanctioned by the Church, so that the ego and individualized superego may often have joined forces in doubting salvation through religious conformity. Such doubts had to be done away with, had to be persecuted and extinguished. They were the greatest threat to the individual's integration. One way to eliminate this threat was to project the conflict onto the Jews. In the Middle Ages, the most frequent accusation made against Jews, and the one which aroused the greatest hatred, was that they had desecrated the host. Closely related was the other accusation that they had committed ritual murders, used children they had killed to say a black mass.

The example of the Marannos (Spanish Jews converted to Catholicism) shows that these accusations reflected a very probable origin of anti-Semitism at that time, namely the Christian's fear of being a bad Catholic (more so, at least, than modern accusations indicate the real reasons for modern anti-Semitism). These Spanish Jews were notoriously wealthy as well as culturally and politically influential, and aside from religious accusations, their wealth, too, was held against them.[2] Still a change of religion put an end to their persecution, provided they really meant it. As soon as Spanish Jews became Catholics, they were not only permitted

[1] Thus the superego which forced them to take a stand against the temporary Church was not strong enough to assert its absolute independence. On the other hand, the Protestant reformers, and their forerunners from Wycliffe on, seem to have had more individualized superegos which permitted them to supplement faith with their own observations in taking a stand against Church and pope. But in this sense they were rather precursors of modern man than typically medieval and once the reforms they inaugurated were established, modern times had begun.

[2] The modern accusation of clannishness (the one most frequently used by the men in the sample) was absent in medieval anti-Semitism, probably because the modern sense of isolation and the fear of alienation were not then prevalent.

to retain status and wealth, but were frequently known to increase in both.

In modern times when religious appeals have been introduced as a basis for the persecution of Jews, they have nearly always fallen flat.[3] Religious fear, or such inner conflicts as are based on it, is just no longer important enough to motivate large masses. Again and again ritual murder stories have been circulated, but have never been widely believed, or at least not in urban centers. The only places where they were lent some credence and led to persecutions were in eastern Europe, where economic, political, and religious organization was still very similar to that of the Middle Ages (the last time in the notorious Beilis case of 1911). Religious conversion which protected Spanish Jews was ultimately of little help to Jews in Germany. Thus although in the two examples, the German and the Spanish, both religious and economic accusations were used, the religious was more basic in the Middle Ages, while it is insignificant in modern times. On the other hand, the economic accusation seems all-important in modern times. The racial issue raised in National Socialist Germany seems but a return to the Middle Ages with racialism taking the place of religion. But into this new "religion" one cannot be "admitted"—the infidel, the man of a lower race, must be extinguished.

While the ethos of medieval society was largely religious, that of the men studied was largely economic. By and large, the latter considered income as the main status-providing factor. Security itself was experienced mainly as economic—as job or income security—and even those men who valued intellectual achievement viewed it chiefly as an economic asset.

The men strove little for religious salvation, but they certainly wished for economic security which was even more important to them than higher income, as some of them stated themselves. But economic security is not easily achieved in a competitive society. Moreover, the notion is widespread that in a competitive society everyone can better his status if he tries hard enough. This, of course, puts an added psychological burden on the man who does not even achieve an occupational position which he thinks will assure his economic well-being. In addition to not attaining needed security, he also experiences a blow to his self-esteem.

Thus the person who experiences a lowering of income is doubly deprived. He is dissatisfied with himself and in addition must fear for his economic welfare. Frustration therefore accumulates and presses for

---

[3] Throughout the interviews when reasons for the dislike of Jews were mentioned, references to religion were almost totally absent.

discharge in those men who experience downward mobility. To such men, ethnic discrimination offers a convenient outlet. But the fourth chapter has shown that it was not only those who experienced a lowering of economic status who were prejudiced, but also those who were stationary in that respect, although there was a significant difference in the intensity of intolerance between these two groups. In terms of existing society even the men whose status was unchanged had reason to be fearful, although they needed, in general, to be less anxious than those on the downgrade. The no-mobility group had failed to live up to the challenge that one better oneself which is inherent in competitive society. Although many social scientists would agree that to remain stationary in our society often indicates that a man has made good in competition, such an attitude is not yet part of the economic ethos. Therefore such men are not really at peace; their self-esteem, too, is threatened, though considerably less so than that of a member of the downwardly mobile group. Thus, among other reasons, even the stationary group took advantage of ethnic discrimination as a channel for the discharge of accumulated hostility. On the other hand, the upwardly mobile group, for their part, had gained enough courage from recent successes to feel they might weather a future depression which they, too, nevertheless feared.

Early in the book (Chapter III) it was mentioned that among the group studied there seemed to be a tendency to select the Jews as the group on whom to project those superego demands making for conflict within the individual, and that the character of anti-Semitism was strongly influenced by such projections. The intolerant men felt that the Jews were successful in those areas where they themselves had failed to make good. Their superegos—in line with the economic ethos of society —required that they increase their earnings and rise in the hierarchy of status. Against these demands, which they could not fulfill, the stationary and particularly the downwardly mobile group defended their egos by pointing to the Jews. It was the Jews, they claimed, who exercised undue control, possessed the money, and thus prevented their own success.

But these same groups among the sample were also the ones who were considerably more intolerant of Negroes than were the men who had risen economically. They could hardly accuse the Negroes of controlling them and thus blocking their advance, nor could they accuse them of possessing the money. Moreover, it has been pointed out that unacceptable id tendencies were most frequently projected onto Negroes, and these tendencies were certainly not required by the social ethos. If the specific form of intolerance in a given society is a function of that social structure and if the character of modern anti-Semitism is conditioned by the structure of modern society, the same must also hold true for intolerance toward the Negro. While the economic and social ethos which was evident among the sample generally required that a man should work hard, earn good money, and in that way better his status, by the same token it rejected tendencies toward laziness, lack of orderliness and cleanliness, unreliability, immorality, and loss of property through neglect.[4]

The type of accusations directed against the Negroes and the manner in which individual tendencies are projected onto that group are highly influenced by social mores. These mores decree which tendencies are unacceptable and which must be integrated and, if that is not possible, which must be eliminated. Those men who had risen occupationally (and to some degree those who had remained stationary) seem to have felt they had complied with the social ethos and thus felt less threatened by their instinctual desires. With their achievement they showed both the world and themselves that their rejected id tendencies interfered in no way with their doing their "duty." Their wish to "take things easy" was obviously no hindrance to their well-being and therefore implied considerably less of a threat to their integration than it did to the no-mobility or downwardly mobile groups. In this connection it might also be mentioned that members of the sample were part of the age group of which occupational improvement is even more expected than of younger or older men—the first being considered beginners, the latter definitely settled. The veterans studied were men enjoying their "best" years—those years, according to prevalent notions, which should be used to climb in the social hierarchy.

Obviously a man who is convinced that his stationary, or even downward socioeconomic position is only temporary can view his position with greater equanimity than one who is more or less convinced it is permanent. He will be able to maintain his integration despite superego pressure for greater achievment. On the other hand, a person who views his occupational potential with pessimism, who fears that an impending change in the business cycle will lead to a loss of his present earning power, will be unable to integrate his superego's pressure and less able to permit himself even those id gratifications which someone more relatively secure can afford to enjoy with ease.

The degree to which a person is haunted by fear depends in good

---

[4] The accusation that the presence of Negroes depreciates the value of property usually carries the definite connotation that such depreciation is due to willful neglect. To lose money or to occasion depreciation through chance rarely arouses the disgust which is created by supposedly willful negligence.

measure on what he feels is expected of him, either by himself or by others. Perhaps in the Middle Ages the man who felt sure he was saved was relatively free from fear and could therefore integrate the comparatively small amounts of aggression he might otherwise have discharged in ethnic hostility. On the other hand, by persecuting the unbelievers the man who feared his damnation might have tried to demonstrate to himself, to others—and, he may have hoped, to God—that he was not as bad a Christian as he feared. He, too, might have been persecuting another "doubting" man so that he might temporarily forget his own doubts. At the same time such persecution allowed him to discharge some of the hostility which was partially created by his fear of damnation, a fear which arose from his doubts. According to this study, many fears now related to intolerance are of an economic nature, hence can be approached rationally and, perhaps, dissolved. In many ways the situation is better in modern times, where few fears are related to the inaccessible supernatural. There are still ways to demonstrate to a person that he may feel secure about his economic future—or there would be if a constant increase in earning power, and success in competition were no longer a feature of economic security—while there was no way, in the Middle Ages, of assuring a man of salvation. Of course, this holds true only in so far as, and as long as the economic system with its vastness, complexity, and lack of individual responsibility or comprehension of the consequences of economic actions is not experienced by the individual as equally incomprehensible and overpowering as the supernatural appeared to the man of the Middle Ages.

THE INDIVIDUAL

After so much has been said about the economic concomitants of intolerance it should again be stressed that the comparison of objective army experiences and their subjective evaluation (Chapter V) has shown that objective reality seemed comparatively less important in shaping interethnic attitudes than the personal frame of reference within which objective reality is experienced. Despite the insecurities of the present day, quite a number of the veterans had egos which were adequate enough to master economic anxieties so that they were not forced to evaluate past, present, and future experiences as deprivational. They were relatively free of fear and found it possible to be optimistic even in adverse circumstances (combat, threat of depression, etc.). Such optimism and the self-confidence and self-respect which go with it, as well as the parallel ability to control hostility, all originate in fortunate childhood experiences. Positive relationships to parents and other members of the primary group and sufficient gratification of instinctual needs during childhood seem to equip a child with sufficient emotional strength to grow into an adult who feels able to master the difficulties of contemporary life.[5] Thus, in more than one way, anxiety about the future and the discharge of aggression in hostile action is a two-generation problem. The individual who has experienced even relative security in childhood will probably have acquired a personality structure which permits him to weather even relatively great frustrations and insecurities without experiencing them as a threat to his personal integration. He will not need to bolster his integration through the mechanism of projection, or the explosive and irrational discharge of hostility against members of an outgroup. On the other hand, a child born into a family which experiences actual deprivation during the child's most formative years will, in addition to actual deprivation, most probably be raised in an atmosphere of emotional insecurity. He will be unable to view his life experiences optimistically and thus every positive experience will lose much of its reassuring, ego-strengthening value. Conversely, every negative experience will seem according to expectation and thus even more deprivational and overpowering.[6]

[5] Clinical observations of severely disturbed children permit several interesting inferences on the consequences of actual and emotional deprivation during infancy and childhood. Children who on initial examination showed comparable degrees of disturbance, nevertheless showed marked differences in improvement during psychiatric treatment, depending chiefly on their past life experiences. Children who had suffered severe actual deprivation because they had been raised in submarginal families or in orphanages soon improved markedly. The abundant gratification of instinctual and interpersonal needs, as provided by the new environment, during treatment —they lived in a psychiatric institution—permitted them to modify their outlook on life quite rapidly. They learned soon enough that past deprivations were only one of many possible kinds of experiences and realized that life has more to offer than they had once thought. Hence, they did their best to adjust to it. On the other hand, children of well-to-do families who had always enjoyed abundance with regard to food and shelter—children who, as a matter of fact, had often been resentfully "overprotected" and in whose case "good" care covered up for intense rejection—these children took very much longer to conceive of the gratification offered at the treatment institution as anything desirable. Clinically speaking, their task was much more complex when compared to that of the "orphans." It was easier for the economically deprived children to change their outlook on life once—contrary to previous expectations—abundant gratification was regularly available. The same offer, and even its acceptance, remained ungratifying to the emotionally deprived children of well-to-do parents. Such offerings and whatever else was done for them were evaluated in terms of their old, pessimistic frame of reference and were, hence, of no positive value.

[6] In Germany, it was not the middle-aged group of men who had served in the first World War, and many of whom had experienced great losses in the after-war years, who furnished Hitler with his most ardent followers, although the leader himself and his officers came from that group. The bulk of the middle-aged men, despite the

Viewed as a two-generation problem, most of the men in the sample were not second generation in terms of insecurity. They were born into relatively stable and, relatively speaking, more secure families and were well out of their most formative years before the depression hit their parents. During their own infancy, many of their parents had been very optimistic about the economic future. The impact of the depression shook some of the men while they were adolescents, both physically, in terms of lowered family income, and emotionally, due to parental fears and insecurity. Those who were already somewhat insecure due to previous experiences probably became fixed in their insecurity and pessimism; and they were the ones who became the more intolerant adults.

In this study an effort was made to establish the association between intolerance and isolated social, economic, and psychological factors; but the results should not be misconstrued as implying that these factors per se account for intolerance. On the contrary, they are only varying attributes of a total Gestalt, formed by the individual's total personality and the social structure in which he finds himself. The interplay between personality structure and those forces originating in the social field seemed to condition the presence, the absence, and the nature of intolerance.

Thus if the personality is very strong, or if, for particular personal reasons, the individual is strongly committed to tolerance or intolerance, the influence of the social field in respect to tolerance or intolerance is relatively small. The weaker the personality, the stronger becomes the influence of the social field. On the basis of a purely psychological hypothesis, namely that ethnic intolerance is nothing but a cathartic outlet for hostility, it might be assumed that catharsis could be effected by dis-

---

downward mobility they had generally experienced, manned the *Reichsbanner* and the *Stahlhelm* (the liberal and the conservative military organizations) and not the SS. In part, this can be explained by the fact that they had, in their childhood, experienced the relative stability which characterized Germany at the turn of the century; most of their families had in fact improved in economic status during those years.

The sons of these men had been infants when their fathers were away at war. Their early childhood was often characterized by instability; food had been scarce, and their mothers, in addition to worrying about their husbands, had been working in war factories to keep the family going. They were still boys or had grown into early adolescence when their own and their parents' hopes for a better life after the war were terribly shattered by inflation, deflation, and unemployment. As young men in the Thirties, they could not believe they would ever be able to secure a decent life for themselves through their own efforts. Therefore they had to rely on a strong "leader," a father figure, to give them the emotional and economic security which their own fathers had been unable to provide. They had also to discharge the frustrations and hostility which had accumulated over a long period of insecurity and suffering, if they wished to retain their tenuous integration. Explosive action against minorities was then a convenient outlet.

charging all hostility against a single group and that all other available groups could then go free. This study seems to show (and the combination of anti-Negro, anti-Jewish, and anti-Catholic feeling in certain southern areas seems to corroborate it) that the singling out of one group for hostile discharge seems to be ruled out by the social context.

The difference between anti-Jewish and anti-Negro attitudes, as it emerged in this study, also belies the assumption that ethnic intolerance is purely psychological in origin and hence beyond the reach of social reform. On the other hand, the association of intolerance with subjective rather than objective deprivation speaks against its purely social origin. Nor can the argument be accepted that ethnic intolerance cannot be dispensed with as an outlet for hostility. Hostility is continuously accumulating in the anxious and the insecure, and cannot be discharged in single or infrequent explosions. With rare exceptions it is not possible to discharge the accumulation of years of hostility, particularly if it did not originate in a particular person whose death or removal alone might yield a cathartic relief. Violent outbursts of ethnic intolerance are still so relatively rare, and provide so few of the intolerant men with direct or vicarious outlet, that the rationalization of the need for ethnic discrimination seems untenable. Moreover, it should be realized that while ethnic hostility only rarely provides full outlet for hostility, it frequently adds to already existing frustrations. Compared to the underlying hostility toward Jews and Negroes which some of the subjects revealed, the outlets of verbal animosity and an occasional physical aggression of little consequence seemed quite insufficient. On the other hand, a mental preoccupation with the hated minority together with a felt inability to do anything about it seemed to add more to the frustration of the very intolerant than it gave outlet for hostility.[7] For these reasons it does not seem true that ethnic hostility is incorrigible because it originates in the hostile personality and is needed as an outlet. Less hostility and less continuous frustration would accumulate if the intolerant person were forced to recognize once and for all that this outlet was no longer available. Some intolerant men would have to find other outlets, but many others would learn to integrate those hostile tendencies which they now try forever and in vain to discharge against ethnic minorities.

---

[7] In seeking to understand prejudice, tolerant persons who reject ethnic hostility for valid reasons, as well as ethnic minorities who suffer from discrimination, often fail to realize that intolerant persons labor under an undischarged hostility which accumulates in them precisely because they are prejudiced. They experience constant frustration since they feel unable to do anything about a minority which they experience as a threat.

On the other hand, it seems invalid to argue that intolerant personality structures can no longer be changed and that similar changes in the future could be achieved only through a different form of personality formation.

The German example has certainly shown that radical changes in the social order produced deep-reaching if not necessarily permanent or desirable changes in the personality, although one must admit that it seems easier to disintegrate personality structure than to influence it toward higher integration.[8] Nevertheless, it is untrue to assume that nothing can be done about an existing generation and that all hopes for tolerance must rest with the future. Clinical experience also demonstrates that considerably greater and more permanently effective in producing modifications of personality structure than the extreme methods of National Socialism are those modifications of the environment which make it reassuring, secure, comprehensible, and thus manageable for the young individual. Such environments and their gentle but powerful challenge to identify with persons offering gratification and, therefore, to restrain hostility, produce changes in personality which are far-reaching indeed. This they do partly by reducing frustrations which derive from the environment, and partly by providing amply for all needs which can be satisfied. Under such conditions, little additional hostility is created, and existing or developing controls and powers of integration prove sufficient to contain it.[9] As one of many indications, it suggests that environmental changes may well be able to produce changes in personality structure and hence in intolerance.

As long as there are personality structures which remain poorly integrated—first because of upbringing and later because of too much tension created by insecurity and frustration—and as long as the individual's upbringing prevents him from acquiring adequate controls, for so long will society have to offer outlets for the discharge of hostility. On the other hand, as long as society continues to permit or to condone such hostile discharge, the individual will not be forced to integrate his hostilities, or to control them.

[8] For example, see Bettelheim, B.: "Individual and Mass Behavior in Extreme Situations," *Journal of Abnormal and Social Psychology* 38: 417-452, 1943.

[9] Even outside of deliberately planned environments, significant changes in personality structure due to changes in environment are constantly being observed. Among the most obvious but dramatic instances are the immigrants to this country who experienced far-reaching changes in personality during the process of adjusting to a socially and culturally different setting.

TOWARD THE FUTURE

The highest degrees of association established in this study were those between intolerance on the one hand and feelings of deprivation and downward social mobility on the other. The deprivations so highly associated with intolerance were not by and large of a predominantly private nature, such as having fallen out with one's family or being unable to have children, but ones very closely related to adverse economic experiences, or a fear of their recurrence.

Social mobility, in this study, has been measured by occupational position. Future changes in the industrial and administrative organization of our economy will partially determine new patterns of mobility. Of particular relevance will be those changes which result in the displacement of occupational groups. These trends, of course, are difficult to measure and hazardous to predict. To date, for example, there has been more speculation than data on the displacement of the middle classes. If such displacement were a fact, it would be extremely significant, not only for interethnic relations of the future but for political stability in general. Even more important is the contention that a general trend is developing toward the limitation of upward mobility in our society, although the picture in this respect is still confused, and far from being definite.

Economic apprehensions felt by men in the sample were shown to exist even before the actual onset of an economic depression. A sizable number of the veterans were beset by such anxieties during a period of high-level employment (at the time of the interview). While democratically minded individuals and organizations are well aware that another depression is likely to increase intolerance, they are not equally aware that rational appeals for tolerance which operate within the context of existing apprehensions are not likely to have lasting effects. These observations become even more pointed when one considers those findings in the study which indicate that even a shift from low to moderate apprehension about unemployment (let alone actual unemployment) may considerably increase the frequency and intensity of ethnic intolerance (see p. 80).

The economic goals of social action are thus clear: an adjusted annual wage to do away with fears of seasonal unemployment, stabilization of employment, and an extension of social security. In the absence of comprehensive and successful attempts to move in that direction, it remains doubtful whether programs oriented specifically toward interethnic issues are at all relevant for changing ethnic relations. But even if this economic program were to be carried out, it would remain insufficient unless a change in the economic ethos took place at the same time. Self-respect and respect for the community must be divorced from upward social mobility, and continuous incitement by the media of mass communication toward the acquisition of new and more expensive commodities (as the tangible symbols of social status) must decrease. Otherwise, new desires are being constantly created which must as constantly be satisfied or lead to new frustration.

Perhaps more relevant, therefore, and open for immediate consideration is the evaluation of mobility and occupational status by the individual and by society. In terms of future planning, it might seem desirable to teach greater acceptance of the facts of occupational status and opportunity as they now exist in the United States, and social consensus ought to be built within that framework. Of course, downward mobility cannot and should not be made acceptable. But values concerned with occupational status which are a function of unbridled aspirations leave much to be desired. It is relevant, in this context, that intolerance was also rather concentrated in that small minority whose rate of upward mobility was higher than the "norm" for the sample. These men were more strongly motivated than the rest, in terms of social mobility—and they were more intolerant. In a democratic society, the goal of indoctrination cannot well be mere acceptance of one's occupational status. But education in relative values, an emphasis on the greater desirability of interpersonal, emotional, and cultural values may be highly in order. They may prove, in the final analysis, to be more satisfactory—given the minimum basis of an adequate standard of living—than unending competition. Moreover, these cultural values are more likely to entail demands for the integration of hostility than does the competitive spirit. If such goals seem utopian, then in a democratic society the demand should at least be raised that the mass media of communication reappraise the overwhelming emphasis on the glorification of high and unattainable occupational status and its associated values.[10]

Of course, the acceptance of one's occupational status, and the effort to gain self-esteem and a sense of personal worth in other than the economic sphere will be possible only if the individual feels assured of his economic position. In this connection it should not be overlooked that the intolerant men tended to reject the controlling institutions of society and also tended to fear unemployment, war, and so on. One may wonder if

---

[10] One movie devoted to combatting anti-Semitism can hardly counteract the effects of countless others which raise the aspirations of its audience beyond any level they are likely to attain.

their attitudes toward societal institutions would have been as rejecting if they could have relied on society, through its institutions, to alleviate their economic fears.

The social and economic goals outlined above, although probably attainable without fundamental changes in the social structure, seem remote at the moment. That they seem far distant should not discourage one from looking toward social action as a principal means of alleviating intolerance. However, as a basis for social action designed to reduce ethnic intolerance, it should be recalled that the hypothesis linking tolerance to the submission to (if not acceptance of) the institutions of social control tended to be confirmed. Moreover, with the exception of the most intolerant, the vast majority of the veterans studied were ready and willing to obey law and order. Although the outspokenly intolerant men demanded more restrictive legislation, they too, by and large, were ready to abide by the law of the land. The greater overall degree of intolerance toward Negroes merely underscores this observation: anti-Semitism is less acceptable and is therefore less common. If the majority of the population, like the majority of the sample, submit to external control, then the task at hand is to change the complexion of these external controls as they relate to interethnic practices.

Among the sample, true independence of judgment on political, economic, religious, and social matters seemed as rare as in matters of ethnic relations. There, too, the men tended to follow the prevailing prejudices of their group. It was not as though ethnic relations was the only area of personal interaction which was comparatively less accessible to rational control. Such behavior has probably been typical for broad masses of the population at all times. The absence of integrated patterns in dealing with ethnic problems is nothing unique. Just as patterns of tolerance and intolerance seemed somewhat generalized in so far as those more tolerant of the Jews also tended to be more tolerant of the Negroes, so also, the patterns of revolt and control seemed also to be more or less generalized. Those men who were better able to control themselves, or more ready to accept or to submit to external control, did so not only with regard to tolerance, but also with regard to many other areas of social interaction.

With the waning of the influence of the church, the family, and other traditional forces, the legal system and its supporting institutions stand out as a basic symbol of external control. Even the dominant elements of the business community make every effort to perpetuate their group norms through the legal system. Of equal importance are the courts and the local police system which are accepted as the personalization of certain aspects of the law. Over and above all these institutions stands the growing power of the state with its external control of the individual in most of his public and much of his private activities. The growth of state power arises from the declining ability of the various segments of industrialized society to regulate themselves. The state thereby becomes a basic source of norms and operates its power to a significant degree through legal channels. Thus the law and the courts stand within our legal system as an immediate focal point for changing some of the basic norms of interpersonal contact outside the primary group, including those of interethnic relations. This is especially significant for those members of society who rely mainly on external authority for the source of their norms.[11] Litigation in 1948 over restrictive covenants clearly indicates some of the potentialities of this source of change.

The legal alteration of norms and their interpretation by the courts does not of course imply that legal decisions will establish the basis for a new consensus on interethnic relations. The long-range effects of abolishing restrictive covenants are not at all certain, for legal norms are essentially negative and minimal in import. The ability of the southern states to circumvent the poll tax decisions of the Supreme Court stands as a classic example. But in a legalistic society such as ours, the legal decision is still a basic and powerful weapon for social change.

How new laws, or the new and different interpretation of existing laws are received, depends largely on how the people are prepared for such changes. On the whole, the educational system (like the law) has tended to reflect rather than to set the norms of our society. Recently, though, there have been signs of dissatisfaction with this situation and some tendencies toward greater initiative can be observed. There is little doubt that at present, education provides the most hopeful long-term approach for changing interethnic relations—though not necessarily education which takes the form of exhortation. But education which supplies only factual information will be of little value, unless there already exists in the person to be educated a frame of mind which permits him to accept this information in line with the intentions of the educator. For example, statements as to the basic similarity of whites and Negroes will be of no value—and may even create the boomerang of greater resistance—to the person who feels that nothing is more basic than outer appearance, ac-

---

[11] According to the observations of a social scientist who did group educational work with juvenile offenders in the 1947 interracial housing riots, the argument which most impressed the young rock-throwers of South Chicago was what the Supreme Court had to say about equal rights in the protection of property.

ceptance by society, or economic success. His own experience tells him that in the question of basic characteristics the Negro is obviously different; his skin is dark, he is not accepted in society, and is notoriously handicapped in economic affairs. The argument that personality characteristics which the educator has in mind, such as willingness to serve others or to live by correct moral values, are èqually common among white people and Negroes will have little strength if the values of the intolerant are based chiefly or solely on economic success. The argument will only convince him that the educator does not understand what is really important, and this conviction—defensive as it may be—will prompt him to discount all further statements by the educator.

Education for better ethnic relations must reach deeper levels than can be touched by factual information. Education for ethnic tolerance must influence "basic" personality traits, such as tendencies to view life experiences as rewarding rather than deprivational. This can best be achieved when the influence of such education makes itself felt during the process of personality formation. In considering the latter, we have moved to some degree from the area of social institutions to that of psychological influences originating in the private sphere. Education as a formal social institution and an influence on the young seems thus to stand between society at large and the individual just ready to enter society from the shelter of the family group.

Education for tolerance must reach the child before he is of school age since that is the age during which the rudimentary personality is first formed and those tendencies first developed which become more rigid as the individual approaches the age of maturity.

In our society, generally speaking, the hostile discharge of tension is not too rigorously inhibited. Individuals do what they can to free themselves of their tensions through discharge unless, during their formative years, they have acquired the ability to store, or to integrate them. Moreover, only a limited amount of the excess tension which can neither be stored nor integrated is discharged into socially acceptable channels, and of this, the most frequently chosen form is that of interpersonal hostility. (It should be stressed that interethnic hostility is a borderland between socially acceptable and inacceptable means of discharging hostility interpersonally.) Hence to promote the tendency to restrain discharge of hostility only if it is directed in socially inacceptable channels is dangerous from the point of view of tolerance, since it is society which predicates what is socially acceptable. Once society has decreed that interethnic hostility is acceptable—instead of overlooking, denying, or condoning it—then tension will be freely discharged into interethnic hostility, as was demonstrated by the German example and by wartime attitudes toward the Nisei. Tolerant attitudes will be assured only if the vast majority of the population tends to deal with their tensions by storage or integration rather than by discharge.

The formation of such tendencies, one way or another, takes place in early childhood, during the age of personality formation. At this age the child receives the imprint of early experiences and his patterns of interpersonal relationships are prepared for the future. As an adult, he may copy or recreate the interpersonal patterns experienced during childhood or he may prefer those of an opposite nature in a reaction-formation against unpleasant early experiences; or finally he may combine these and other reactions into still another pattern. At this early age, when the techniques of relationships are acquired, the young child is also encountering all those difficulties which are connected with exploring and understanding the outer world, and of learning to master his inner tensions. These problems, and many others simultaneously experienced, can be eased, and the tensions created by them reduced to a manageable level, if the child feels sufficiently protected by gratifying—and hence most reassuring—interpersonal relationships. Only then will the child learn to recognize that he can master his own inner tensions by integration, and that hostile discharge is not only unnecessary but also undesirable, since it interferes with a highly valued interpersonal relationship to a parent. On the other hand, if this relationship is not gratifying, there is little reason for learning control and the child first manifests hostility toward his parent and later toward others. Eventually, under the latter conditions, immediate hostile discharge may be established as the preferred relief for inner difficulties.[12]

[12] Prevalent attitudes held by many parents who fear their children may not succeed in this competitive society, run directly counter to sound psychological behavior. The small boy who runs to his mother because he has been hurt in a street fight is often sent back without the comfort he asked for and is told to go back and stand his ground. Actually, because of his defeat, he has already been swamped by unmasterable tension, which he expressed in his tears, and has come to his mother to help him in integrating these tensions; i.e., his behavior, in effect, seems to say: "I have been defeated, but you, through your action, can show me this was not an important defeat, since you, the most important person in the world, remain unaffected by it. If you show me that this was an unimportant event, I'll be able to integrate my tension." The mother who sends her son back to fight, forces him into hostile discharge of a tension which is now truly beyond his ability to master, since rejection by the mother, or at least the absence of her protection, is now added to the initial defeat. This is only one example of how the child's natural tendencies toward integration (which he realizes is the safer way, since he does not know whether aggressiveness may not lead to a more serious defeat) are thwarted and he is directed back toward hostile discharge of his tensions against others.

The individual who has learned in his childhood that emotional difficulties can be relieved through gratifying interpersonal relationships within the family circle will in all likelihood grow into a mature person who will seek and find relief in the sphere of his private relations from the tensions accumulating in the outside world. Moreover, he is probably an individual who as a child has experienced respect by those around him. Therefore, later in life, he will rely less for his self-respect on the whims and favors of foremen, or on promotions handed down by the boss. Since he finds self-assurance within himself and his family, economic and political dependency on outsiders will be less of a threat and hence create fewer tensions.[13] Finally, he will probably be able to seek gratification for his self-esteem in self-chosen activities of a cultural or social nature in which he can engage in relative independence of what others may think.

By contrast, an individual who has not been able to develop a well-integrated personality will take advantage of any opportunity which offers itself for the hostile discharge of tension, since discharge he must have. He will be intolerant of those groups against whom hostility may safely be directed, including ethnic minorities; the evidence of this and other studies indicates that propaganda for tolerance of itself will remain largely ineffectual in changing the basic patterns of his behavior. Economic, political, and interpersonal insecurities, lack of self-respect, and the absence of meaningful life activities will continue to create unmanageable tensions. Those tensions created through insecurity in interpersonal relationships are themselves a major factor in intolerance. No interpersonal relationship, including love, can withstand the destructive consequences of inadequate controls. Modern life invariably creates tensions, and if they are discharged against the love partner, love is soon destroyed and frustration in the most private sphere adds its weight to all others.

[13] The question may be raised as to how such a personality structure would affect a democracy. Would it make for greater autonomy and independence of judgment (and therefore an active and responsible electorate) or would satisfaction with life in the private sphere foster indifference to public affairs (and therefore a citizenry easily manipulated for good or for ill)? Such people might tend to remain unexcited by societal issues which they would consider in a matter-of-fact fashion. On the other hand, their self-respect and sense of justice would force them—possibly despite an initial hesitation to enter the political arena—to fight for the autonomy of the individual, that is, against regimentation or injustice, and for democracy. In this fight they would be more effective than those who are motivated—and handicapped— by anxiety or social resentment. In any event, we have not yet known a society of wholly autonomous individuals, so that all speculation on this question remains hazardous.

Tolerance propaganda, if at all effective, may persuade an individual to abandon one outlet for hostility. But while this may result in the protection of a particular minority, the matter does not end there. If the new ways of discharging tensions are not more desirable from a social point of view, then the efforts of the tolerance propaganda have been wasted. Moreover, mere changes in outlet are easily reversible. A temporary end to the flow of tolerance propaganda, less watchfulness on the part of controlling institutions, an increase in intolerance propaganda, or simply an increase in the tensions which press for discharge, may all undo such tenuous redirection of hostility. But even redirection is difficult to achieve, since the discrimination of each minority serves its particular function in the psychic economy of the intolerant. (See Chapters III and VIII for a discussion of this problem.)

A more important social objective seems to be to eliminate the psychological need to discharge hostility. In this connection the ego-bolstering aspects of ethnic discrimination should not be overlooked. To some degree, it is also this element which makes it attractive even to well-educated persons and to polite society. By the same token, ethnic intolerance becomes acceptable to men whose integration would forbid them to project inacceptable tendencies onto minorities, or to those who would never accuse minorities of behavior which is either common to all men or the result of discrimination. While these men do not necessarily discriminate against members of the minority, they enjoy a vague feeling of superiority, for ethnic discrimination seems to indicate there are others below them. In the case of the actively intolerant person, this feeling is often initially developed out of an unconscious fear of social inferiority. Nothing outrages an individual more than efforts to convince him of his equality with the discriminated group, because they deprive him of the mechanism he has developed for retaining self-respect and without which he cannot maintain his integration. Against such threats he must defend himself as best he can.[14]

---

[14] The behavior of SS guards in German concentration camps tended to follow such patterns. If prisoners of an "inferior" race, particularly Jews, groveled before an SS guard they succeeded only in arousing his disgust. After having made sport of such prisoners, he often exterminated them soon enough. Feeling superior to people so obviously inferior was no boon to his self-respect. If, on the other hand, such prisoners made him feel their actual superiority, or showed him up in his ignorance, he became violently angry because he was being deprived of his much-needed feeling of superiority. Such prisoners were often killed on the spot. But a prisoner who showed through his behavior that he was a man of some value—who without fawning or arrogance accepted the SS guard as his superior in a matter-of-fact way—was as safe as any person could be in a concentration camp. As a matter of fact, with individual guards, such a Jewish prisoner often fared much better than a too subservient German pris-

The problem of mitigating interethnic hostility from the point of view of the individual's personality-formation reduces itself to a twofold approach: the provision of more adequate discharge of tension and the development of more integrated personalities. Persons of more adequate integration would not only be able to manage relatively large amounts of tension, but their ego strength and self-esteem would no longer depend on vicarious, external support. These suggestions parallel those mentioned earlier, in the field of social action. Ethnic tolerance presupposes a societal structure which generates less tension in the individual, which controls their discharge more adequately, and which, most important of all, permits the development of integrated personalities of adequate ego strength. This it does by not confronting individuals with unattainable or contradictory goals, and by not creating desires which can rarely be satisfied.

The less reliable of these two psychological approaches is the provision of more adequate outlets for the discharge of tension. Present-day society, and particularly the mores of the group studied, approves in the main of only one such outlet: successful competition. The less likely the chances grow for success, the more this once possible outlet turns into a source of additional tension. True, there is another mode of discharging tension which is also accepted by society, namely discharge through motility. Biogenetically speaking this is the first form of discharge, and in the temper tantrum the young child uses it to explode all unmasterable tension. As the individual grows up, the integrative tendencies of the ego no longer permit such random motility and it is sublimated into sports and similar activities. Unfortunately, even in sports, where the only purpose should be discharge of tension through motility, competition creeps in, which brings additional tensions to all but the winners. Moreover, the conception of sports as a direct participation activity is too often replaced by that of passive observation by the spectator.[15] The professionalization

---

oner. (A German prisoner who displayed his superiority over an SS guard wrote his own death warrant no less than a Jew.) The reason was that only a man who showed his worth and nevertheless accepted the SS man's superiority—a man who knew his place and kept it—only such a man could provide the SS guard with the emotional experience he needed for maintaining his self-respect. Only then could the guard enjoy the conviction that he was actually superior to a man in whose case such superiority really meant something.

[15] In this way the temper tantrum as a total experience of screaming and moving is then separated into the moving of the performers and the shouting of the spectators, which offers little enough relief to any of the latter. (With the growing popularity of television, currently most valued for the transmission of sporting events, the role of the spectator is even further reduced. Without the support of the crowds at the stadium a man would perhaps feel foolish rooting enthusiastically in his own parlor.)

of performers discourages the public at large from personal efforts, which often seem ludicrous to the individual when compared to those of the performing expert. Even more basic from the point of view of relief through motility is the increasing mechanization of the modern factory system. The endless repetition of movements in a mechanical way creates more tension than can safely be discharged through their means.[16]

According to psychoanalytical theory, the main adult avenue for the discharge of tension is that of interpersonally gratifying sexual relations.[17] The same body of theories maintains that anxiety (which was found to be strongly associated with intolerance) is a direct or indirect consequence of inhibited sexuality. It may seem doubtful, in a society as complex as ours and with its countless sources of anxiety, whether all tensions can actually be discharged in sexual activity. But there seems little doubt that if two people enjoy a mutually gratifying sexual relationship, under normal circumstances the remaining tensions can be integrated with relatively greater ease.

Even the most adequate provisions for the discharge of tension into socially acceptable channels will not do away with the hostility which underlies ethnic intolerance, but might go a long way toward mitigating its more violent features. Propaganda and planning for direct rather than vicarious discharge of tensions through motility seems feasible and might provide some relief of those forces which otherwise press for interpersonal discharge. More difficult to approach or to modify are patterns of sexual discharge. Sexual activities, however, which are accompanied by feelings of guilt or anxiety often create more tensions than they relieve. There seems little doubt that the dissemination of adequate information about contemporary sexual practices might tend to decrease anxiety in those who for personal reasons prefer to engage in nongenital, nonheterosexual, or extramarital sexual activities. Such decrease in anxiety may be

---

[16] Before the era of mechanization, occupations such as farming used to provide almost unlimited possibilities for the discharge of tension through motility, except that the hard labor then required precluded any relief. Thus while modern conveniences, for the first time in the history of technology, have provided relief from exhaustion, technology itself deprives work of nearly all its potentials for discharge of tension. In addition, it creates new and formerly unknown tensions through the blow to their self-respect which human beings experience when they are degraded to perform with the regularity and repetitiousness of a tool.

[17] The qualification "interpersonally gratifying" should be emphasized. Frequently it is assumed that sexual discharge in itself constitutes release. This is by no means so. Intercourse frequently has an aggressive rather than a benign meaning and is little concerned with seeking the partner's permanent love through gratifying his sexual desires. Sexual relations entered mainly for the purpose of demonstrating one's superiority, or of testing one's virility, will provide neither partner with total release from tension and may well create additional anxiety or hostility.

achieved by showing such individuals that they are not alone in their deviation, and indirectly by perhaps leading to a more tolerant attitude in those who as vocation or avocation persecute the deviate individual.

Perhaps more fruitful in the elimination of ethnic intolerance would be efforts leading toward more integrated personalities. The discharge of tension depends mainly on societal factors, and can easily be interfered with by society; recent history has demonstrated how rapidly such societal changes can now be engineered. But the individual's ability to integrate his tensions is relatively independent of societal interference. That requires fundamental changes in the structure of the personality of the individual. On the basis of our present knowledge such changes can hardly be achieved in the mature individual, at least not short of psychotherapy, and even that is successful only in selected cases. Hence to attack ethnic intolerance from the point of view of personality formation seems to require social action that will insure that the personalities of the next generation are so structured that they have a maximum ability to integrate tensions and are ready and able to discharge the remainder in ways that are not harmful to outgroups. The building up of such personalities must begin at birth and must continue through adolescence; as a point of departure there is little doubt that the most important task would be to influence those who mould the child in his earliest, most formative years. This is obviously not the place for a treatise on child rearing. It should be repeated, however, that the men who recalled their childhood as having been happy tended to be the most tolerant.

In our society, an increasing number of parents are genuinely interested in problems of child rearing. The educator does not need to go after such parents, they seek him out if they have any hope that he will relieve their anxieties about whether they are bringing their children up properly and whether they are good parents. More and more parents, for example, are discarding the rigid feeding schedules imposed by so-called experts, for more flexible behavior in which they follow the natural leads given by the child. As a result, both parent and child derive much gratification from the change. The parents have thus freed themselves of a prejudice which interfered with their enjoying their children, and the child is protected from a source of possibly permanent anxiety.[18] Parents who permit the child to regulate his life according to his own rhythm of

[18] Of course when other experts continually threaten the parent through the means of mass communication by inferring that unless he gives his child this or that new food preparation the child's health will not be what it should, then the parent who cannot afford buying all new items on the market is thrown into anxiety which affects his relation to his child.

growth and intellectual development have made great strides toward developing integrated personalities in their children. They are also learning to eliminate the threatening "wait till father comes home" attitude which destroyed the optimistic hope in many children that their next life experience would be a pleasant one.

These examples may show that even without centrally planned and directed efforts, progress in child rearing is being made toward the development of more integrated persons. If society does not thwart these efforts by increasing the tensions to be integrated even faster than the efforts to shape more integrated personalities are proceeding, then the modern methods of child rearing will produce some effects. But these changes in child rearing must truly reach the large masses of the population if such an end is to be accomplished.

In any case it seems simpler, and more feasible, to influence parental attitudes toward children, when compared with the efforts needed for assuring a stable economy free from the fear of war and unemployment.

It cannot be emphasized too strongly that efforts to modify parental attitudes will remain ineffectual in their most important aspects if they proceed outside of direct interpersonal context. Interpersonal techniques are not learned from books, or by listening to radio performances, nor even by listening to lectures. Interpersonal relations by definition are two-way relations either between student and teacher or among students themselves. Techniques applied according to the best prescriptions only mechanize mother-child relations instead of vitalizing them unless these techniques have been acquired through a process of living.[19]

[19] Discussion groups for expectant mothers and mothers of small children have proved quite successful in modifying their attitudes. They had to be congenial groups, and had to meet regularly for many months. Only then could what was initially just the prescription of a so-called expert become a mutually gratifying process of living. In one such group a recurrent anxiety of the mothers was the fear that their babies were not eating enough. It was only with reluctance that they accepted the advice of the group leader who suggested that whatever the eating habits of their children might be, forcing them to eat much, or what were considered vitally needed fares, would not produce the desired effect, and that being less fearful might prove more successful. But at first, forcing the child to eat was only exchanged for tense watching to see whether he would eat when he was not being forced. Only after some of the general fears connected with bringing up children had been worked through—particularly after such fears as whether the mother would be recognized as a good mother by her husband, her own mother, or her mother-in-law were repeatedly discussed—did it become possible to return to the mother's basic fear about the child's health. Then it was also possible to deal with her fear more realistically, by asking, for example, what the child's weight was, and how it related to norms of weight. The amusement of the group as a whole increased when, month after month, mothers admitted that their "noneating" babies were either perfectly normal in weight or a bit over the norm. The mutual interest of mothers in this group for one another's problems was a demonstration that the interpersonal techniques they had acquired at the meetings were being immediately applied in life situations.

These remarks in brief outline can do no more than indicate the direction in which efforts to combat ethnic intolerance might be guided. They seem far too tentative to be formally summarized, as though they were recommendations which should follow with logical stringency from the objective data and the critical evaluations forming the bulk of this report. This study, in the end, was but an investigation of existing attitudes, and not one of plans for future policy in interethnic relations.

It is our conviction that better ethnic relations are possible within our society, and that modern education, particularly the education of the small child, could be so improved that fewer of them would need to mature into intolerant adults. If we bring our children up wisely they will not only be happier, but will also be able to live more successfully with one another. That it seems possible to raise a generation which will be relatively free of ethnic intolerance is not only a hope, but a real possibility, and hence a great challenge.

Man's best hope is still the next generation. But the challenge of controlling personality development should not be used for a diversion of efforts from a comprehensive and immediate program of social reform. If we succeed in achieving both social reform and education for personal integration, we shall not only have better ethnic relations, but also a better society. The one cannot be had without the other.

APPENDIX

I. THE INTERVIEW

This study was based on the so-called "open-ended interview." In this type of interview the questions are designed to stimulate the respondent to reply not with "yes" or "no" or a short factual statement, but to give a fairly elaborated response. If the respondent does not voluntarily offer additional associative material, probes are used to evoke it.

The use of this type of intensive interview, and the requirements of a systematic analysis of its contents made it essential that the interview situations be as highly comparable as possible. Care had to be taken that efforts at standardization were not so rigid that they interfered with the flow of associative material, or with keeping the interviewee interested and in good rapport. The elements of the interview situation singled out for the standardization were: (1) the person of the interviewer, (2) the method of approaching the subject, (3) the place of the interview, (4) the method of asking the predetermined questions and of probing for associative material, and (5) the technique for recording the entire interview. The time period during which the interviews took place was reasonably short so that changes in the political and economic situation or in other world events would be held constant for all members of the sample.

1. *Person of the Interviewer.* An effort was made to use as few interviewers as possible so that this factor too might be kept fairly constant. Because each interview and its recording took a long time and because by spreading the interviews over many weeks another extraneous factor would have been introduced, it was necessary to use six interviewers. The interviewers were all women from twenty-five to thirty-five years of age. Because of the character of the interview situation, it is possible that there was at least one area of life experience in which the veterans' attitudes were not fully revealed, namely their attitudes toward wives or girl friends. However, this was an area of relatively low significance in the context of this study.

At the outset, all the interviewers were made aware of the problem of their own bias in a series of group discussions on the schedule. At the same time, they were given an opportunity to express their opinions on ethnic attitudes and other matters to be discussed at the interviews. During the trial run of interviews great emphasis was placed on the control and elimination of interview bias, and a study of the final interview records showed no evidence of consistent bias.

2. *Method of Approaching Subjects.* A standardized procedure for establishing contact with the veteran was employed. (See pages 12-13.) During the initial contact a number of veterans asked why they had been selected. The standard answer was that the names selected for the survey were picked at random from lists of veterans. In fact, the veterans were told that every ninetieth veteran (which was the sample) was being interviewed; in virtually all cases this allayed suspicions.

3. *Place of the Interview.* The majority of the interviews took place at the homes of the interviewees. Where this was not appropriate, the subject was interviewed in a private office, at the downtown branch of the University. In the latter case, continued privacy so essential for successful interviewing was assured. When the veteran was interviewed in his home, rapport was simple to maintain because the subject felt more at ease in the familiar surroundings, but making sure of complete and continued privacy was more difficult. When interviewed at the University office, some veterans felt more self-conscious during the initial portion of the interview.

4. *Method of Asking Questions and Probing for Associations.* Basically, the interview (pages 213-219) consisted of over 160 standardized questions. In addition, twenty-four factual questions were asked. The standardized procedure for administering the questions contained the following elements: Each fixed question was asked in a verbatim fashion. If no answer was forthcoming, it was repeated in the original form. Partial answers were followed by neutral probes for fuller responses. (A neutral probe was a colorless phrase, ranging from "huh" to "what do you mean by that?" or the repetition of a phrase used by the veteran himself.) Certain questions were always carried further by neutral probes because of their special importance for the study. If at any point in the interview, whether by association or after probing on the part of the interviewer, the subject brought forth irrelevant material he was not interrupted but permitted to continue as long as he wished. If he produced material which was irrelevant to the questions, but relevant to the objectives of the interview, the interviewer was instructed to encourage the fullest responses by means of probes.

5. *Recording the Interview.* A complete interview transcript based on the interviewer's stenographic notes made during the interview was prepared immediately after the interview. The transcript included a report on each of the neutral probes, and which of the questions had had to be repeated. Material offered spontaneously by the subject was recorded in that section of the interview where it was offered. Later, such material was cross-referenced to the question it was more closely related to, so that the content analysis of each question might be exhaustive.

6. *Timing of Interviews.* Many questions dealing with political events were asked in order to gain added indications of the nature of the subject's anxiety and the character of his hostilities. Such questions dealt with problems of price control, the occupation of Japan and Germany, relief for war-devastated nations, and the like. Since opinions on these problems are subject to rapid change as objective conditions also change, an effort was made to conclude all interviews within a short span of time. Some factors were beyond the control of the interviewers and interfered somewhat with this objective. For instance, interviewees broke or postponed appointments. The interviews began on April 1, 1946 and were completed in June of that year—a time span of three months.

II. SAMPLING PROCEDURE

The sampling procedure was designed to yield a random sample of male army veterans of enlisted rank who were residents of the city of Chicago. Special definitions were introduced to delimit the population and to make the sample more homogeneous.

1. Veterans who were officers were eliminated since their war experiences were sharply at variance with those of the enlisted men. Moreover, most of them came from social and economic backgrounds which differed from those of the enlisted men.

2. Naval and marine personnel were excluded since the basis of their recruitment and their wartime experiences were sharply at variance with those of enlisted soldiers. Members of the women's auxiliary services were likewise excluded.

3. Men over thirty-five years of age were not included. This was necessary because the definition of overage in the army varied greatly as draft procedures were altered. By selecting men up to the age of thirty-five, it was not necessary to deal with those men whose army careers were limited simply to a stay within the continental United States until the rules for overaged men were changed.

4. A veteran was arbitrarily defined as a soldier who had been in the army for at least six months. It was felt that service for a shorter period of service would have been too brief for a man to have developed common identifications and to have shared experiences common to the rest of the sample.

5. Members of those main ethnic groups onto whom hostility is most often projected were not included; that is, Negroes, Jews, Chinese, Japanese, and Mexicans. No attempt was made to eliminate other ethnic or nationality groups which find themselves subject to varying degrees of prejudice. As a result, the following distribution of ethnic origin (father's origin) was encountered:

TABLE 1(A)

DISTRIBUTION OF ETHNIC ORIGIN AMONG THE SAMPLE

	Number	Percentage
Poland	31	21
Ireland	27	18
Germany; Austria	18	12
Italy	18	12
Great Britain	14	9
Czechoslovakia	8	5
The Balkans	7	5
Other	27	18
Total	150	100

6. The length of time between demobilization and the date of interview was held as constant as possible. To test some of the hypotheses it was essential that the veteran should have had some opportunity to face the problems of adjustment to civilian life. The timing of discharge from the United States Army

made it advisable that for the purposes of this study sampling should begin after August, 1945, since before that time only wounded soldiers and a very small number of combat troops had been discharged. It was about August, 1945 that mass discharges began. The sampling period was therefore limited to August through November, 1945, and the interviews were carried out six to eight months after discharge.

The sampling technique employed was to obtain a random sample falling within these definitions. This was made possible by the existence of a central file of photostatic copies of veterans' discharge records which was maintained by the Recorder of Cook County (which included the city of Chicago). At the time of discharge from the United States Army, each veteran was issued a certificate attesting to his service in the armed forces. It was impressed on the veteran that in order to legally complete his discharge, it was necessary to register a copy of his discharge certificate with the appropriate civilian author- ities. The process of actually depositing a copy with the Recorder was a volun- tary one. No data were available on the number of veterans who failed to comply with this routine, but statements by draft officials indicated that the County Records were almost complete except perhaps for a small margin of deviants.

During the period sampled more than 15,000 veterans registered their dis- charge papers. Tabulations of a random sampling of these records showed that one-third of this number were outside of the sample because of branch of serv- ice, age, sex, officer status, or the like. Therefore it was decided to select at random one out of every ninety of the total veteran population, or one out of every sixty veterans falling within the definitions of the sample.

The discharge records in the County Recorder's office are filed serially by date of registration and without any special classification system that might tend to introduce a bias in random sampling. Therefore, every ninetieth case was examined. If the case fell within the limits of the sample, it was noted as a respondent to be interviewed; if not then the next case was taken. By this method enough names were drawn to fill the sample and to replace the refusals.

Every effort was made to keep to the original sample although certain prob- lems obviously prevented achieving such a goal. The interviewing staff was in- structed to carry out at least three attempts (including home visits) to locate and communicate with each subject. It was found that most of the failures to obtain total compliance arose not from refusal, but from the fact that veterans who had registered their discharge papers in Chicago had moved to other cities. In all, total compliance failed by about 14 per cent due to refusals and other such reasons.

One special problem presented itself in connection with the elimination of members of ethnic minorities. Negroes were readily eliminated since their dis- charge records bore that information. Chinese and Japanese names were quite readily discernible. In the case of Jews keys to ethnic identity are not clear-cut. Though their number was slight, they presented a problem, especially since the interviewer could make no slightest attempt to discover whether they were Jewish or not during the initial contacting. Therefore, little was done to eliminate them from the sample; instead, the interviewer was instructed that if during the course of the interview, it emerged that the subject was a Jew, the interview was to be terminated. Two such interviews occurred and these subjects were replaced.

III. COMMENTS ON THE INTERVIEW SITUATION

Social researchers have often advocated gathering data on the respondents' own view of the interview as a further aid in evaluating attitude data. To obtain such data is frequently difficult, and particularly so at the end of a long interview, when the subject is beginning to tire. For one-third of the sample, however, an adequate opportunity was provided for such inquiry during the course of a follow-up study.

In this second interview a number of general questions were asked to determine what meaning the subject attributed to the interview. There was a wide variation of responses ranging from expressions of genuine satisfaction with the cathartic aspects of the interview to outright suspicion of the whole procedure. In general, however, it appeared that the occurrence and procedures of attitude surveying had become relatively familiar to the public at large. Therefore, a survey which sought generally to inquire into the personal problems as well as a wide complex of public attitudes of the subject was accepted rather matter-of-factly with an admixture of interest or indifference. The element of indifference arose from the feeling expressed by a minority of the subjects that few or no practical results would be forthcoming generally, or for themselves in particular.

TABLE 2(A)

VETERANS' REACTIONS TO THE INTERVIEW

	Tolerant	Intolerant to some Degree	Total
	No.	No.	No.
Positive affect toward the interview	8	12	20
Neutral	14	11	25
Negative	1	6	7
Other	3	1	4
	26	30	56

In all, fifty-six veterans answered questions on their conception of the interview situation. Their reactions to the interview were classified as: (a) positive, (b) negative, or (c) showing mild interest to indifference. Only seven men were manifestly negative in their reactions. The above Table 2(A) presents the responses of the subjects according to their degree of anti-Semitism. It is interesting to note that the interview situation was viewed negatively to a higher degree by those veterans who displayed greater amounts of intolerance.

Suspicion as to the purpose of the interview was limited to intolerant veterans and does not therefore appear to have interfered with their expression of intolerance. Typical were such responses as:

"At first I was kind of leery about answering questions. You figure you got freedom of speech, but sometimes you wonder."

"I really don't know what. I think there's more behind it—some organization or political party is behind it. Everything has a purpose—just like the army—if we wanted to take an objective we didn't go straight to it, but a roundabout way. I think this is the same thing."

In one case, suspicion was mixed with general confusion:

"Well, I'll tell you—some of these questions were rather stupid. Such as how to keep industry going, and another, what we thought of our officers. If we told half of what we thought we'd be shot for treason."

Manifest statements of positive attitudes, which were three times as numerous as negative ones, were more evenly distributed between tolerant and intolerant veterans. Some veterans experienced the relief of catharsis and said as much:

"It lets you get off your mind what you think of army life and the rest of the problems. I think you should have more questions on the army, their way of living, etc. There's too much difference between the officers and the enlisted men."

More important in explaining a clear positive reaction were statements of twelve veterans who felt it was proper and useful to interview veterans in order to give expression to their needs and wants. For example:

"I guess it's a good idea to find out what the different fellows think. If more people thought about things and tried to do something, it would be better. But the trouble is nobody cares about anything."

Here was a man who according to the interview seemed lost and aimless; nevertheless, he not only felt that the interview offered an opportunity for self-expression, but that it proved somebody was interested in him. Another said:

"I think it's very good, like I talk to my friends. We agree on a lot of things, but we don't always agree. . . . I think all sorts of things to find out what people are thinking are a good thing."

In one case, a veteran showed considerable objectivity in his response. He reversed the procedure indicating that the interview helped clarify civilian opinion for him.

"It's interesting to know what the people want to know about the veteran."

In a sample this size, it was to be expected that at least one man would point out:

"I imagine most universities want to publish some sort of findings. Someone's always working up something like that, wanting to publish some sort of findings—a cross section of what groups think of sundry questions."

Finally, it should be noted that the intense anti-Semites merely took these questions as an additional opportunity to verbalize their hostility.

"And from all indications, it would seem the country itself thinks there's a racial problem in the U. S. Most of your questions are foolish. I'll bet they'll only come to one conclusion; there's only one thing to do—shoot the Jews."

And:

"Well I'm not sorry I answered. I gave my true opinions and I'm not afraid of what I said. After all, the nigger knows they'll always be crucified—and why. I'm not against talking to niggers and Jews—I have several times—I talk to them at work and joke with them, but as for living next door to them or going around with them, I can't see that."

IV. DEFINING THE PATTERNS OF INTOLERANCE

In analyzing the interview for expressions of hostility, a clear distinction could be made between descriptive statements and demands for restrictions against a particular group. Despite the value judgments they contained, statements such as the following were considered descriptive:

"The Negroes smell badly regardless of the amount of soap they use; it's just a physical difference between them and us white people."

or

"The Jews always seem to get to the top; and that's because they stick together and help one another."

Quite different from these were demands for aggressive action such as the following:

"The way to solve the Jewish problem is to get a Hitler over here, and then forget about the whole business once and for all."

Negative descriptions and stereotypes about minorities might appear with or without restrictive demands. However, restrictive demands against a minority almost never appear without negative descriptions and stereotypes. In evaluating restrictive demands it was noted whether they emerged spontaneously or only on question.

In order to determine the types of anti-Semitic attitudes which could be sampled by the interview instrument, a series of interviews were conducted with a group of veterans not included in the final sample. These interviews revealed, as far as anti-Semitic attitudes were concerned, that it would be useful to isolate four types of attitude patterns which would form a continuum from tolerance to intolerance. These attitude patterns were called: *tolerant, stereotyped anti-Semitic, outspokenly anti-Semitic,* and *intensely anti-Semitic.*

This method of classification took into consideration the frequency of stereo-types, the presence or absence of restrictive demands, and whether they were spontaneously elicited. All four types are defined in Chapter II, page 13.

In the light of the preliminary study, the interview was so constructed that the various patterns of ethnic intolerance could be delimited with precision and objectivity. For example, if the intensely anti-Semitic subject was to be differentiated from the outspokenly anti-Semitic one on the basis that his restrictive demands revealed themselves more spontaneously, then it became important to decide at which point in the interview restrictive statements were no longer considered to be spontaneous but to be elicited. Similarly, the question arose as to where the line should be drawn between the tolerant and the stereotyped anti-Semite, for even the most tolerant person is not entirely free of occasionally stereotyped thinking in problems of interethnic relations.

In order to allow for spontaneous expression of intolerance, the initial part of the interview was free of direct questions on ethnic minorities. Five indirect questions which made no specific mention of ethnic minorities were included; these questions were designed to permit the subject to reveal spontaneous hostile demands against minority groups. Questions in the central portion of the interview were designed to evoke stereotyped thinking on interethnic problems if such thought-patterns were present. The final section included ten direct questions enabling the subject to express a preference for restricting minority groups. Responses to these questions made it possible to differentiate between the various types of intolerance and to determine whether the veterans were persistent and consistent in their tolerance attitudes.

The responses to these questions and the subjects' spontaneous ethnic statements and stereotypes were listed on a continuum. This permitted grouping of their responses, on the basis of our definitions, as falling into the class of the intense, the outspoken, the stereotyped, or the tolerant veterans. Within each category the traits were arranged in terms of the order of their appearance in the interview. It then became possible to construct an overall chart. This chart was designed to present the full range of statements about ethnic groups and to include frequency data for those attitude traits which had a frequency occurrence. (See charts B and C which present the data in summary form.) The chart provided a convenient key to the data and this, together with the definitions, made it possible to set precise limits for each type.

Since the veterans were divided into four categories on the basis of their attitudes towards Jews, it became necessary to select three lines which would divide the categories from one another. These limits between the categories of intolerance were set arbitrarily, although in keeping with the basic assumptions and consistent with the inner logic of the data. These dividing lines separated first, the intense from the outspoken veterans; second, the outspoken from the stereotyped veterans; and third, the stereotyped from the tolerant veterans.

1. *Delimitation of the Intense Anti-Semite from the Outspoken Anti-Semite.* As noted above, approximately 160 questions were asked at each interview, not including the neutral probes whose number varied from individual to individual. The first forty questions contained nothing which would normally

Chart B

DISTRIBUTION OF ANTI-SEMITIC ATTITUDES

Legend

Column
- (1) Spontaneous restrictive response (groups)
- (2) Spontaneous restrictive response (persons)
- (3) Spontaneous restrictive response (general)
- (4) Elicited restrictions (general)
- (5) Elicited restrictions (deportation)
- (6) Elicited restrictions (intermarriage)
- (7) Elicited restrictions (housing)
- (8) Elicited restrictions (employment)
- (9) Spontaneous stereotypes
- (10) Elicited stereotypes
- (11) Total number of stereotypes
- (12) Grounds for tolerance
    - A Denial of differences between Jews and non-Jews
    - B Acceptance of differences between Jews and non-Jews
    - C Indifference
- (13) Index of anti-Semitism
    - 1 Tolerant
    - 2 Stereotyped
    - 3 Outspokenly anti-Semitic
    - 4 Intensely anti-Semitic

	Intense			Outspoken					Stereotyped			Tolerant	Index
	(1)	(2)	(3)	(4)	(5)	(6)	(7)	(8)	(9)	(10)	(11)	(12)	(13)
1	—	x	x	x	x	—	x	—	x	x	11	—	4
2	x	—	—	x	—	x	x	—	x	x	8	—	4
3	x	x	x	x	x	—	x	x	x	x	14	—	4
4	x	—	—	x	x	x	—	x	x	x	9	—	4
5	x	—	x	x	x	—	x	x	x	x	8	—	4
6	—	—	x	x	—	—	—	—	x	x	6	—	4
7	—	—	—	x	—	—	x	x	x	x	7	—	3
8	—	—	—	x	—	—	—	x	x	x	7	—	3
9	—	—	—	x	x	x	—	x	x	x	10	—	3
10	—	—	—	x	x	—	—	—	x	x	2	—	3
11	—	—	—	x	x	—	—	—	x	x	4	—	3
12	—	—	—	x	—	—	—	—	x	x	8	—	3
13	—	—	—	x	x	—	—	—	—	x	1	A	3
14	—	—	—	x	x	—	x	—	x	x	3	—	3
15	—	—	—	x	x	—	x	—	x	x	9	—	3

CHART B—(*Continued*)

Intense			Outspoken					Stereotyped			Tolerant	Index
(1)	(2)	(3)	(4)	(5)	(6)	(7)	(8)	(9)	(10)	(11)	(12)	(13)
16 —	—	—	x	—	—	—	—	x	x	9	—	3
17 —	—	—	x	—	—	—	—	—	x	4	—	3
18 —	—	—	x	x	—	x	x	x	x	7	—	3
19 —	—	—	x	x	—	x	—	x	x	10	—	3
20 —	—	—	x	x	—	—	—	—	x	2	—	3
21 —	—	—	x	—	—	—	—	x	x	6	—	3
22 —	—	—	x	—	—	x	—	x	x	2	—	3
23 —	—	—	—	x	x	—	—	x	x	4	—	3
24 —	—	—	—	x	—	—	—	—	x	2	—	3
25 —	—	—	x	x	—	—	—	x	x	4	—	3
26 —	—	—	x	—	—	—	—	x	x	6	—	3
27 —	—	—	x	—	x	x	x	x	x	10	—	3
28 —	—	—	x	x	—	—	—	x	x	7	—	3
29 —	—	—	x	x	—	x	—	x	x	8	—	3
30 —	—	—	x	x	—	—	—	x	x	17	—	3
31 —	—	—	x	x	x	—	x	x	x	6	—	3
32[a] —	—	x	—	—	—	—	—	x	x	3	—	3
33 —	—	—	x	—	—	x	—	x	x	8	—	3
34 —	—	—	x	x	x	x	x	x	x	7	—	3
35 —	—	—	x	—	—	—	—	x	x	3	—	3
36 —	—	—	x	x	—	x	—	x	x	12	—	3
37 —	—	—	x	x	—	x	x	x	x	7	—	3
38 —	—	—	x	—	—	—	x	x	x	6	—	3
39 —	—	—	x	x	—	—	—	x	x	6	—	3
40 —	—	—	x	—	—	—	—	x	x	9	—	3
41 —	—	—	x	x	—	—	—	x	x	3	—	3
42 —	—	—	x	x	x	—	—	x	—	1	—	3
43 —	—	—	x	x	x	x	—	x	x	7	—	3
44 —	—	—	x	x	—	—	—	x	x	6	—	3
45 —	—	—	x	x	—	—	—	—	—	—	—	3
46 —	—	—	x	x	—	—	—	x	x	7	—	3
47 —	—	—	x	x	—	x	—	x	x	8	—	3
48 —	—	—	—	—	—	—	—	x	x	4	—	2
49 —	—	—	—	—	—	—	—	x	x	5	B	2
50 —	—	—	—	—	—	—	—	x	x	4	—	2
51[b] —	—	—	—	—	—	—	—	—	—	—	—	2
52 —	—	—	—	—	—	—	—	x	x	7	—	2
53 —	—	—	—	—	—	—	—	x	x	3	—	2
54 —	—	—	—	—	—	—	—	x	x	2	—	2
55 —	—	—	—	—	—	—	—	—	x	3	—	2

CHART B—(*Continued*)

	Intense			Outspoken					Stereotyped			Tolerant	Index
	(1)	(2)	(3)	(4)	(5)	(6)	(7)	(8)	(9)	(10)	(11)	(12)	(13)
56	—	—	—	—	—	—	—	—	x	x	7	—	2
57	—	—	—	—	—	—	—	—	x	x	5	—	2
58	—	—	—	—	—	—	—	x	x	x	5	—	2
59	—	—	—	—	—	—	—	—	x	x	3	—	2
60ᵃ	—	—	—	—	—	—	—	—	x	x	1	—	2
61	—	—	—	—	—	—	—	—	x	x	9	B	2
62	—	—	—	—	—	—	—	—	x	x	4	B	2
63	—	—	—	—	—	—	—	x	x	x	8	—	2
64	—	—	—	—	—	—	—	—	—	x	2	—	2
65	—	—	—	—	—	—	—	—	x	x	9	B	2
66	—	—	—	—	—	—	—	—	x	x	7	B	2
67	—	—	—	—	—	—	—	—	x	x	5	—	2
68	—	—	—	—	—	—	—	—	x	x	3	A	2
69	—	—	—	—	—	—	—	—	x	x	5	B	2
70	—	—	—	—	—	—	x	—	x	x	7	A	2
71	—	—	—	—	—	—	—	—	x	x	8	B	2
72	—	—	—	—	—	—	—	—	—	x	3	B	2
73	—	—	—	—	—	—	—	—	x	x	5	B	2
74	—	—	—	—	—	—	—	—	x	x	4	B	2
75	—	—	—	—	—	—	—	—	x	x	3	B	2
76	—	—	—	—	—	—	—	—	x	—	5	B	2
77	—	—	—	—	—	—	—	—	x	x	10	B	2
78	—	—	—	—	—	—	—	—	x	x	5	B	2
79	—	—	—	—	—	—	—	—	x	—	2	—	2
80	—	—	—	—	—	—	—	—	x	x	5	A	2
81	—	—	—	—	—	—	—	—	x	x	3	—	2
82	—	—	—	—	—	—	—	—	x	—	5	A	2
83	—	—	—	—	—	—	—	—	x	x	4	B	2
84	—	—	—	—	—	—	—	—	x	x	6	—	2
85	—	—	—	—	—	—	—	—	x	x	3	A	2
86	—	—	—	—	—	—	—	—	x	x	8	A	2
87	—	—	—	—	—	—	—	—	x	x	6	B	2
88	—	—	—	—	—	—	—	—	x	x	6	—	2
89	—	—	—	—	—	—	—	—	x	x	3	—	2
90	—	—	—	—	—	—	—	—	—	—	—	A	1
91	—	—	—	—	—	—	—	—	—	—	—	B	1
92	—	—	—	—	—	—	—	—	—	—	—	A	1
93	—	—	—	—	—	—	—	—	—	—	—	A	1
94	—	—	—	—	—	—	—	—	x	—	1	B	1
95	—	—	—	—	—	—	—	—	x	—	2	B	1

CHART B—(*Continued*)

	Intense			Outspoken					Stereotyped			Tol-erant	Index
	(1)	(2)	(3)	(4)	(5)	(6)	(7)	(8)	(9)	(10)	(11)	(12)	(13)
96	—	—	—	—	—	—	—	—	x	x	1	C	1
97	—	—	—	—	—	—	—	—	x	x	1	C	1
98	—	—	—	—	—	—	—	—	—	—	—	A	1
99	—	—	—	—	—	—	—	—	—	—	—	A	1
100	—	—	—	—	—	—	—	—	—	x	1	A	1
101	—	—	—	—	—	—	—	—	—	—	—	A	1
102	—	—	—	—	—	—	—	—	—	—	—	A	1
103	—	—	—	—	—	—	—	—	—	—	—	A	1
104	—	—	—	—	—	—	—	—	—	x	1	A	1
105	—	—	—	—	—	—	—	—	—	—	—	B	1
106	—	—	—	—	—	—	—	—	x	x	2	—	1
107	—	—	—	—	—	—	—	—	—	—	—	B	1
108	—	—	—	—	—	—	—	—	x	—	1	A	1
109	—	—	—	—	—	—	—	—	—	—	—	A	1
110	—	—	—	—	—	—	—	—	—	—	—	—	1
111	—	—	—	—	—	—	—	—	x	—	1	B	1
112	—	—	—	—	—	—	—	—	x	x	2	B	1
113	—	—	—	—	—	—	—	—	—	—	—	A	1
114	—	—	—	—	—	—	—	—	x	x	2	B	1
115	—	—	—	—	—	—	—	—	—	—	—	C	1
116	—	—	—	—	—	—	—	—	—	x	1	A	1
117	—	—	—	—	—	—	—	—	—	—	—	A	1
118	—	—	—	—	—	—	—	—	—	—	—	A	1
119	—	—	—	—	—	—	—	—	—	—	—	A	1
120	—	—	—	—	—	—	—	—	—	—	—	A	1
121	—	—	—	—	—	—	—	—	—	—	—	A	1
122	—	—	—	—	—	—	—	—	—	—	—	D	1
123	—	—	—	—	—	—	—	—	—	—	—	A	1
124	—	—	—	—	—	—	—	—	—	x	1	A	1
125	—	—	—	—	—	—	—	—	x	—	1	B	1
126	—	—	—	—	—	—	—	—	—	—	—	B	1
127	—	—	—	—	—	—	—	—	x	x	2	B	1
128	—	—	—	—	—	—	—	—	—	—	—	B	1
129	—	—	—	—	—	—	—	—	—	—	—	A	1
130	—	—	—	—	—	—	—	—	—	—	—	A	1
131	—	—	—	—	—	—	—	—	—	x	1	A	1
132	—	—	—	—	—	—	—	—	—	x	1	B	1
133	—	—	—	—	—	—	—	—	—	—	—	A	1
134	—	—	—	—	—	—	—	—	—	x	1	A	1
135	—	—	—	—	—	—	—	—	—	—	—	B	1

CHART B—(*Continued*)

	Intense				*Outspoken*					*Stereotyped*			*Tol- erant*	*Index*
	(1)	(2)	(3)	(4)	(5)	(6)	(7)	(8)	(9)	(10)	(11)	(12)	(13)
136	—	—	—	—	—	—	—	—	x	x	2	A	1
137	—	—	—	—	—	—	—	—	—	—	—	A	1
138	—	—	—	—	—	—	—	—	x	—	2	B	1
139	—	—	—	—	—	—	—	—	—	—	—	A	1
140	—	—	—	—	—	—	—	—	x	—	2	B	1
141	—	—	—	—	—	—	—	—	—	—	—	A	1
142	—	—	—	—	—	—	—	—	—	—	—	C	1
143	—	—	—	—	—	—	—	—	—	—	—	C	1
144	—	—	—	—	—	—	—	—	—	—	—	A	1
145	—	—	—	—	—	—	—	—	—	—	—	A	1
146	—	—	—	—	—	—	—	—	x	x	2	A	1
147	—	—	—	—	—	—	—	—	—	—	—	A	1
148	—	—	—	—	—	—	—	—	—	—	—	B	1
149	—	—	—	—	—	—	—	—	—	—	—	A	1
150	—	—	—	—	—	—	—	—	—	—	—	A	1

[a] Limited responses in latter half of the interview.
[b] Refused to answer but responses indicative of stereotyped anti-Semitism.

be interpreted as pertaining directly or indirectly to ethnic relations. However, five of the questions presented an opportunity for expression to those who tended to respond readily with interethnic hostility to questions of a general nature. They also permitted the expression of a demand or desire for restrictive actions. They were:

"Are there any organizations or groups of people whom you feel might be harmful to the country unless they are curbed?"

"Are there any groups of people you think are trying to get ahead at the expense of people like you?"

"What will interfere with our having a decent life?"

"Who do you think runs the government? What kind of people are they?"

"As things stand, would you say that some people get all the breaks and others get none?"

Subjects who mentioned the Jews in response to one of the first two questions were considered intensely anti-Semitic. If a subject responded to any one of the last three questions with *elaborated restrictive* comments, he was also considered to be intensely anti-Semitic. (See Col. 2 and Col. 3 on Chart B.)

Subjects who advocated restrictions against the Jews on any of the items which directly referred to the Jews throughout the remainder of the interview, or on direct questions, were considered to be outspokenly anti-Semitic.

2. *Delimitation of the Outspoken Anti-Semite from the Stereotyped Anti-Semite.* After the first forty nonethnic questions had been asked, six groups of questions were asked toward the end of the interview which were directly related to ethnic problems. They were so designed that responses could reveal whether a subject advocated restrictive action against the Jews. They also resulted in other types of hostile remarks about the Jews. The six main questions were the following:

> "(In a depression) if there are not enough jobs to go around, who should have the first chance at them?" (After the veteran had stated his preference, several probes were used. Among them were the following: "What about native Americans? And what about Gentiles?")

> "What do you think should be done about the Jews in this country?"

> "Should Jews be forced to leave the country?"

> "Should Jews be prevented from intermarriage?"

> "Would you object to a Jew moving in next door to your house?"

> "Would you be willing to have a Jew work on the job that you are doing?"

Responding to any one of these questions with discriminatory recommendations classified the subject as an outspoken anti-Semite. (The dividing line fell between Col. 8 and Col. 9 on Chart B.)

3. *Delimitation of the Stereotyped Anti-Semite from the Tolerant Veteran.* Eight questions were asked whose answers could have revealed anti-Semitic stereotypes. Most of these questions dealt with army experiences, For example, the veterans were asked who the "goldbrickers" in their outfit were and whether the Jews made good soldiers. In addition, the complete interview was combed for stereotypes which appeared as associative material. Stereotypes were analyzed in terms of their frequency and the distribution of the symbols employed. The total number of stereotypes made it possible to decide whether a subject should be categorized as a stereotyped anti-Semite or as a tolerant veteran. The next problem was to establish the maximum number of responses containing stereotypes which would still permit a subject to be considered as belonging in the category of tolerant veterans.

To arrive at such a number was not as difficult and the delimitation not as arbitrary as they may seem on the basis of a priori considerations. A careful inspection of the interviews revealed that it was possible to draw a convincing line of division between the tolerant and the intolerant veterans. The most important index with regard to tolerance proved to be the veteran's answer to the final direct question, "What shall be done with the Jews in this country?" The response to this question was markedly different in the case of veterans who had previously used a larger number of stereotypes from the responses of those who had used only isolated stereotypes. Subjects who used no stereotypes, or at most one or two stereotypes, usually elaborated their answer to this question in such a way as to suggest that Jews should not be treated differently from the rest of the population. Veterans who had previously used more stereotypes either failed to elaborate their answers voluntarily, or supported their "tolerant" position by acknowledging that they were willing to accept the Jews *regardless of their difference*.

On the basis of this observation it was decided to classify a veteran as tolerant if he used *not more than two isolated stereotypes* and if he expressed *no restrictive demands* at any point in the interview.

The index as a whole should find its justification by the manner in which the data fitted into the scheme. It is additionally supported by the analysis of how certain traits correlated with the types of intolerance as measured by the index.

As mentioned above, this procedure was designed to measure a subject's degree of intolerance on the basis of his total response and by arranging all responses so as to form a continuum. One of the underlying assumptions was that higher degrees of intolerance contained the characteristics of intolerance which could also be found on the lower levels of intolerance. Thus the outspokenly anti-Semitic subject was supposed to show, in addition to his particular traits, those of the stereotyped anti-Semite. The intensely anti-Semitic subject was expected to display the attitudes of both the stereotyped and the outspoken anti-Semite plus the distinguishing element of a spontaneous appearance and a greater violence of such attitudes. This typology was suggested by the pre-test. Therefore the interview as a standardized instrument was so constructed that it would elicit responses which when systematically analyzed would permit such an ordering of respondents. The analysis of the results seems to indicate that the instrument was adequate in terms of this criterion. The number of cases which did not fit into the "scale" was very small, and in most cases it was possible to isolate particular conditions which explained why that was so.

The items in the interview dealing with Jewish topics were arranged in descending order of intensity on Chart B. Where the required number of items was present, the subject was classified as intensely anti-Semitic. The absence of all of them would indicate a completely tolerant attitude. It was possible to determine into which class an individual fell by noting where on the continuum the first intolerant trait appeared. It was assumed that ideally after the first trait of ethnic intolerance appeared, all the other traits would follow without interruption. The number of violations of this rule could be taken as a measure of the adequacy or inadequacy of the scheme of analysis. Such violations of this rule appeared in less than 5 per cent of the total number of cases.

Similar dividing lines were set up to delimit areas within the continuum of anti-Negro attitudes. Some modification of the definitions used in delimiting areas of anti-Semitism became necessary, but the same general procedure was applied (see Chart C).

In delimiting the "intensely" anti-Negro,[1] the spontaneity of restrictive comments was again used as the basis for categorizing. In addition, those who answered affirmatively to the question, "Should the Negroes be deported?" were classified in this group.

The most important revision of definitions was that the distinction between the outspoken and stereotyped categories was dropped. Instead, two groups of outspokenly anti-Negro veterans were isolated. First, those who made clear and unqualified demands for restrictive action with regard to the Negro were classifiable, according to the previous set of definitions, in the outspokenly anti-Negro category. These were classified as outspokenly anti-Negro, Type A. However, a number of veterans who made restrictive demands, spontaneously modified them by advocating equal opportunities and facilities under conditions of segregation. Responses of this nature were in answer to the generalized question, "What do you think ought to be done about the Negro in this country?" Veterans who responded in this way were classified as outspokenly anti-Negro, Type B. The form of their intolerance was clearly different from that of Type A. On the other hand, stereotyped thinking about the Negro unaccompanied by some form of restrictive demands almost never occurred. Stereotyped thinking about the Negro took the form of requests for segregation rather than expressions of mere negative valuations.

Therefore in relating social and economic factors to the degree of Negro intolerance as indicated by the position on the continuum, the latter type of outspoken intolerance (Type B) was included with the few veterans who displayed only stereotyped thinking about the Negro.

CHART C

DISTRIBUTION OF ANTI-NEGRO ATTITUDES

Legend

Column
(1) Spontaneous restrictive responses (all types)
(2) Elicited restrictions (deportation)
(3) Elicited restrictions (general)
    (Code O refers to expressions of equal opportunities under segregated conditions)
(4) Elicited restrictions (intermarriage)
(5) Elicited restrictions (housing)
(6) Elicited restrictions (employment)
(7) Spontaneous stereotypes
(8) Elicited stereotypes
(9) Total number of stereotypes
(10) Grounds for tolerance
    A Denial of differences between Negroes and non-Negroes
    B Acceptance of differences between Negroes and non-Negroes

[1] The term "intensely" anti-Negro is a shorthand notation for veterans who had intensely anti-Negro attitudes; likewise "outspokenly" anti-Negro refers to veterans who had outspokenly anti-Negro attitudes, etc.

(11) Index of anti-Negro attitudes
    1 Tolerant
    2 Stereotyped
    3 Outspoken anti-Negro
      A Demands restrictions
      B Demands segregation but equal rights and opportunities
    4 Intensely anti-Negro

	Intense		Outspoken				Stereotyped			Tolerant	Index
	(1)	(2)	(3)	(4)	(5)	(6)	(7)	(8)	(9)	(10)	(11)
1	x	x	x	—	x	—	—	x	1	—	4
2	—	x	x	x	x	x	x	x	14	—	4
3	—	x	x	x	x	x	x	x	4	—	4
4	—	x	x	—	x	x	x	x	7	—	4
5	—	x	x	x	x	x	x	x	9	—	4
6	—	x	x	x	x	x	x	x	3	—	4
7	—	x	x	x	x	x	x	x	7	—	4
8	—	x	x	x	x	x	x	x	20	—	4
9	—	x	x	x	x	x	x	x	9	—	4
10	—	x	x	x	x	x	x	x	6	—	4
11	—	x	x	x	x	x	x	x	4	—	4
12	—	x	x	x	x	x	x	x	9	—	4
13	—	x	x	x	x	x	x	x	5	—	4
14	—	x	x	x	x	x	x	x	4	—	4
15	—	x	x	x	—	—	x	x	3	—	4
16	—	x	x	x	x	x	x	x	7	—	4
17	—	x	x	x	x	x	x	x	8	—	4
18	x	x	x	x	x	x	x	x	5	—	4
19	—	x	—	x	x	x	x	x	5	—	4
20	x	x	x	x	x	x	—	x	4	—	4
21	x	x	x	x	x	x	x	x	7	—	4
22	—	x	x	x	x	—	x	x	5	—	4
23	x	x	x	x	x	x	x	—	1	—	4
24	x	x	x	x	x	—	x	x	4	—	4
25	—	—	x	x	x	—	x	x	5	—	3A
26	—	—	x	x	x	—	x	x	5	—	3A
27	—	—	x	—	x	—	—	x	1	—	3A
28	—	—	x	x	x	x	x	x	2	—	3A
29	—	—	x	x	x	x	x	x	6	—	3A
30	—	—	x	x	x	x	x	x	2	—	3A
31	—	—	x	x	x	—	x	x	7	—	3A
32	—	—	x	—	x	x	x	x	3	—	3A
33	—	—	x	x	x	x	x	—	1	—	3A
34	—	—	x	—	x	x	—	x	1	—	3A

CHART C—(Continued)

	Intense			Outspoken				Stereotyped			Tol-erant	Index
	(1)	(2)	(3)	(4)	(5)	(6)	(7)	(8)	(9)	(10)	(11)
35	—	—	x	x	—	—	x	x	5	—	3A
36	—	—	x	x	x	x	x	x	4	—	3A
37	—	—	x	x	x	x	x	x	6	—	3A
38	—	—	x	x	x	—	x	x	4	—	3A
39	—	—	x	x	x	x	x	x	7	—	3A
40	—	—	x	x	—	—	x	—	1	—	3A
41	—	—	x	x	x	x	x	x	5	—	3A
42	—	—	x	x	x	x	—	—	0	—	3A
43	—	—	x	—	x	x	x	x	4	—	3A
44	—	—	x	x	x	—	x	x	6	—	3A
45	—	—	x	x	x	—	x	x	6	—	3A
46	—	—	x	x	x	x	—	x	4	—	3A
47	—	—	x	x	x	x	—	x	3	—	3A
48	—	—	x	x	x	x	x	x	2	—	3A
49	—	—	x	x	x	x	x	x	4	—	3A
50	—	—	x	x	x	x	x	x	8	—	3A
51	—	—	x	x	x	x	x	x	4	—	3A
52	—	—	x	x	x	x	x	x	12	—	3A
53	—	—	x	x	x	x	x	x	10	—	3A
54	—	—	x	x	x	x	x	x	9	—	3A
55	—	—	x	—	—	—	—	x	2	—	3A
56	—	—	x	x	x	x	x	x	5	—	3A
57	—	—	x	x	x	—	x	x	6	—	3A
58	—	—	x	x	x	x	x	x	10	—	3A
59	—	—	x	x	x	x	x	x	7	—	3A
60	—	—	x	x	x	x	x	x	10	—	3A
61	—	—	x	x	x	—	x	—	2	—	3A
62	—	—	x	x	x	—	x	—	5	—	3A
63	—	—	x	x	x	x	—	x	3	—	3A
64	—	—	x	x	x	x	x	x	4	—	3A
65	—	—	x	x	x	x	x	x	5	—	3A
66	—	—	x	—	x	—	x	x	4	—	3A
67	—	—	x	x	x	x	x	x	6	—	3A
68	—	—	x	x	x	—	x	x	4	—	3A
69	—	—	x	—	x	x	x	x	3	—	3A
70	—	x	—	x	x	x	x	x	3	—	3A
71	—	—	x	x	x	—	—	x	1	—	3A
72	—	—	x	x	x	x	—	x	3	—	3A
73	—	—	x	x	x	x	x	x	6	—	3A

CHART C—(*Continued*)

	Intense		Outspoken				Stereotyped			Tol-erant	Index
	(1)	(2)	(3)	(4)	(5)	(6)	(7)	(8)	(9)	(10)	(11)
74	—	—	x	—	x	—	x	x	5	—	3A
75	—	—	x	x	x	x	—	x	2	—	3A
76	—	—	x	x	x	x	x	x	4	—	3A
77	—	—	x	x	x	x	x	x	6	—	3A
78	—	—	x	x	x	x	x	x	4	—	3A
79	—	—	x	x	x	x	x	x	3	—	3A
80	—	—	x	x	x	x	x	x	4	—	3A
81	—	—	x	—	x	—	x	x	1	—	3A
82	—	—	x	x	x	x	x	x	5	—	3A
83	—	—	x	—	x	—	x	x	5	—	3A
84	—	—	x	x	x	x	—	x	3	—	3A
85	—	—	x	x	x	x	x	x	7	—	3A
86	—	—	x	x	x	—	—	x	2	—	3A
87	—	—	x	x	x	x	x	x	5	B	3A
88	—	—	x	x	x	x	x	x	5	—	3A
89	—	—	x	x	—	x	x	x	7	—	3A
90	—	—	x	x	x	x	x	x	4	—	3A
91	—	—	x	x	x	—	x	x	3	A	3A
92	—	—	x	—	x	x	x	x	6	—	3A
93	—	—	x	x	x	x	x	x	5	—	3A
94	—	—	x	x	x	—	x	x	3	—	3A
95	—	—	x	—	x	—	x	x	2	—	3A
96	—	—	x	x	x	—	x	x	2	—	3A
97	—	—	x	x	x	x	x	—	2	—	3A
98	—	—	x	—	x	x	x	x	6	—	3A
99	—	—	0	—	x	x	x	x	6	—	3B
100	—	—	0	x	x	x	x	x	4	—	3B
101	—	—	0	—	x	—	—	—	0	—	3B
102	—	—	0	x	x	—	—	x	3	—	3B
103	—	—	0	—	x	—	—	x	1	—	3B
104	—	—	0	x	x	x	x	x	6	—	3B
105	—	—	0	x	—	—	—	—	0	—	3B
106	—	—	0	—	x	—	x	—	3	—	3B
107	—	—	0	—	x	—	—	—	0	—	3B
108	—	—	0	x	x	—	—	—	2	—	3B
109	—	—	0	x	x	x	—	x	2	—	3B
110	—	—	0	—	x	—	x	x	3	—	3B
111	—	—	0	x	x	x	—	x	1	—	3B
112	—	—	0	x	x	—	x	—	1	A	3B

DYNAMICS OF PREJUDICE

CHART C—(Continued)

	Intense		Outspoken				Stereotyped			Tol-erant	Index
	(1)	(2)	(3)	(4)	(5)	(6)	(7)	(8)	(9)	(10)	(11)
113	—	—	0	x	—	—	x	—	1	—	3B
114	—	—	0	x	x	—	x	x	3	—	3B
115	—	—	0	x	x	—	x	x	4	—	3B
116	—	—	0	x	x	—	x	x	5	—	3B
117	—	—	0	—	x	—	x	x	2	—	3B
118	—	—	0	x	x	—	x	—	1	A	3B
119	—	—	0	x	x	—	x	x	5	A	3B
120	—	—	0	—	—	x	x	x	4	—	3B
121	—	—	0	x	x	x	x	x	4	—	3B
122	—	—	0	x	x	x	x	x	5	—	3B
123	—	—	0	x	x	—	x	x	1	—	3B
124	—	—	0	x	—	—	x	—	2	—	3B
125	—	—	0	x	x	—	—	x	2	—	3B
126	—	—	0	x	—	—	x	x	6	—	3B
127	—	—	0	x	x	x	—	x	2	—	3B
128	—	—	0	x	x	x	—	x	3	—	3B
129	—	—	0	x	x	—	—	x	1	—	3B
130	—	—	0	—	x	—	—	—	0	—	3B
131	—	—	0	x	—	—	x	—	2	—	3B
132	—	—	—	—	x	—	x	x	3	—	2
133	—	—	—	x	—	—	x	x	7	—	2
134	—	—	—	x	x	—	—	x	3	—	2
135	—	—	—	x	x	—	—	x	2	—	2
136	—	—	—	—	—	x	—	x	2	B	2
137	—	—	—	x	x	—	—	x	1	—	2
138	—	—	—	—	—	—	—	x	3	A	2
139	—	—	—	x	—	—	—	—	0	A	1
140	—	—	—	x	—	—	—	—	0	A	1
141	—	—	—	x	—	—	—	—	0	B	1
142	—	—	—	—	—	—	—	x	1	A	1
143	—	—	—	—	—	—	—	—	0	B	1
144	—	—	—	—	—	—	—	—	0	—	1
145	—	—	—	—	—	—	—	—	0	A	1
146	—	—	—	—	—	—	—	x	1	A	1
147	—	—	—	—	—	—	—	—	0	A	1
148	—	—	—	x	—	—	—	x	1	A	1
149	—	—	—	—	—	—	—	—	0	A	1
150	—	—	—	x	—	—	—	—	0	A	1

V. RELIABILITY OF ANALYTIC PROCEDURES

An examination of the literature on the analysis of open-ended interviews reveals a lack of progress toward the development of a suitable methodology. Advocates of the open-ended interview admit that the problem of analyzing its intensive data remains relatively unsolved, that is, the problem of translating the interview record into rigorous statistical categories of analysis. Lazarsfeld[2] states candidly:

> "We shall agree that a well-conducted open-ended interview gives us a fascinating wealth of information on the attitude of a single respondent. When it comes to the statistical analysis of many open-ended interviews, the matter is already not so simple. It is in the nature of this technique that just the most valuable details of open-ended interviews become difficult to compare with the answers obtained in another interview. It can safely be said that the proponents of the open-ended interview technique have made much more progress in the conduct of the interviews than in their statistical analysis."

In particular, the few references make no mention of the problem of reliability in existing methods of analysis. It is most striking that in the literature on intensive interviews no cognizance is taken of experiences and techniques developed in the study of mass communications, particularly that of content analysis. The interview record is a form of communications, and therefore, should be subject to analysis in much the same way that communications content is analyzed. This is particularly the case since the various types of content analysis have attempted to deal with the reliability of their procedures.

Lasswell[3] has brought this problem to the fore. Apparently the study of interpersonal relationships is held back by the absence of satisfactory categories for the description and comparison of symbols. He therefore suggests that communications be classified into categories according to the understandings which prevail among those who issued the communications, or to whom they are directed. (In the case of the interview, it would be in terms of the meanings of the respondent.)

The analyst may use a single symbol, an assertion, a sentence, a paragraph (or even a larger flow of communications) as his unit of analysis.[4] (In the case of an intensive interview, he may use the responses to a single question, or to a number of questions, or a whole page of the interview.) Each reference or unit of analysis is classified according to explicit definitions or criteria; the definitions and criteria are obtained from the hypotheses being tested. (Lasswell has suggested and used the criteria of indulgence and deprivation; but this is only one set of criteria.) The next step is to determine the frequency

[2] Lazarsfeld, Paul F.: "The Controversy Over Detailed Interviews—An Offer for Negotiation," *Public Opinion Quarterly*, VIII: 38-60, 1944.

[3] Lasswell, Harold: "A Provisional Classification of Symbol Data," *Psychiatry* I: 197, 1938.

[4] Lasswell, Harold: *Analyzing the Content of Mass Communications: A Brief Introduction*, Washington: Experimental Division for the Study of War Time Communications, Library of Congress 1942.

with which these categories appear in any flow of communications. Fundamentally, the method of content analysis depends on the reliability of the judgments of different analysts in applying the same criteria to a given document or interview. It should be noted that this is the problem of reliability implicit in the procedures described by practitioners of the open-ended interview.[5] If the methodologists of open-ended and intensive interviews were explicit in this respect, they would cite reliability data indicating the degree to which more than one analyst agreed on the application of the categories of analysis. That contents can be reliably analyzed in this fashion has been shown by numerous studies. The degree of reliability depends on the unit of analysis and the explicitness with which the criteria and definitions are made.[6] A number of unpublished studies by the Office of Radio Research may be considered as moving in the direction of the systematic analysis of intensive interview data.[7]

Therefore, the central problem in the application of content analysis procedures to intensive interviews is to take the responses to specific questions or groups of questions and to classify them reliably under a systematic set of criteria or categories.

Two points are central in this process of content analysis: (1) The classification system (the "code") cannot be determined completely before the interviews are gathered, although in the main the hypotheses and the pre-test supply the major outlines; (2) The reliable classification of a given response means that two or more analysts using the same explicit categories are able to produce a satisfactorily high degree of agreement in their analytical judgments, and that their judgments do not vary with time.

When the interviewing was completed for this study, 20 per cent of the cases were read. For each question or group of questions, all possible alternative answers supplied the basis for constructing a category system (the "code").[8] Three types of categories were devised: (A) symbol categories, (B) assertion or proposition categories, and (C) analytic categories.

(A) In some cases the "code" merely called for noting the presence or absence of a particular list of *symbols*. For example, the question asking "Who do you think gained through the war?" produced the following category system:

1. We, we all.
2. The people, my country.
3. Nobody.
4. The officers.
5. Big business.
6. Those men who stayed at home.
7. Others.

[5] Skott, H. E.: "Attitude Research in the Department of Agriculture," *Public Opinion Quarterly*, VII: 280-292, 1943.

[6] Janis, Irving L., Fadner, Raymond H., and Janowitz, Morris: "Reliability of a Content Analysis Technique," *Public Opinion Quarterly*, VII: 293-96, 1943.

[7] In particular, Berelson, Bernard: "The Quantitative Analysis of Case Records: An Experimental Study," *Psychiatry*, X: 395-403, 1948.

[8] The category system which was developed to encompass questions both individually and in selected groups filled more than sixty typewritten pages.

(B)   In other cases the response required the categorizing of an *assertion or statement*. For example: "How did the fellows feel about religion?" The code for this question was:

1. Soldiers were more religious in combat; there were no atheists in foxholes.
2. Most soldiers followed their civilian habits.
3. Like everything else; everybody feels a little different; everybody had his own opinions.
4. Most soldiers didn't go to church; no one in the army was really religious.
5. Other.
6. Don't know.

Frequently, the responses did not employ these explicit assertions so that supplementary rules had to be constructed.

Many questions which might have been asked in a "yes" or "no" fashion were asked as open-ended questions in order to produce fuller and more representative responses. For example: "How were the Jews treated in the army?" This made the coding procedure of assertions more elaborate. The categories employed for this question were:

1. They were treated just like anyone.
2. They were treated very well (matter-of-fact).
3. They were treated very well because they always got soft jobs and special privileges.
4. They always watched out for themselves; talked themselves into good jobs.
5. The Jews were not treated too well because they held all the good jobs, and special privileges, and were disliked by the boys for this.

Because of the detail of analysis, assertion analysis developed into complicated classification systems where the question required it. For example: "If we have a large amount of unemployment, what will that do to you and your family?" Responses were coded as follows:

1. Unemployment would mean nothing to a person like me.
2. Won't do much.
3. Depends.
4. We will probably be able to get along on a reduced level; my wages will be reduced.
5. Will affect us very much; would have to go on relief; will put us in a bad fix.
6. People like me will starve.
7. Don't know.

Or, "Do you think that what the government has been doing these days is affecting the liberties of the ordinary people?"

1. We don't have any liberties.
2. The government is affecting our liberties (generally).
3. The government is affecting our liberties (mentions specific ways).
4. The government is not affecting our liberties to any great extent.
5. These restrictions are necessary; are helpful.
6. We have our freedom.
7. Some Americans have too much freedom; they don't appreciate their freedom.

8. Other.

9. Don't know.

In the final presentation of results, sub-categories of this type were often combined for special purposes.

(C) Certain questions were classified according to judgments not readily discernible from the manifest content but dependent on *analytical definitions*. For example, the series of questions on political parties, in addition to being coded for professed party affiliation, were classified according to the following criteria, after clear definitions and examples were established. Code: Attitude toward political parties in general.

1. Feeling of general deprivation (due to disregard by the leaders, incompetency, or deliberate manipulation).

2. Feeling of indulgence (due to benevolence or competency).

3. Indeterminate.

The reliability of the coding procedure was dependent ultimately on the ability of trained analysts who were familiar with the definitions to apply them to the 150 cases and independently to produce comparable results. To this end, only four analysts participated in the task, two of whom carried out the bulk of the work. All four were totally familiar with the various aspects of the study and had wide experience in social research, particularly in attitude research. To test the procedure, four of the most abstract and complicated sets of categories were tested. In all, 400 judgments drawn from one-third of the sample were made by one analyst. The same data were "coded" independently by another analyst. The classification systems tested were: (1) expressions of personal competency; (2) acceptance of present status in economic matters; (3) demands for collective vs. individual action; (4) economic apprehensions. The analysis of errors is tabulated below:

TABLE 3(A)

RELIABILITY OF ANALYTIC PROCEDURE

	No. of Differences Between Two Analysts	Total No. of Judgments	Percentage Error
1. Competency	5	100	5.0
2. Acceptance of present status	12	100	12.0
3. Demands for action	10	150	7.0
4. Apprehensions	4	50	8.0
Total	31	400	7.7

The total percentage of error for the 400 judgments was about 8. It should be noted that the largest number of errors occurred in the category on the veteran's acceptance of his present status. The overall percentage error was considered strikingly small and therefore warranted confidence in the procedure of analysis, especially since these categories were typical of the most difficult aspects of the coding procedures. Actually the data produced by the categories included under "acceptance of present status" were not employed in this report, so that the percentage error may be considered to have been even smaller.

VI. SCHEDULE OF INTERVIEW QUESTIONS

1. How do you think things are going to turn out now that the war is over?
1.1. Why do you think so?

2. What do you think can be done to insure a decent life for us?
2.1. Why do you think that?
2.2. What are the chances that ——— will happen?
2.3. Who should do it?

3. What will interfere with our having a decent life?
3.1. What can be done about it?
3.2. Who should do it?

4. Now that the veterans are back, how do you think they are going to get along?
4.1. Why do you think that?
4.2. What are the main gripes of the veterans?

5. Do you think enough is being done for the veterans now?
5.1. Why do you say that?
5.2. (If not enough) What should be done for the veterans?
5.3. Who should do it?
5.4. Are there any groups of people you think are trying to get ahead at the expense of people like you?

6. Which party do you think is better for the veteran?
6.1. In what way will the ——— party be better for the veteran?
6.2. How about your parents? What party do, or did, they favor?
6.3. How could our government be improved?
6.4. Do you think that what the government has been doing these days is affecting the liberties of the ordinary people?

7. Do you think the ordinary individual has any chance to influence politics nowadays?
7.1. (If "yes") How does the ordinary individual influence politics?
    (If "no") How could the ordinary individual influence politics?
7.2. Who do you think runs the government?
7.3. What kind of people are they?
7.4. Are there any organizations or groups of people who you feel might be harmful to the country unless they are curbed?

8. Are you a member of any veterans' organization?
8.1. (If "yes") Why do you prefer that (or those) organizations?
8.2. (If not a member) Why don't you belong to any of these veterans' organizations?

9. We have been talking about how to get a decent life in America, but as things stand, would you say that some people get all the breaks, and others get none?
9.1. Which groups get all the breaks?
9.2. Are there any others?
9.3. Do you think they deserve them?
9.4. Why do you think so?

10. If we have unemployment how bad will it be?
10.1. If we have a large amount of unemployment what will that do to you and your family?
10.2. What did you and your family experience during the last depression of 1929?
10.3. What's gone wrong with America that we run into depressions?
10.4. What can be done about it?
10.5. If there are not enough jobs to go around, who should have the first chance at them?
10.51. What about veterans, white people, Gentiles, native-born Americans, people who have seniority on the job?
10.6. Why would you say that (for each)?

11. What are you working at now?
11.1. Are you satisfied with your present position?
11.2. Why?
11.3. What job do you want to get into now?
11.4. What do you think the chances are for this?
11.5. Why?
11.6. What occupation would you like to get into as your life's work?

12. About how much money would you want to be making a year?
12.1. What do you think the chances are for that?
12.2. Why?

13. Do you happen to be married? (If "yes" ask 14. to 15.3.)
13.1. (If single) Have you thought of getting married?
     (If engaged or planning to get married, ask 14.4. to 15.3.)
13.2. Are you living alone or with your family?
13.3. Is this a satisfactory arrangement?
13.4. Why "yes" or "no"?
13.5. Why don't you plan to get married?

14. (If veteran is married ask) Have you and your wife been able to continue your home life the way you wanted it since your discharge?
14.1. Why?
14.2. What things can you think of that would improve your home life?
14.3. How many children do you have?
14.4. How many children would you like to have?
14.5. What do you think is the best way of bringing up your children?
14.6. Do you think the ways of bringing up children have changed since your parents' time?

14.7. Would you bring your children up the way your mother and father brought you up?

14.8. How do you think you can get children to behave?

14.9. How did your parents do it?

14.10. Do you think that was the right way of going about it?

15. What do you think about wives working?

15.1. Why "yes" or "no"?

15.2. Did your mother ever work?

15.3. How did your dad feel about women working?

16. We've been talking about how you would like your life to be now; do you think the time you spent in the army set you back in any way?

16.1. By the way, how long were you in the army?

16.2. What type of army service did you see? (Type of work; how long

16.21-4. for each; amount of combat; special decorations.)

16.3. What did you lose by being in the army?

16.4 If you lost, who gained through the war?

17. How did you feel about going into the army?

17.1. Why?

17.2. What did you like most about army life?

17.3. What did you like least about army life?

17.4. Do you feel that you got a bad break in your army career?

17.5. How is that?

17.6. Do you feel that army life changed you in any way?

17.7. How is that?

18. In your experience in the army, what kind of fellows were the "goldbrickers"?

19. How did the fellows in your outfit get along with the officers?

19.1. What was wrong with the officers?

19.2. Do you think promotions were decided upon fairly?

19.3. Why?

19.4. Do you fellows feel that army discipline was too strict?

19.5. In what way?

19.6. In general, do you feel that officers deserve the special privileges which they get?

19.7. Why?

19.8. How do you feel about saluting officers?

20.1. Do you find you miss the fellows in your outfit?

20.2. Was your outfit one where everybody got along together?

20.3. Who were the troublemakers?

20.4. What kind of fellows were they?

20.5. Is there anything about army life that you miss now?

20.6. When you were in the army, did you feel the civilians treated you right?

20.7. In what way?

21.   How did the fellows feel about religion?

21.1.   Did you notice any change in their attitude towards religion?

21.2.   Do you think your attitude toward religion was changed in any way by army life?

21.3.   How about going to church?

21.31.   Do you think you go to church more or less than you did before you entered the army?

21.4.   May I ask what denomination you are?

21.5.   May I ask what denomination your mother and father were?

21.51.   How important was religion in your family?

22.   Do you go around with a crowd regularly?

22.1.   Is it the same crowd you went out with before the war?

22.2.   Do your parents approve?

22.3.   Do you keep in touch with your brothers and sisters who do not live with you?

22.4.   Do you keep in touch with any of your army buddies?

23.   Do you think civilians respect and understand the veterans?

23.1.   How is that?

24.   In view of what the war has cost you fellows and the rest of the country, do you think it was worthwhile?

24.1.   Do you think the German and Japanese wars were equally necessary?

24.2.   Why?

24.3.   What did we gain or lose by the European war?

24.4.   What did we gain or lose by the Japanese war?

24.5.   What do you think are the chances for a long peace?

24.6.   What would you say were the biggest threats coming from outside the United States?

24.7.   Do you think there are any threats to peace inside this country?

24.8.   Can anything be done to guarantee peace? What?

25.   Do you think we should help other countries get on their feet with food, manufactured products, etc?

25.1.   Which ones?

25.2.   When you were in the army, did you get into contact with foreigners?

25.3.   What ones?

25.4.   What do you think about them?

25.5.   What should we do with Germany? Japan?

25.6.   What should be done about the refugees who have come to this country?

25.7.   Should more be let in?

26.   How were the Mexicans treated in the army?

27.   How were the Negroes treated in the army?

27.1.   Did the Negroes make good soldiers?

27.2.   How did the fellows in your outfit get along with Negroes?

27.3.   What do you think should be done about the Negro in this country?

28. How were the Jews treated in the army?
28.1. Did the Jews make good soldiers?
28.2. How did the fellows in your outfit get along with the Jews?
28.3. What do you think should be done about the Jews in this country?

29. Should Negroes be forced to leave the country?
29.1. Should Negroes be prevented from intermarriage?
29.2. Would you object to a Negro moving in next door to your house?
29.3. Would you be willing to have a Negro work on the same job that you are doing?
29.4. Would you eat in a restaurant where Negroes were served?

30. Should Jews be forced to leave the country?
30.1. Should Jews be prevented from intermarriage?
30.2. Would you object to a Jew moving in next door to your house?
30.3. Would you be willing to have a Jew work on the same job that you are doing?
30.4. Would you eat in a restaurant where Jews were served?
30.5. What should be done with the Japanese in this country?

ASKED AT THE END OF THE INTERVIEW

1. How old are you?
2. Where were you born? (City and state.)
3. Where did you live before you joined the army?
4. When were you demobilized?
5. What was your rank at the time of discharge?
6. How long have you lived at your present address?
7. Married, single, separated, divorced, how many times married?
8. How long married?
9. If not married, with whom are you living?
9.1. How much education have you had?
10. Are your parents living or dead? If dead, when?
11. Are there any divorces in your family?
12. How many brothers and sisters do you have? (Record sibling relationships.)
13. Where was your father born?
14. Where was your mother born? (If either parent was born in the U. S., determine ethnic stock by question, "From where did your father's family come?")
15. What is your father's occupation?
16. What is his present income?
17. What was your occupation and salary before you entered the army?
18. What is your present salary?
19. What organizations did you belong to before the war?
20. What organizations do you belong to now?
21. What is your favorite newspaper?

21.1.   What is your favorite radio program?
21.2.   What is your favorite magazine?
22.   By the way, which political party do you favor?

VII. SUPPLEMENTARY TABLES

A. Tables dealing with attitudes toward Jews.

TABLE 4(A)

RELIGIOUS DENOMINATION OF VETERANS' PARENTS

	Parents both Catholic		Parents both Protestant		Parents both Gr. Orth.		Parents of different denomination		Total
	No.	Per-centage	No.	Per-centage	No.	Per-centage	No.	Per-centage	No.
Tolerant	39	40	14	45	0	—	8	40	61
Stereotyped	26	27	9	29	1	—	6	30	42
Outspoken & Intense	32	33	8	26	1	—	6	30	47
Total	97		31		2		20		150

TABLE 5(A)

"DO YOU THINK YOUR ATTITUDE TOWARD RELIGION WAS CHANGED

IN ANY WAY BY ARMY LIFE?"

	Tolerant		Stereotyped		Outspoken and Intense		Total	
	No.	%	No.	%	No.	%	No.	%
It was strengthened	15	25	10	24	19	40	44	29
It's the same	38	62	26	62	21	45	85	57
I'm less religious now	7	11	4	9	4	9	15	10
Indeterminate	1	2	2	5	3	6	6	4
Total	61		42		47		150	

Table 6(A)

Ethnic Origin of Parents

	Both parents born in U.S.		One parent born in U.S.		Neither parent born in U.S.		Total
	No.	Percentage	No.	Percentage	No.	Percentage	No.
Tolerant	24	44	9	36	28	40	61
Stereotyped	16	29	5	20	21	30	42
Outspoken and Intense	15	27	11	44	21	30	47
Total	55		25		70		150

Table 7(A)

Salary Range

	No.	Percentage
Less than $1,500	1	1
$1,501 to $2,000	29	19
$2,001 to $2,500	29	19
$2,501 to $3,000	43	29
$3,001 to $3,500	20	13
$3,501 to $4,000	4	3
$4,001 to $4,500	0	0
Over $4,500	4	3
Unemployed	7	5
Student	8	5
No data	5	3
Total	150	100

TABLE 8(A)
CURRENT OCCUPATION

	No.	Percentage
Professional	3	2
Prof. and Managerial	5	3
Clerk and Kindred	27	18
Skilled	20	13
Semi-skilled	62	42
Unskilled	11	7
Unemployed	7	5
Student	9	6
On-the-job-training	6	4
Total	150	100

TABLE 9(A)
TYPE OF ARMY SERVICE

	Combat		Combat support		Noncombat		Total
	No.	Percentage	No.	Percentage	No.	Percentage	No.
Tolerant	22	41	12	40	27	40	61
Stereotyped	18	34	6	20	18	27	42
Outspoken & Intense	13	25	12	40	22	33	47
Total	53		30		67		150

TABLE 10(A)
ILLNESS AND INJURY DURING SERVICE[a]

	Wounded		Combat exhaustion		Noncombat illness or accident		None		Total
	No.	Per-centage	No.	Per-centage	No.	Per-centage	No.	Per-centage	No.
Tolerant	11	42	1	—	8	32	43	44	63
Stereotyped	9	35	2	—	5	20	26	26	42
Outspoken & Intense	6	23	1	—	12	48	30	30	49
Total	26		4		25		99		

[a] Multiple entries possible.

TABLE 11(A)

LENGTH OF ARMY SERVICE

	1–3 years		3–4 years		4 and more		Total
	No.	Percentage	No.	Percentage	No.	Percentage	No.
Tolerant	14	36	30	48	17	35	61
Stereotyped	12	31	16	26	14	29	42
Outspoken & Intense	13	33	16	26	18	36	47
Total	39		62		49		150

TABLE 12(A)

"NOW THAT THE VETERANS ARE BACK, HOW DO YOU THINK THEY ARE GOING TO GET ALONG?"

	Tolerant		Stereotyped		Outspoken and Intense		Total	
	No.	Per-centage	No.	Per-centage	No.	Per-centage	No.	Per-centage
Well	38	62	14	33	19	40	71	47
Badly	11	18	12	29	15	32	38	25
Other	11	18	15	36	10	22	36	24
Don't know	1	2	1	2	3	6	5	4
Total	61		42		47		150	

B. Tables dealing with attitudes toward Negroes.

TABLE 13(A)

ANTI-NEGRO ATTITUDE AND ETHNIC ORIGIN OF PARENTS

	Both parents born in U.S.		One parent born in U.S.		Neither parent born in U.S.		Total
	No.	Percentage	No.	Percentage	No.	Percentage	No.
Tolerant	7	13	1	4	4	6	12
Stereotyped	15	27	5	20	20	29	40
Outspoken	25	45	14	56	35	50	74
Intense	8	15	5	20	11	15	24
Total	55		25		70		150

DYNAMICS OF PREJUDICE

TABLE 14(A)

ANTI-NEGRO ATTITUDE AND AGE

	Under 28		29–36		Total
	No.	Percentage	No.	Percentage	No.
Tolerant	6	7	6	10	12
Stereotyped	21	22	19	35	40
Outspoken	52	55	22	39	74
Intense	15	16	9	16	24
Total	94		56		150

TABLE 15(A)

ANTI-NEGRO ATTITUDE AND EDUCATION

	Up to some high school		Completed high school		Some college or more		Total
	No.	Percentage	No.	Percentage	No.	Percentage	No.
Tolerant	2	3	5	13	5	13	12
Stereotyped	16	25	10	22	14	36	40
Outspoken	32	49	27	57	15	38	74
Intense	15	23	4	8	5	13	24
Total	65		46		39		150

TABLE 16(A)

ANTI-NEGRO ATTITUDE AND PARTY AFFILIATION

	Democratic		Republican		Total
	No.	Percentage	No.	Percentage	No.
Tolerant	3	6	1	4	4
Stereotyped	14	29	6	24	20
Outspoken	26	53	12	48	38
Intense	6	12	6	24	12
Total	49		25		74

TABLE 17(A)

ANTI-NEGRO ATTITUDE AND RELIGIOUS DENOMINATION

	Catholic		Protestant		Greek Orth.		No present religious denomination		Total
	No.	Per-centage	No.	Per-centage	No.	Per-centage	No.	Per-centage	No.
Tolerant	8	8	3	9	0	—	1	8	12
Stereotyped	23	22	10	30	2	—	5	42	40
Outspoken	57	55	14	43	0	—	3	25	74
Intense	15	15	6	18	0	—	3	25	24
Total	103		33		2		12		150

TABLE 18(A)

ANTI-NEGRO ATTITUDE AND FAVORITE NEWSPAPER

	Tolerant and Stereotyped		Outspoken and Intense		Total	
	No.	Per Cent	No.	Per Cent	No.	Per Cent
Chicago Times	10	20	39	80	49	100
Chicago Tribune	14	30	33	60	47	100
Daily News	12	50	12	50	24	100
Herald-American	6	29	15	71	21	100
Chicago Sun	6	43	8	57	14	100

TABLE 19(A)

ANTI-NEGRO ATTITUDE AND DIVORCE IN VETERAN'S FAMILY

	No divorces		One or more divorces		Total
	No.	Percentage	No.	Percentage	No.
Tolerant	12	9	0	0	12
Stereotyped	38	29	2	12	40
Outspoken	64	48	10	59	74
Intense	19	14	5	29	24
Total	133		17		150

TABLE 20(A)

ANTI-NEGRO ATTITUDE AND CURRENT SALARY

	Under $3,000		Over $3,000		Total
	No.	Percentage	No.	Percentage	No.
Tolerant	7	7	2	7	9
Stereotyped	27	26	4	14	31
Outspoken	49	48	19	68	68
Intense	19	19	3	11	22
Total	102		28		130

TABLE 21(A)

ANTI-NEGRO ATTITUDE AND SOCIOECONOMIC STATUS

	Unskilled; semi-skilled		Top Four Groups[a]		Total
	No.	Percentage	No.	Percentage	No.
Tolerant and Stereotyped	20	25	32	46	52
Outspoken	42	53	32	46	74
Intense	18	22	6	8	24
Total	80		70		150

[a] Includes students; on-the-job training

INDEX

INDEX

Ackerman, Nathan, 53
Adolescence, 57
Adorno, Theodore, 67
Age, 3, 14-17, 152-53
Allport, Floyd H., 70
Allport, Gordon, 112
Altus, W. D., 71
"American Dilemma," 13
American Institute of Public Opinion, 8n, 12n
American Jewish Committee, 4, 12n, 101ff
Analytic categories, 314, 316-17
Analytic procedures, reliability of, 323-25
Anti-Negro attitudes, 11-14, 22-23, 71-72, 130-35
Anti-Semitism, 4-11, 23
  and age, 152-53
  compared with anti-Negro attitudes, 130-35
  and educational level, 153-54
  and family composition, 156-57
  in Germany, 80-81, 136n, 138, 146-47n, 152-53, 158, 160, 162, 164-65, 199, 270, 274n, 277, 285-86n
  in the Middle Ages, 268-70, 273
  and nativity of parents, 157-58
  and political affiliation, 156
  polls on, 111-12, 152f, 160n
  and reading and listening habits, 158-59, 253
  and religion, 154-56
  and social mobility, 160-65
  and sociometric status, 159-60, 270-73

  and world events, 153
Anxiety, 53ff, 69-71, 198
Army discipline, 201-204
Army experience, 166-77
  anti-Negro, 256-57
  deprivation caused by, 166ff
  effect of, 147-51, 156
  types of, 167
Assertion categories, 314, 315-16
Assimilation, 43-44
Attitudes
  toward authority, 75
  changes in, 3-14
  toward Jews, 4-11, 23, 80
  toward Negroes, 11-14, 22-23, 80
  parental, 208-10, 221, 274-75, 283, 288-89
  and personal controls, 91
  and personality variables, 79-80
  political, 189-97, 205ff
  racial, 11-14, 71-72, 246-48
  religious, 154-56, 200-201, 259-60, 262, 268-70, 273
Authoritarianism, 67-69, 74
Authority
  army, 201-204
  religious, 76-77, 200-201
  societal, 73ff, 204-208
Authority constellations, 199ff
Axline, Virginia M., 73

Bendix, Reinhard, 38n
Berelson, Bernard R., 46n, 159n, 314n
Bettelheim, Bruno, 147n, 277n
Bird, B., 52

SPECIAL MESSAGE TO READERS

This book is published under the auspices of

THE ULVERSCROFT FOUNDATION

(registered charity No. 264873 UK)

Established in 1972 to provide funds for research, diagnosis and treatment of eye diseases. Examples of contributions made are: —

A Children's Assessment Unit at Moorfield's Hospital, London.

•

Twin operating theatres at the Western Ophthalmic Hospital, London.

•

A Chair of Ophthalmology at the Royal Australian College of Ophthalmologists.

•

The Ulverscroft Children's Eye Unit at the Great Ormond Street Hospital For Sick Children, London.

You can help further the work of the Foundation by making a donation or leaving a legacy. Every contribution, no matter how small, is received with gratitude. Please write for details to:

THE ULVERSCROFT FOUNDATION,
The Green, Bradgate Road, Anstey,
Leicester LE7 7FU, England.
Telephone: (0116) 236 4325

In Australia write to:
THE ULVERSCROFT FOUNDATION,
c/o The Royal Australian and New Zealand College of Ophthalmologists,
94-98 Chalmers Street, Surry Hills,
N.S.W. 2010, Australia

Derek Johns has been a bookseller, editor and publisher and now works as a literary agent in London.

WINTERING

Arriving at harvest time in a sleepy village in the shadow of Glastonbury Tor, the Palmer family is making a fresh start — with a new job for recently bankrupted Jim, and a new life for Margaret and the children, Billy and Sarah. At first it's a smaller, slower world, but even before winter has arrived, opportunities open up — especially for Jim, with his eye for easy money and a pretty face. However, in such a small town nothing goes unobserved, either by the locals or by Billy, who is about to start dreaming of girls . . .